THE LOEB CLASSICAL LIBRARY

FOUNDED BY JAMES LOEB, LL.D.

EDITED BY

G. P. GOOLD, PH.D.

PREVIOUS EDITORS

† T. E. PAGE, C.H., LITT.D.   † E. CAPPS, PH.D., LL.D.

† W. H. D. ROUSE, LITT.D.   † L. A. POST, L.H.D.

E. H. WARMINGTON, M.A., F.R.HIST.SOC.

CLAUDIAN

I

135

CLAUDIAN

WITH AN ENGLISH TRANSLATION BY
MAURICE PLATNAUER
SOMETIME HONORARY SCHOLAR OF NEW COLLEGE, OXFORD
ASSISTANT MASTER AT WINCHESTER COLLEGE

IN TWO VOLUMES

I

CAMBRIDGE, MASSACHUSETTS
HARVARD UNIVERSITY PRESS
LONDON
WILLIAM HEINEMANN LTD
MCMLXXVI

American
ISBN 0-674-99150-8

British
ISBN 0 434 99135 x

First printed 1922
Reprinted 1956, 1963, 1976

Printed in Great Britain

CONTENTS OF VOLUME I

V

CONTENTS

INTRODUCTION

CLAUDIUS CLAUDIANUS may be called the last poet of classical Rome. He was born about the year 370 A.D. and died within a decade of the sack of the city by Alaric in 410. The thirty to forty odd years which comprised his life were some of the most momentous in the history of Rome. Valentinian and Valens were emperors respectively of the West and the East when he was born, and while the former was engaged in constant warfare with the northern tribes of Alamanni, Quadi and Sarmatians, whose advances the skill of his general, Theodosius, had managed to check, the latter was being reserved for unsuccessful battle with an enemy still more deadly.

It is about the year 370 that we begin to hear of the Huns. The first people to fall a victim to their eastward aggression were the Alans, next came the Ostrogoths, whose king, Hermanric, was driven to suicide; and by 375 the Visigoths were threatened with a similar fate. Hemmed in by the advancing flood of Huns and the stationary power of Rome this people, after a vain attempt to ally itself with the latter, was forced into arms against her. An indecisive battle with the generals of Valens (377) was followed by a crushing Roman defeat in the succeeding year (August 9, 378) at Adrianople, where

Valens himself, but recently returned from his Persian war, lost his life.

Gratian and his half-brother, Valentinian II., who had become Augusti upon the death of their father, Valentinian I., in 375, would have had little power of themselves to withstand the victorious Goths and Rome might well have fallen thirty years before she did, had it not been for the force of character and the military skill of that same Theodosius whose successes against the Alamanni have already been mentioned. Theodosius was summoned from his retirement in Spain and made Augustus (January 19, 379). During the next three years he succeeded, with the help of the Frankish generals, Bauto and Arbogast, in gradually driving the Goths northward, and so relieved the barbarian pressure on the Eastern Empire and its capital. In 381 Athanaric, the Gothic king, sued in person for peace at Constantinople and there did homage to the emperor. In the following year the Visigoths became allies of Rome and, for a time at least, the danger was averted.

Meanwhile the West was faring not much better. Gratian, after an uneasy reign, was murdered in 383 by the British pretender, Magnus Maximus. From 383 to 387 Maximus was joint ruler of the West with Valentinian II., whom he had left in command of Italy rather from motives of policy than of clemency ; but in the latter year he threw off the mask and, crossing the Alps, descended upon his colleague whose court was at Milan. Valentinian fled to Thessalonica and there threw himself on the mercy of Theodosius. Once more that general was to save the situation.

Maximus was defeated by him at Aquileia and
put to death, while Arbogast recovered Gaul by
means of an almost bloodless campaign (388).

The next scene in the drama is the murder at
Vienne on May 15, 392, of the feeble Valentinian at
the instigation of Arbogast. Arbogast's triumph was,
however, short-lived. Not daring himself, a Frank,
to assume the purple he invested therewith his
secretary, the Roman Eugenius, intending to govern
the West with Eugenius as a mere figure-head.
Once more, and now for the last time, Theodosius
saved the cause of legitimacy by defeating Eugenius
at the battle of the Frigidus[1] in September 394.
Eugenius was executed but Arbogast made good his
escape, only to fall a few weeks later by his own hand.

Theodosius himself died on January 17, 395, leaving
his two sons, Arcadius and Honorius, emperors of
the East and West respectively. Arcadius was but
a tool in the hands of his praetorian prefect, Rufinus,
whose character is drawn with such venomous
ferocity in Claudian's two poems. Almost equally
powerful and scarcely less corrupt seems to have
been that other victim of Claudian's splenetic verses,
the eunuch chamberlain Eutropius, who became
consul in the year 399. Both these men suffered a
violent end : Eutropius, in spite of the pleadings of
S. John Chrysostom, was put to death by Gainas,
the commander of the Gothic troops in the East ;
Rufinus was torn to pieces in the presence of Arcadius
himself by his Eastern troops.[2] The instigator of

---

[1] *Cf.* vii. 99 *et sqq.*

[2] v. 348 *et sqq.* S. Jerome (*Ep.* lx.) refers to his death
and tells how his head was carried on a pike to Constan-
tinople.

this just murder was Claudian's hero, Stilicho the Vandal.

Stilicho, who had been one of Theodosius' generals, had been put in command of the troops sent to oppose Alaric, the Visigoth, when the latter had broken away from his allegiance to Rome and was spreading devastation throughout Thrace, Macedonia and Thessaly. He was successful in his campaign, but, upon his marching south into Greece, in order to rid that country also of its Gothic invaders, he was forbidden by Rufinus to advance any farther. There can be little doubt that the murder of Rufinus was Stilicho's answer.

In spite of a subsequent victory over Alaric near Elis in the year 397, Stilicho's success can have been but a partial one, for we find the Visigoth general occupying the post of Master of the Soldiery in Illyricum, the withholding of which office had been the main cause of his defection. Possibly, too, the revolt of Gildo in Africa had something to do with the unsatisfactory termination of the Visigothic war. It is interesting to observe the dependence of Italy on African corn, a dependence of which in the first century of the Christian era Vespasian, and right at the end of the second the pretender Pescennius Niger, threatened to make use. If we can credit the details of Claudian's poem on the war (No. xv.), Rome was very shortly reduced to a state of semi-starvation by Gildo's holding up of the corn fleet, and, but for Stilicho's prompt action in sending Gildo's own brother, Mascezel, to put down the rebellion, the situation might have become even more critical. The poet, it may be remarked, was in an awkward position with regard to the war for, though the real credit of victory was clearly due to Mascezel (*cf.* xv. 380 *et sqq.*), he nevertheless wished to attribute it to his hero Stilicho, and, as Stilicho had Mascezel executed [1] later in that same year (Gildo had been defeated at Tabraca July 31, 398), he prudently did not write, or perhaps suppressed, Book II.

Stilicho, who had married Serena, niece and adoptive daughter of Theodosius, still further secured his position by giving his daughter, Maria, in marriage to the young Emperor Honorius in the year 398. This " father-in-law and son-in-law of an emperor," as Claudian is never wearied of calling him, did the country of his adoption a signal service by the defeat at Pollentia on Easter Day (April 6), 402, of Alaric, who, for reasons of which we really know nothing, had again proved unfaithful to Rome and had invaded and laid waste Italy in the winter of 401–402.

The battle of Pollentia was the last important event in Claudian's lifetime. He seems to have died in 404, four years before the murder of Stilicho by the jealous Honorius and six before the sack of Rome by Alaric—a disaster which Stilicho [2] alone, perhaps, might have averted.

So much for the historical background of the life of the poet. Of the details of his career we are not well informed. Something, indeed, we can gather from the pages of the poet himself, though it is not much, but besides this we have to guide us only Hesychius of Miletus' short

---

[1] Or at least connived at his death ; see Zosimus v. 11. 5.

[2] For an adverse (and probably unfair) view of Stilicho see Jerome, *Ep.* cxxiii. § 17.

article in Suidas' lexicon, a brief mention in the
Chronicle of 395, and (a curious survival) the in-
scription [1] under the statue which, as he himself tells
us,[2] emperor and senate had made in his honour and
set up in the Forum of Trajan. We are ignorant even
of the date of his birth and can only conjecture that
it was about the year 370. Of the place of his birth
we are equally uninformed by contemporary and
credible testimony, but there can be little doubt
that he came from Egypt,[3] probably from Alexandria
itself. We have, for what it is worth, the word of

[1] *C.I.L.* vi. 1710 (= Dessau 2949). Now in the Naples
Museum.

[Cl.] Claudiani v.c. | [Cla]udio Claudiano v.c., tri | [bu]no
et notario, inter ceteras | [de]centes artes prae[g]loriosissimo
| [po]etarum, licet ad memoriam sem|piternam carmina
ab eodem | scripta sufficiant, adtamen | testimonii gratia ob
iudicii sui | [f]idem, dd. nn. Arcadius et Honorius | [fe-]
licissimi et doctissimi | imperatores senatu petente | statuam
in foro divi Traiani | erigi collocarique iusserunt.

Εἰν ἐνὶ Βιργιλίοιο νόον | καὶ Μοῦσαν Ὁμήρου |
  Κλαυδιανὸν Ῥώμη καὶ | βασιλῆς ἔθεσαν.

v.c.=vir clarissimus, *i.e.* (roughly) The Rt. Hon. dd. nn.
=domini nostri. The inscription may be translated:—To
Claudius Claudianus v.c., son of Claudius Claudianus v.c.,
tribune and notary (*i.e.* Permanent Secretary), master of the
ennobling arts but above all a poet and most famous of poets,
though his own poems are enough to ensure his immortality,
yet, in thankful memory of his discretion and loyalty, their
serene and learned majesties, the Emperors Arcadius and
Honorius have, at the instance of the senate, bidden this
statue to be raised and set up in the Forum of the Emperor
Trajan of blessed memory.

Rome and her kings—to one who has combined
A Homer's music with a Vergil's mind.

[2] xxv. 7.
[3] John Lydus (*De magistr.* i. 47) writes οὗτος ὁ Παφλαγών,
but this, as Birt has shown, is merely an abusive appellation.

xii

Suidas and the lines of Sidonius Apollinaris,[1] which clearly refer to Claudian and which give Canopus as the place of his birth. (Canopus is almost certainly to be taken as synonymous with Egypt.) But besides these two statements we have only to look at his interest in things Egyptian, *e.g.* his poems on the Nile, the Phoenix, etc., at such passages as his account of the rites at Memphis,[2] at such phrases as " nostro cognite Nilo," [3] to see that the poet is an Egyptian himself. It is probable that, whether or not he spent all his early life in Egypt, Claudian did not visit Rome until 394. We know from his own statement [4] that his first essays in literature were all of them written in Greek and that it was not until the year 395 that he started to write Latin. It is not unlikely, therefore, that his change of country and of literary language were more or less contemporaneous, and it is highly probable that he was in Rome before January 3, 395, on which day his friends the Anicii (Probinus and Olybrius) entered upon their consulship. Speaking, moreover, of Stilicho's consulship in 400 Claudian mentions a five years' *absence*.[5] Not long after January 3, 395, Claudian seems to have betaken himself to the court at Milan, and it is from there that he sends letters to Probinus and Olybrius.[6] Here the poet seems to have stayed for five years, and here he seems to

[1] Sid. Ap. *Carm.* ix. 274.
[2] viii. 570 *et sqq.*
[3] Carm. min. corp. xix. 3 : *cf.* also Carm. min. corp. xxii. 20.
[4] Carm. min. corp. xli. 13.
[5] xxiii. 23.
[6] Carm. min. corp. xl. and xli. ; see ref. to Via Flaminia in xl. 8.

have won for himself a position of some importance.
As we see from the inscription quoted above, he
became *vir clarissimus, tribunus et notarius,* and, as he
does not continue further along the road of honours
(does not, for instance, become a *vir spectabilis*) we
must suppose that he served in some capacity on
Stilicho's private staff. No doubt he became a sort
of poet laureate.

It is probable that the "De raptu" was written
during the first two years of his sojourn at the court
of Milan. The poem is dedicated, or addressed, to
Florentinus,[1] who was *praefectus urbi* from August
395 to the end of 397 when he fell into disgrace with
Stilicho. It is to this circumstance that we are to
attribute the unfinished state of Claudian's poem.

The Emperor Honorius became consul for the
third time on January 3, 396, and on this occasion
Claudian read his Panegyric in the emperor's pres-
ence.[2]

Some five weeks before this event another of
greater importance had occurred in the East. This
was the murder of Rufinus, the praetorian prefect,
amid the circumstances that have been related
above. The date of the composition of Claudian's
two poems "In Rufinum" is certainly to be placed
within the years 395-397, and the mention of a
"tenuem moram"[3] makes it probable that Book II.
was written considerably later than Book I.; the
references, moreover, in the Preface to Book II. to
a victory of Stilicho clearly point to that general's
defeat of the Goths near Elis in 397.

To the year 398 belong the Panegyric on the

---

[1] Praef. ii. 50.

[2] vi. 17.   [3] iv. 15.

fourth consulship of Honorius and the poems cele-
brating the marriage of the emperor to Stilicho's
daughter, Maria. We have already seen that the
Gildo episode and Claudian's poem on that subject
are to be attributed to this same year.

The consuls for the year 399 were both, in different
ways, considered worthy of the poet's pen. Perhaps
the most savage of all his poems was directed against
Eutropius, the eunuch chamberlain, whose claim to
the consulship the West never recognized,[1] while a
Panegyric on Flavius Manlius Theodorus made
amends for an abusive epigram which the usually
more politic Claudian had previously levelled at
him.[2]

At the end of 399, or possibly at the beginning of
400, Claudian returned to Rome [3] where, probably
in February,[4] he recited his poem on the consulship
of Stilicho ; and we have no reason for supposing
that the poet left the capital from this time on until
his departure for his ill-starred journey four years
later. In the year 402,[5] as has already been men-
tioned, Stilicho defeated Alaric at Pollentia, and
Claudian recited his poem on the Gothic war some-
time during the summer of the same year. The
scene of the recitation seems to have been the
Bibliotheca Templi Apollinis.[6] It was in this year,
too, that the poet reached the summit of his great-

---

[1] *Cf.* xxii. 291 *et sqq.*
[2] Carm. min. xxi.
[3] xxiii. 23.
[4] So Birt, *Praef.* p. xlii. note 1.
[5] It should perhaps be mentioned that this date is dis-
puted : see Crees, *Claudian as an Historical Authority,*
pp. 175 *et sqq.*
[6] xxv. 4 " Pythia . . . domus."

ness in the dedication of the statue which, as we have seen, was accorded to him by the wishes of the emperor and at the demand of the senate.

The last of Claudian's datable public poems is that on the sixth consulship of Honorius. It was composed probably towards the end of 403 and recited in Rome on (or after) the occasion of the emperor's triumphant entry into the city. The emperor had just returned after inflicting a defeat on the Goths at Verona in the summer of 403. It is reasonable to suppose that this triumphant entry (to which the poem refers in some detail, ll. 331-639) took place on the day on which the emperor assumed the consular office, viz. January 3, 404.

In the year 404 Claudian seems to have married some protégée of Serena's. Of the two poems addressed to her the " Laus Serenae " is clearly the earlier, and we may take the other, the " Epistola ad Serenam," to be the last poem Claudian ever wrote. It is a poem which seems to have been written on his honeymoon, during the course of which he died.[1]

It is not easy to arrive at any just estimate of Claudian as a writer, partly because of an inevitable tendency to confuse relative with absolute standards, and partly (and it is saying much the same thing in other words) because it is so hard to separate Claudian the poet from Claudian the manipulator of the Latin language. If we compare his latinity with that of his contemporaries (with the possible exception of Rutilius) or with that of such a poet as Sidonius Apollinaris, who came not much more

[1] This suggestion is Vollmer's: see his article on Claudian in Pauly-Wissowa, III. ii. p. 2655.

than half a century after him, it is hard to withhold our admiration from a writer who could, at least as far as his language is concerned, challenge comparison with poets such as Valerius Flaccus, Silius Italicus, and Statius—poets who flourished about three centuries before him.[1] I doubt whether, subject matter set aside, Claudian might not deceive the very elect into thinking him a contemporary of Statius, with whose *Silvae* his own shorter poems have much in common.

Even as a poet Claudian is not always despicable, His descriptions are often clever, *e.g.* the Aponus, and many passages in the " De raptu." [2] His treatment of somewhat commonplace and often threadbare themes is not seldom successful—for example, the poem on the Phoenix and a four-line description of the horses of the dawn in the Panegyric on Honorius' fourth consulship [3]—and he has a happy knack of phrase-making which often relieves a tedious page :

> ille vel aerata Danaën in turre latentem
> eliceret [4]

he says of the pander Eutropius.

But perhaps Claudian's forte is invective. The panegyrics (with the doubtful exception of that on

[1] Still more striking is the comparison of Claudian's latinity with that of his contemporary, the authoress of the frankly colloquial *Peregrinatio ad loca sancta* (see Grandgent, *Vulgar Latin*, p. 5 : Wölfflin, "Über die Latinität der P. ad l. sancta," in *Archiv für lat. Lexikographie*, iv. 259).
[2] It is not impossible that this poem is a translation or at least an adaptation of a Greek (Alexandrine) original. So Förster, *Der Raub und die Rückkehr der Persephone*, Stuttgart, 1874.
[3] viii. 561-4 (dawns seem to suit him : *cf.* i. 1-6).
[4] xviii. 82, 83.

Manlius, which is certainly brighter than the others)
are uniformly dull, but the poems on Rufinus and
Eutropius are, though doubtless in the worst of
taste, at least in parts amusing.

Claudian's faults are easy to find. He mistook
memory for inspiration and so is often wordy and
tedious, as for instance in his three poems on Stilicho's
consulship.[1] Worse than this he is frequently ob-
scure and involved—witness his seven poems on the
drop of water contained within the rock crystal.[2]
The besetting sin, too, of almost all post-Virgilian
Roman poets, I mean a " conceited " frigidity, is one
into which he is particularly liable to fall. Examples
are almost too numerous to cite but the following
are typical : " nusquam totiensque sepultus "[3] of
the body of Rufinus, torn limb from limb by the
infuriated soldiery ; " caudamque in puppe re-
torquens Ad proram iacet usque leo "[4] of one of
the animals brought from Africa for the games at
Stilicho's triumph ; " saevusque Damastor, Ad de-
pellendos iaculum cum quaereret hostes, Germani
rigidum misit pro rupe cadaver "[5] of the giant
Pallas turned to stone by the Gorgon's head on
Minerva's shield. Consider, too, the remarkable

---

[1] Honourable exception should be made of xxi. 291 *et sqq.*
—one of the best and most sincere things Claudian ever
wrote.

[2] It is worth observing that not infrequently Claudian is
making " tentamina," or writing alternative lines : *e.g.*
Carm. min. corp. vii. 1 and 2, and almost certainly the four
lines of id. vi. v. is quite likely " a trial " for some such
passage as xv. 523.

[3] v. 453.

[4] xxiv. 357-8.

[5] Carm. min. corp. liii. 101-3.

statement that Stilicho, in swimming the Addua, showed greater bravery than Horatius Cocles because, while the latter swam away from Lars Porsenna, the former "dabat . . . Geticis pectora bellis." [1]

Two of the poems are interesting as touching upon Christianity (Carm. min. corp. xxxii. "De salvatore," and l. "In Iacobum"). The second of these two poems can scarcely be held to be serious, and although the first is unobjectionable it cannot be said to stamp its author as a sincere Christian. Orosius [2] and S. Augustine [3] both declare him to have been a heathen, but it is probable that, like his master Stilicho, Claudian rendered the new and orthodox religion at least lip-service.

It seems likely that after the death of Claudian (404) and that of his hero, Stilicho, the political poems (with the exception of the Panegyric on Probinus and Olybrius,[4] which did not concern Stilicho) were collected and published separately. The "Carmina minora" may have been published about the same time. The subsequent conflation of these two portions came to be known as "Claudianus maior," the "De raptu" being "Claudianus minor."

The MSS. of Claudian's poems fall into two main classes :

(1) Those which Birt refers to as the *Codices*

---

[1] xxviii. 490.
[2] vii. 35 "Paganus pervicacissimus."
[2] *Civ. dei*, v. 26 "a Christi numine alienus."
[4] This poem does not seem to have been associated with the others till the 12th century.

maiores and which contain the bulk of the poems but seldom the " De raptu."

(2) Those which Birt calls the *Codices minores* and which contain (generally exclusively) the " De raptu."

Class (1) may be again divided into (*a*) MSS. proper ; (*b*) excerpts. I give Birt's abbreviations.

(*a*) The most important are :

> R = Cod. Veronensis 163. 9th century.
>> Contains only the " Carmina minora."
>
> G = Cod. Sangallensis S n. 429. 9th century.
>> Contains only the (Latin) " Giganto-machia."
>
> G (*sic*) = Cod. Reginensis 123. 11th century.
>> Contains only " De Nilo."
>
> V = Cod. Vaticanus 2809. 12th century.
>
> P = Cod. Parisinus lat. 18,552. 12th or 13th century.
>> Contains all the " Carmina maiora " except (as usual) the " De raptu " and " Pan. Prob. et Olyb." No " minora."
>
> C = Cod. Bruxellensis 5380-4. (?) 12th-13th century.
>
> Π = Cod. Parisinus lat. 8082. 13th century.
>> This is Heinsius' " Regius." The MS. once belonged to Petrarch and still bears his name.
>
> B = Cod. Neapolitanus Borbonicus 1111 E 47. 13th century.
>
> A = Cod. Ambrosianus S 66. 15th century.
>> Contains all the " maiora " except the " De raptu " and " Pan. Prob. et Olyb."
>
> J = Cod. Cantabrigiensis coll. Trinitatis 0.3.22. 13th century.

Besides these are many inferior MSS. referred to collectively by Birt as ς.

(*b*) Consists of :

E = Excerpta Florentina. 15th century.
e = Excerpta Gyraldina 16th century.

Each of them resembles the other closely and both come from a common parent.

Under (*b*) may further be mentioned the Basel edition of Isengrin (1534), which preserves an independent tradition.

Birt postulates an archetype (Ω), dating between 6th and 9th centuries, and two main " streams," *x* and *y* ; *y* being again subdivided into *w* and *z*.

The following is the family " tree." Letters enclosed in brackets refer to non-existent MSS.

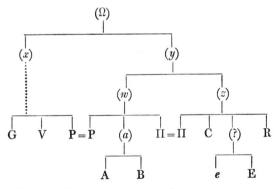

Of class (2) may be mentioned :

S = Cod. Parisinus lat. 15,005. 13th or 14th century.

C = Cod. Cantabrigiensis coll. corp. Christi 228. 13th century.

D = Cod. Musei Britannici 6042. 13th century.

W = Cod. Antverpiensis iii. 59. 12th or 13th century.

F = Cod. Florentinus bibl. St. Crucis. 12th century.

A }
B } = Codd. Oxonienses Bodleiani. (?) 13th century.

V = Cod. Antverpiensis N. 71. 14th century.

It is to be observed that in Birt's edition, and in any other that accepts his " sigla," A B C and V stand for different mss. according to whether they refer, or do not refer, to the " De raptu."

Some mss. contain scholia but none of these go back before the 12th or even the 13th century.

The chief editions of Claudian are as follows :

Ed. princeps :
　Celsanus, Vicenza, 1482.
　Ugolentus, Parma, 1500.
　Parrhasius, Milan, 1500.
　Camers, Vienna, 1510.
Aldine ed. (Asulanus), 1523.
Isengrin ed. (Michael Bentinus), Basel, 1534.[1]
　Claverius, Paris, 1602.

Like Bentinus, Claverius used certain mss. (in his case those of the library of Cuiacius) unknown to us.[2]

---

[1] See section on mss.

[2] Koch, *De codicibus Cuiacianis quibus in edendo Claudiano Claverius usus est*, Marburg, 1889.

INTRODUCTION

Plantin ed. (Scaliger), 1603.
Elzevir ed. (Heinsius), Leyden, 1650.
   Amsterdam, 1665.
Barth, Hanau, 1612.
   Frankfort, 1650.
Delphin ed. (Pyrrho), Paris, 1677.
Burmann, Amsterdam, 1760.
König, Göttingen, 1808.

These last three have good explanatory notes.

The first critical edition is that of L. Jeep (Leipzig, 1876–79).

In 1892 Birt published what must be considered as the standard edition of Claudian—vol. x. in the *Monumenta Germaniae historica* series. Birt was the first to put the text of Claudian on a firm footing, and it is his edition that I have followed, appending critical notes only where I differ from him.[1]

The latest edition of Claudian is that of Koch (Teubner, Leipzig, 1893). Koch was long associated with Birt in his researches into textual questions connected with Claudian, and his text is substantially the same as that of Birt.

---

[1] I should like if possible to anticipate criticism by frankly stating that the text of this edition makes no claims to being based on scientific principles. I have followed Birt not because I think him invariably right but because his is at present the standard text. Where I differ from him (and this is but in a few places) I do so not because I prefer the authority of another MS. or because I am convinced of the rightness of a conjecture, but because Birt's conservatism commits him (in my opinion) to untranslatable readings, in which cases my choice of a variant is arbitrary. Of the principle of *difficilior lectio* I pragmatically take no account.

INTRODUCTION

So far as I know, there is no English prose translation of Claudian already in the field, though various of his poems, notably the " De raptu," have found many verse translators, and in 1817 his complete works were put into English verse by A. Hawkins. An Italian version was published by Domenico Grillo in Venice in 1716, a German one by Wedekind in Darmstadt in 1868, and there exist two French prose translations, one by MM. Delatour and Geruzez (éd. Nisard, Paris, 1850) and one by M. Héguin de Guerle (Garnier frères, Collection Panckoucke, Paris, 1865).

Of Claudiana may be mentioned Vogt, *De Claudiani carminum quae Stilichonem praedicant fide historica* (1863) ; Ney, *Vindictae Claudianeae* (1865) ; T. Hodgkin's *Claudian, the last of the Roman Poets* (1875) ; E. Arens' *Quaestiones Claudianae* (1894) ; two studies by A. Parravicini, (1) *Studio di retorica sulle opere di Claudio Claudiano* (1905), and (2) *I Panegirici di Claudiano* (1909) ; J. H. E. Crees' *Claudian as an Historical Authority* (Cambridge Historical Essays, No. 17, 1908) ; Professor Postgate's article on the editions of Birt and Koch in the *Class. Rev.* (vol. ix. pp. 162 *et sqq.*), and the same scholar's Emendations in the *Class. Quarterly* of 1910 (pp. 257 *et sqq.*). Reference may also be made to Professor Bury's appendix to vol. iii. of his edition of Gibbon (1897, under " Claudian ") and to Harvard Studies in Classical Philology, vol. xxx. *The Encomiums of Claudius Claudianus.* Vollmer's article in Pauly-Wissowa's Lexicon is a mine of information, but for completeness Birt's introduction (over 200 pp. long) stands alone

The curious may find an interesting light thrown

on Claudian and his circle by Sudermann's play, *Die
Lobgesänge des Claudian* (Berlin, 1914).

All Claudian's genuine works are translated in the
present volumes with the exception of the two-line
fragment " De Lanario " (Birt, c.m.c. lii [lxxxviii.)].
The appendix " vel spuria vel suspecta continens "
has been rejected both by Birt and Koch, and I
have in this followed their example. The eight
Greek poems attributed to Claudian are at least of
doubtful authenticity, though Birt certainly makes
out a good case for the " Gigantomachia " (a fragment
of 77 lines). The remainder consists of short epi-
grams, two on the well-worn theme of the water
enclosed in the crystal and two Christian ones.
These last are almost certainly not the work of
Claudius Claudianus but of Claudianus Mamertus,
presbyter of Vienne *circ.* 474 A.D. We know from
Sidonius (*Ep.* iv. 3. 8) that this Claudian was a
writer of sacred poetry both in Greek and Latin
—indeed the famous " Pange lingua " is attributed
to him.

A word should perhaps be said as to the numbering
of the poems.

It is much to be regretted that Birt did not cut
adrift from Gesner's system, or at least that he
only did so in the " Carmina minora." The resultant
discrepancy in his (and Koch's) edition between the
order of the poems and their numbering is un-
doubtedly a nuisance, but I have not felt justified,
in so slight a work as the present one, in departing
from the now traditional arrangement.

INTRODUCTION

I wish, in conclusion, to express my thanks to my colleagues, Mr. R. L. A. Du Pontet and Mr. E. H. Blakeney : to the first for valuable suggestions on several obscure points, and to the second for help in reading the proofs.

MAURICE PLATNAUER.

WINCHESTER, *September* 1921.

CLAUDIAN

CLAUDII CLAUDIANI CARMINA

PANEGYRICUS DICTUS PROBINO ET OLYBRIO CONSULIBUS

I

Sol, qui flammigeris mundum complexus habenis
volvis inexhausto redeuntia saecula motu,
sparge diem meliore coma crinemque repexi
blandius elato surgant temone iugales
efflantes roseum frenis spumantibus ignem.
iam nova germanis vestigia torqueat annus
consulibus, laetique petant exordia menses.
  Scis genus Auchenium, nec te latuere potentes
Anniadae; nam saepe soles ductoribus illis
instaurare vias et cursibus addere nomen.   10
his neque per dubium pendet Fortuna favorem
nec novit mutare vices, sed fixus in omnes
cognatos procedit honos.   quemcumque require
hac de stirpe virum : certum est de consule nasci.

---

¹ Probinus and Olybrius, the consuls for 395 (they were
brothers), both belonged to the Anician gens, of which
Auchenius became an alternative gentile name, Anicius
becoming, in these cases, the *praenomen*. Many members
of this family had been, and were to be, consuls: *e.g.* Anicius
Auchenius Bassus in A.D. 408. The Annian gens was

THE POEMS OF CLAUDIAN

PANEGYRIC ON THE CONSULS PROBINUS AND OLYBRIUS

I

Sun, that encirclest the world with reins of flame
and rollest in ceaseless motion the revolving centuries,
scatter thy light with kindlier beams and let thy
coursers, their manes combed and they breathing
forth a rosy flame from their foaming bits, climb
the heavens more jocund in their loftier drawn
chariot. Now let the year bend its new steps for
the consul brothers and the glad months take their
beginning.

Thou wottest of the Auchenian[1] race nor are the
powerful Anniadae unknown to thee, for thou oft
hast started thy yearly journey with them as consuls
and hast given their name to thy revolution. For
them Fortune neither hangs on uncertain favour nor
changes, but honours, firmly fixed, pass to all their
kin. Select what man thou wilt from their family,
'tis certain he is a consul's son. Their ancestors are

related by intermarriage to the Anician : *e.g.* Annius Bassus
(cos. 331) who married the daughter of Annius Anicius
Iulianus (cos. 322).

per fasces numerantur avi semperque renata   15
nobilitate virent, et prolem fata sequuntur
continuum simili servantia lege tenorem.
nec quisquam procerum temptat, licet aere vetusto
floreat et claro cingatur Roma senatu,
se iactare parem ; sed, prima sede relicta   20
Aucheniis, de iure licet certare secundo :
haud secus ac tacitam Luna regnante per Arcton
sidereae cedunt acies, cum fratre retuso
aemulus adversis flagraverit ignibus orbis ;
tunc iubar Arcturi languet, tunc fulva Leonis   25
ira perit, Plaustro iam rara intermicat Arctos
indignata tegi, iam caligantibus armis
debilis Orion dextram miratur inertem.
    Quem prius adgrediar ?   veteris quis facta Probini
nesciat aut nimias laudes ignoret Olybri ?   30
    Vivit adhuc completque vagis sermonibus aures
gloria fusa Probi, quam non ventura silebunt
lustra nec ignota rapiet sub nube vetustas.
illum fama vehit trans aequora transque remotas
Tethyos ambages Atlanteosque recessus.   35
audiit et gelido si quem Maeotia pascit
sub Iove vel calido si quis coniunctus in axe
nascentem te, Nile, bibit.   virtutibus ille
Fortunam domuit numquamque levantibus alte
intumuit rebus ; sed mens circumflua luxu   40
noverat intactum vitio servare rigorem.
hic non divitias nigrantibus abdidit antris
nec tenebris damnavit opes ; sed largior imbre
sueverat innumeras hominum ditare catervas.

---

[1] Probus was born about 332 and died about 390. He
was (among many other things) proconsul of Africa and
praefectus of Illyricum.

counted by the fasces (for each has held them), the same recurring honours crown them, and a like destiny awaits their children in unbroken succession. No noble, though he boast of the brazen statues of his ancestors, though Rome be thronged with senators, no noble, I say, dare boast himself their equal. Give the first place to the Auchenii and let who will contest the second. It is as when the moon queens it in the calm northern sky and her orb gleams with brightness equal to that of her brother whose light she reflects; for then the starry hosts give place, Arcturus' beam grows dim and tawny Leo loses his angry glint, far-spaced shine the Bear's stars in the Wain, wroth at their eclipse, Orion's shafts grow dark as he looks in feeble amaze at his strengthless arm.

Which shall I speak of first? Who has not heard of the deeds of Probinus of ancient lineage, who knows not the endless praise of Olybrius?

The far-flung fame of Probus[1] and his sire lives yet and fills all ears with widespread discourse: the years to come shall not silence it nor time o'ercloud or put an end to it. His great name carries him beyond the seas, beyond Ocean's distant windings and Atlas' mountain caverns. If any live beneath the frozen sky by Maeotis' banks, or any, near neighbours of the torrid zone, drink Nile's stripling stream, they, too, have heard. Fortune yielded to his virtues, but never was he puffed up with success that engenders pride. Though his life was surrounded with luxury he knew how to preserve his uprightness uncorrupted. He did not hide his wealth in dark cellars nor condemn his riches to the nether gloom, but in showers more abundant than rain would ever enrich countless numbers of

5

quippe velut denso currentia munera nimbo   45
cernere semper erat, populis undare penates,
adsiduos intrare inopes, remeare beatos.
praeceps illa manus fluvios superabat Hiberos
aurea dona vomens (sic vix [1] tellure revulsa
sollicitis fodiens miratur collibus aurum),   50
quantum stagna Tagi rudibus stillantia venis
effluxere decus, quanto pretiosa metalli
Hermi ripa micat, quantas per Lydia culta
despumat rutilas dives Pactolus harenas.

   Non, mihi centenis pateant si vocibus ora   55
multifidusque ruat centum per pectora Phoebus,
acta Probi narrare queam, quot in ordine gentes
rexerit, ad summi quotiens fastigia iuris
venerit, Italiae late cum frena teneret
Illyricosque sinus et quos arat Africa campos.   60
sed nati vicere patrem solique merentur
victores audire Probi.   non contigit illi
talis honor, prima cum parte viresceret aevi,
nec consul cum fratre fuit.   vos nulla fatigat
cura diu maiora petens, non anxia mentem   65
spes agit et longo tendit praecordia voto :
coepistis quo finis erat.   primordia vestra
vix pauci meruere senes, metasque tenetis
ante genas dulces quam flos iuvenilis inumbret
oraque ridenti lanugine vestiat aetas.   70
tu, precor, ignarum doceas, Parnasia, vatem,
quis deus ambobus tanti sit muneris auctor.

   Postquam fulmineis impellens viribus hostem
belliger Augustus trepidas laxaverat Alpes,

   [1] *MSS.* si quis; *Birt suggests* sic vix; *possibly* ecquis *should be read. Postgate* (*C. Q. iv. p. 258*) quae vix . . . miretur . . . Astur

6

men. The thick cloud of his generosity was ever
big with gifts, full and overflowing with clients was
his mansion, and thereinto there poured a stream
of paupers to issue forth again rich men. His prodigal
hand outdid Spain's rivers in scattering gifts of gold
(scarce so much precious metal dazzles the gaze of
the miner delving in the vexed bowels of the earth),
exceeding all the gold dust carried down by Tagus'
water trickling from unsmelted lodes, the glittering
ore that enriches Hermus' banks, the golden sand
that rich Pactolus in flood deposits over the plains
of Lydia.

Could my words issue from a hundred mouths,
could Phoebus' manifold inspiration breathe through
a hundred breasts, even so I could not tell of Probus'
deeds, of all the people his ordered governance
ruled, of the many times he rose to the highest
honours, when he held the reins of broad-acred Italy,
the Illyrian coast, and Africa's lands. But his sons
o'ershadowed their sire and they alone deserve to
be called Probus' vanquishers. No such honour
befell Probus in his youth : he was never consul with
his brother. You ambition, ever o'ervaulting itself,
pricks not ; no anxious hopes afflict your minds
or keep your hearts in long suspense. You have
begun where most end : but few seniors have attained
to your earliest office. You have finished your race
e'er the full flower of youth has crowned your gentle
cheeks or adolescence clothed your faces with its
pleasant down. Do thou, my Muse, tell their
ignorant poet what god it was granted such a boon
to the twain.

When the warlike emperor had with the thunder-
bolt of his might put his enemy to flight and freed

Roma Probo cupiens dignas persolvere grates   75
sedula pro natis dominum flexura rogando
ire parat.   famuli currum iunxere volantem
Impetus horribilisque Metus, qui semper agentes
proelia cum fremitu Romam comitantur anhelo,
sive petat Parthos seu cuspide turbet Hydaspen.   80
hic ligat axe rotas ; hic sub iuga ferrea nectit
cornipedes rigidisque docet servire lupatis.
ipsa, triumphatis qua possidet aethera regnis,
adsilit innuptae ritus imitata Minervae.
nam neque caesariem crinali stringere cultu   85
colla nec ornatu patitur mollire retorto ;
dextrum nuda latus, niveos exerta lacertos,
audacem retegit mammam, laxumque coercens
mordet gemma sinum ; nodus, qui sublevat ensem,
album puniceo pectus discriminat ostro.   90
miscetur decori virtus pulcherque severo
armatur terrore pudor, galeaeque minaci
flava cruentarum praetenditur umbra iubarum,
et formidato clipeus Titana lacessit
lumine . quem tota variarat Mulciber arte.   95
hic patrius Mavortis amor fetusque notantur
Romulei ; pius amnis inest et belua nutrix ;
electro Tiberis, pueri formantur in auro ;
fingunt aera lupam ; Mavors adamante coruscat.

    Iam simul emissis rapido velocior Euro   100
fertur equis ; strident Zephyri cursuque rotarum
saucia dividuis clarescunt nubila sulcis.
nec traxere moras, sed lapsu protinus uno,

the Alps from fear, Rome, anxious worthily to thank her Probus, hastened to beg the Emperor's favour for that hero's sons. Her slaves, Shock and horrid Fear, yoked her winged chariot; 'tis they who ever attend Rome with loud-voiced roar, setting wars afoot, whether she battle against the Parthians or vex Hydaspes' stream with her spear. The one fastens the wheels to the hubs, the other drives the horses beneath the iron yoke and makes them obey the stubborn bit. Rome herself in the guise of the virgin goddess Minerva soars aloft on the road by which she takes possession of the sky after triumphing over the realms of earth. She will not have her hair bound with a comb nor her neck made effeminate with a twisted necklace. Her right side is bare; her snowy shoulder exposed; her brooch fastens her flowing garments but loosely and boldly shows her breast: the belt that supports her sword throws a strip of scarlet across her fair skin. She looks as good as she is fair, chaste beauty armed with awe; her threatening helm of blood-red plumes casts a dark shadow and her shield challenges the sun in its fearful brilliance, that shield which Vulcan forged with all the subtlety of his skill. In it are depicted the children Romulus and Remus, and their loving father Mars, Tiber's reverent stream, and the wolf that was their nurse; Tiber is embossed in electrum, the children in pure gold, brazen is the wolf, and Mars fashioned of flashing steel.

And now Rome, loosing both her steeds together, flies swifter than the fleet east wind; the Zephyrs shrill and the clouds, cleft with the track of the wheels, glow in separate furrows. What matchless speed! One pinion's stroke and they reach their

9

quem poscunt, tetigere locum : qua fine sub imo
angustant aditum curvis anfractibus Alpes   105
claustraque congestis scopulis durissima tendunt,
non alia reseranda manu, sed pervia tantum
Augusto geminisque fidem mentita tyrannis.
semirutae turres avulsaque moenia fumant ;
crescunt in cumulum strages vallemque profundam
aequavere iugis ; stagnant inmersa cruore   111
corpora ; turbantur permixto funere manes.

Haud procul exhausto laetus certamine victor
caespite gramineo consederat arbore fultus
adclines umeros ; dominum gavisa coronat   115
terra suum, surguntque toris maioribus herbae.
sudor adhuc per membra calet creberque recurrit
halitus et placidi radiant in casside vultus :
qualis letifera populatus caede Gelonos
procubat horrendus Getico Gradivus in arvo ;   120
exuvias Bellona levat, Bellona tepentes
pulvere solvit equos, inmensaque cornus in hastam
porrigitur tremulisque ferit splendoribus Hebrum.

Ut stetit ante ducem discussas Roma per auras,
conscia ter sonuit rupes et inhorruit atrum   125
maiestate nemus.   prior hic : " o numen amicum "
dux ait " et legum genetrix longeque regendo
circumfusa polo consors ac dicta Tonantis,
dic agedum, quae causa viae ?   cur deseris arces
Ausonias caelumque tuum ?   dic, maxima rerum ! 130

---

[1] Maximus and Eugenius.   See Introduction, p. ix.

goal: it is there where in their furthermost parts the Alps narrow their approaches into tortuous valleys and extend their adamantine bars of piled-up rocks. No other hand could unlock that gate, as, to their cost, those two tyrants[1] found; to the Emperor only they offer a way. The smoke of towers o'erthrown and of ruined fortresses ascends to heaven. Slaughtered men are piled up on a heap and bring the lowest valley equal with the hills; corpses welter in their blood; the very shades are confounded with the inrush of the slain.

Close at hand the victor, Theodosius, happy that his warfare is accomplished, sits upon the green sward, his shoulders leaning against a tree. Triumphant earth crowned her lord and flowers sprang up from prouder banks. The sweat is still warm upon his body, his breath comes panting, but calm shines his countenance beneath his helmet. Such is Mars, when with deadly slaughter he has devastated the Geloni and thereafter rests, a dread figure, in the Getic plain, while Bellona, goddess of war, lightens him of his armour and unyokes his dust-stained coursers; an outstretched spear, a huge cornel trunk, arms his hand and flashes its tremulous splendour over Hebrus' stream.

When Rome had ended her airy journey and now stood before her lord, thrice thundered the conscious rocks and the black wood shuddered in awe. First to speak was the hero: " Goddess and friend, mother of laws, thou whose empire is conterminous with heaven, thou that art called the consort of the Thunderer, say what hath caused thy coming: why leavest thou the towns of Italy and thy native clime? Say, queen of the world. Were it thy

11

non ego vel Libycos cessem tolerare labores
Sarmaticosve pati medio sub frigore Cauros,
si tu, Roma, velis ; pro te quascumque per oras
ibimus et nulla sub tempestate timentes
solstitio Meroën, bruma temptabimus Histrum." 135
    Tum regina refert : " non me latet, inclite rector,
quod tua pro Latio victricia castra laborant
nec quod servitium rursus Furiaeque rebelles
edomitae paribus sub te cecidere triumphis.
sed precor hoc donum cum libertate recenti   140
adicias, si vera manet reverentia nostri.
sunt mihi pubentes alto de semine fratres,
pignora cara Probi, festa quos luce creatos
ipsa meo fovi gremio.   cunabula parvis
ipsa dedi, cum matris onus Lucina beatum   145
solveret et magnos proferrent sidera partus.
his ego nec Decios pulchros fortesve Metellos ✦
praetulerim, non, qui Poenum domuere ferocem,
Scipiadas Gallisque genus fatale Camillos.
Pieriis pollent studiis multoque redundant   150
eloquio ; nec desidiis dapibusve paratis
indulgere iuvat nec tanta licentia vitae
adripit aut mores aetas lasciva relaxat :
sed gravibus curis animum sortita senilem
ignea longaevo frenatur corde iuventus.   155
illis, quam propriam ducunt ab origine, sortem
oramus praebere velis annique futurum
devoveas venientis iter.   non improba posco,
non insueta dabis : domus haec de more requirit.
adnue : sic nobis Scythicus famuletur Araxes,   160
12

wish I would not shrink from toiling neath a Libyan sun nor from the cold winds of a Russian midwinter. At thy behest I will traverse all lands and fearing no season of the year will hazard Meroë in summer and the Danube in winter."

Then the Queen answered : "Full well know I, far-famed ruler, that thy victorious armies toil for Italy, and that once again servitude and furious rebels have given way before thee, overthrown in one and the same battle. Yet I pray thee add to our late won liberty this further boon, if in very truth thou still reverest me. There are among my citizens two young brothers of noble lineage, the dearly loved sons of Probus, born on a festal day and reared in my own bosom. 'Twas I gave the little ones their cradles when the goddess of childbirth freed their mother's womb from its blessed burden and heaven brought to light her glorious offspring. To these I would not prefer the noble Decii nor the brave Metelli, no, nor the Scipios who overcame the warlike Carthaginians nor the Camilli, that family fraught with ruin for the Gauls. The Muses have endowed them with full measure of their skill ; their eloquence knows no bounds. Theirs not to wanton in sloth and banquets spread ; unbridled pleasure tempts them not, nor can the lure of youth undermine their characters. Gaining from weighty cares an old man's mind, their fiery youth is bridled by a greybeard's wisdom. That fortune to which their birth entitles them I beg thee assure them and appoint for them the path of the coming year. 'Tis no unreasonable request and will be no unheard-of boon. Their birth demands it should be so. Grant it ; so may Scythian Araxes be our vassal

sic Rhenus per utrumque latus, Medisque subactis
nostra Semiramiae timeant insignia turres ;
sic fluat attonitus Romana per oppida Ganges."

    Ductor ad haec : " optata iubes ultroque volentem,
diva, rogas ; non haec precibus temptanda fuissent.
usque adeone meam condunt oblivia mentem,   166
ut pigeat meminisse Probi, quo vindice totam
vidimus Hesperiam fessasque resurgere gentes ?
ante dabunt hiemes Nilum, per flumina dammae
errabunt glacieque niger damnabitur Indus,   170
ante Thyesteis iterum conterrita mensis
intercisa dies refugos vertetur in ortus,
quam Probus a nostro possit discedere sensu."

    Dixerat et velox iam nuntius advolat urbem.
extemplo strepuere chori collesque canoris   175
plausibus impulsi septena voce resultant.
laetatur veneranda parens et pollice docto
iam parat auratas trabeas cinctusque micantes
stamine, quod molli tondent de stipite Seres
frondea lanigerae carpentes vellera silvae,   180
et longum tenues tractus producit in aurum
filaque concreto cogit squalere metallo :
qualis purpureas praebebat candida vestes
numinibus Latona suis, cum sacra redirent
ad loca nutricis iam non errantia Deli,   185
illa feros saltus et desolata relinquens
Maenala lassato certis venatibus arcu,
Phoebus adhuc nigris rorantia tela venenis
extincto Pythone gerens ; tunc insula notos

14

and Rhine's either bank; so may the Mede be o'erthrown and the towers that Semiramis built yield to our standards, while amazèd Ganges flows between Roman cities."

To this the king: "Goddess, thou biddest me do what I would fain do and askest a boon that I wish to grant: thy entreaties were not needed for this. Does forgetfulness so wholly cloud my mind that I will not remember Probus, beneath whose leadership I have seen all Italy and her war-weary peoples come again to prosperity? Winter shall cause Nile's rising, hinds shall make rivers their element, dark-flowing Indus shall be ice-bound, terror-stricken once again by the banquet of Thyestes the sun shall stay his course and fly for refuge back into the east, all this ere Probus can fade from my memory."

He spake, and now the speedy messenger hies him to Rome. Straightway the choirs chant and the seven hills re-echo their tuneful applause. Joy is in the heart of that aged mother whose skilled fingers now make ready gold-embroidered vestment and garments agleam with the thread which the Seres comb out from their delicate plants, gathering the leafy fleece of the wool-bearing trees. These long threads she draws out to an equal length with the threads of gold and by intertwining them makes one golden cord; as fair Latona gave scarlet garments to her divine offspring when they returned to the now firm-fixèd shrine of Delos their foster-island, Diana leaving the forest glades and bleak Maenalus, her unerring bow wearied with much hunting, and Phoebus bearing the sword still dripping with black venom from the slaughtered Python. Then their dear island laved the feet of its acknow-

lambit amica pedes ridetque Aegaeus alumnis   190
lenior et blando testatur gaudia fluctu.

   Sic Proba praecipuo natos exornat amictu :
quae decorat mundum, cuius Romana potestas
fetibus augetur.   credas ex aethere lapsam
stare Pudicitiam vel sacro ture vocatam   195
Iunonem Inachiis oculos advertere templis.
talem nulla refert antiquis pagina libris
nec Latiae cecinere tubae nec Graeca vetustas.
coniuge digna Probo ; nam tantum coetibus extat
femineis, quantum supereminet ille maritos.   200
ceu sibi certantes, sexus quid possit uterque,
hunc legere torum.   taceat Nereida nuptam
Pelion.   o duplici fecundam consule matrem
felicemque uterum, qui nomina parturit annis !

   Ut sceptrum gessere manu membrisque rigentes
aptavere togas, signum dat summus hiulca   206
nube Pater gratamque facem per inane rotantes
prospera vibrati tonuerunt omina nimbi.
accepit sonitus curvis Tiberinus in antris
ima valle sedens.   adrectis auribus haesit,   210
unde repentinus populi fragor.   ilicet herbis
pallentes thalamos et structa cubilia musco
deserit ac Nymphis urnam commendat erilem.
illi glauca nitent hirsuto lumina vultu
caeruleis infecta notis, reddentia patrem   215
Oceanum ; crispo densantur gramine colla ;
vertice luxuriat toto crinalis harundo,

---

   [1] Anicia Faltonia Proba.   She was still alive in 410 and
according to Procopius (*Bell. Vand.* i. 2) opened the
gates of Rome to Alaric.

ledged deities, the Aegean smiled more gently on
its nurslings, the Aegean whose soft ripples bore
witness to its joy.

So Proba[1] adorns her children with vestment
rare, Proba, the world's glory, by whose increase
the power of Rome, too, is increased. You would
have thought her Modesty's self fallen from heaven
or Juno, summoned by sacred incense, turning her
eyes on the shrines of Argos. No page in ancient
story tells of such a mother, no Latin Muse nor
old Grecian tale. Worthy is she of Probus for
a husband, for he surpassed all husbands as she all
wives. 'Twas as though in rivalry either sex had
done its uttermost and so brought about this mar-
riage. Let Pelion vaunt no more that Nereid bride.[2]
Happy thou that art the mother of consuls twain,
blessed thy womb whose offspring have given the
year their name for its own.

So soon as their hands held the sceptres and the
jewel-studded togas had enfolded their limbs the
almighty Sire vouchsafes a sign with riven cloud
and the shaken heavens, projecting a welcoming
flash through the void, thundered with prosperous
omen. Father Tiber, seated in that low valley,
heard the sound in his labyrinthine cave. He stays
with ears pricked up wondering whence this sudden
popular clamour comes. Straightway he leaves his
couch of green leaves, his mossy bed, and entrusts
his urn to his attendant nymphs. Grey eyes flecked
with blue shine out from his shaggy countenance,
recalling his father Oceanus; thick curlèd grasses
cover his neck and lush sedge crowns his head.

[2] Thetis, daughter of Nereus, was married to Peleus on
Mount Pelion in Thessaly.

quam neque fas Zephyris frangi nec sole perustam
aestivo candore mori ; sed vivida frondet
aequaevum complexa caput.   taurina levantur   220
cornua temporibus raucos sudantia rivos ;
distillant per pectus aquae ; frons hispida manat
imbribus ; in liquidos fontes se barba repectit.
palla graves umeros velat, quam neverat uxor
Ilia percurrens vitreas sub gurgite telas.   225
  Est in Romuleo procumbens insula Thybri
qua medius geminas interfluit alveus urbes
discretas subeunte freto, pariterque minantes
ardua turrigerae surgunt in culmina ripae.
hic stetit et subitum prospexit ab aggere votum: 230
unanimos [1] fratres iuncto stipante senatu
ire forum strictasque procul radiare secures
atque uno biiuges tolli de limine fasces.
obstupuit visu suspensaque gaudia vocem
oppressam tenuere diu ; mox incohat ore :   235
  " Respice, si tales iactas aluisse fluentis,
Eurota Spartane, tuis.   quid protulit aequum
falsus olor, valido quamvis decernere caestu
noverit et ratibus saevas arcere procellas ?
en nova Ledaeis suboles fulgentior astris,   240
ecce mei cives, quorum iam Signifer optat
adventum stellisque parat convexa futuris.
iam per noctivagos dominetur Olybrius axes
pro Polluce rubens, pro Castore flamma Probini.

  [1] *Birt, following* MSS., unanimes ; *Koch* unanimos

---

  [1] Jupiter, who courted Leda in the form of a swan,
becoming by her the father of Helen, Clytemnestra, Castor
and Pollux. These latter two were the patrons of the ring—
hence "decernere caestu " (l. 238); and of sailors—hence
" arcere procellas " (l. 239).

This the Zephyrs may not break nor the summer
sun scorch to withering; it lives and burgeons
around those brows immortal as itself. From
his temples sprout horns like those of a bull; from
these pour babbling streamlets; water drips upon
his breast, showers pour down his hair-crowned
forehead, flowing rivers from his parted beard.
There clothes his massy shoulders a cloak woven by
his wife Ilia, who threaded the crystalline loom
beneath the flood.

There lies in Roman Tiber's stream an island
where the central flood washes as 'twere two cities
parted by the sundering waters : with equal threaten-
ing height the tower-clad banks rise in lofty build-
ings. Here stood Tiber and from this eminence
beheld his prayer of a sudden fulfilled, saw the
twin-souled brothers enter the Forum amid the
press of thronging senators, the bared axes gleam
afar and both sets of fasces brought forth from one
threshold. He stood amazed at the sight and for a
long time incredulous joy held his voice in check.
Yet soon he thus began :

" Behold, Eurotas, river of Sparta, boastest thou
that thy streams have ever nurtured such as these ?
Did that false swan[1] beget a child to rival them,
though 'tis true his sons could fight with the heavy
glove and save ships from cruel tempests ? Behold
new offspring outshining the stars to which Leda
gave birth, men of my city for whose coming the
Zodiac is now awatch, making ready his hollow
tract of sky for a constellation that is to be. Hence-
forth let Olybrius rule the nightly sky, shedding
his ruddy light where Pollux once shone, and
where glinted Castor's fires there let glitter Probinus'

ipsi vela regent, ipsis donantibus auras   245
navita tranquillo moderabitur aequore pinum.
nunc pateras libare deis, nunc solvere multo
nectare corda libet.   niveos iam pandite coetus,
Naides, et totum violis praetexite fontem ;
mella ferant silvae ; iam profluat ebrius amnis   250
mutatis in vina vadis ; iam sponte per agros
sudent inriguae spirantia balsama venae !
currat, qui sociae roget in convivia mensae
indigenas Fluvios, Italis quicumque suberrant
montibus Alpinasque bibunt de more pruinas :   255
Vulturnusque rapax et Nar vitiatus odoro
sulphure tardatusque suis erroribus Ufens
et Phaëthonteae perpessus damna ruinae
Eridanus flavaeque terens querceta Maricae
Liris et Oebaliae qui temperat arva Galaesus.   260
semper honoratus nostris celebrabitur undis
iste dies, semper dapibus recoletur opimis."

     Sic ait et Nymphae patris praecepta secutae
tecta parant epulis ostroque infecta corusco
umida gemmiferis inluxit regia mensis.   265

     O bene signatum fraterno nomine tempus !
o consanguineis felix auctoribus annus,
incipe quadrifidum Phoebi torquere laborem.
prima tibi procedat hiems non frigore torpens,
non canas vestita nives, non aspera ventis,   270
sed tepido calefacta Noto ; ver inde serenum
protinus et liquidi clementior aura Favoni
pratis te croceis pingat ; te messibus aestas

flame. These shall direct men's sails and vouchsafe those breezes whereby the sailor shall guide his bark o'er the calm ocean. Let us now pour libation to the new gods and ease our hearts with copious draughts of nectar. Naiads, now spread your snowy bands, wreath every spring with violets. Let the woods bring forth honey and the drunken river roll, its waters changed to wine ; let the watering streams that vein the fields give off the scent of balsam spice. Let one run and invite to the feast and banquet-board all the rivers of our land, even all that wander beneath the mountains of Italy and drink as their portion the Alpine snows, swift Vulturnus and Nar infected with ill-smelling sulphur, Ufens whose meanderings delay his course and Eridanus into whose waters Phaëthon fell headlong ; Liris who laves Marica's golden oak groves and Galaesus who tempers the fields of Sparta's colony Tarentum. This day shall always be held in honour and observed by our rivers and its anniversary ever celebrated with rich feastings."

So spake he, and the Nymphs, obeying their sire's behest, made ready the rooms for the banquet, and the watery palace, ablaze with gleaming purple, shone with jewelled tables.

O happy months to bear these brothers' name ! O year blessed to own such a pair as overlords, begin thou to turn the laborious wheel of Phoebus' four-fold circle. First let thy winter pursue its course, sans numbing cold, not clothed in white snow nor torn by rough blasts, but warmed with the south wind's breath : next, be thy spring calm from the outset and let the limpid west wind's gentler breeze flood thy meads with yellow flowers.

induat autumnusque madentibus ambiat uvis.

omni nobilior lustro, tibi gloria soli   275

contigit exactum numquam memorata per aevum,

germanos habuisse duces ; te cuncta loquetur

tellus ; te variis scribent in floribus Horae

longaque perpetui ducent in saecula fasti.

PANEGYRIC ON PROBINUS AND OLYBRIUS

May summer crown thee with harvest and autumn store thee with luscious grapes. An honour that no age has ever yet known, a privilege never yet heard of in times gone by, this has been thine and thine alone—to have had brothers as thy consuls. The whole world shall tell of thee, the Hours shall inscribe thy name in various flowers, and age-long annals hand thy fame down through the long centuries.

IN RUFINUM LIBER PRIMUS

INCIPIT PRAEFATIO

(II)

Phoebeo domitus Python cum decidit arcu
    membraque Cirrhaeo fudit anhela iugo,
qui spiris tegeret montes, hauriret hiatu
    flumina, sanguineis tangeret astra iubis :
iam liber Parnasus erat nexuque soluto   5
    coeperat erecta surgere fronde nemus
concussaeque diu spatiosis tractibus orni
    securas ventis explicuere comas
et qui vipereo spumavit saepe veneno
    Cephisos nitidis purior ibat aquis.   10
omnis " io Paean " regio sonat ; omnia Phoebum
    rura canunt ; tripodas plenior aura rotat,
auditoque procul Musarum carmine dulci
    ad Themidis coëunt antra severa dei.

Nunc alio domini telis Pythone perempto   15
    convenit ad nostram sacra caterva lyram,
qui stabilem servans Augustis fratribus orbem
    iustitia pacem, viribus arma regit.

24

THE FIRST BOOK AGAINST RUFINUS

PREFACE

(II)

When Python had fallen, laid low by the arrow of Phoebus, his dying limbs outspread o'er Cirrha's heights—Python, whose coils covered whole mountains, whose maw swallowed rivers and whose bloody crest touched the stars — then Parnassus was free and the woods, their serpent fetters shaken off, began to grow tall with lofty trees. The mountain-ashes, long shaken by the dragon's sinuous coils, spread their leaves securely to the breeze, and Cephisus, who had so often foamed with his poisonous venom, now flowed a purer stream with limpid wave. The whole country echoed with the cry, " hail, Healer ": every land sang Phoebus' praise. A fuller wind shakes the tripod, and the gods, hearing the Muses' sweet song from afar off, gather in the dread caverns of Themis.

A blessed band comes together to hear my song, now that a second Python has been slain by the weapons of that master of ours who made the rule of the brother Emperors hold the world steady, observing justice in peace and showing vigour in war.

LIBER I

(III)

Saepe mihi dubiam traxit sententia mentem,
curarent superi terras an nullus inesset
rector et incerto fluerent mortalia casu.
nam cum dispositi quaesissem foedera mundi
praescriptosque mari fines annisque meatus   5
et lucis noctisque vices : tunc omnia rebar
consilio firmata dei, qui lege moveri
sidera, qui fruges diverso tempore nasci,
qui variam Phoeben alieno iusserit igni
compleri Solemque suo, porrexerit undis   10
litora, tellurem medio libraverit axe.
sed cum res hominum tanta caligine volvi
adspicerem laetosque diu florere nocentes
vexarique pios, rursus labefacta cadebat
relligio causaeque viam non sponte sequebar   15
alterius, vacuo quae currere semina motu
adfirmat magnumque novas per inane figuras
fortuna non arte regi, quae numina sensu
ambiguo vel nulla putat vel nescia nostri.

---

[1] Epicureanism.

BOOK I

(III)

My mind has often wavered between two opinions :
have the gods a care for the world or is there no
ruler therein and do mortal things drift as dubious
chance dictates ? For when I investigated the laws
and the ordinances of heaven and observed the sea's
appointed limits, the year's fixed cycle and the
alternation of light and darkness, then methought
everything was ordained according to the direction
of a God who had bidden the stars move by fixed
laws, plants grow at different seasons, the changing
moon fulfil her circle with borrowed light and the
sun shine by his own, who spread the shore before
the waves and balanced the world in the centre of
the firmament. But when I saw the impenetrable
mist which surrounds human affairs, the wicked
happy and long prosperous and the good discom-
forted, then in turn my belief in God was weakened
and failed, and even against mine own will I embraced
the tenets of that other philosophy [1] which teaches
that atoms drift in purposeless motion and that new
forms throughout the vast void are shaped by chance
and not design—that philosophy which believes in
God in an ambiguous sense, or holds that there be
no gods, or that they are careless of our doings. At

27

abstulit hunc tandem Rufini poena tumultum   20
absolvitque deos.   iam non ad culmina rerum
iniustos crevisse queror ; tolluntur in altum,
ut lapsu graviore ruant.   vos pandite vati,
Pierides, quo tanta lues eruperit ortu.

    Invidiae quondam stimulis incanduit atrox   25
Allecto, placidas late cum cerneret urbes.
protinus infernas ad limina taetra sorores
concilium deforme vocat.   glomerantur in unum
innumerae pestes Erebi, quascumque sinistro
Nox genuit fetu : nutrix Discordia belli,   30
imperiosa Fames, leto vicina Senectus
impatiensque sui Morbus Livorque secundis
anxius et scisso maerens velamine Luctus
et Timor et caeco praeceps Audacia vultu
et Luxus populator opum, quem semper adhaerens 35
infelix humili gressu comitatur Egestas,
foedaque Avaritiae complexae pectora matris
insomnes longo veniunt examine Curae.
complentur vario ferrata sedilia coetu
torvaque collectis stipatur curia monstris.   40
Allecto stetit in mediis vulgusque tacere
iussit et obstantes in tergum reppulit angues
perque umeros errare dedit.   tum corde sub imo
inclusam rabidis patefecit vocibus iram :

    " Sicine tranquillo produci saecula cursu,   45
sic fortunatas patiemur vivere gentes ?
quae nova corrupit nostros clementia mores ?
quo rabies innata perit ? quid inania prosunt
verbera ? quid facibus nequiquam cingimur atris ?

last Rufinus' fate has dispelled this uncertainty and freed the gods from this imputation. No longer can I complain that the unrighteous man reaches the highest pinnacle of success. He is raised aloft that he may be hurled down in more headlong ruin. Muses, unfold to your poet whence sprang this grievous pest.

Dire Allecto once kindled with jealous wrath on seeing widespread peace among the cities of men. Straightway she summons the hideous council of the nether-world sisters to her foul palace gates. Hell's numberless monsters are gathered together, Night's children of ill-omened birth. Discord, mother of war, imperious Hunger, Age, near neighbour to Death; Disease, whose life is a burden to himself; Envy that brooks not another's prosperity, woeful Sorrow with rent garments; Fear and foolhardy Rashness with sightless eyes; Luxury, destroyer of wealth, to whose side ever clings unhappy Want with humble tread, and the long company of sleepless Cares, hanging round the foul neck of their mother Avarice. The iron seats are filled with all this rout and the grim chamber is thronged with the monstrous crowd. Allecto stood in their midst and called for silence, thrusting behind her back the snaky hair that swept her face and letting it play over her shoulders. Then with mad utterance she unlocked the anger deep hidden in her heart.

"Shall we allow the centuries to roll on in this even tenour, and man to live thus blessed? What novel kindliness has corrupted our characters? Where is our inbred fury? Of what use the lash with none to suffer beneath it? Why this purposeless girdle of smoky torches? Sluggards, ye,

heu nimis ignavae, quas Iuppiter arcet Olympo, 50
Theodosius terris. en aurea nascitur aetas,
en proles antiqua redit. Concordia, Virtus
eumque Fide Pietas alta cervice vagantur
insignemque canunt nostra de plebe triumphum.
pro dolor ! ipsa mihi liquidas delapsa per auras 55
Iustitia insultat vitiisque a stirpe recisis
elicit oppressas tenebroso carcere leges.
at nos indecores longo torpebimus aevo
omnibus eiectae regnis !   agnoscite tandem
quid Furias deceat ; consuetas sumite vires 60
conventuque nefas tanto decernite dignum.
iam cupio Stygiis invadere nubibus astra,
iam flatu violare diem, laxare profundo
frena mari, fluvios ruptis inmittere ripis
et rerum vexare fidem."
                Sic fata cruentum 65
mugiit et totos serpentum erexit hiatus
noxiaque effudit concusso crine venena.
anceps motus erat vulgi.   pars maxima bellum
indicit superis, pars Ditis iura veretur,
dissensuque alitur rumor : ceu murmurat alti 70
impacata quies pelagi, cum flamine fracto
durat adhuc saevitque tumor dubiumque per aestum
lassa recedentis fluitant vestigia venti.
   Improba mox surgit tristi de sede Megaera,
quam penes insani fremitus animique profanus 75
error et undantes spumis furialibus irae :
non nisi quaesitum cognata caede cruorem
inlicitumve bibit, patrius quem fuderit ensis,

whom Jove has excluded from heaven, Theodosius from earth. Lo! a golden age begins; lo! the old breed of men returns. Peace and Godliness, Love and Honour hold high their heads throughout the world and sing a proud song of triumph over our conquered folk. Justice herself (oh the pity of it!), down-gliding through the limpid air, exults over me and, now that crime has been cut down to the roots, frees law from the dark prison wherein she lay oppressed. Shall we, expelled from every land, lie this long age in shameful torpor? Ere it be too late recognize a Fury's duty: resume your wonted strength and decree a crime worthy of this august assembly. Fain would I shroud the stars in Stygian darkness, smirch the light of day with our breath, unbridle the ocean deeps, hurl rivers against their shattered banks, and break the bonds of the universe."

So spake she with cruel roar and uproused every gaping serpent mouth as she shook her snaky locks and scattered their baneful poison. Of two minds was the band of her sisters. The greater number was for declaring war upon heaven, yet some respected still the ordinances of Dis and the uproar grew by reason of their dissension, even as the sea's calm is not at once restored, but the deep still thunders when, for all the wind be dropped, the swelling tide yet flows, and the last weary winds of the departing storm play o'er the tossing waves.

Thereupon cruel Megaera rose from her funereal seat, mistress she of madness' howlings and impious ill and wrath bathed in fury's foam. No blood her drink but that flowing from kindred slaughter and forbidden crime, shed by a father's, by a brother's

quem dederint fratres ; haec terruit Herculis ora
et defensores terrarum polluit arcus,   80
haec Athamanteae direxit spicula dextrae,
haec Agamemnonios inter bacchata penates
alternis lusit iugulis ; hac auspice taedae
Oedipoden matri, natae iunxere Thyesten.
quae tunc horrisonis effatur talia dictis :   85
    " Signa quidem, sociae, divos attollere contra
nec fas est nec posse reor ; sed laedere mundum
si libet et populis commune intendere letum.
est mihi prodigium cunctis inmanius hydris,
tigride mobilius feta, violentius Austris   90
acribus, Euripi fulvis incertius undis
Rufinus, quem prima meo de matre cadentem
suscepi gremio.   parvus reptavit in isto
saepe sinu teneroque per ardua colla volutus
ubera quaesivit fletu linguisque trisulcis   95
mollia lambentes finxerunt membra cerastae ;
meque etiam tradente dolos artesque nocendi
edidicit : simulare fidem sensusque minaces
protegere et blando fraudem praetexere risu,
plenus saevitiae lucrique cupidine fervens.   100
non Tartesiacis illum satiaret harenis
tempestas pretiosa Tagi, non stagna rubentis
aurea Pactoli ; totumque exhauserit Hermum,
ardebit maiore siti.   quam fallere mentes
doctus et unanimos odiis turbare sodales !   105
talem progenies hominum si prisca tulisset,
Perithoum fugeret Theseus, offensus Orestem
desereret Pylades, odisset Castora Pollux.
ipsa quidem fateor vinci rapidoque magistram

---

¹ Athamas, king of Orchomenus, murdered his son
Learchus in a fit of madness.
32

sword. 'Twas she made e'en Hercules afraid and brought shame upon that bow that had freed the world of monsters ; she aimed the arrow in Athamas'[1] hand : she took her pleasure in murder after murder, a mad fury in Agamemnon's palace ; beneath her auspices wedlock mated Oedipus with his mother and Thyestes with his daughter. Thus then she speaks with dread-sounding words :

" To raise our standards against the gods, my sisters, is neither right nor, methinks, possible ; but hurt the world we may, if such our wish, and bring an universal destruction upon its inhabitants. I have a monster more savage than the hydra brood, swifter than the mother tigress, fiercer than the south wind's blast, more treacherous than Euripus' yellow flood—Rufinus. I was the first to gather him, a new-born babe, to my bosom. Often did the child nestle in mine embrace and seek my breast, his arms thrown about my neck in a flood of infant tears. My snakes shaped his soft limbs licking them with their three-forked tongues. I taught him guile whereby he learnt the arts of injury and deceit, how to conceal the intended menace and cover his treachery with a smile, full-filled with savagery and hot with lust of gain. Him nor the sands of rich Tagus' flood by Tartessus' town could satisfy nor the golden waters of ruddy Pactolus ; should he drink all Hermus' stream he would parch with the greedier thirst. How skilled to deceive and wreck friendships with hate ! Had that old generation of men produced such an one as he, Theseus had fled Pirithous, Pylades deserted Orestes in wrath, Pollux hated Castor. I confess myself his inferior : his quick genius has outstripped

praevenit ingenio ; nec plus sermone morabor :   110
solus habet scelerum quidquid possedimus omnes.
hunc ego, si vestrae res est accommoda turbae,
regalem ad summi producam principis aulam.
sit licet ipse Numa gravior, sit denique Minos,
cedet et insidiis nostri flectetur alumni."   115
   Orantem sequitur clamor cunctaeque profanas
porrexere manus inventaque tristia laudant.
illa ubi caeruleo vestes conexuit angue
nodavitque adamante comas, Phlegethonta sonorum
poscit et ambusto flagrantis ab aggere ripae   120
ingentem piceo succendit gurgite pinum
pigraque veloces per Tartara concutit alas.
   Est locus extremum pandit qua Gallia litus
Oceani praetentus aquis, ubi fertur Ulixes
sanguine libato populum movisse silentem.   125
illic umbrarum tenui stridore volantum
flebilis auditur questus ; simulacra coloni
pallida defunctasque vident migrare figuras.
hinc dea prosiluit Phoebique egressa serenos
infecit radios ululatuque aethera rupit   130
terrifico : sentit ferale Britannia murmur
et Senonum quatit arva fragor revolutaque Tethys
substitit et Rhenus proiecta torpuit urna.
tunc in canitiem mutatis sponte colubris
longaevum mentita senem rugisque seueras   135
persulcata genas et ficto languida passu
invadit muros Elusae, notissima dudum

---

[1] Their territory lay some sixty miles S.E. of Paris.   Its
chief town was Agedincum (mod. Sens).
[2] Elusa (the modern Eauze in the Department of Gers)
was the birthplace of Rufinus (*cf.* Zosim. iv. 51. 1).
34

his preceptress : in a word (that I waste not your time further) all the wickedness that is ours in common is his alone. Him will I introduce, if the plan commend itself to you, to the kingly palace of the emperor of the world. Be he wiser than Numa, be he Minos' self, needs must he yield and succumb to the treachery of my foster child."

A shout followed her words : all stretched forth their impious hands and applauded the awful plot. When Megaera had gathered together her dress with the black serpent that girdled her, and bound her hair with combs of steel, she approached the sounding stream of Phlegethon, and seizing a tall pine-tree from the scorched summit of the flaming bank kindled it in the pitchy flood, then plied her swift wings o'er sluggish Tartarus.

There is a place where Gaul stretches her furthermost shore spread out before the waves of Ocean : 'tis there that Ulysses is said to have called up the silent ghosts with a libation of blood. There is heard the mournful weeping of the spirits of the dead as they flit by with faint sound of wings, and the inhabitants see the pale ghosts pass and the shades of the dead. 'Twas from here the goddess leapt forth, dimmed the sun's fair beams and clave the sky with horrid howlings. Britain felt the deadly sound, the noise shook the country of the Senones,[1] Tethys stayed her tide, and Rhine let fall his urn and shrank his stream. Thereupon, in the guise of an old man, her serpent locks changed at her desire to snowy hair, her dread cheeks furrowed with many a wrinkle and feigning weariness in her gait she enters the walls of Elusa,[2] in search of the house she had long known so well. Long

35

tecta petens, oculisque diu liventibus haesit
peiorem mirata virum, tum talia fatur :
    " Otia te, Rufine, iuvant frustraque iuventae   140
consumis florem patriis inglorius arvis ?
heu nescis quid fata tibi, quid sidera debent,
quid Fortuna parat : toto dominabere mundo,
si parere velis ! artus ne sperne seniles !
namque mihi magicae vires aevique futuri   145
praescius ardor inest ; novi quo Thessala cantu
eripiat lunare iubar, quid signa sagacis
Aegypti valeant, qua gens Chaldaea vocatis
imperet arte deis, nec me latuere fluentes
arboribus suci funestarumque potestas   150
herbarum, quidquid letali gramine pollens
Caucasus et Scythicae vernant in crimina¹ rupes,
quas legit Medea ferox et callida Circe.
saepius horrendos manes sacrisque litavi
nocturnis Hecaten et condita funera traxi   155
carminibus victura meis, multosque canendo,
quamvis Parcarum restarent fila, peremi.
ire vagas quercus et fulmen stare coegi
versaque non prono curvavi flumina lapsu
in fontes reditura suos. ne vana locutum   160
me fortasse putes, mutatos cerne penates."
dixerat, et niveae (mirum !) coepere columnae
ditari subitoque trabes lucere metallo.
    Inlecebris capitur nimiumque elatus avaro
pascitur aspectu. sic rex ad prima tumebat   165

---

¹ gramina *E* : *other codd.* gramine. *Birt. conjectures*
toxica, *Heinsius* carmina. *I take Postgate's* crimina

she stood and gazed with jealous eyes, marvelling at a man worse than herself; then spake she thus: "Does ease content thee, Rufinus? Wastest thou in vain the flower of thy youth inglorious thus in thy father's fields? Thou knowest not what fate and the stars owe thee, what fortune makes ready. So thou wilt obey me thou shalt be lord of the whole world. Despise not an old man's feeble limbs: I have the gift of magic and the fire of prophecy is within me. I have learned the incantations wherewith Thessalian witches pull down the bright moon, I know the meaning of the wise Egyptians' runes, the art whereby the Chaldeans impose their will upon the subject gods, the various saps that flow within trees and the power of deadly herbs; all those that grow on Caucasus rich in poisonous plants, or, to man's bane, clothe the crags of Scythia; herbs such as cruel Medea gathered and curious Circe. Often in nocturnal rites have I sought to propitiate the dread ghosts and Hecate, and recalled the shades of buried men to live again by my magic: many, too, has my wizardry brought to destruction though the Fates had yet somewhat of their life's thread to spin. I have caused oaks to walk and the thunderbolt to stay his course, aye, and made rivers reverse their course and flow backwards to their fount. Lest thou perchance think these be but idle boasts behold the change of thine own house." At these words the white pillars, to his amazement, began to turn into gold and the beams of a sudden to shine with metal.

His senses are captured by the bait, and, thrilled beyond measure, he feasts his greedy eyes on the sight. So Midas, king of Lydia, swelled at first

Maeonius, pulchro cum verteret omnia tactu ;
sed postquam riguisse dapes fulvamque revinctos
in glaciem vidit latices, tum munus acerbum
sensit et inviso votum damnavit in auro.
ergo animi victus " sequimur quocumque vocabis, 170
seu tu vir seu numen " ait, patriaque relicta
Eoas Furiae iussu tendebat ad arces
instabilesque olim Symplegadas et freta remis
inclita Thessalicis, celsa qua Bosphorus urbe
splendet et Odrysiis Asiam discriminat oris.   175

   Ut longum permensus iter ductusque maligno
stamine fatorum claram subrepsit in aulam,
ilicet ambitio nasci, discedere rectum,
venum cuncta dari ; profert arcana, clientes
fallit et ambitos a principe vendit honores.   180
ingeminat crimen, commoti pectoris ignem
nutrit et exiguum stimulando vulnus acerbat.
ac velut innumeros amnes accedere Nereus
nescit et undantem quamvis hinc hauriat Histrum,
hinc bibat aestivum septeno gurgite Nilum,   185
par semper similisque manet : sic fluctibus auri
expleri calor ille nequit.   cuicumque monile
contextum gemmis aut praedia culta fuissent,
Rufino populandus erat, dominoque parabat
exitium fecundus ager ; metuenda colonis   190
fertilitas : laribus pellit, detrudit avitis
38

with pride when he found he could transform everything he touched to gold: but when he beheld his food grow rigid and his drink harden into golden ice then he understood that this gift was a bane and in his loathing for the gold cursed his prayer. Thus Rufinus, overcome, cried out: "Whithersoever thou summonest me I follow, be thou man or god." Then at the Fury's bidding he left his fatherland and approached the cities of the East, threading the once floating Symplegades and the seas renowned for the voyage of the Argo, ship of Thessaly, till he came to where, beneath its high-walled town, the gleaming Bosporus separates Asia from the Thracian coast.

When he had completed this long journey and, led by the evil thread of the fates, had won his way into the far-famed palace, then did ambition straightway come to birth and right was no more. Everything had its price. He betrayed secrets, deceived dependents, and sold honours that had been wheedled from the emperor. He followed up one crime with another, heaping fuel on the inflamed mind and probing and embittering the erstwhile trivial wound. And yet, as Nereus knows no addition from the infinitude of rivers that flow into him and though here he drains Danube's wave and there Nile's summer flood with its sevenfold mouth, yet ever remains his same and constant self, so Rufinus' thirst knew no abatement for all the streams of gold that flowed in upon him. Had any a necklace studded with jewels or a fertile demesne he was sure prey for Rufinus: a rich property assured the ruin of its own possessor: fertility was the husbandman's bane. He drives them from their homes, expels them from the lands their sires had

finibus ; aut aufert vivis aut occupat heres
congestae cumulantur opes orbisque ruinas
accipit una domus : populi servire coacti
plenaque privato succumbunt oppida regno.   195

    Quo, vesane, ruis ? teneas utrumque licebit
Oceanum, laxet rutilos tibi Lydia fontes,
iungatur solium Croesi Cyrique tiara :
numquam dives eris, numquam satiabere quaestu.
semper inops quicumque cupit. contentus honesto
Fabricius parvo spernebat munera regum   201
sudabatque gravi consul Serranus aratro
et casa pugnaces Curios angusta tegebat.
haec mihi paupertas opulentior, haec mihi tecta
culminibus maiora tuis. ibi quaerit inanes   205
luxuries nocitura cibos ; hic donat inemptas
terra dapes. rapiunt Tyrios ibi vellera sucos
et picturatae saturantur murice vestes ;
hic radiant flores et prati viva voluptas
ingenio variata suo. fulgentibus illic   210
surgunt strata toris ; hic mollis panditur herba
sollicitum curis non abruptura soporem.
turba salutantum latas ibi perstrepit aedes ;
hic avium cantus, labentis murmura rivi.
vivitur exiguo melius ; natura beatis   215
omnibus esse dedit, si quis cognoverit uti.
haec si nota forent, frueremur simplice cultu,
classica non gemerent, non stridula fraxinus iret,
nec ventus quateret puppes nec machina muros.

left them, either wresting them from the living owners or fastening upon them as an inheritor. Massed riches are piled up and a single house receives the plunder of a world; whole peoples are forced into slavery, and thronging cities bow beneath the tyranny of a private man.

Madman, what shall be the end? Though thou possess either Ocean, though Lydia pour forth for thee her golden waters, though thou join Croesus' throne to Cyrus' crown, yet shalt thou never be rich nor ever contented with thy booty. The greedy man is always poor. Fabricius, happy in his honourable poverty, despised the gifts of monarchs; the consul Serranus sweated at his heavy plough and a small cottage gave shelter to the warlike Curii. To my mind such poverty as this is richer than thy wealth, such a home greater than thy palaces. There pernicious luxury seeks for the food that satisfieth not; here the earth provides a banquet for which is nought to pay. With thee wool absorbs the dyes of Tyre; thy patterned clothes are stained with purple; here are bright flowers and the meadow's breathing charm which owes its varied hues but to itself. There are beds piled on glittering bedsteads; here stretches the soft grass, that breaks not sleep with anxious cares. There a crowd of clients dins through the spacious halls, here is song of birds and the murmur of the gliding stream. A frugal life is best. Nature has given the opportunity of happiness to all, knew they but how to use it. Had we realized this we should now have been enjoying a simple life, no trumpets would be sounding, no whistling spear would speed, no ship be buffeted by the wind, no siege-engine overthrow battlements.

Crescebat scelerata sitis praedaeque recentis   220
incestus flagrabat amor, nullusque petendi
cogendive pudor : crebris periuria nectit
blanditiis ; sociat perituro foedere dextras.
si semel e tantis poscenti quisque negasset,
effera praetumido quatiebat corda furore.   225
quae sic Gaetuli iaculo percussa leaena
aut Hyrcana premens raptorem belua partus
aut serpens calcata furit ? iurata deorum
maiestas teritur ; nusquam reverentia mensae.
non coniunx, non ipse simul, non pignora caesa   230
sufficiunt odiis ; non extinxisse propinquos,
non notos egisse sat est ; exscindere cives
funditus et nomen gentis delere laborat.
nec celeri perimit leto ; crudelibus ante
suppliciis fruitur ; cruciatus, vincla, tenebras   235
dilato mucrone parat. pro saevior ense
parcendi rabies concessaque vita dolori !
mors adeone parum est ? causis fallacibus instat,
arguit attonitos se iudice. cetera segnis,
ad facinus velox, penitus regione remotas   240
impiger ire vias : non illum Sirius ardens
brumave Riphaeo stridens Aquilone retardat.
effera torquebant avidae praecordia curae,
effugeret ne quis gladios neu perderet ullum
Augusto miserante nefas. non flectitur annis,   245
non aetate labat : iuvenum rorantia colla
ante patrum vultus stricta cecidere securi ;

THE FIRST BOOK AGAINST RUFINUS

Still grew Rufinus' wicked greed, and his impious passion for new-won wealth blazed yet fiercer; no feeling of shame kept him from demanding and extorting money. He combines perjury with ceaseless cajolery, ratifying with a hand-clasp the bond he purposes to break. Should any dare to refuse his demand for one thing out of so many, his fierce heart would be stirred with swelling wrath. Was ever lioness wounded with a Gaetulian's spear, or Hyrcan tiger pursuing the robber of her young, was ever bruisèd serpent so fierce? He swears by the majesty of the gods and tramples on his oath. He reverences not the laws of hospitality. To kill a wife and her husband with her and her children sates not his anger; 'tis not enough to slaughter relations and drive friends into exile; he strives to destroy every citizen of Rome and to blot out the very name of our race. Nor does he even slay with a swift death; ere that he enjoys the infliction of cruel torture; the rack, the chain, the lightless cell, these he sets before the final blow. Why, this remission is more savage, more madly cruel, than the sword—this grant of life that agony may accompany it! Is death not enough for him? With treacherous charges he attacks; dazed wretches find him at once accuser and judge. Slow to all else he is swift to crime and tireless to visit the ends of the earth in its pursuit. Neither the Dog-star's heat nor the wintry blasts of the Thracian north wind detain him. Feverish anxiety torments his cruel heart lest any escape his sword, or an emperor's pardon lose him an opportunity for injury. Neither age nor youth can move his pity: before their father's eyes his bloody axe severs boys' heads

ibat grandaevus nato moriente superstes
post trabeas exul.   quis prodere tanta relatu
funera, quis caedes possit deflere nefandas ?   250
quid tale inmanes umquam gessisse feruntur
vel Sinis Isthmiaca pinu vel rupe profunda
Sciron vel Phalaris tauro vel carcere Sulla ?
o mites Diomedis equi !   Busiridis arae
clementes !   iam Cinna pius, iam Spartace segnis 255
Rufino collatus eris !
                              Deiecerat omnes
occultis odiis terror tacitique sepultos
suspirant gemitus indignarique verentur.
at non magnanimi virtus Stilichonis eodem
fracta metu ; solus medio sed turbine rerum   260
contra letiferos rictus contraque rapacem
movit tela feram, volucris non praepete cursu
vectus equi, non Pegaseis adiutus habenis.
hic cunctis optata quies, hic sola pericli
turris erat clipeusque trucem porrectus in hostem,
hic profugis sedes adversaque signa furori,   266
servandis hic castra bonis.
                              Hucusque minatus
haerebat retroque fuga cedebat inerti :
haud secus hiberno tumidus cum vertice torrens
saxa rotat volvitque nemus pontesque revellit,   270
frangitur obiectu scopuli quaerensque meatum
spumat et inlisa montem circumtonat unda.
   Qua dignum te laude feram, qui paene ruenti

from their bodies; an aged man, once a consul, survived the murder of his son but to be driven into exile. Who can bring himself to tell of so many murders, who can adequately mourn such impious slaughter? Do men tell that cruel Sinis of Corinth e'er wrought such wickedness with his pine-tree, or Sciron with his precipitous rock, or Phalaris with his brazen bull, or Sulla with his prison? O gentle horses of Diomede! O pitiful altars of Busiris! Henceforth, compared with Rufinus thou, Cinna, shalt be loving, and thou, Spartacus, a sluggard.

All were a prey to terror, for men knew not where next his hidden hatred would break forth, they sob in silence for the tears they dare not shed and fear to show their indignation. Yet is not the spirit of great-hearted Stilicho broken by this same fear. Alone amid the general calamity he took arms against this monster of greed and his devouring maw, though not borne on the swift course of any wingèd steed nor aided by Pegasus' reins. In him all found the quiet they longed for, he was their one defence in danger, their shield out-held against the fierce foe, the exile's sanctuary, standard confronting the madness of Rufinus, fortress for the protection of the good.

Thus far Rufinus advanced his threats and stayed; then fell back in coward flight: even as a torrent swollen with winter rains rolls down great stones in its course, overwhelms woods, tears away bridges, yet is broken by a jutting rock, and, seeking a way through, foams and thunders about the cliff with shattered waves.

How can I praise thee worthily, thou who sus-

45

lapsuroque tuos umeros obieceris orbi ?
te nobis trepidae sidus ceu dulce carinae   275
ostendere dei, geminis quae lassa procellis
tunditur et victo trahitur iam caeca magistro.
Inachius Rubro perhibetur in aequore Perseus
Neptuni domuisse pecus, sed tutior alis :
te non penna vehit ; rigida cum Gorgone Perseus :
tu non vipereo defensus crine Medusae ;   281
illum vilis amor suspensae virginis egit :
te Romana salus.   taceat superata vetustas,
Herculeos conferre tuis iam desinat actus.
una Cleonaeum pascebat silva leonem ;   285
Arcadiae saltum vastabat dentibus unum
saevus aper, tuque o compressa matre rebellans
non ultra Libyae fines, Antaee, nocebas,
solaque fulmineo resonabat Creta iuvenco
Lernaeamque virens obsederat hydra paludem.   290
hoc monstrum non una palus, non una tremebat
insula, sed Latia quidquid dicione subactum
vivit, et a primis Ganges horrebat Hiberis.
hoc neque Geryon triplex nec turbidus Orci
ianitor aequabit nec si concurrat in unum   295
vis hydrae Scyllaeque fames et flamma Chimaerae.
    Certamen sublime diu, sed moribus impar
virtutum scelerumque fuit.   iugulare minatur :
tu prohibes ; ditem spoliat : tu reddis egenti ;
eruit : instauras ; accendit proelia : vincis.   300

tainedst with thy shoulders the tottering world in
its threatened fall? The gods gave thee to us
as they show a welcome star to frightened mariners
whose weary bark is buffeted with storms of wind
and wave and drifts with blind course now that
her steersman is beaten. Perseus, descendant of
Inachus, is said to have overcome Neptune's monsters
in the Red Sea, but he was helped by his wings;
no wing bore thee aloft: Perseus was armed with
the Gorgons' head that turneth all to stone; the
snaky locks of Medusa protected not thee. His
motive was but the love of a chained girl, thine the
salvation of Rome. The days of old are surpassed;
let them keep silence and cease to compare Hercules'
labours with thine. 'Twas but one wood that
sheltered the lion of Cleonae, the savage boar's
tusks laid waste a single Arcadian vale, and thou,
rebel Antaeus, holding thy mother earth in thine
embrace, didst no hurt beyond the borders of Africa.
Crete alone re-echoed to the bellowings of the fire-
breathing bull, and the green hydra beleaguered no
more than Lerna's lake. But this monster Rufinus
terrified not one lake nor one island: whatsoever
lives beneath the Roman rule, from distant Spain
to Ganges' stream, was in fear of him. Neither
triple Geryon nor Hell's fierce janitor can vie with
him nor could the conjoined terrors of powerful
Hydra, ravenous Scylla, and fiery Chimaera.

Long hung the contest in suspense, but the struggle
betwixt vice and virtue was ill-matched in character.
Rufinus threatens slaughter, thou stayest his hand;
he robs the rich, thou givest back to the poor; he
overthrows, thou restorest; he sets wars afoot, thou
winnest them. As a pestilence, growing from day

ac velut infecto morbus crudescere caelo
incipiens primos pecudum depascitur artus,
mox populos urbesque rapit ventisque perustis
corruptos Stygiam pestem desudat in amnes :
sic avidus praedo iam non per singula saevit.   305
sed sceptris inferre minas omnique perempto
milite Romanas ardet prosternere vires,
iamque Getas Histrumque movet Scythiamque
          receptat
auxilio traditque suas hostilibus armis
relliquias.   mixtis descendit Sarmata Dacis   310
et qui cornipedes in pocula vulnerat audax
Massagetes caesamque bibens Maeotin Alanus
membraque qui ferro gaudet pinxisse Gelonus,
Rufino collecta manus.   vetat ille domari
innectitque moras et congrua tempora differt.   315
nam tua cum Geticas stravisset dextra catervas,
ulta ducis socii letum, parsque una maneret
debilior facilisque capi, tunc impius ille
proditor imperii coniuratusque Getarum
distulit instantes eluso principe pugnas   320
Hunorum laturus opem, quos adfore bello
norat et invisis mox se coniungere castris.

   Est genus extremos Scythiae vergentis in ortus
trans gelidum Tanain, quo non famosius ullum
Arctos alit.   turpes habitus obscaenaque visu   325
corpora ; mens duro numquam cessura labori ;
praeda cibus, vitanda Ceres frontemque secari

---

[1] Here and throughout his poems Claudian refers to the
Visigoths as the Getae.
[2] *Cf.* Introduction, p. x.
48

to day by reason of the infected air, fastens first
upon the bodies of animals but soon sweeps away
peoples and cities, and when the winds blow hot
spreads its hellish poison to the polluted streams,
so the ambitious rebel marks down no private prey,
but hurls his eager threats at kings, and seeks to
destroy Rome's army and overthrow her might.
Now he stirs up the Getae[1] and the tribes on
Danube's banks, allies himself with Scythia and
exposes what few his cruelties have spared to the
sword of the enemy. There march against us a
mixed horde of Sarmatians and Dacians, the
Massagetes who cruelly wound their horses that
they may drink their blood, the Alans who break the
ice and drink the waters of Maeotis' lake, and the
Geloni who tattoo their limbs : these form Rufinus'
army. And he brooks not their defeat ; he
frames delays and postpones the fitting season for
battle. For when thy right hand, Stilicho, had
scattered the Getic bands and avenged the death
of thy brother general, when one section of Rufinus'
army was thus weakened and made an easy prey,
then that foul traitor, that conspirator with the
Getae, tricked the emperor and put off the instant
day of battle, meaning to ally himself with the
Huns, who, as he knew, would fight and quickly join
the enemies of Rome.[2]

These Huns are a tribe who live on the extreme
eastern borders of Scythia, beyond frozen Tanais ;
most infamous of all the children of the north.
Hideous to look upon are their faces and loathsome
their bodies, but indefatigable is their spirit. The
chase supplies their food ; bread they will not eat.
They love to slash their faces and hold it a

ludus et occisos pulchrum iurare parentes.
nec plus nubigenas duplex natura biformes
cognatis aptavit equis ; acerrima nullo   330
ordine mobilitas insperatique recursus.

     Quos tamen impavidus contra spumantis ad Hebri
tendis aquas, sic ante tubas aciemque precatus :
" Mavors, nubifero seu tu procumbis in Haemo
seu te cana gelu Rhodope seu remige Medo   335
sollicitatus Athos seu caligantia nigris
ilicibus Pangaea tenent, accingere mecum
et Thracas defende tuos   si laetior adsit
gloria, vestita spoliis donabere quercu."

     Audiit illa pater scopulisque nivalibus Haemi   340
surgit et hortatur celeres clamore ministros :
" fer galeam, Bellona, mihi nexusque rotarum
tende, Pavor.   frenet rapidos Formido iugales.
festinas urgete manus.   meus ecce paratur
ad bellum Stilicho, qui me de more tropaeis   345
ditat et hostiles suspendit in arbore cristas.
communes semper litui, communia nobis
signa canunt iunctoque sequor tentoria curru."
sic fatus campo insiluit lateque fugatas
hinc Stilicho turmas, illinc Gradivus agebat   350
et clipeis et mole pares ; stat cassis utrique
sidereis hirsuta iubis loricaque cursu
aestuat et largo saturatur vulnere cornus.

     Acrior interea voto multisque Megaera
luxuriata malis maestam deprendit in arce   355
50

righteous act to swear by their murdered parents. Their double nature fitted not better the twi-formed Centaurs to the horses that were parts of them. Disorderly, but of incredible swiftness, they often return to the fight when little expected.

Fearless, however, against such forces, thou, Stilicho, approachest the waters of foaming Hebrus and thus prayest ere the trumpets sound and the fight begins: "Mars, whether thou reclinest on cloud-capped Haemus, or frost-white Rhodope holdeth thee, or Athos, severed to give passage to the Persian fleet, or Pangaeus, gloomy with dark holm-oaks, gird thyself at my side and defend thine own land of Thrace. If victory smile on us, thy meed shall be an oak stump adorned with spoils."

The Father heard his prayer and rose from the snowy peaks of Haemus shouting commands to his speedy servants: "Bellona, bring my helmet; fasten me, Panic, the wheels upon my chariot; harness my swift horses, Fear. Hasten: speed on your work. See, my Stilicho makes him ready for war; Stilicho whose habit it is to load me with rich trophies and hang upon the oak the plumed helmets of his enemies. For us together the trumpets ever sound the call to battle; yoking my chariot I follow wheresoever he pitch his camp." So spake he and leapt upon the plain, and on this side Stilicho scattered the enemy bands in broadcast flight and on that Mars; alike the twain in accoutrement and stature. The helmets of either tower with bristling crests, their breastplates flash as they speed along and their spears take their fill of widely dealt wounds.

Meanwhile Megaera, more eager now she has got her way, and revelling in this widespread

Iustitiam diroque prior sic ore lacessit :
" en tibi prisca quies renovataque saecula rursus,
ut rebare, vigent ? en nostra potentia cessit
nec locus est usquam Furiis ? huc lumina flecte.
adspice barbaricis iaceant quot moenia flammis,   360
quas mihi Rufinus strages quantumque cruoris
praebeat et quantis epulentur caedibus hydri.
linque homines sortemque meam, pete sidera ; notis
Autumni te redde plagis, qua vergit in Austrum
Signifer ; aestivo sedes vicina Leoni   365
iam pridem gelidaeque vacant confinia Librae.
atque utinam per magna sequi convexa liceret ! "

   Diva refert : " non ulterius bacchabere demens.
iam poenas tuus iste dabit, iam debitus ultor
inminet, et, terras qui nunc ipsumque fatigat   370
aethera, non vili moriens condetur harena.
iamque aderit laeto promissus Honorius aevo
nec forti genitore minor nec fratre corusco,
qui subiget Medos, qui cuspide proteret Indos.
sub iuga venturi reges ; calcabitur asper   375
Phasis equo pontemque pati cogetur Araxes,
tuque simul gravibus ferri religata catenis
expellere die debellatasque draconum
tonsa comas imo barathri claudere recessu.
tum tellus communis erit, tum limite nullo   380
52

calamity, comes upon Justice sad at heart in her palace, and thus provokes her with horrid utterance: " Is this that old reign of peace; this the return of that golden age thou fondly hopedst had come to pass ? Is our power gone, and no place now left for the Furies ? Turn thine eyes this way. See how many cities the barbarians' fires have laid low, how vast a slaughter, how much blood Rufinus hath procured for me, and on what widespread death my serpents gorge themselves. Leave thou the world of men ; that lot is mine. Mount to the stars, return to that well-known tract of Autumn sky where the Standard-bearer dips towards the south. The space next to the summer constellation of the Lion, the neighbourhood of the winter Balance has long been empty. And would I could now follow thee through the dome of heaven."

The goddess made answer : " Thou shalt rage no further, mad that thou art. Now shall thy creature receive his due, the destined avenger hangs over him, and he who now wearies land and the very sky shall die, though no handful of dust shall cover his corpse. Soon shall come Honorius, promised of old to this fortunate age, brave as his father Theodosius, brilliant as his brother Arcadius ; he shall subdue the Medes and overthrow the Indians with his spear. Kings shall pass under his yoke, frozen Phasis shall bear his horses' hooves, and Araxes submit perforce to be bridged by him. Then too shalt thou be bound with heavy chains of iron and cast out from the light of day and imprisoned in the nethermost pit, thy snaky locks overcome and shorn from thy head. Then the world shall be owned by all in common, no field marked off from another

discernetur ager ; nec vomere sulcus adunco
findetur : subitis messor gaudebit aristis.
rorabunt querceta favis ; stagnantia passim
vina fluent oleique lacus ; nec murice tinctis
velleribus quaeretur honos, sed sponte rubebunt 385
attonito pastore greges pontumque per omnem
ridebunt virides gemmis nascentibus algae."

by any dividing boundary, no furrow cleft with bended ploughshare; for the husbandman shall rejoice in corn that springs untended. Oak groves shall drip with honey, streams of wine well up on every side, lakes of oil abound. No price shall be asked for fleeces dyed scarlet, but of themselves shall the flocks grow red to the astonishment of the shepherd, and in every sea the green seaweed will laugh with flashing jewels."

IN RUFINUM LIBER SECUNDUS

INCIPIT PRAEFATIO

(IV)

Pandite defensum reduces Helicona sorores,
   pandite ; permissis iam licet ire choris :
nulla per Aonios hostilis bucina campos
   carmina mugitu deteriore vetat.
tu quoque securis pulsa formidine Delphis   5
   floribus ultorem, Delie, cinge tuum.
nullus Castalios latices et praescia fati
   flumina polluto barbarus ore bibit.
Alpheus late rubuit Siculumque per aequor
   sanguineas belli rettulit unda notas   10
agnovitque novos absens Arethusa triumphos
   et Geticam sensit teste cruore necem.

Inmensis, Stilicho, succedant otia curis
   et nostrae patiens corda remitte lyrae,
nec pudeat longos interrupisse labores   15
   et tenuem Musis constituisse moram.
fertur et indomitus tandem post proelia Mavors
   lassa per Odrysias fundere membra nives
oblitusque sui posita clementior hasta
   Pieriis aures pacificare modis.   . 20

---

[1] A reference to Stilicho's campaign against Alaric in the
Peloponnese in 397 (see Introduction, p. x).

THE SECOND BOOK AGAINST RUFINUS

PREFACE

(IV)

Return, ye Muses, and throw open rescued
Helicon ; now again may your company gather
there. Nowhere now in Italy does the hostile trumpet
forbid song with its viler bray. Do thou too, Delian
Apollo, now that Delphi is safe and fear has been
dispelled, wreath thy avenger's head with flowers.
No savage foe sets profane lips to Castalia's spring
or those prophetic streams. Alpheus'[1] flood ran
all his length red with slaughter and the waves
bore the bloody marks of war across the Sicilian
sea ; whereby Arethusa, though herself not present,
recognized the triumphs freshly won and knew of
the slaughter of the Getae, to which that blood bore
witness.

Let peace, Stilicho, succeed these age-long labours
and ease thine heart by graciously listening to my
song. Think it no shame to interrupt thy long toil
and to consecrate a few moments to the Muses. Even
unwearying Mars is said to have stretched his tired
limbs on the snowy Thracian plain when at last
the battle was ended, and, unmindful of his wonted
fierceness, to have laid aside his spear in gentler
mood, soothing his ear with the Muses' melody.

57

LIBER II

(V)

Iam post edomitas Alpes defensaque regna
Hesperiae merita complexus sede parentem
auctior adiecto fulgebat sidere mundus,
iamque tuis, Stilicho, Romana potentia curis
et rerum commissus apex, tibi credita fratrum   5
utraque maiestas geminaeque exercitus aulae.
Rufinus (neque enim patiuntur saeva quietem
crimina pollutaeque negant arescere fauces)
infandis iterum terras accendere bellis
incohat et solito pacem vexare tumultu.   10
haec etiam secum : " quanam ratione tuebor
spem vitae fragilem ?   qua tot depellere fluctus
arte queam ? premor hinc odiis, hinc milite cingor.
heu quid agam ? non arma mihi, non principis ullus
auxiliatur amor.   matura pericula surgunt   15
undique et impositi radiant cervicibus enses.
quid restat, nisi cuncta novo confundere luctu
insontesque meae populos miscere ruinae ?
everso iuvat orbe mori ; solacia leto

---

¹ Theodosius died in January 395, not long after his
defeat of Eugenius at the Frigidus River (near Aquileia),
September 5-6, 394 (see Introduction, p. ix).
58

BOOK II

(V)

After the subjugation of the Alpine tribes and the salvation of the kingdoms of Italy the heavens welcomed the Emperor Theodosius [1] to the place of honour due to his worth, and so shone the brighter by the addition of another star. Then was the power of Rome entrusted to thy care, Stilicho; in thy hands was placed the governance of the world. The brothers' twin majesty and the armies of either royal court were given into thy charge. But Rufinus (for cruelty and crime brook not peace, and a tainted mouth will not forgo its draughts of blood), Rufinus, I say, began once more to inflame the world with wicked wars and to disturb peace with accustomed sedition. Thus to himself: "How shall I assure my slender hopes of survival? By what means beat back the rising storm? On all sides are hate and the threat of arms. What am I to do? No help can I find in soldier's weapon or emperor's favour. Instant dangers ring me round and a gleaming sword hangs above my head. What is left but to plunge the world into fresh troubles and draw down innocent peoples in my ruin? Gladly will I perish if the world does too; general destruction shall console me for

exitium commune dabit nec territus ante   20
discedam : cum luce simul linquenda potestas."
   Haec fatus, ventis veluti si frena resolvat
Aeolus, abrupto gentes sic obice fudit
laxavitque viam bellis et, nequa maneret
inmunis regio, cladem divisit in orbem   25
disposuitque nefas. alii per terga ferocis
Danuvii solidata ruunt expertaque remos
frangunt stagna rotis ; alii per Caspia claustra
Armeniasque nives inopino tramite ducti
invadunt Orientis opes. iam pascua fumant   30
Cappadocum volucrumque parens Argaeus equorum,
iam rubet altus Halys nec se defendit iniquo
monte Cilix. Syriae tractus vastantur amoeni
adsuetumque choris et laeta plebe canorum
proterit imbellem sonipes hostilis Orontem.   35
hinc planctus Asiae ; Geticis Europa catervis
ludibrio praedaeque datur frondentis ad usque
Dalmatiae fines : omnis quae mobile Ponti
aequor et Adriacas tellus interiacet undas
squalet inops pecudum, nullis habitata colonis,   40
instar anhelantis Libyae, quae torrida semper
solibus humano nescit mansuescere cultu.
Thessalus ardet ager ; reticet pastore fugato
Pelion ; Emathias ignis populatur aristas.
nam plaga Pannoniae miserandaque moenia Thracum
arvaque Mysorum iam nulli flebile damnum,   46
sed cursus sollemnis erat campusque furori
expositus, sensumque malis detraxerat usus.
eheu quam brevibus pereunt ingentia fatis !
60

mine own death, nor will I die (for I am no coward)
till I have accomplished this. I will not lay down
my power before my life."

So spake he, and as if Aeolus unchained the winds
so he, breaking their bonds, let loose the nations,
clearing the way for war ; and, that no land should
be free therefrom, apportioned ruin throughout
the world, parcelling out destruction. Some pour
across the frozen surface of swift-flowing Danube
and break with the chariot wheel what erstwhile
knew but the oar ; others invade the wealthy East,
led through the Caspian Gates and over the Armenian
snows by a newly-discovered pass. The fields of
Cappadocia reek with slaughter ; Argaeus, father
of swift horses, is laid waste. Halys' deep waters
run red and the Cilician cannot defend himself
in his precipitous mountains. The pleasant plains of
Syria are devastated, and the enemy's cavalry
thunders along the banks of Orontes, home hitherto
of the dance and of a happy people's song. Hence
comes mourning to Asia, while Europe is left to be
the sport and prey of Getic hordes even to the borders
of fertile Dalmatia. All that tract of land lying
between the stormy Euxine and the Adriatic is laid
waste and plundered, no inhabitants dwell there ;
'tis like torrid Africa whose sun-scorched plains never
grow kindlier through human tillage. Thessaly
is afire ; Pelion silent, his shepherds put to flight ;
flames bring destruction on Macedonia's crops.
For Pannonia's plain, the Thracians' helpless cities,
the fields of Mysia were ruined but now none wept ;
year by year came the invader, unsheltered was the
countryside from havoc and custom had robbed
suffering of its sting. Alas, in how swift ruin perish

imperium tanto quaesitum sanguine, tanto   50
servatum, quod mille ducum peperere labores,
quod tantis Romana manus contexuit annis,
proditor unus iners angusto tempore vertit.

Urbs etiam, magnae quae ducitur aemula Romae
et Calchedonias contra despectat harenas,   55
iam non finitimo Martis terrore movetur,
sed propius lucere faces et rauca sonare
cornua vibratisque peti fastigia telis
adspicit.   hi vigili muros statione tueri,
hi iunctis properant portus munire carinis.   60
obsessa tamen ille ferus laetatur in urbe
exultatque malis summaeque ex culmine turris
impia vicini cernit spectacula campi :
vinctas ire nurus, nunc in vada proxima mergi
seminecem, hunc subito percussum vulnere labi   65
dum fugit, hunc animam portis efflare sub ipsis ;
nec canos prodesse seni puerique cruore
maternos undare sinus.   inmensa voluptas
et risus plerumque subit ; dolor afficit unus,
quod feriat non ipse manu.   videt omnia late   70
exceptis incensa suis et crimine tanto
luxuriat carumque sibi non abnuit hostem ;
iactabatque ultro, quod soli castra paterent
sermonumque foret vicibus permissa potestas.
egregii quotiens exisset foederis auctor,   75
stipatur sociis, circumque armata clientum

---

¹ Constantinople.

even the greatest things! An empire won and kept at the expense of so much bloodshed, born from the toils of countless leaders, knit together through so many years by Roman hands, one coward traitor overthrew in the twinkling of an eye.

That city,[1] too, called of men the rival of great Rome, that looks across to Chalcedon's strand, is stricken now with terror at no neighbouring war; nearer home it observes the flash of torches, the trumpet's call, and its own roofs the target for an enemy's artillery. Some guard the walls with watchful outposts, others hasten to fortify the harbour with a chain of ships. But fierce Rufinus is full of joy in the leaguered city and exults in its misfortunes, gazing at the awful spectacle of the surrounding country from the summit of a lofty tower. He watches the procession of women in chains, sees one poor half-dead wretch drowned in the water hard by, another, stricken as he fled, sink down beneath the sudden wound, another breathe out his life at the tower's very gates; he rejoices that no respect is shown to grey hairs and that mother's breasts are drenched with their children's blood. Great is his pleasure thereat; from time to time he laughs and knows but one regret—that it is not his own hand that strikes. He sees the whole countryside (except for his own lands) ablaze, and has joy of his great wickedness, making no secret of the fact that the city's foes are his friends. It is his boast, moreover, that to him alone the enemy camp opened its gates, and that there was allowed right of parley between them. Whene'er he issued forth to arrange some wondrous truce his companions thronged him round and an armed band of depen-

63

agmina privatis ibant famulantia signis ;
ipse inter medios, ne qua de parte relinquat
barbariem, revocat fulvas in pectora pelles
frenaque et inmanes pharetras arcusque sonoros   80
adsimulat mentemque palam proclamat amictu,
nec pudet Ausonios currus et iura regentem
sumere deformes ritus vestemque Getarum ;
insignemque habitum Latii mutare coactae
maerent captivae pellito iudice leges.   85

    Quis populi tum vultus erat ! quae murmura furtim !
(nam miseris ne flere quidem aut lenire dolorem
colloquiis impune licet) : " quonam usque feremus
exitiale iugum ?   durae quis terminus umquam
sortis erit ?   quis nos funesto turbine rerum   90
aut tantis solvet lacrimis, quos barbarus illinc,
hinc Rufinus agit, quibus arva fretumque negatur ?
magna quidem per rura lues, sed maior oberrat
intra tecta timor.   tandem succurre ruenti
heu patriae, Stilicho !   dilecta hic pignora certe,   95
hic domus, hic thalamis primum genialibus omen,
hic tibi felices erexit regia taedas.
vel solus sperate veni.   te proelia viso
languescent avidique cadet dementia monstri."

    Talibus urgetur discors Aurora procellis.   100
at Stilicho, Zephyris cum primum bruma remitti
et iuga diffusis nudari coepta pruinis,
partibus Italiae tuta sub pace relictis
utraque castra movens Phoebi properabat ad ortus,

64

dents danced attendance on a civilian's standards.
Rufinus himself in their midst drapes tawny skins of
beasts about his breast (thorough in his barbarity),
and uses harness and huge quivers and twanging bows
like those of the Getae—his dress openly showing the
temper of his mind. One who drives a consul's
chariot and enjoys a consul's powers has no shame to
adopt the manners and dress of barbarians ; Roman
law, obliged to change her noble garment, mourns
her slavery to a skin-clad judge.

What looks then on men's faces ! What furtive
murmurs ! For, poor wretches, they could not even
weep nor, without risk, ease their grief in converse.
" How long shall we bear this deadly yoke ? What
end shall there ever be to our hard lot ? Who will free
us from this death-fraught anarchy, this day of tears ?
On this side the barbarian hems us in, on that
Rufinus oppresses us ; land and sea are alike denied
us. A pestilence stalks through the country : yes,
but a deadlier terror haunts our houses. Stilicho,
delay no more but succour thy dying land ; of a
truth here are thy children, here thy home, here
were taken those first auspices for thy marriage,
so blessed with children, here the palace was illu-
mined with the torches of happy wedlock. Nay,
come even though alone, thou for whom we long ;
wars will perish at thy sight and the ravening
monster's rage subside."

Such were the tempests that vexed the turbulent
East. But so soon as ever winter had given place
to the winds of spring and the hills began to lose
their covering of snow, Stilicho, leaving the fields of
Italy in peace and safety, set in motion his two armies
and hastened to the lands of the sunrise, combining

Gallica discretis Eoaque robora turmis 105
amplexus.   numquam tantae dicione sub una
convenere manus nec tot discrimina vocum :
illinc Armeniae vibratis crinibus alae
herbida collectae facili velamina nodo ;
inde truces flavo comitantur vertice Galli, 110
quos Rhodanus velox, Araris quos tardior ambit
et quos nascentes explorat gurgite Rhenus
quosque rigat retro pernicior unda Garunnae,
Oceani pleno quotiens impellitur aestu.
mens eadem cunctis animique recentia ponunt 115
vulnera ; non odit victus victorve superbit.
et quamvis praesens tumor et civilia nuper
classica bellatrixque etiamnunc ira caleret,
in ducis eximii conspiravere favorem.
haud aliter Xerxen toto simul orbe secutus 120
narratur rapuisse vagos exercitus amnes
et telis umbrasse diem, cum classibus iret
per scopulos tectumque pedes contemneret aequor.

   Vix Alpes egressus erat nec iam amplius errat
barbarus adventumque timens se cogit in unam 125
planitiem tutoque includit pascua gyro :
tum duplici fossa non exuperabile vallum
asperat alternis sudibus murique locata
in speciem caesis obtendit plaustra iuvencis.

   At procul exanguis Rufinum perculit horror ; 130
infectae pallore genae ; stetit ore gelato
incertus peteretne fugam, veniamne subactus

the so different squadrons of Gaul and of the East.
Never before did there meet together under one command such numerous bands, never in one army such a babel of tongues.   Here were curly-haired Armenian cavalry, their green cloaks fastened with a loose knot, fierce Gauls with golden locks accompanied them, some from the banks of the swift-flowing Rhone, or the more sluggish Saône, some whose infant bodies Rhine's flood had laved, or who had been washed by the waves of the Garonne that flow more rapidly towards, than from, their source, whenever they are driven back by Ocean's full tide.   One common purpose inspires them all ; grudges lately harboured are laid aside ; the vanquished feels no hate, the victor shows no pride.   And despite of present unrest, of the trumpet's late challenge to civil strife, and of warlike rage still aglow, yet were all at one in their support of their great leader.   So it is said that the army that followed Xerxes, gathered into one from all quarters of the world, drank up whole rivers in their courses, obscured the sun with the rain of their arrows, passed through mountains on board ship, and walked the bridged sea with contemptuous foot.

Scarce had Stilicho crossed the Alps when the barbarian hordes began to restrict their forays and for fear of his approach gathered together in the plain and enclosed their pasture lands within a defensive ring.   They then built an impregnable fortification with a double moat, planted stakes two deep at intervals along its summit and set wagons rigged with ox-hide all round like a wall.

Panic fear seized upon Rufinus as he saw this from afar, and his cheeks grew pale.   He stood with ice-cold face, not knowing whether to fly, to own himself

posceret an fidos sese transferret in hostes.
quid nunc divitiae, quid fulvi vasta metalli
congeries, quid purpureis effulta columnis   135
atria prolataeve iuvant ad sidera moles ?
audit iter numeratque dies spatioque viarum
metitur vitam. torquetur pace futura
nec recipit somnos et saepe cubilibus amens
excutitur poenamque luit formidine poenae.   140
sed redit in rabiem scelerumque inmane resumit
ingenium sacrasque fores praedivitis aulae
intrat et Arcadium mixto terrore precatur :

    " Per fratris regale iubar, per facta parentis
aetherii floremque tui te deprecor aevi,   145
eripe me gladiis ; liceat Stilichonis iniquas
evitare minas. in nostram Gallia caedem
coniurata venit. quidquid rigat ultima Tethys,
extremos ultra volitat gens si qua Britannos,
mota mihi. tantis capiendi credimur armis ?   150
tot signis unum petitur caput ? unde cruoris
ista sitis ? geminum caeli sibi vindicat axem
et nullum vult esse parem. succumbere poscit
cuncta sibi : regit Italiam Libyamque coercet ;
Hispanis Gallisque iubet ; non orbita solis,   155
non illum natura capit. quascumque paravit
hic Augustus opes et quas post bella recepit,
solus habet, possessa semel nec reddere curat.
scilicet ille quidem tranquilla pace fruatur ;
nos premat obsidio ? quid partem invadere temptat ?
deserat Illyricos fines ; Eoa remittat   161

beaten and sue for mercy, or go over to an enemy whose good faith his treachery had assured. Of what use now were his riches, his vast stores of golden ore, his halls upheld with red marble pillars, his sky-towering palace? He hears of Stilicho's march and counts the days, measuring his term of life according to the distance of his enemy from him. He is troubled with thoughts of coming peace and cannot sleep, often starts up distraught from his bed and suffers as punishment the fear of punishment. But his fury repossesses him and, regaining his genius for crime, he enters the sacred portal of the rich palace and addresses Arcadius with prayers and threats: " By thy brother's royal star, by the deeds of thy divine sire and the flower of thine own age, I beg thee deliver me from the edge of the sword ; let me escape the cruel threatenings of Stilicho. All Gaul is sworn to my destruction. Tethys' extreme coasts, the wandering tribes beyond the farthest Britons are stirred up against me. Am I thought fit prey for all those armies ? Are so many standards advanced against a solitary man ? Whence comes this lust for blood ? Stilicho lays claim to either hemisphere and will brook no equal. The world forsooth must lie at his feet. Italy is his kingdom, Libya his dominion, Spain and Gaul his empire. The sun's path circumscribes him not, no nor the whole universe. All the wealth collected here by Theo-dosius or received by him after the war is Stilicho's alone, and he has small mind to restore what he has once acquired. Is he to enjoy his gains in peace and quietness while 'tis mine to stand a siege ? Why should he encroach on thy share ? Let him leave Illyria, send back his Eastern troops, divide the

agmina ; fraternas ex aequo dividat hastas,
nec sceptri tantum fueris, sed militis heres.
quodsi dissimulas nostrae succurrere morti
nec prohibere paras, Manes et sidera testor : 165
haec cervix non sola cadet ; miscebitur alter
sanguis ; nec Stygias ferar incomitatus ad undas
nec mea securus ridebit funera victor ! "

Haec ubi, dictatur facinus missusque repente
qui ferat extortas invito principe voces. 170

Interea Stilicho iam laetior hoste propinquo
nec multo spatii distantibus aequore vallis
pugnandi cupidas accendit voce cohortes.
Armeniis frons laeva datur ; per cornua Gallos
dexteriora locat. spumis ignescere frena, 175
pulveris extolli nimbos lateque videres
surgere purpureis undantes anguibus hastas
serpentumque vago caelum saevire volatu.
implet Thessaliam ferri nitor antraque docti
cornipedis, teneroque amnis reptatus Achilli 180
et nemus Oetaeum radiat. clamore nivalis
Ossa tonat pulsoque fragor geminatur Olympo.
intumuit virtus et lucis prodigus arsit
impetus ; haud illos rupes, haud alta vetarent
flumina : praecipiti stravissent omnia cursu. 185

Si tunc his animis acies collata fuisset,
prodita non tantas vidisset Graecia caedes,
oppida semoto Pelopeia Marte vigerent,

hosts fairly between the two brothers, and do thou
not be heir to the sceptre only but to thy forces. But
if thou neglect to come to mine aid and make not
ready to prevent my death, this head of mine shall
not fall alone—by the dead and the stars I swear it.
The blood of another shall be mingled with mine.
I will not go unaccompanied to the waters of Styx nor
shall the victor be free to exult in my death."

So saying he dictates a treasonable letter and
sends therewith an emissary to bear the message
extorted from the emperor's unwilling lips.

Meanwhile Stilicho, exulting in the thought of
advancing upon the foe and of the narrow stretch
of country that separated him from the fortifications,
inflames with his words the hearts of his troops
already thirsting for battle. On the left wing are
posted the Armenians, farther to the right the
Gauls. A beholder might have seen bits covered
with warm foam, clouds of dust uprising, and on all
sides waving banners bearing the device of a scarlet
dragon ; the very air seemed to teem with these
fierce flying monsters. The glint of steel fills all
Thessaly and the cave of the wise Centaur ; the
river whose banks supported Achilles' baby footsteps
and the forests of Oeta are agleam with arms, snowy
Ossa re-echoes to the sound and Olympus smitten
therewith sends it back twofold. Hearts beat high
with a courage that is lavish of life. Neither precipice
nor deep river could check their advance: their head-
long speed would have overthrown all barriers.

If the two armies had then joined battle in this
temper ruined Greece would not have witnessed such
disaster as she did, the cities of the Peloponnese would
still have been flourishing untouched by the hand

starent Arcadiae, starent Lacedaemonis arces ;
non mare fumasset geminum flagrante Corintho   190
nec fera Cecropiae traxissent vincula matres.
illa dies potuit nostris imponere finem
cladibus et sceleris causas auferre futuri.
invida pro quantum rapuit Fortuna triumphum !
inter equos interque tubas mandata feruntur   195
regia et armati veniunt ductoris ad aures.

  Obstupuit ; simul ira virum, simul obruit ingens
maeror et ignavo tantum licuisse nocenti
miratur. dubios anceps sententia volvit
eventus : peragat pugnas an fortia coepta   200
deserat ? Illyricis ardet succurrere damnis ;
praeceptis obstare timet. reverentia frangit
virtutis stimulos : hinc publica commoda suadent,
hinc metus invidiae. tandem indignatus ad astra
extollit palmas et ab imo pectore fatur :   205

  " Numina Romanis necdum satiata ruinis,
si iuvat imperium penitus de stirpe revelli,
uno si placuit deleri saecula lapsu,
si piget humani generis, prorumpat in arva
libertas effrena maris vel limite iusto   210
devius errantes Phaëthon confundat habenas.
cur per Rufinum geritur ? procumbere mundum
hoc auctore pudet. mediis revocamur ab armis
(pro dolor !) et strictos deponere cogimur enses.
vos, arsurae urbes perituraque moenia, testor :   215
cedo equidem et miserum permitto casibus orbem
flectite signa, duces. redeat iam miles Eous.

of war, Arcadia and Sparta's citadel would have remained unravaged. Burning Corinth would not have heated the waves of her two seas, nor would cruel chains have led in captivity the matrons of Athens. That day might have set an end to our disasters and destroyed the seeds of future calamities. For shame, envious Fortune, of what a triumph didst thou rob us! The kingly mandate came to Stilicho in arms amid the cavalry and the trumpets' din.

He stood amazed; anger and great grief o'erwhelm the hero and he wonders that such power for ill is allowed a coward. His wavering mind ponders the uncertain issue: shall he continue his advance or fail his brave beginnings? He longs to stem Illyria's ruin but fears to disobey orders. Loyalty annuls the prickings-on of valour. The public good urges him one way, fear of the emperor's displeasure another. At length in his distress he raises his hands to heaven and speaks from deep within his heart: " Ye gods not yet glutted with Rome's destruction, if ye will that our empire be utterly uprooted, if ye have resolved to blot out all the centuries with one blow, if ye repent you of the race of man, then let the sea's unrestrained fury burst forth upon the land or let Phaëthon, deviating from his ordained course, drive his straying chariot at random. Shall Rufinus be your tool? 'Twere shame that such an one should be the author of the world's destruction. O the grief of it! recalled in mid fight; forced to lay down the swords we have drawn! Cities marked out for the flames, walls doomed to destruction, I call you to witness: see, I retire; I leave the unhappy world to its fate. Turn your banners, captains; to your homes, soldiers of the east. Needs must we obey.

parendum est.   taceant litui.   prohibete sagittas.
parcite contiguo—Rufinus praecipit !—hosti."

His dictis omnes una fremuere manipli   220
quantum non Italo percussa Ceraunia fluctu,
quantum non madidis elisa tonitrua Cauris,
secernique negant ereptaque proelia poscunt,
insignemque ducem populus defendit uterque
et sibi quisque trahit.   magno certatur amore,   225
alternamque fidem non inlaudata lacessit
seditio talique simul clamore queruntur :

   " Quis mihi nudatos enses, quis tela lacertis
excutit et solvi curvatos imperat arcus ?
quisnam audet stricto leges imponere ferro ?   230
inflammata semel nescit mitescere virtus.
iam mihi barbaricos sitientia pila cruores
sponte volant ultroque manus mucrone furenti
ducitur et siccum gladium vagina recusat.
non patiar.   semperne Getis discordia nostra   235
proderit ?   en iterum belli civilis imago !
quid consanguineas acies, quid dividis olim
concordes aquilas ?   non dissociabile corpus
coniunctumque sumus.   te qua libet ire sequemur.
te vel Hyperboreo damnatam sidere Thylen,   240
te vel ad incensas Libyae comitabor harenas.
Indorum si stagna petas Rubrique recessus
litoris, auriferum veniam poturus Hydaspen ;
si calcare Notum secretaque noscere Nili
nascentis iubeas, mundum post terga relinquam ;   245

74

THE SECOND BOOK AGAINST RUFINUS

Silence, ye clarions ; men, forbear to shoot. The foe is at hand, spare him ; 'tis Rufinus' command."

At these words an unanimous roar went up from all the companies. With less din are the cliffs of Ceraunia buffeted by the Italian sea or the thunders evoked from the western winds' wet storm-clouds. They will not separate, and demand the battle of which they have been defrauded. East and west claim the leadership of that illustrious chief. It is a contest of affection ; insubordination that none can blame threatens to sap the loyalty of both armies who thus utter their common complaint: "Who is it robs us of our drawn swords ? Who strikes the lance from our hand and bids us unstring the bent bow ? Who dares dictate to an army under arms ? Valour once roused knows no abatement. Spears thirsting for barbarian blood cast themselves from out our hands ; our headlong blades force our vengeful arms to follow them ; our very scabbards refuse to sheath an unblooded sword. I will not bear it. Shall the Getae ever profit by our dissension ? Behold once more the shadow of civil war. Why dost thou seek to separate armies whose blood is one, standards of immemorial alliance ? We are a body one and indivisible. Thee will we follow whithersoever thou goest ; thee will we accompany even as far as Thule lying icebound beneath the pole-star, or to the burning sands of Libya. Should thy path be by the waters of Ind, or the bays of the Red Sea,[1] I would go drink Hydaspes' golden stream. Shouldst thou bid me fare south and search out the hidden sources of the stripling Nile, I would leave behind me the world

[1] By the *mare rubrum* the ancients meant the Indian Ocean. The Hydaspes is the modern Jhylum.

et quocumque loco Stilicho tentoria figat,
haec patria est."
                    Dux inde vetat : " desistite, quaeso.
atque avidam differte manum. cadat iste minacis
invidiae cumulus. non est victoria tanti,
ut videar vicisse mihi. vos fida iuventus   250
ite, mei quondam socii." nec plura locutus
flexit iter : vacuo qualis discedit hiatu
impatiens remeare leo, quem plurima cuspis
et pastorales pepulerunt igne catervae,
inclinatque iubas demissaque lumina velat   255
et trepidas maesto rimatur murmure silvas.

  Ut sese legio vidit disiuncta relinqui,
ingentem tollit gemitum galeasque solutis
umectat lacrimis pressamque morantia vocem
thoracum validos pulsant suspiria nexus :   260
" tradimur, heu, tantumque sequi prohibemur
    amorem ! "
exclamant. " spernisne tuas, dux optime, dextras,
quas tibi victrices totiens Bellona probavit ?
nos adeo viles ? adeo felicior axis
Hesperius, meruit qui te rectore teneri ?   265
quid nobis patriam, quid cara revisere tandem
pignora dilectosve iuvat coluisse penates ?
te sine dulce nihil. iam formidata tyranni
tempestas subeunda mihi, qui forte nefandas
iam parat insidias, qui nos aut turpibus Hunis 270
aut impacatis famulos praebebit Alanis ;
quamquam non adeo robur defecerit omne
tantave gestandi fuerit penuria ferri.
tu, licet occiduo maneas sub cardine caeli,

I know. Wheresoever Stilicho plants his tent there is my fatherland."

But Stilicho said them nay : " Cease, I beg you," he cried, " stay your eager hands. Suffer to disperse the mountain of hatred that towers over me. I hold not victory so dear that I would fain seem to win it for myself. Loyal gentlemen, so long my fellow-soldiers, get you gone." He said no more but turned away, as a lion loath to retire makes off with empty maw when the serried spears and the burning branches in the hands of the shepherd band drive him back and he droops his mane and closes his downcast eyes and with a disappointed roar pushes his way through the trembling forest.

When the armies saw that they had been parted and left, they groaned deeply and bedewed their helmets with a stream of tears. The sighs that refused egress to their smothered words shook the strong fastenings of their breastplates. " We are betrayed," they cried, " and forbidden to follow him we love so well. Dost thou despise, matchless chief, thine own right hands which have so often won thee the victory ? Are we thus vile ? Is the Western sky to be the happier which has won the right to enjoy thy rule ? What boots it to return to our country, to see once more our children dear after so long an absence, to live again in the home we love ? Without thee is no joy. Now must I face the tyrant's dread wrath ; mayhap e'en now he is making ready against me some wicked snare and will make me a slave to the foul Huns or restless Alans. Yet is not my strength altogether perished nor so complete my powerlessness to wield the sword. Rest thou beneath the sun's westering course, Stilicho, thou art still

tu mihi dux semper, Stilicho, nostramque vel absens
experiere fidem.   dabitur tibi debita pridem   276
victima : promissis longe placabere sacris."

   Tristior Haemoniis miles digressus ab oris
tangebat Macetum fines murosque subibat,
Thessalonica, tuos.   sensu dolor haeret in alto   280
abditus et tacitas vindictae praestruit iras,
spectaturque favens odiis locus aptaque leto
tempora.   nec quisquam tanta de pube repertus,
proderet incautis qui corda minantia verbis.
quae non posteritas, quae non mirabitur aetas   285
tanti consilium vulgi potuisse taceri
aut facinus tam grande tegi mentisque calorem
non sermone viae, non inter pocula rumpi ?
aequalis tantam tenuit constantia turbam
et fuit arcanum populo.   percurritur Haemus,   290
deseritur Rhodope Thracumque per ardua tendunt,
donec ad Herculei perventum nominis urbem.

   Ut cessisse ducem, propius venisse cohortes
cognita Rufino, magna cervice triumphat
omnia tuta ratus sceptrumque capessere fervet   295
et coniuratos hortatur voce clientes :
" vicimus, expulimus, facilis iam copia regni.
nullus ab hoste timor.   quis enim, quem poscere solum
horruit, hunc tanto munitum milite vincat ?
quis ferat armatum, quem non superavit inermem ?
i nunc, exitium nobis meditare remotus   301

---

[1] Probably Heraclea, at the west end of the Propontis.

ever our general, and though we be not together
thou shalt still know our loyalty. Long has a victim
been owed thee ; he shall be sacrificed and thou
placated by an immolation promised of old."

Sad at heart the army left Thessaly, reached the
borders of Macedon, and arrived before the walls
of Thessalonica. Indignation deep hid in their
hearts prepares the silent wrath of revenge. They
look for a place where they may wreak their
vengeance and a moment propitious for the blow,
and of all that vast army not one is found to divulge
with incautious speech his heart's intent. What
succeeding age and time but will marvel that a plot
so widespread could be kept hid, a deed of such
vast import concealed ; that the ardour of their
minds was not rendered of no avail by the chance
word of a soldier on the march or a drunkard's
babbling ? But discretion ruled all alike and the
people's secret was kept. The army crossed the
Hebrus, left Rhodope behind, and struck across the
uplands of Thrace until it came to the city called
after Hercules.[1]

When Rufinus learned that Stilicho had retired
and that his troops were approaching he held his
head high in triumph, believing everything safe, and,
anxious to seize the power, inflamed his traitorous
minions with this speech : "We have conquered ;
have driven off our enemy ; empire is within my
grasp, nor have we anything to fear from the foe.
Will one who dared not approach me when I stood
alone defeat me now that I am strengthened by
the addition of so great a force ? Who could stand
against him armed whom unarmed he could not
conquer ? Plot my destruction in exile, friend

incassum, Stilicho, dum nos longissima tellus
dividat et mediis Nereus interstrepat undis.
Alpinas transire tibi me sospite rupes
haud dabitur. iaculis illinc me figere tempta.   305
quaere ferox ensem, qui nostra ad moenia tendi
possit ab Italia. non te documenta priorum,
non exempla vetant ? quisnam conatus adire
has iactat vitasse manus ? detrusimus orbe
te medio tantisque simul spoliavimus armis.   310
nunc epulis tempus, socii, nunc larga parare
munera donandumque novis legionibus aurum !
opportuna meis oritur lux crastina votis.
quod nolit rex ipse velit iubeatque coactus
in partem mihi regna dari. contingat in uno   315
privati fugisse modum crimenque tyranni."

  Talibus adclamat dictis infame nocentum
concilium, qui perpetuis crevere rapinis
et quos una facit Rufino causa sodales,
inlicitum duxisse nihil ; funesta tacere   320
nexus amicitiae. iamiam conubia laeti
despondent aliena sibi frustraque vicissim
promittunt, quae quisque petat, quas devoret urbes.

  Coeperat humanos alto sopire labores
nox gremio, nigrasque sopor diffuderat alas.   325
ille diu curis animum stimulantibus aegre
labitur in somnos. toto vix corde quierat,
ecce videt diras adludere protinus umbras,

Stilicho. What harm can that do so long as a vast stretch of country divide us and Nereus' waves thunder between? Thou shalt have no chance of crossing the rocky Alps while I live. Transfix me from thence with thine arrows, if thou canst. Seek in thy fury a sword that from Italy shall reach my city's walls. Does not the experience and the example of those who have tried before deter thee? Who that has dared approach can boast escape from my hands? I have driven thee from the centre of the civilized world and at the same time deprived thee of thy great army. Now, my friends, is come the time for feasting and making ready bountiful gifts and bestowing gold upon these new legions. To-morrow's light dawns prosperously for my purpose. Needs must the emperor will what he would not and bid a portion of his empire to be given to me. Mine alone be the happy fortune to rise above a private estate and yet escape the charge of tyranny."

To such words they shout acclaim — that vile band of traitors, waxed fat on plunder, whom one principle makes fellows with Rufinus, the holding nothing unlawful, and whose bond of friendship is to guard guilt in silence. Straightway they joyfully promise themselves foreign wives and all to no purpose forecast the booty they will win and the cities they will sack.

Night had begun to soothe human toils in her deep bosom and sleep had spread his black wings when Rufinus, whose mind had long been a prey to anxiety, sank into a troubled slumber. Scarce had quiet fastened on his heart when, lo, he sees flit before his eyes the dread ghosts of those whom he

quas dedit ipse neci ; quarum quae clarior una
visa loqui : " pro ! surge toro. quid plurima volvis 330
anxius ?   haec requiem rebus finemque labori
adlatura dies : omni iam plebe redibis
altior et laeti manibus portabere vulgi.
has canit ambages.   occulto fallitur ille
omine nec capitis sentit praesagia fixi.   335

    Iam summum radiis stringebat Lucifer Haemum
festinamque rotam solito properantior urget
tandem Rufini visurus funera Titan :
desiluit stratis densaeque capacia turbae
atria regifico iussit splendere paratu   340
exceptura dapes et, quod post vota daretur,
insculpi propriis aurum fatale figuris.
ipse salutatum reduces post proelia turmas
iam regale tumens et principe celsior ibat
collaque femineo solvebat mollia gestu   345
imperii certus, tegeret ceu purpura dudum
corpus et ardentes ambirent tempora gemmae.

    Urbis ab angusto tractu, qua vergit in austrum,
planities vicina patet : nam cetera pontus
circuit exiguo dirimi se limite passus.   350
hic ultrix acies ornatu lucida Martis
explicuit cuneos.   pedites in parte sinistra
consistunt.   equites illinc poscentia cursum
ora reluctantur pressis sedare lupatis ;
hinc alii saevum cristato vertice nutant   355
et tremulos umeris gaudent vibrare colores,
quos operit formatque chalybs ; coniuncta per artem

had killed. Of them one, more distinct than the rest, seemed thus to address him: " Up from thy couch ! why schemes thine anxious mind further ? This coming day shall bring thee rest and end thy toils. High above the people shalt thou be raised, and happy crowds shall carry thee in their arms." Such was the ambiguous prophecy of the ghost, but Rufinus observed not the hidden omen and saw not it foretold the elevation of his severed head upon a spear.

Now Lucifer touched the peak of Haemus with his rays and Titan urged his hastening wheel quicker than his wont, so soon to see at last the death of Rufinus. Rufinus himself leapt from his bed and bade make ready the capacious palace with regal splendour in preparation for the feast ; the gold to be given in largesse he ordered to be stamped with his own fateful image. Himself went to welcome the troops returning from the battle in kingly pride and arrogance above a prince's. Sure now of empire he wore a woman's raiment about his neck ; as though the purple already clothed his limbs and the jewelled crown blazed upon his brow.

Hard by a crowded quarter of the city of Constantinople, towards the south, there lies a plain. The rest is surrounded by the sea which here allows itself to be parted by a narrow way. Here the avenging army, bright with the panoply of the war god, disposes its squadrons. On the left stands the infantry. Over against them the cavalry seek to restrain their eager steeds by holding tight the reins. Here nod the savage waving plumes whose wearers rejoice to shake the flashing colours of their shoulder-armour ; for steel clothes them on and gives them their shape ; the limbs within

flexilis inductis animatur lamina membris;
horribiles visu : credas simulacra moveri
ferrea cognatoque viros spirare metallo.   360
par vestitus equis : ferrata fronte minantur
ferratosque levant securi vulneris armos.
diviso stat quisque loco, metuenda voluptas
cernenti pulcherque timor, spirisque remissis
mansuescunt varii vento cessante dracones.   365
  Augustus veneranda prior vexilla salutat.
Rufinus sequitur, quo fallere cuncta solebat
callidus adfatu, devotaque brachia laudat ;
nomine quemque vocat ; natos patresque reversis
nuntiat incolumes. illi dum plurima ficto   370
certatim sermone petunt, extendere longos
a tergo flexus insperatoque suprema
circuitu sociare parant ; decrescere campus
incipit, et clipeis in se redeuntia iunctis
curvo paulatim sinuantur cornua ductu :   375
sic ligat inmensa virides indagine saltus
venator ; sic attonitos ad litora pisces
aequoreus populator agit rarosque plagarum
contrahit anfractus et hiantes colligit oras.
excludunt alios. cingi se fervidus ille   380
nescit adhuc graviterque adprensa veste morantem
increpat Augustum : scandat sublime tribunal,
participem sceptri, socium declaret honoris—
cum subito stringunt gladios ; vox desuper ingens
infremuit : "nobis etiam, deterrime, nobis   385

---

¹ Claudian refers to the devices emblazoned upon the
banners.

give life to the armour's pliant scales so artfully
conjoined, and strike terror into the beholder. 'Tis
as though iron statues moved and men lived cast
from that same metal. The horses are armed in
the same way; their heads are encased in threaten-
ing iron, their forequarters move beneath steel
plates protecting them from wounds; each stands
alone, a pleasure yet a dread to behold, beautiful,
yet terrible, and as the wind drops the parti-
coloured dragons[1] sink with relaxing coils into
repose.

The emperor first salutes the hallowed standards;
Rufinus follows him, speaking with that crafty voice
wherewith he deceived all, praising their devoted
arms and addressing each by name. He tells those
who have returned that their sons and fathers are
still alive. The soldiers, observing a feigned rivalry
in asking questions, begin to extend their long lines
behind his back and to join up the ends so as to
form a circle unnoticed by Rufinus. The space in
the centre grows smaller and the wings meeting with
serried shields gradually form into one lessening
circle. Even so the huntsman surrounds the grassy
glades with his widespread snares: so the spoiler
of the ocean drives to land the frightened fish,
narrowing the circuit of his nets and closing up all
possible ways of egress. All others they exclude.
In his eagerness he notes not yet that he is being
surrounded and, strongly seizing his robe, chides
the hesitating emperor: let him mount the lofty
platform and declare him sharer in his sceptre,
partaker in his dignities — when suddenly they
draw their swords and above the rest there rang
out a mighty voice: "Basest of the base, didst

sperasti famulas imponere posse catenas ?
unde redi nescis ?   patiarne audire satelles,
qui leges aliis libertatemque reduxi ?
bis domitum civile nefas, bis rupimus Alpes.
tot nos bella docent nulli servire tyranno."   390

   Deriguit.   spes nulla fugae ; seges undique ferri
circumfusa micat ; dextra laevaque revinctus
haesit et ensiferae stupuit mucrone coronae,
ut fera, quae nuper montes amisit avitos
altorumque exul nemorum damnatur harenae   395
muneribus, commota ruit ; vir murmure contra
hortatur nixusque genu venabula tendit ;
illa pavet strepitus cuneosque erecta theatri
respicit et tanti miratur sibila vulgi.

   Unus per medios audendi pronior ense   400
prosilit exerto dictisque et vulnere torvus
impetit : " hac Stilicho, quem iactas pellere, dextra
te ferit ; hoc absens invadit viscera ferro."
sic fatur meritoque latus transverberat ictu.

   Felix illa manus, talem quae prima cruorem   405
hauserit et fessi poenam libaverit orbis !
mox omnes laniant hastis artusque trementes
dilacerant ; uno tot corpore tela tepescunt
et non infecto puduit mucrone reverti.

thou hope to cast upon *us* the yoke of slavery ?
Knowest thou not whence I return ? Shall I allow
myself to be called another's servant, I who gave
laws to others and restored the reign of liberty ?
Two civil wars have I quenched, twice forced the
barrier of the Alps. These many battles have taught
me to serve no tyrant."

Rufinus stood rooted to earth. There is no hope
of escape, for a forest of flashing spears hems
him in. Shut in on the right hand and on the left
he stood and gazed in wonder on the drawn blades
of the armed throng ; as a beast who has lately left
his native hills, driven in exile from the wooded
mountains and condemned to the gladiatorial shows,
rushes into the arena while over against him
the gladiator, heartened by the crowd's applause
kneels and holds out his spear. The beast, alarmed
at the noise, gazes with head erect upon the rows
of seats in the amphitheatre and hears with amaze-
ment the murmuring of the crowd.

Then one more daring than the rest drew his
sword and leapt forward from the crowd and with
fierce words and flashing eye rushed upon Rufinus
crying : " It is the hand of Stilicho whom thou
vauntest that thou didst expel that smites thee ;
his sword, which thou thoughtest far away, that
pierces thy heart." So spake he and transfixed
Rufinus' side with a well-deserved thrust.

Happy the hand that first spilt such vile blood
and poured out vengeance for a world made weary.
Straightway all pierce him with their spears and
tear quivering limb from limb ; one single body
warms all these weapons with its blood ; shame
to him whose sword returns unstained therewith.

87

hi vultus avidos et adhuc spirantia vellunt   410
lumina, truncatos alii rapuere lacertos.
amputat ille pedes, umerum quatit ille solutis
nexibus ; hic fracti reserat curvamina dorsi ;
hic iecur, hic cordis fibras, hic pandit anhelas
pulmonis latebras.   spatium non invenit ira   415
nec locus est odiis.   consumpto funere vix tum
deseritur sparsumque perit per tela cadaver.
sic mons Aonius rubuit, cum Penthea ferrent
Maenades aut subito mutatum Actaeona cornu
traderet insanis Latonia visa Molossis.   420
criminibusne tuis credis, Fortuna, mederi
et male donatum certas aequare favorem
suppliciis ?   una tot milia morte rependis ?
eversis agedum Rufinum divide terris.
da caput Odrysiis, truncum mereantur Achivi.   425
quid reliquis dabitur ? nec singula membra peremptis
sufficiunt populis.

                   Vacuo plebs undique muro
iam secura fluit ; senibus non obstitit aetas
virginibusve pudor ; viduae, quibus ille maritos
abstulit, orbataeque ruunt ad gaudia matres   430
insultantque alacres.   laceros iuvat ire per artus
pressaque calcato vestigia sanguine tingui.
nec minus adsiduis flagrant elidere saxis
prodigiale caput, quod iam de cuspide summa

They stamp on that face of greed and while yet he lives pluck out his eyes; others seize and carry off his severed arms. One cuts off his foot, another wrenches a shoulder from the torn sinews; one lays bare the ribs of the cleft spine, another his liver, his heart, his still panting lungs. There is not space enough to satisfy their anger nor room to wreak their hate. Scarce when his death had been accomplished do they leave him; his body is hacked in pieces and the fragments borne on the soldiers' spears. Thus red with blood ran the Boeotian mountain when the Maenads caused Pentheus' destruction or when Latona's daughter seen by Actaeon betrayed the huntsman, suddenly transformed into a stag, to the fury of her Molossian hounds. Dost thou hope, Fortune, thus to right thy wrongs? Seekest thou to atone by this meting out of punishment for favour ill bestowed? Dost thou with one death make payment for ten thousand murders? Come, portion out Rufinus' corpse among the lands he has wronged. Give the Thracians his head; let Greece have as her due his body. What shall be given the rest? Give but a limb apiece, there are not enough for the peoples he has ruined.

The citizens leave the town and hasten exulting to the spot from every quarter, old men and girls among them whom nor age nor sex could keep at home. Widows whose husbands he had killed, mothers whose children he had murdered hurry to the joyful scene with eager steps. They are fain to trample the torn limbs and stain their deep pressed feet with the blood. So, too, they eagerly hurl a shower of stones at the monstrous head, nodding from the summit of the spear that transfixed it as it

nutabat digna rediens ad moenia pompa.   435
dextera quin etiam ludo concessa vagatur
aera petens poenasque animi persolvit avari
terribili lucro vivosque imitata retentus
cogitur adductis digitos inflectere nervis.

Desinat elatis quisquam confidere rebus   440
instabilesque deos ac lubrica numina discat.
illa manus, quae sceptra sibi gestanda parabat,
cuius se totiens summisit ad oscula supplex
nobilitas, inhumata diu miseroque revulsa
corpore feralem quaestum post fata reposcit.   445
adspiciat quisquis nimium sublata secundis
colla gerit : triviis calcandus spargitur ecce,
qui sibi pyramidas, qui non cedentia templis
ornatura suos extruxit culmina manes,
et qui Sidonio velari credidit ostro,   450
nudus pascit aves. iacet en, qui possidet orbem,
exiguae telluris inops et pulvere raro
per partes tegitur nusquam totiensque sepultus.

Senserunt convexa necem tellusque nefandum
amolitur onus iam respirantibus astris.   455
infernos gravat umbra lacus. pater Aeacus horret
intrantemque etiam latratu Cerberus urget.
tunc animae, quas ille fero sub iure peremit,
circumstant nigrique trahunt ad iudicis urnam
infesto fremitu : veluti pastoris in ora   460
commotae glomerantur apes, qui dulcia raptu
mella vehit, pennasque cient et spicula tendunt
et tenuis saxi per propugnacula cinctae

was carried back in merited splendour to the city.
Nay his hand too, made over to their mockery, goes
a-begging for alms, and with its awful gains pays
the penalty for his greedy soul, while forced, in
mimicry of its living clutch, to draw up the fingers
by their sinews.

Put not now your trust in prosperity ; learn that
the gods are inconstant and heaven untrustworthy.
That hand which sought to wield a sceptre, which a
humbled nobility stooped so often to kiss, now torn
from its wretched trunk and left long unburied
begs after death a baneful alms. Let him gaze
on this whoso carries his head high in pride of pros-
perity, see trodden under foot at the cross-roads
him who built pyramids for himself and a tomb,
large as a temple, to the glory of his own ghost.
He who trusted to be clothed in Tyrian purple is
now a naked corpse and food for birds. See, he
who owns the world lies denied six foot of earth,
half covered with a sprinkling of dust, given no
grave yet given so many.

Heaven knew of his death and earth is freed of
her hated burden, now that the stars can breathe
again. His shade oppresses the rivers of Hell.
Old Aeacus shudders and Cerberus bays to stop,
in this case, the *entry* of a ghost. Then those shades
which he had sent to death beneath his cruel laws
flock round him and hale him away with horrid
shoutings to the tribunal of the gloomy judge : even
as bees whom a shepherd has disturbed swarm round
his head when he would rob them of their sweet
honey, and flutter their wings and put forth their
stings, making them ready for battle in the fast-
nesses of their little rock, and seek to defend the

rimosam patriam dilectaque pumicis antra
defendunt pronoque favos examine velant.   465
    Est locus infaustis quo conciliantur in unum
Cocytos Phlegethonque vadis ; inamoenus uterque
alveus ; hic volvit lacrimas, hic igne redundat.
turris per geminos, flammis vicinior, amnes
porrigitur solidoque rigens adamante sinistrum   470
proluit igne latus ; dextro Cocytia findit
aequora triste gemens et fletu concita plangit.
huc post emeritam mortalia saecula vitam
deveniunt. ibi nulla manent discrimina fati,
nullus honos vanoque exutum nomine regem   475
proturbat plebeius egens. quaesitor in alto
conspicuus solio pertemptat crimina Minos
et iustis dirimit sontes. quos nolle fateri
viderit, ad rigidi transmittit verbera fratris.
nam iuxta Rhadamanthys agit. cum gesta superni
curriculi totosque diu perspexerit actus,   481
exaequat damnum meritis et muta ferarum
cogit vincla pati. truculentos ingerit ursis
praedonesque lupis ; fallaces vulpibus addit.
at qui desidia semper vinoque gravatus,   485
indulgens Veneri, voluit torpescere luxu,
hunc suis inmundi pingues detrudit in artus.
qui iusto plus esse loquax arcanaque suevit
prodere, piscosas fertur victurus in undas,
ut nimiam pensent aeterna silentia vocem.   490
quos ubi per varias annis ter mille figuras
egit, Lethaeo purgatos flumine tandem
rursus ad humanae revocat primordia formae.

crevices of their home, their beloved pumice-stone cave, swarming over the honeycombs therein.

There is a place where the unhallowed rivers of Cocytus and Phlegethon mingle their dread streams of tears and fire. Between the rivers yet nearer to that of Phlegethon there juts a tower stiff with solid adamant that bathes its left side in the flames; its right hand wall extends into Cocytus' stream and echoes the lamentation of the river of tears. Hither come all the children of men whose life is ended; here there abide no marks of earthly fortune; no reverence is shown; the common beggar ousts the king, now stripped of his empty title. Seen afar on his lofty throne the judge Minos examines the charges and separates the wicked from the righteous. Those whom he sees unwilling to confess their sins he remits to the lash of his stern brother; for he, Rhadamanthus, is busy close at hand. When he has closely examined the deeds of their earthly life and all that they did therein, he suits the punishment to their crimes and makes them undergo the bonds of dumb animals. The spirits of the cruel enter into bears, of the rapacious into wolves, of the treacherous into foxes. Those, on the other hand, who were ever sunk in sloth, sodden with wine, given to venery, sluggish from excesses, he compelled to enter the fat bodies of filthy swine. Was any above measure talkative, a betrayer of secrets, he was carried off, a fish, to live in the waters amid his kind, that in eternal silence he might atone for his garrulity. When for thrice a thousand years he had forced these through countless diverse shapes, he sends them back once more to the beginnings of human form purged at last with Lethe's stream.

Tum quoque, dum lites Stygiique negotia solvit
dura fori veteresque reos ex ordine quaerit,   495
Rufinum procul ecce notat visuque severo
lustrat et ex imo concussa sede profatur :

" Huc superum labes, huc insatiabilis auri
proluvies pretioque nihil non ause parato,
quodque mihi summum scelus est, huc improbe legum
venditor, Arctoi stimulator perfide Martis !   501
cuius ob innumeras strages angustus Averni
iam sinus et plena lassatur portitor alno.
quid demens manifesta negas ? en pectus inustae
deformant maculae vitiisque inolevit imago   505
nec sese commissa tegunt. genus omne dolorum
in te ferre libet : dubio tibi pendula rupes
inmineat lapsu, volucer te torqueat axis,
te refugi fallant latices atque ore natanti
arescat decepta sitis, dapibusque relictis   510
in tua mansurus migret praecordia vultur.
quamquam omnes alii, quos haec tormenta fatigant,
pars quota sunt, Rufine, tui ! quid tale vel audax
fulmine Salmoneus vel lingua Tantalus egit
aut inconsulto Tityos deliquit amore ?   515
cunctorum si facta simul iungantur in unum,
praecedes numero. cui tanta piacula quisquam
supplicio conferre valet ? quid denique dignum
omnibus inveniam, vincant cum singula poenas ?
tollite de mediis animarum dedecus umbris.   520
adspexisse sat est. oculis iam parcite nostris
et Ditis purgate domos. agitate flagellis

THE SECOND BOOK AGAINST RUFINUS

So then while he settles these suits, dread business of that infernal court, while he examines in due order the criminals of old, he marks afar Rufinus, scans him with a stern scrutiny and speaks, shaking his throne to its foundation. " Hither, Rufinus, scourge of the world, bottomless sink of gold who wouldst dare aught for money ; hither conscienceless seller of justice (that crime of crimes), faithless cause of that northern war whose thousand slaughtered victims now throng Hell's narrow entry and weigh down Charon's crowded barque. Madman, why deny what all know ? The foul stains of wickedness are branded upon thy heart, thy crimes have made their impress on thy spirit and thy sins cannot be hid. Right glad I am to sentence thee to every kind of punishment. O'er thee shall hang the threatening rock the moment of whose fall thou knowest not. The circling wheel shall rack thee. Thy lips the stream's waves shall flee, thirst shall parch thee to whose chin its elusive waters mount. The vulture shall leave his former prey and feast for ever on thy heart. And yet all these, Rufinus, whom the like punishments torment, how paltry their wickedness compared with thine ! Did bold Salmoneus' thunderbolt or Tantalus' tongue ever do like wrong or Tityos so offend with his mad love ? Join all their crimes together yet wilt thou surpass them. What sufficient atonement can be found for such wickedness ? What to match thy sum of crimes whose single misdeeds outmatch all punishment ? Shades, remove from this our ghostly company that presence that disgraces it. To have seen once is enough. Have mercy now on our eyes, and cleanse the realm of Dis. Drive

trans Styga, trans Erebum, vacuo mandate barathro
infra Titanum tenebras infraque recessus
Tartareos ipsumque[1] Chaos, qua noctis opacae   525
fundamenta latent ; praeceps ibi mersus anhelet,
dum rotat astra polus, feriunt dum litora venti."

[1] MSS. *have* nostrumque

him with whips beyond the Styx, beyond Erebus;
thrust him down into the empty pit beneath the
lightless prison of the Titans, below the depths of
Tartarus and Chaos' own realm, where lie the
foundations of thickest midnight ; deep hidden there
let him live while ever the vault of heaven carries
round the stars and the winds beat upon the land."

DE BELLO GILDONICO

LIBER I

(XV)

Redditus imperiis Auster subiectaque rursus
alterius convexa poli. rector sub uno
conspirat geminus frenis communibus orbis.
iunximus Europen Libyae. concordia fratrum
plena redit. patriis solum quod defuit armis,   5
tertius occubuit nati virtute tyrannus.
horret adhuc animus manifestaque gaudia differt,
dum stupet et tanto cunctatur credere voto.
necdum Cinyphias exercitus attigit oras :
iam domitus Gildo. nullis victoria nodis   10
haesit, non spatio terrae, non obice ponti.
congressum profugum captum vox nuntiat una
rumoremque sui praevenit laurea belli.
quo, precor, haec effecta deo ? robusta vetusque
tempore tam parvo potuit dementia vinci ?   15
quem veniens indixit hiems, ver perculit hostem.

---

[1] For the details of Gildo's rebellion see Introduction,
p. x.
[2] The Cinyps is a river in Libya; *cf.* Virg. *Georg.*
iii. 312.

THE WAR AGAINST GILDO[1]

BOOK I

(XV)

The kingdom of the south is restored to our empire, the sky of that other hemisphere is once more brought into subjection. East and West live in amity and concord beneath the sway of one ruler. We have joined Europe again to Africa, and unswerving singleness of purpose unites the brother emperors. The would-be third participant of empire has fallen before the prowess of Honorius the son —that one victory that failed to grace the arms of Theodosius, the father. Still is my mind troubled and admits not the universal joy for very amazement, nor can believe the fulfilment of its heartfelt prayers. Not yet had the army landed upon Africa's[2] coasts when Gildo yielded to defeat. No difficulties delayed our victorious arms, neither length of march nor intervening ocean. One and the same word brings news of the conflict, the flight, the capture of Gildo. The news of victory outstripped the news of the war that occasioned it. What god wrought this for us? Could madness so strong, so deep-seated be overcome so soon? The enemy whom early winter brought upon us, spring destroyed.

Exitium iam Roma timens et fessa negatis
frugibus ad rapidi limen tendebat Olympi
non solito vultu nec qualis iura Britannis
dividit aut trepidos summittit fascibus Indos.   20
vox tenuis tardique gradus oculique iacentes
interius ; fugere genae ; ieiuna lacertos
exedit macies.   umeris vix sustinet aegris
squalentem clipeum ; laxata casside prodit
canitiem plenamque trahit rubiginis hastam.   25
attigit ut tandem caelum genibusque Tonantis
procubuit, tales orditur maesta querellas :

" Si mea mansuris meruerunt moenia nasci,
Iuppiter, auguriis, si stant inmota Sibyllae
carmina, Tarpeias si necdum respuis arces :   30
advenio supplex, non ut proculcet Araxen
consul ovans nostraeve premant pharetrata secures
Susa, nec ut Rubris aquilas figamus harenis.
haec nobis, haec ante dabas ; nunc pabula tantum
Roma precor.   miserere tuae, pater optime, gentis, 35
extremam defende famem.   satiavimus iram
si qua fuit ; lugenda Getis et flenda Suebis
hausimus ; ipsa meos horreret Parthia casus.
quid referam morbive luem tumulosve repletos
stragibus et crebras corrupto sidere mortes ?   40
aut fluvium per tecta vagum summisque minatum
collibus ? ingentes vexi summersa carinas
remorumque sonos et Pyrrhae saecula sensi.

" Ei mihi, quo Latiae vires urbisque potestas
100

THE WAR AGAINST GILDO, I

Rome, the goddess, fearing for her city's destruction and weak with corn withheld, hastened to the threshold of revolving Olympus with looks unlike her own; not with such countenance does she assign laws to the Britons, or subject the frightened Indians to her rule. Feeble her voice, slow her step, her eyes deep buried. Her cheeks were sunken and hunger had wasted her limbs. Scarce can her weak shoulders support her unpolished shield. Her ill-fitting helmet shows her grey hairs and the spear she carries is a mass of rust. At last she reaches heaven and falls at the Thunderer's feet and utters this mournful complaint: "If prophecy rightly foretold the permanence of the rising walls of Rome; if the Sibyl's verse is unalterable; if thou art not yet wearied of our city and the Capitol, I come to thee as a suppliant. My prayer is not that a consul may march in triumph along Araxes' banks, nor that Rome's power may crush the archer Persians and Susa their capital, nor yet that we may plant our standards on the Red Sea's strand. All this thou grantedst us of old. 'Tis but food I, Rome, ask for now; father, take pity on thy chosen race and ease us of this hunger unto death. Whatever thy displeasure, we have surely sated it. The very Getae and Suebi would pity our sufferings; Parthia's self would shudder at my disasters. What need have I to mention the pestilence, the heaps of corpses, the numberless deaths wherewith the very air is corrupted? Why tell of Tiber's flooded stream, sweeping betwixt roofs and threatening the very hills? My submerged city has borne mighty ships, echoed the sound of oars, and experienced Pyrrha's flood.

"Woe is me, whither are fled the power of Latium

decidit ! in qualem paulatim fluximus umbram !　45
armato quondam populo patrumque vigebam
conciliis ; domui terras urbesque revinxi
legibus : ad solem victrix utrumque cucurri.
postquam iura ferox in se communia Caesar
transtulit et lapsi mores desuetaque priscis　50
artibus in gremium pacis servile recessi,
tot mihi pro meritis Libyam Nilumque dedere,
ut dominam plebem bellatoremque senatum
classibus aestivis alerent geminoque vicissim
litore diversi complerent horrea venti.　55
stabat certa salus : Memphis si forte negasset,
pensabam Pharium Gaetulis messibus annum,
frugiferas certare rates lateque videbam
Punica Niliacis concurrere carbasa velis.
cum subiit par Roma mihi divisaque sumpsit　60
aequales Aurora togas, Aegyptia rura
in partem cessere novae.　spes unica nobis
restabat Libyae, quae vix aegreque fovebat ;
solo ducta Noto, numquam secura futuri,
semper inops, ventique fidem poscebat et anni.　65
hanc quoque nunc Gildo rapuit sub fine cadentis
autumni.　pavido metimur caerula voto,
puppis si qua venit, si quid fortasse potenti
vel pudor extorsit domino vel praedo reliquit.
pascimur arbitrio Mauri nec debita reddi,　70

---

[1] Claudian means that the African corn-supply was not
always to be relied upon because (1) there might be a bad
season, (2) there might be unfavourable winds.

and the might of Rome ? To what a shadow of our former glory are we by gradual decline arrived ! Time was when my men bore arms and my greybeards met in council ; mistress of the world was I and lawgiver to mankind. From rising to setting sun I sped in triumph. When proud Caesar had transferred my people's power to himself, when manners became corrupt and forgetful of war's old discipline I declined into the servile lap of peace, the emperors rewarded me with Africa and Egypt that they might nourish the sovereign people and the Senate, arbiter of peace and war, by means of summer-sped fleets, and that the winds, blowing alternately from either shore, should fill our granaries with corn. Our provisioning was secure. Should Memphis perchance have denied us food, I would make up for the failure of Egypt's harvest by the African supply. I saw competition between grainbearing vessels, and where'er I looked I beheld the fleet of Carthage strive in rivalry with that of the Nile. When a second Rome arose and the Eastern Empire assumed the toga of the West, Egypt fell beneath that new sway. Africa remained our only hope and scarcely did she suffice to feed us, whose corn-ships none but the south wind wafted across. Her promise for the future was insecure, as, ever helpless, she demanded the loyalty of the wind and of the season.[1] This province, too, Gildo seized towards the close of autumn. Anxiously and prayerfully we scan the blue sea to glance a coming sail in the fond hope that perchance a sense of shame has extorted somewhat from the powerful tyrant, or the conqueror left some corner unconquered. We are fed at the pleasure of the Moor,

sed sua concedi iactat gaudetque diurnos
ut famulae praebere cibos vitamque famemque
librat barbarico fastu vulgique superbit
fletibus et tantae suspendit fata ruinae.
Romuleas vendit segetes et possidet arva   75
vulneribus quaesita meis.   ideone tot annos
flebile cum tumida bellum Carthagine gessi ?
idcirco voluit contempta luce reverti
Regulus ? hoc damnis, genitor, Cannensibus emi ?
incassum totiens lituis navalibus arsit   80
Hispanum Siculumque fretum vastataque tellus
totque duces caesi ruptaque emissus ab Alpe
Poenus et attonitae iam proximus Hannibal urbi ?
scilicet ut domitis frueretur barbarus Afris,
muro sustinui Martem noctesque cruentas   85
Collina pro turre tuli ?   Gildonis ad usum
Carthago ter victa ruit ?   hoc mille gementis
Italiae clades impensaque saecula bellis,
hoc Fabius fortisque mihi Marcellus agebant,
ut Gildo cumularet opes ?   haurire venena   90
compulimus dirum Syphacem fractumque Metello
traximus inmanem Marii sub vincla Iugurtham,
et Numidae Gildonis erunt ?   pro funera tanta,
pro labor ! in Bocchi regnum sudavit uterque
Scipio.   Romano vicistis sanguine Mauri.   95
ille diu miles populus, qui praefuit orbi,
qui trabeas et sceptra dabat, quem semper in armis
horribilem gentes, placidum sensere subactae,

---

¹ Bocchus, properly a king of Mauritania, stands here
typically for any native monarch.

who boasts that he does not repay a debt but that
he gives us of his own, and rejoices to apportion out
my daily food to me, as though I were his slave ;
with a barbarian's pride he weighs me life or death
by hunger, triumphs in a people's tears, and holds
above our heads an universal destruction. He
sells Rome's crops and possesses land won by my
wounds. Was it for this that I waged lamentable
war with proud Carthage for so many years ? For
this that Regulus reckoned his life as naught and
would fain return to his captors ? Is this my reward,
father, for my losses on Cannae's field ? Have the
Spanish and Sicilian seas resounded so often to our
navies' clarion for naught ? For naught my lands
been laid waste, so many of my generals slain, the
Carthaginian invader broken his way through the
Alps, Hannibal approached my affrighted capital ?
Have I kept the foe at bay with my walls and spent
nights of slaughter before the Colline gate to enable
a barbarian to reap the fruits of conquered Africa ?
Has thrice-conquered Carthage fallen for Gildo's
benefit ? Was this the object of mourning Italy's
thousand disasters, of centuries spent in war, of
Fabius' and Marcellus' deeds of daring—that Gildo
should heap him up riches ? We forced cruel
Syphax to drink poison, drove fierce Iugurtha,
whose power Metellus had broken, beneath Marius'
yoke—and shall Africa be Gildo's ? Alas for our
toil and those many deaths : the two Scipios have
laboured, it seems, to further Bocchus'[1] native rule ;
Roman blood has given victory to the Moors. That
long warlike race, lord of the world, that appointed
consuls and kings, whom foreign nations found ever
formidable in war, though gentle once they had

nunc inhonorus egens perfert miserabile pacis
supplicium nulloque palam circumdatus hoste   100
obsessi discrimen habet.   per singula letum
impendet momenta mihi dubitandaque pauci
praescribunt alimenta dies.   heu prospera fata !
quid mihi septenos montes turbamque dedistis,
quae parvo non possit ali ?   felicior essem   105
angustis opibus ; mallem tolerare Sabinos
et Veios ; brevior duxi securius aevum.
ipsa nocet moles.   utinam remeare liceret
ad veteres fines et moenia pauperis Anci.
sufficerent Etrusca mihi Campanaque culta   110
et Quincti Curiique seges, patriaeque petenti
rusticus inferret proprias dictator aristas.
    " Nunc quid agam ?   Libyam Gildo tenet, altera
        Nilum.
ast ego, quae terras umeris pontumque subegi,
deseror : emeritae iam praemia nulla senectae.   115
di, quibus iratis crevi, succurrite tandem,
exorate patrem ; tuque o si sponte per altum
vecta Palatinis mutasti collibus Idam
praelatoque lavas Phrygios Almone leones,
maternis precibus natum iam flecte, Cybebe.   120
sin prohibent Parcae falsisque elusa vetustas
auspiciis, alio saltem prosternite casu
et poenae mutate genus.   Porsenna reducat
Tarquinios ; renovet ferales Allia pugnas ;
me potius saevi manibus permittite Pyrrhi,   125

---

[1] Doubtless a reference to Cincinnatus.
[2] Claudian means by "*altera*" the Eastern Empire.

been subdued, dishonoured now and poverty-stricken, bends beneath the cruel lash of peace, and though not openly beleaguered by any foe yet has all the hazard of a siege. Destruction threatens me hourly; a few days will set a limit to my uncertain food-supply. Out upon thee, prosperity! Why hast thou given me seven hills and such a population as a small supply cannot nourish? Happier I, had my power been less. Better to have put up with the Sabines and Veii; in narrower bonds I passed securer days. My very magnitude undoes me; would that I could return to my former boundaries and the walls of poor Ancus. Enough for me then would be the ploughlands of Etruria and Campania, the farms of Cincinnatus and Curius, and at his country's prayer the rustic dictator [1] would bring his home-grown wheat.

"What am I to do now? Gildo holds Libya, another [2] Egypt; while I, who subdued land and sea with my strong arm, am left to perish. Veteran of so many wars, can I claim no reward in mine old age? Ye gods in whose despite, it seems, I increased, now aid me at the last; pray Jove for me. And thou, Cybele, if ever of thine own free will thou wert carried over the sea and in exchange for Mount Ida tookest the hills of Rome and didst bathe thy Phrygian lions in Almo's more favoured stream, move now thy son [3] with a mother's entreaties. But if the fates forbid and our first founder was misled by augury untrue, o'erwhelm me at least in some different ruin, and change the nature of my punishment. Let Porsenna bring back the Tarquins; let Allia renew her bloody battle. Let me fall rather into the hands of cruel

[3] *i.e.* Jupiter.

me Senonum furiis, Brenni me reddite flammis.
cuncta fame leviora mihi."
                                    Sic fata refusis
obticuit lacrimis.   mater Cytherea parensque
flet Mavors sanctaeque memor Tritonia Vestae,
nec Cybele sicco nec stabat lumine Iuno.   130
maerent indigetes et si quos Roma recepit
aut dedit ipsa deos.   genitor iam corde remitti
coeperat et sacrum dextra sedare tumultum,
cum procul insanis quatiens ululatibus axem
et contusa genas mediis adparet in astris   135
Africa : rescissae vestes et spicea passim
serta iacent ; lacero crinales vertice dentes
et fractum pendebat ebur, talique superbas
inrupit clamore fores :
                        " Quid magne moraris
Iuppiter avulso nexu pelagique solutis   140
legibus iratum populis inmittere fratrem ?
mergi prima peto ; veniant praerupta Pachyno
aequora, laxatis subsidant Syrtibus urbes.
si mihi Gildonem nequeunt abducere fata,
me rape Gildoni.   felicior illa perustae   145
pars Libyae, nimio quae se munita calore
defendit tantique vacat secura tyranni.
crescat zona rubens ; medius flagrantis Olympi
me quoque limes agat ; melius deserta iacebo
vomeris impatiens.   pulsis dominentur aristis   150
dipsades et sitiens attollat glaeba cerastas.
quid me temperies iuvit ? quid mitior aether ?
Gildoni fecunda fui.   iam solis habenae

---

[1] *i.e.* the Palladium, the image of Pallas (= Minerva),
rescued by Metellus from the burning temple of Vesta,
241 B.C.

Pyrrhus; abandon me to the fury of the Senones
or the flames of Brennus. Welcome all this rather
than to starve!"

So spake she, and upwelling tears choked her voice.
Venus, mother of Aeneas, wept, and Mars, father of
Romulus and Minerva, mindful of Vesta's sacred
charge.[1] Nor Cybele nor Juno stood with dry eyes.
The heroes mourn and all the gods whose worship
Rome received from without or herself inaugurated.
And now began the heart of Jove to soften. With
hand outstretched he was checking the murmurings of
the gods when, shaking heaven with distraught cries,
Africa, her cheeks torn, appeared in the distance
advancing amid the stars. Torn was her raiment,
scattered her crown of corn. Her head was wounded
and the ivory comb that secured her hair hung
loose and broken. She rushed into Heaven's
halls shouting thus: "Great Jove, why delayest
thou to loose the bonds of sea, to break its
decree and hurl thy brother[2] in wrath against
the land? May I be the first to be overwhelmed.
Welcome the broken waters from Pachynus' cape;
sink my cities in the freed Syrtes. If so be fate
cannot rid me of Gildo, rid Gildo of me. Happier
that region of Libya that defends itself by means
of its own excessive heat and thus knows not the
irksome rule of so savage a tyrant. Let the torrid
zone spread. Let the midmost path of the scorching
sky burn me also. Better I lay a desert nor ever
suffered the plough. Let the dust-snake lord it in
a cornless land and the thirsty earth give birth to
nought but vipers. What avails me a healthy
climate, a milder air? My fruitfulness is but for

[2] *i.e.* Neptune.

bis senas torquent hiemes, cervicibus ex quo
haeret triste iugum. nostris iam luctibus ille   155
consenuit regnumque sibi tot vindicat annos.
atque utinam regnum !   privato iure tenemur
exigui specie fundi.   quod Nilus et Atlas
dissidet, occiduis quod Gadibus arida Barce
quodque Paraetonio secedit litore Tingi,   160
hoc sibi transcripsit proprium.   pars tertia mundi
unius praedonis ager.

         " Distantibus idem
inter se vitiis cinctus : quodcumque profunda
traxit avaritia, luxu peiore refundit.
instat terribilis vivis, morientibus heres,   165
virginibus raptor, thalamis obscaenus adulter.
nulla quies : oritur praeda cessante libido,
divitibusque dies et nox metuenda maritis.
quisquis vel locuples pulchra vel coniuge notus,
crimine pulsatur falso ; si crimina desunt,   170
accitus conviva perit.   mors nulla refugit
artificem : varios sucos spumasque requirit
serpentum virides et adhuc ignota novercis
gramina.   si quisquam vultu praesentia damnet
liberiusve gemat, dapibus crudelis in ipsis   175
emicat ad nutum stricto mucrone minister.
fixus quisque toro tacita formidine libat
carnifices epulas incertaque pocula pallens
haurit et intentos capiti circumspicit enses.
splendet Tartareo furialis mensa paratu   180
caede madens, atrox gladio, suspecta veneno.

---

¹ Tangiers.

Gildo. Twelve courses has the sun's chariot run since first I wore this sorry yoke. He has now grown old amid our miseries and these many years have set their seal upon his rule. Rule—would it were rule : a private owner possesses me, as it had been some pelting farm. From Nile to Atlas' mount, from scorched Barce to western Gades, from Tingi [1] to Egypt's coast Gildo has appropriated the land as his own. A third of the world belongs to one robber-chief.

" He is a prey to the most diverse vices : whatsoe'er his bottomless greed has stolen, a yet more insatiable profligacy squanders. He is the terror of the living, the heir of the dead, the violator of the unwed, and the foul corrupter of the marriage-bed. He is never quiet ; when greed is sated lust is rampant ; day is a misery to the rich, night to the married. Is any wealthy or known to possess a beautiful wife, he is overwhelmed by some trumped-up charge. If no charge be brought against him, he is asked to a banquet and there murdered. No form of death but is known to this artist in crime. He investigates the properties of different poisons and serpents' livid venom and knows of deadly herbs unknown even to stepmothers. If any condemns what he sees by a look or sighs with too much freedom, at the very festal board out darts some henchman with drawn sword at a nod from his master. Each glued to his seat tastes in silent fear of the deadly banquet ; drains, pale of face, the treacherous cup, and looks around at the weapons that threaten his life. The deadly board is decked in infernal splendour, wet with slaughter, dreadful with fear of sword and suspected poison. When wine has

ut vino calefacta Venus, tum saevior ardet
luxuries, mixtis redolent unguenta coronis :
crinitos inter famulos pubemque canoram
orbatas iubet ire nurus nuperque peremptis   185
adridere viris.   Phalarim tormentaque flammae
profuit et Siculi mugitus ferre iuvenci
quam tales audire choros.   nec damna pudoris
turpia sufficiunt : Mauris clarissima quaeque
fastidita datur.   media Carthagine ductae   190
barbara Sidoniae subeunt conubia matres ;
Aethiopem nobis generum, Nasamona maritum
ingerit ; exterret cunabula discolor infans.
his fretus sociis ipso iam principe maior
incedit ; peditum praecurrunt agmina longe ;   195
circumdant equitum turmae regesque clientes,
quos nostris ditat spoliis.   proturbat avita
quemque domo ; veteres detrudit rure colonos.
exiliis dispersa feror.   numquamne reverti
fas erit errantesque solo iam reddere cives ? "   200

    Iret adhuc in verba dolor, ni Iuppiter alto
coepisset solio (voces adamante notabat
Atropos et Lachesis iungebat stamina dictis) :
" nec te, Roma, diu nec te patiemur inultam,
Africa. communem prosternet Honorius hostem. 205
pergite securae.   vestrum vis nulla tenorem
separat et soli famulabitur Africa Romae."

    Dixit et adflavit Romam meliore iuventa.
continuo redit ille vigor seniique colorem
mutavere comae.   solidatam crista resurgens   210

inflamed the passions, his lust rages more savagely;
'midst the mingled smell of scents and flowers,
'midst curled minions and youthful choirs he bids
go sport the widowed wives whose husbands he
but a moment ago has murdered. Better Phalaris
and the torments of his furnace, better to listen to
the bellowings of the Sicilian bull than to such
songs as these. Nor is the base sacrifice of their
good name enough. When tired of each noblest
matron Gildo hands her over to the Moors. Married
in Carthage city these Sidonian mothers needs must
mate with barbarians. He thrusts upon me an
Ethiopian as a son-in-law, a Berber as a husband.
The hideous half-breed child affrights its cradle.
Thanks to those base allies his state is more regal
than that of the emperor himself. Before him goes
a body of foot-soldiers, squadrons of cavalry surround
him and client kings whom he enriches with our
spoils. He drives one and all from their ancestral
houses and expels husbandmen from farms so long
theirs. My people are scattered in exile. Are my
citizens never to return from their wanderings
to their native soil?"

She would have spoken further in her grief had
not Jove begun from his lofty throne—Atropos
wrote down his words in adamant and Lachesis spun
them in with her thread—" Neither thou, Rome,
nor yet thou, Africa, will we suffer to go long un-
avenged. Honorius shall disperse your common foe.
Go in peace. No violence shall part your companion-
ship; Africa shall serve Rome, and Rome alone."

He spake and breathed into Rome a youth renewed.
Straightway her former strength returned, and her
hair put off its grey of eld; her helmet grew solid,

erexit galeam clipeique recanduit orbis
et levis excussa micuit rubigine cornus.
    Umentes iam noctis equos Lethaeaque Somnus
frena regens tacito volvebat sidera curru.
iam duo divorum proceres, maiorque minorque   215
Theodosii, pacem laturi gentibus ibant,
qui Iovis arcanos monitus mandataque ferrent
fratribus et geminis sancirent foedera regnis :
sic cum praecipites artem vicere procellae
adsiduoque gemens undarum verbere nutat   220
descensura ratis, caeca sub nocte vocati
naufraga Ledaei sustentant vela Lacones.
circulus ut patuit Lunae, secuere meatus
diversos : Italas senior tendebat in oras ;
at pater, intrantem Pontum qua Bosphorus artat,
Arcadii thalamis urbique inlapsus Eoae.   226
quem simulac vidit natus (nam clara nitebat
Cynthia), permixto tremuerunt gaudia fletu
complexuque fovens, quos non speraverat, artus
" O mihi post Alpes nunc primum reddite," dixit, 230
" unde tuis optatus ades ? da tangere dextram,
qua gentes cecidere ferae. quis tale removit
praesidium terris ? ut te mortalia pridem
implorant longeque pium fortemque requirunt ! "
    Cui pater in tales rupit suspiria voces :   235
" hoc erat ? in fratres medio discordia Mauro
nascitur et mundus germanaque dissidet aula ?

---

[1] Theodosius the younger is, of course, Theodosius I.,
the Emperor (see Introduction, p. vii). Theodosius the
elder was his father. He was an able and trusted general of
Valentinian I., who restored quiet in Britain (368–370),
defeated the Alamanni (370), and crushed the revolt of
Firmus, Gildo's brother (see line 333 of this poem) in
Africa (? 372–374). His death was brought about by Mero-
baudes, Gratian's minister (cf. viii. 26-9).

upright stood the plumes, the round shield shone once more, and gone was every trace of rust from her wingèd, gleaming spear.

Sleep was now driving the dew-drenched steeds of night, guiding them with the reins of Lethe and carrying round the stars in her silent course, when the elder and the younger Theodosius,[1] chief among the heroes divine, came to bring peace to men. They bore Jove's secret message and mandate to the two brothers and ratified the treaty between the two empires. So when at dead of night the driving tempest has brought the helmsman's skill to nought and the sinking ship groans and shudders at the waves' ceaseless shock, Leda's Spartan-born sons sustain the foundering bark in answer to the sailors' prayers. At the rise of the full moon the twain parted. The elder directed his steps towards the coasts of Italy, the younger visited the couch of Arcadius, gliding down to that Eastern city where Bosporus narrows the entrance to the Euxine. As soon as the son saw his father (for the moon was shining brightly), he wept, yet trembled for joy, and embracing that form he had little hoped ever to embrace again, said: " O thou restored now to me for the first time since thy triumphs in the Alps, whence comest thou to thy loving son? Let me touch that hand that has conquered so many barbarian races! Who hath robbed the world of such a defender? How long a while has mankind prayed thine aid, and missed thy goodness and thy might!"

Sighing, the father made answer: " Was it for this? Is a Moor become a cause of discord between two brothers? Does the empire and court of the

Gildonisne salus tanti sit palma furoris?
scilicet egregius morum magnoque tuendus
et cuius meritis pietas in fratre recedat!   240
invito [1] genitore, vide, civile calebat
discidium; dubio stabant Romana sub ictu;
quis procul Armenius vel quis Maeotide ripa
rex ignotus agit, qui me non iuvit euntem
auxilio? fovere Getae, venere Geloni.   245
solus at hic non puppe data, non milite misso
subsedit fluitante fide. si signa petisset
obvia, detecto summissius hoste dolerem :
restitit in speculis fati turbaque reductus
libravit geminas eventu iudice vires   250
ad rerum momenta cliens seseque daturus
victori; fortuna simul cum mente pependit.
o si non cupidis essem praereptus ab astris,
exemplum sequerer Tulli laniandaque dumis
impia diversis aptarem membra quadrigis.   255
germani nunc usque tui responsa colebat :
en iterum calcat. tali te credere monstro
post patrem fratremque paras? sed magna rependit
inque tuam sortem numerosas transtulit urbes!
ergo fas pretio cedet? mercede placebit   260
proditio? taceo, laesi quod transfuga fratris,
quod levis ingenio. quamvis discrimine summo
proditor adportet suspensa morte salutem
numquam gratus erit. damnamus luce reperta

---

[1] MSS. in primo; *Birt suggests* invito, *Koch* infirmo

East quarrel with those of the West? Can Gildo's
salvation be fit guerdon for this mad rivalry? Great
no doubt are his virtues, great should be the price
paid to preserve them and such his merits as to
banish affection in a brother. Look you, though I,
thy sire, willed it not, civil war raged; the fortunes of
Rome stood on a razor's edge. Was there a distant
king of Armenia, an unknown monarch by Maeotis'
shore but sent aid to mine enterprises? The Getae
gave me succour, the Geloni came to my assistance.
Gildo alone sent not a man, not a ship, but waited
the issue in wavering loyalty. Had he sought the
confronting host as an open foe my wrath had been
less bitter. He stood apart on Fortune's watch-
tower and, withdrawn from the throng, weighed this
side against that, meaning to let the event decide him,
dependent upon the turn things might take and ready
to embrace the side of the victor. His fortune hung in
the balance as well as his intention. Had I not been
hurried to heaven by the impatient stars I would have
followed the example of Tullus Hostilius and dragged
the impious wretch limb from limb fastened to
chariots driven different ways through thorn bushes.[1]
Up to this time he has owed obedience to thy commands,
now behold he spurns his commands. After thy
father's and thy brother's fate art thou ready to
trust thyself to such a villain? Is thine answer that
he maketh great return and hath brought over many
cities to thine allegiance? Shall honour, then, give
place to utility? Can gain render treachery welcome?
I make no mention of his cruel betrayal of thy brother;
of his fickle nature; were a traitor to bring safety
even when at peril's height death threatened, never
shall he win gratitude. When our life is saved

perfidiam nec nos patimur committere tali.   265
hoc genus emptori cives cum moenibus offert,
hoc vendit patriam.   plerique in tempus abusi
mox odere tamen : tenuit sic Graia Philippus
oppida ; Pellaeo libertas concidit auro.
Romani scelerum semper sprevere ministros.   270
noxia pollicitum domino miscere venena
Fabricius regi nudata fraude remisit,
infesto quem Marte petit, bellumque negavit
per famuli patrare nefas, ductosque Camillus
trans murum pueros obsessae reddidit urbi.   275

    " Traduntur poenis alii, cum proelia tollunt ;
hic manet ut moveat ?   quod respuit alter in hostem,
suscipis in fratrem ? longi pro dedecus aevi !
cui placet, australes Gildo condonat habenas
tantaque mutatos sequitur provincia mores.   280
quaslibet ad partes animus nutaverit anceps,
transfundit secum Libyam refluumque malignus
commodat imperium.   Mauri fuit Africa munus.
tollite Massylas fraudes, removete bilingues
insidias et verba soli spirantia virus.   285
ne consanguineis certetur comminus armis,
ne, precor. haec trucibus Thebis, haec digna Mycenis ;
in Mauros hoc crimen eat.

                        " Quid noster iniquum
molitur Stilicho ?   quando non ille iubenti
paruit ? an quisquam nobis devinctior extat ?   290

118

we condemn the treachery nor brook to entrust ourselves to such protection. 'Tis this sort that offers for purchase cities and their inhabitants, that sells its fatherland. Most make use of such for the moment but soon learn to hate them. 'Twas thus that Philip held the cities of Greece ; liberty fell before the attack of Macedonian gold. Rome has ever despised the ministers of guilt. Fabricius, discovering the plot, sent back to King Pyrrhus the slave who had promised to mingle deadly poison for his lord; fierce war raged between them, but Fabricius refused to end it by means of the treachery of a slave. Camillus, too, gave back to the beleaguered city the boys brought to his camp from out the walls.

" These were consigned to punishment for seeking to put an end to wars. Is Gildo to live that he may kindle them ? Takest thou such measures against thy brother as another would disdain to take against an enemy ? O shame for unending ages ! Gildo entrusts the governance of the south to whom he will ; the great province of Africa obeys a tyrant's whim. To whichever side his fickle mind inclines, he carries Libya over with him and malignantly subjects it to a rule shifting as the tide. Africa was the gift of the Moor. Away with the trickery of the Massyli, their treacherous wiles and their words that breathe forth the poison of their land. Let not brother wage war on brother, I pray. That were worthy of cruel Thebes and Mycenae ; let that accusation be levelled against the Moors.

" What wrong is Stilicho devising ? when did he fail in his obedience ? than him what more loyal

119

ut sileam varios mecum quos gesserit actus,
quae vidi post fata, loquar.   cum divus abirem,
res incompositas (fateor) tumidasque reliqui.
stringebat vetitos etiamnum exercitus enses
Alpinis odiis, alternaque iurgia victi   295
victoresque dabant.   vix haec amentia nostris
excubiis, nedum puero rectore quiesset.
heu quantum timui vobis, quid libera tanti
militis auderet moles, cum patre remoto
ferveret iam laeta novis !   dissensus acerbus   300
et gravior consensus erat.   tunc ipse paterna
successit pietate mihi tenerumque rudemque
fovit et in veros eduxit principis annos,
Rufinumque tibi, quem tu tremuisse fateris,
depulit.   hunc solum memorem solumque fidelem 305
experior.   volui si quid, dum vita maneret,
aut visus voluisse, gerit ;   venerabilis illi
ceu praesens numenque vocor.   si tanta recusas,
at soceri reverere faces, at respice fratris
conubium pignusque meae regale Serenae.   310
debueras etiam fraternis obvius ire
hostibus, ille tuis.   quae gens, quis Rhenus et Hister
vos opibus iunctos conspirantesque tulisset ?
sed tantum permitte, cadat.   nil poscimus ultra.
ille licet sese praetentis Syrtibus armet   315
oppositoque Atlante tegat, licet arva referta
anguibus et solis medios obiecerit aestus :
120

supporter have we ? I will not mention the various
brave deeds he did while yet with me ; of those
only I will tell which I saw after my death. When
I was raised to heaven disorder—I admit it—and
tumult did I leave behind me. The army was still
drawing the forbidden sword in that Alpine war,
and conquerors and conquered gave alternate cause
for dissension. Scarce could this madness have been
calmed by my vigilance, much less by a boy's rule.
Ah, how I feared for you what the uncontrolled
might of such vast armies might dare, when, your
sire removed, there came the fevered delight in
change ! Dangerous was discord, more dangerous
still unanimity. 'Twas then that Stilicho took
my place in paternal love for thee, tended thine
immature youth, and brought thee to the years
and estate of an emperor. 'Twas he drove back
Rufinus whom thou didst confess thou fearedst.
Gratitude and loyalty I find in him alone. Did
I want or seem to want aught, while yet I
lived he accomplished it. Now I am dead he
worships me as worthy of veneration and an ever
present helper. If the thought of his goodness
move thee not, at least show respect to thy brother's
father-in-law : bethink thee of Honorius' marriage,
the royal espousal of my niece Serena. Thou
oughtest to face thy brother's foes, he thine. Could
any nation, could the combined forces of Rhine and
Danube have stood against you twain allied ?
Enough ! bring about but the defeat of Gildo : I ask
nought else. Though he entrench himself behind the
protecting Syrtes and rely for safety on the inter-
vening ocean ; though he think to be defended by
reason of his serpent-infested country and the fierce

121

novi consilium, novi Stilichonis in omnes
aequalem casus animum : penetrabit harenas,
inveniet virtute viam."

                         Sic divus et inde   320
sic natus : " iussis, genitor, parebitur ultro.
amplector praecepta libens, nec carior alter
cognato Stilichone mihi.　commissa profanus
ille luat ; redeat iam tutior Africa fratri."

    Talia dum longo secum sermone retexunt,   325
Hesperiam pervenit avus castumque cubile
ingreditur, Tyrio quo fusus Honorius ostro
carpebat teneros Maria cum coniuge somnos.
adsistit capiti ; tunc sic per somnia fatur :

    " Tantane devictos tenuit fiducia Mauros,   330
care nepos ? iterum post me coniurat in arma
progenies vesana Iubae bellumque resumit
victoris cum stirpe sui ? Firmumne iacentem
obliti Libyam nostro sudore receptam
rursus habent ? ausus Latio contendere Gildo   335
germani nec fata timet ? nunc ire profecto,
nunc vellem notosque senex ostendere vultus :
nonne meam fugiet Maurus cum viderit umbram ?
quid dubitas ? exsurge toris, invade rebellem,
captivum mihi redde meum. desiste morari.   340
hoc generi fatale tuo : dum sanguis in orbe
noster erit, semper pallebit regia Bocchi.
iungantur spoliis Firmi Gildonis opima ;

---

[1] Firmus, brother of Gildo, had, during the reign of
Valentinian, risen against the oppressive government of
Romanus, count of Africa, and had been defeated by
Theodosius the elder.

sun's mid-day heat, yet well I know Stilicho's in-
genuity—that mind of his equal to any emergency.
He will force his way through the desert, his own
greatness will lead him."

Thus spake the dead emperor, whereon thus
the son answered : " Right willingly, father, will I
fulfil thy commands : ever ready am I to welcome
thy behests. None is dearer to me than my kinsman
Stilicho. Let the impious Gildo atone for his wrongs,
and Africa be restored to my brother still safer
than before."

While father and son thus debated in long converse,
Theodosius the grandfather made his way to Italy
and entered the chaste bedchamber where on his
couch of Tyrian purple Honorius lay in sweet sleep
by the side of his wife Maria. At his head he stood
and thus spake to him in a dream. " What rash
confidence is this, dear grandson, that fills the
conquered Moors ? Does the mad race descended
from Juba, the people whom I subdued, once more
conspire to oppose Rome's power and recommence
the war with its conqueror's grandson ? Have they
forgotten the defeat of Firmus [1] ? Do they think to
repossess Libya won back by the sweat of battle ?
Dares Gildo strive with Rome ? Does he not fear
his brother's fate. Fain would I go myself, old
though I be, and show him the face he knows but
too well. Will not the Moor flee my very shade,
should he behold it ? Why delayest thou ? Up from
thy bed ; attack the rebel ; give me back my
prisoner ; waste no more time. 'Tis Fate's gift to
thy family. While yet the race of Theodosius treads
the earth the palace of Bocchus shall go in fear. Let
the spoils of Gildo be added to those of Firmus ;

exornet geminos Maurusia laurea currus :
una domus totiens una de gente triumphet.   345
di bene, quod tantis interlabentibus annis
servati Firmusque mihi fraterque nepoti."
dixit et adflatus vicino sole refugit.

At iuvenem stimulis inmanibus aemula virtus
exacuit ; iam puppe vehi, iam stagna secare   350
fervet et absentes invadere cuspide Mauros.
tum iubet acciri socerum dextramque vocato
conserit et, quae sit potior sententia, quaerit :

" Per somnos mihi, sancte pater, iam saepe futura
panduntur multaeque canunt praesagia noctes.   355
namque procul Libycos venatu cingere saltus
et iuga rimari canibus Gaetula videbar.
maerebat regio saevi vastata leonis
incursu ; pecudum strages passimque iuvenci
semineces et adhuc infecta mapalia tabo   360
sparsaque sanguineis pastorum funera campis.
adgredior latebras monstri mirumque relatu
conspicio : dilapsus honos, cervice minaces
defluxere iubae ; fractos inglorius armos
supposuit, servile gemens ; iniectaque vincla   365
unguibus et subitae collo sonuere catenae.
nunc etiam paribus secum certare tropaeis
hortator me cogit avus.   quonam usque remoti
cunctamur ?   decuit pridem complere biremes
et pelagi superare moras.   transmittere primus   370
ipse paro ; quaecumque meo gens barbara nutu
stringitur, adveniat : Germania cuncta feratur

---

¹ *i.e.* Stilicho.

let the bays of Mauretania deck chariots twain and one house triumph thus many times over one race. Thanks be to the gods who have interposed so many years between the sacrifice of Firmus to my arms and that of Firmus' brother to those of my grandson." He spake, then fled, as he felt the breath of the approaching dawn.

Then emulous courage roused the emperor with insistent goad. He burns to set sail, to cleave the main, to assail with the spear the distant Moors. So he summons his father-in-law [1] and clasping his hand asks what course of action he advises. " Full often, reverend sire, is the future revealed to me in dreams ; many a night brings prophecy. Methought I surrounded in hunting the distant glades of Africa and scoured the Gaetulian mountains with my hounds. The district was distressed by reason of the incursions of a ravening lion. On all sides were slaughtered beasts and mangled heifers, and still their homesteads ran red with blood, and corpses of many a shepherd lay weltering in the bloody fields. I approached the beast's cave and saw a sight wonderful to relate. Gone was that noble form, drooping on the neck the threatening mane ; there he crouched, defeated, humbled, with slavish moans ; fetters were upon his paws and a chain clanked of a sudden on his neck. Now, too, my grandsire eagerly urges me to rival his triumphs with my own. Why, he asked, did I delay and hesitate so long ? Already my ships should have been manned and the sea's threatened opposition overcome. I myself am ready to cross in the first vessel. Let every foreign nation that is bound beneath my rule come to our aid. Let all Germany be transported and

navibus et socia comitentur classe Sygambri.
pallida translatum iam sentiat Africa Rhenum.   374
an patiar tot probra sedens iuvenisque relinquam
quae tenui rexique puer ?   bis noster ad Alpes
alterius genitor defensus regna cucurrit.
nos praedae faciles insultandique iacemus ? ''
    Finierat.   Stilicho contra cui talia reddit :
'' adversine tubam princeps dignabere Mauri ?   380
auferet ignavus clari solacia leti,
te bellante mori ?   decernet Honorius inde,
hinc Gildo ?   prius astra Chaos miscebit Averno.
vindictam mandasse sat est ; plus nominis horror
quam tuus ensis aget.   minuit praesentia famam. 385
qui stetit aequatur campo, collataque nescit
maiestatem acies.   sed quod magis utile factu
atque hosti gravius (sensus adverte) docebo
est illi patribus, sed non et moribus isdem
Mascezel, fugiens qui dira piacula fratris   390
spesque suas vitamque tuo commisit asylo.
hunc ubi temptatis frustra mactare nequivit
insidiis, patrias in pignora contulit iras
et, quos ipse sinu parvos gestaverat, una
occidit iuvenes inhumataque corpora vulgo   395
dispulit et tumulo cognatas arcuit umbras
naturamque simul fratremque hominemque cruentus
exuit et tenuem caesis invidit harenam.
hoc facinus refugo damnavit sole Mycenas
avertitque diem ; sceleri sed reddidit Atreus   400
126

the Sygambri come with allied fleet. Let trembling Africa now have experience of the dwellers on Rhine's banks. Or shall I sit here and submit to such disgrace? Shall I relinquish, now that I am a man, what I ruled and governed as a boy? Twice my father hurried to the Alps to defend another's realm. Am I to be an easy prey, an object of scorn?"

He ended and Stilicho thus made answer: "Wilt thou, an emperor, deign to challenge a Moor to fight? Is that coward to have the consolation of death in battle at thy hand? Shall Honorius fight on our side and Gildo on the other? Ere that, chaos shall plunge the stars into Hell. 'Tis enough to command his punishment. Thy name shall strike greater terror into him than thy sword. Presence will minish awe; he who stands in the lists admits equality, and struggling hosts regard not majesty. Listen and I will tell thee something at once more profitable for thyself and of more effect against the enemy. Gildo has a brother of like descent but unlike in character, Mascezel, who, avoiding the evil courses of his brother, has entrusted his hopes and his life to thy keeping. When Gildo, after many vain attempts, found no means to kill Mascezel, he turned his anger from the father to the children and slew those whom himself had nursed as infants in his arms; then cast aside their unburied bodies and refused sepulchre to the shades of those that had been his kin. The bloody tyrant stifled all natural feelings, forgot he was a brother, forgot he was a man, and begrudged the slain a handful of dust. 'Twas a like deed brought its ill repute upon Mycenae, that put the sun to rout and turned back the day. But while Atreus paid back crime for crime and had excuse

crimen et infandas excusat coniuge mensas.
hic odium, non poena fuit. te perdita iura,
te pater ultorem, te nudi pulvere manes,
te pietas polluta rogat ; si flentibus aram
et proprium miseris numen statuistis, Athenae, 405
si Pandionias planctu traxere phalanges
Inachides belloque rogos meruere maritis,
si maesto squalore comae lacrimisque senatum
in Numidas pulsus solio commovit Adherbal :
hunc quoque nunc Gildo, tanto quem funere mersit,
hunc doleat venisse ducem seseque minorem   411
supplicibus sciat esse tuis.   quem sede fugavit,
hunc praeceps fugiat, fregit quem clade, tremiscat
agnoscatque suum, trahitur dum victima, fratrem."

Haec ubi sederunt genero, notissima Marti   415
robora, praecipuos electa pube maniplos
disponit portuque rates instaurat Etrusco.
Herculeam suus Alcides Ioviamque cohortem
rex ducit superum, premitur nec signifer ullo
pondere : festinant adeo vexilla moveri.   420
Nervius insequitur meritusque vocabula Felix
dictaque ab Augusto legio nomenque probantes
invicti clipeoque animosi teste Leones.

Dictis ante tamen princeps confirmat ituros

---

¹ A reference to the support given by Theseus, King of
Athens, to Adrastus, King of Argos, when the Thebans had
refused to allow the burial of the Argives slain at Thebes ;
cf. Eur. Supplices.
² Orosius (vii. 36. 6) says Mascezel only had 5000 men.
The legion may have been leg. viii. Augusta. The other
names are those of various numeri (the unit of the post-
Diocletianic army).

for the bloody banquet in the unfaithfulness of his wife, Gildo's motive was hatred, not vengeance. Violated rights, the sorrowing father, the unburied dead, the unnatural crime all call upon thee as avenger. If thou, Athens, didst dedicate an altar to the sorrowing and ordain to those that mourn a special deity, if the women of Argos won to their aid the Athenian phalanx by their tears and bought burial for their slain lords at the price of war;[1] if Adherbal, driven from his throne, roused the Senate against the Numidians by the sad appeal of unkempt locks and by his tears, then let Gildo be sorry that now this man also whom he has crushed by so many murders is come into the field against him, and let him learn that he must bow before thy suppliants. Let Gildo flee headlong before him whom he put to flight and fear him whom he o'erwhelmed with the murder of his children. As he is being dragged off to the slaughter let him recognize his brother's hand."

When this advice had been accepted by his son-in-law, Stilicho made ready for war the most famous regiments in the army, selecting therefrom special companies of picked men; he further prepared the fleet in the harbours of Etruria. Alcides himself commands the Herculean cohort; the king of the gods leads the Jovian. No standard-bearer feels the weight of his eagle, so readily do the very standards press forward. The Nervian cohort follows and the Felix, well deserving its name, the legion, too, named after Augustus, that well called The Un-conquered, and the brave regiment of the Lion[2] to whose name their shields bear witness.

But before they start the emperor, standing upon a platform of earth, heartens them with his words:

aggere conspicuus ; stat circumfusa iuventus   425
nixa hastis pronasque ferox accommodat aures :
   " Gildonem domitura manus, promissa minasque
tempus agi. si quid pro me doluistis, in armis
ostentate mihi ; iusto magnoque triumpho
civiles abolete notas ; sciat orbis Eous   430
sitque palam Gallos causa, non robore vinci.
nec vos, barbariem quamvis collegerit omnem,
terreat. an Mauri fremitum raucosque repulsus
umbonum et vestros passuri comminus enses ?
non contra clipeis tectos gladiisque micantes   435
ibitis : in solis longe fiducia telis.
exarmatus erit, cum missile torserit, hostis.
dextra movet iaculum, praetentat pallia laeva ;
cetera nudus eques. sonipes ignarus habenae ;
virga regit. non ulla fides, non agminis ordo :   440
arma oneri, fuga praesidio. conubia mille ;
non illis generis nexus, non pignora curae :
sed numero languet pietas. haec copia vulgi.
umbratus dux ipse rosis et marcidus ibit
unguentis crudusque cibo titubansque Lyaeo,   445
confectus senio, morbis stuprisque solutus.
excitet incestos turmalis bucina somnos,
imploret citharas cantatricesque choreas
offensus stridore tubae discatque coactus,
quas vigilat Veneri, castris impendere noctes.   450

---

[1] He appeals to the Gallic element of the army to atone for its previous support of Maximus and Eugenius.

leaning upon their spears the soldiers throng around him and attune their ready ears to his inspiring voice. " My men, so soon to bring defeat upon Gildo, now is the time to fulfil your promises and make good your threats. If you felt indignation on my behalf, now take up arms and prove it. Wash out the stain of civil war by means of a great and deserved triumph. Let the empire of the East know, let it be plain to all the world, that Gaul can only owe defeat to the badness of a cause, not to her enemies' strength.[1] Let not Gildo affright you though he have all barbary at his back. Shall Moors stand up against the shock of your clashing shields and the near threat of your swords ? You shall not oppose men armed with shields or shining blades. These savages put their trust in javelins hurled from afar. Once he has discharged his missile the enemy will be disarmed. With his right hand he hurls his spear, with his left he holds his cloak before him ; no other armour has the horseman. His steed knows not the rein ; a whip controls it. Obedience and discipline are unknown in their ranks. Their arms are a burden to them, their salvation lies in flight. Though each has many wives, ties of family bind them not, nor have they any love for their children whose very number causes affection to fail. Such are the troops. The chief will come to battle crowned with roses, drenched with scents, his last feast still undigested ; drunken with wine, foredone with eld, enervated with disease and venery. Let the war trumpet rouse him from a bed of incest, let him beg aid of lutes and choirs, for he likes not the clarion's note, and let him learn (all unwilling) to spend in war nights that he now dedicates to love.

131

" Nonne mori satius, vitae quam ferre pudorem ?
nam quae iam regio restat, si dedita Mauris
regibus Illyricis accesserit Africa damnis ?
ius Latium, quod tunc Meroë Rubroque solebat
Oceano cingi, Tyrrhena clauditur unda ;   455
et cui non Nilus, non intulit India metas,
Romani iam finis erit Trinacria regni.
ite recepturi, praedo quem sustulit, axem
ereptumque Notum ; caput insuperabile rerum
aut ruet in vestris aut stabit Roma lacertis.   460
tot mihi debetis populos, tot rura, tot urbes
amissas.   uno Libyam defendite bello.
vestros imperium remos et vestra sequatur
carbasa.   despectas trans aequora ducite leges.
tertia iam solito cervix mucrone rotetur   465
tandem funereis finem positura tyrannis."
    Omina conveniunt dicto fulvusque Tonantis
armiger a liquida cunctis spectantibus aethra
correptum pedibus curvis innexuit hydrum,
dumque reluctantem morsu partitur obunco,   470
haesit in ungue caput ; truncatus decidit anguis.
ilicet auguriis alacres per saxa citati
torrentesque ruunt ; nec mons aut silva retardat :
pendula ceu parvis moturae bella colonis
ingenti clangore grues aestiva relinquunt   475
Thracia, cum tepido permutant Strymona Nilo :
ordinibus variis per nubila texitur ales
littera pennarumque notis conscribitur aër.
    Ut fluctus tetigere maris, tunc acrior arsit

---

[1] The other two being Maximus and Eugenius.
[2] *i.e.* the Greek Λ.

" Is not death preferable to a life disgraced ? **If,**
in addition to the loss of Illyria, Africa is to be
surrendered to Moorish kings, what lands still remain
to us ? The empire of Italy, once bounded by the
Nile and the Red Sea, is limited to-day by the sea
of Tuscany ; shall Sicily now be the most distant
province of Roman rule, to which in days of old
neither Egypt nor India set an end ? Go : win back
that southern realm a rebel has reft from me. It
depends on your arms whether Rome, the uncon-
querable mistress of the world, stands or falls. You
owe me so many peoples, countries, cities lost.
Fight but one battle in defence of Libya. Let
empire restored attend on your oars and sails. Give
back to Africa the laws of Rome she now disregards.
Let history repeat itself, and the sword smite from
its trunk the head of this third tyrant [1] and so end
at last the series of bloody usurpers."

An omen confirms his word and before the eyes
of all, the tawny bird, armour-bearer of Jove, swoops
down from the open sky and seizes a snake in his
curved talons ; and while the eagle tears his struggling
prey with his hooked beak, his claws are embedded
in its head. The severed body falls to earth. Straight-
way the soldiers come hurrying up, crossing rocks
and streams in their eagerness at the call of this
portent. Neither mountains nor woods delay them.
Even as the cranes leave their summer home of
Thrace clamorously to join issue in doubtful war
with the Pygmies, when they desert the Strymon
for warm-watered Nile, the letter [2] traced by the
speeding line stands out against the clouds and the
heaven is stamped with the figure of their flight.

When they reached the coast still fiercer blazed

impetus ; adripiunt naves ipsique rudentes   480
expediunt et vela legunt et cornua summis
adsociant malis ; quatitur Tyrrhena tumultu
ora nec Alpheae capiunt navalia Pisae :
sic Agamemnoniam vindex cum Graecia classem
solveret, innumeris fervebat vocibus Aulis.   485
non illos strepitus impendentisque procellae
signa nec adventus dubii deterruit Austri.
" vellite " proclamant " socii, iam vellite funem.
per vada Gildonem quamvis adversa petamus.
ad bellum nos trudat hiems per devia ponti.   490
quassatis cupio tellurem figere rostris.
heu nimium segnes, cauta qui mente notatis,
si revolant mergi, graditur si litore cornix.
ora licet maculis adsperserit occiduus sol
lunaque conceptis livescat turgida Cauris   495
et contusa vagos iaculentur sidera crines ;
imbribus umescant Haedi nimbosaque Taurum
ducat Hyas totusque fretis descendat Orion :
certa fides caeli, sed maior Honorius auctor ;
illius auspiciis inmensa per aequora miles,   500
non Plaustris Arctove regor. contemne Booten,
navita, turbinibus mediis permitte carinas.
si mihi tempestas Libyam ventique negabunt,
Augusti Fortuna dabit."
                Iam classis in altum
provehitur ; dextra Ligures, Etruria laeva   505
linquitur et caecis vitatur Corsica saxis.
humanae specie plantae se magna figurat
insula (Sardiniam veteres dixere coloni),
dives ager frugum, Poenos Italosve petenti
134

their enthusiasm. They seize upon the ships and themselves make ready the hawsers ; furl the sails and fix the yards to the masts. Etruria's shore is shaken with their uproar and Arcadian-founded Pisa cannot contain so great a number of ships. So Aulis rang with countless voices what time avenging Greece loosed the cables of Agamemnon's fleet. No storm-blast deterred them nor threat of coming tempest nor the presence of the treacherous south wind. " Seize the rope, fellow-soldiers," they cry, " seize the rope : let us sail against Gildo though the very seas be against us. Let the storm drive us to battle by how crooked so ever a course. Fain would I seize upon that shore though my ships' beaks be shattered. Cowards ye, who cautiously observe whether or no the sea-gulls fly back or the crow pace the beach. What if clouds fleck the face of the setting sun or a stormy moon wear the halo that betokens hurricane ? What if comets wave their spreading tails, or the constellation of the Kids threatens rain, or the cloudy Hyades lead forth the Bull and all Orion sink 'neath the waves ? Put your trust in the sky, but put more in Honorius. Beneath his auspices I, his soldier, range the boundless seas nor look to the Plough or the Bear to guide me. Make no account of Boötes, sailor; launch your bark in mid tempest. If winds and storms deny me Libya, my emperor's fortune will grant it."

The fleet is launched. They pass Liguria on their right hand, Etruria on their left, avoiding the sunken reefs of Corsica. There lies an island formed like a human foot (Sardinia its former inhabitants called it), an island rich in the produce of its fields, and conveniently situated for them who sail either to

opportuna situ : quae pars vicinior Afris,   510
plana solo, ratibus clemens ; quae respicit Arcton,
inmitis, scopulosa, procax subitisque sonora
flatibus ; insanos infamat navita montes.
hic hominum pecudumque lues, sic [1] pestifer aër
saevit et exclusis regnant Aquilonibus Austri.   515
    Quos ubi luctatis procul effugere carinis,
per diversa ruunt sinuosae litora terrae.
pars adit antiqua ductos Carthagine Sulcos ;
partem litoreo complectitur Olbia muro.
urbs Libyam contra Tyrio fundata potenti   520
tenditur in longum Caralis tenuemque per undas
obvia dimittit fracturum flamina collem ;
efficitur portus medium mare, tutaque ventis
omnibus ingenti mansuescunt stagna recessu.
hanc omni petiere manu prorisque reductis   525
suspensa Zephyros expectant classe faventes.

    [1] *Birt, following the* MSS., si.   *Older editions* huic . . .
huic.   *I print* sic

---

    [1] This poem was never properly finished ; see Introduc-
tion, p. xi.

Africa or Italy. The part that faces Africa is flat and affords good anchorage for ships ; the northern shore is inhospitable, rock-bound, stormy, and loud with sudden gales. The sailor curses these wild cliffs. Here the pestilence falls on men and beasts, so plague-ridden and deadly is the air, so omnipotent the South wind and the North winds banished.

When their much buffeted vessels had given a wide berth to these dangers, they came to land at different places on the broken coast-line. Some are beached at Sulci, a city founded by Carthage of old. The sea-wall of Olbia shelters others. The city of Caralis over against the coast of Libya, a colony of great Phoenician Carthage, juts out into the sea and extends into the waves, a little promontory that breaks the force of the opposing winds. Thus in the midst a harbour is found and in a huge bay the quiet waters lie safe from every wind. For this harbour they make with every effort, and reversing their vessels they await the favouring breezes of the west wind with fleet at anchor.[1]

IN EUTROPIUM

LIBER I

(XVIII)

Semiferos partus metuendaque pignora matri
moenibus et mediis auditum nocte luporum
murmur et attonito pecudes pastore locutas
et lapidum duras hiemes nimboque minacem
sanguineo rubuisse Iovem puteosque cruore   5
mutatos visasque polo concurrere lunas
et geminos soles mirari desinat orbis :
omnia cesserunt eunucho consule monstra.
heu terrae caelique pudor ! trabeata per urbes
ostentatur anus titulumque effeminat anni.   10
pandite pontifices Cumanae carmina vatis,
fulmineos sollers Etruria consulat ignes
inmersumque nefas fibris exploret haruspex,
quae nova portendant superi. Nilusne meatu
devius et nostri temptat iam transfuga mundi   15
se Rubro miscere mari ? ruptone Niphate
rursum barbaricis Oriens vastabitur armis ?
an morbi ventura lues ? an nulla colono
responsura seges ? quae tantas expiet iras
victima ? quo diras iugulo placabimus aras ?   20

---

[1] For the consulship of Eutropius see Introduction, p. xv.
[2] A mountain in Armenia.

AGAINST EUTROPIUS

BOOK I

(XVIII)

Let the world cease to wonder at the births of
creatures half human, half bestial, at monstrous
babes that affright their own mothers, at the howling
of wolves heard by night in the cities, at beasts that
speak to their astonied herds, at stones falling
like rain, at the blood-red threatening storm clouds,
at wells of water changed to gore, at moons that
clash in mid heaven and at twin suns. All portents
pale before our eunuch consul. O shame to heaven
and earth ! Our cities behold an old woman decked
in a consul's robe who gives a woman's name to the
year.[1] Open the pages of the Cumaean Sibyl, ye
pontifs ; let wise Etrurian seers consult the light-
ning's flash, and the soothsayer search out the awful
portent hidden in the entrails. What new dread
warning is this the gods give ? Does Nile desert
his bed and leaving Roman soil seek to mix his
waters with those of the Red Sea ? Does cleft
Niphates [2] once more let through a host of eastern
barbarians to ravage our lands ? Does a pestilence
threaten us ? Or shall no harvest repay the farmer ?
What victim can expiate divine anger such as this ?
What offering appease the cruel altars ? The consul's

consule lustrandi fasces ipsoque litandum
prodigio ; quodcumque parant hoc omine fata,
Eutropius cervice luat sic omnia nobis.[1]

   Hoc regni, Fortuna, tenes ? quaenam ista iocandi
saevitia ? humanis quantum bacchabere rebus ?   25
si tibi servili placuit foedare curules
crimine, procedat laxata compede consul,
rupta Quirinales sumant ergastula cinctus ;
da saltem quemcumque virum. discrimina quaedam
sunt famulis splendorque suus, maculamque minorem
condicionis habet, domino qui vixerit uno.   31
si pelagi fluctus, Libyae si discis harenas,
Eutropii numerabis eros. quot iura, quot ille
mutavit tabulas vel quanta vocabula vertit !
nudatus quotiens, medicum dum consulit emptor, 35
ne qua per occultum lateat iactura dolorem !
omnes paenituit pretii venumque redibat,
dum vendi potuit. postquam deforme cadaver
mansit et in rugas totus defluxit aniles,
iam specie doni certatim limine pellunt   40
et foedum ignaris properant obtrudere munus.
tot translata iugis summisit colla, vetustum
servitium semperque novum, nec destitit umquam,
saepe tamen coepit.
                  Cunabula prima cruentis
debet suppliciis ; rapitur castrandus ab ipso   45

---

[1] *Birt begins the new paragraph at* sic, *printing a comma
at* nobis. *Alternatively, read* volvis *for* nobis (*so Cuiacius'
codd.*).

own blood must cleanse the consular insignia, the monster itself must be sacrificed. Whatever it be that fate prepares for us and shows forth by such an omen, let Eutropius' death, I pray, avert it all.

Fortune, is thy power so all-embracing? What is this savage humour of thine? To what lengths wilt thou sport with us poor mortals? If it was thy will to disgrace the consul's chair with a servile occupant let some "consul" come forward with broken chains, let an escaped jail-bird don the robes of Quirinus—but at least give us a man. There are grades even among slaves and a certain dignity; that slave who has served but one master holds a position of less infamy. Canst thou count the waves of the sea, the grains of Africa's sands, if so thou canst number Eutropius' masters. How many owners has he had, in how many sale-catalogues has he appeared, how often has he changed his name! How often has he been stripped while buyer consulted doctor whether there lurked any flaw by reason of some hidden disease! All repented having bought him and he always returned to the slave-market while he could yet fetch a price. When he became but a foul corpse-like body, a mass of senile pendulous flesh, his masters were anxious to rid their houses of him by giving him away as a present and made haste to foist the loathsome gift on an unsuspecting friend. To so many different yokes did he submit his neck, this slave, old in years but ever new to the house; there was no end to his servitude though many beginnings.

He is destined from his very cradle to bloody tortures; straight from his mother's womb he is hurried away to be made a eunuch; no sooner born

ubere ; suscipiunt matris post viscera poenae.
advolat Armenius certo mucrone recisos
edoctus mollire mares damnoque nefandum
aucturus pretium ; fecundum corporis imbrem [1]
sedibus exhaurit geminis unoque sub ictu   50
eripit officium patris nomenque mariti.
ambiguus vitae iacuit, penitusque supremum
in cerebrum secti traxerunt frigora nervi.

   Laudemusne manum, quae vires abstulit hosti,
an potius fato causam tribuisse queramur ?   55
profuerat mansisse virum ; felicior extat
opprobrio ; serviret adhuc, si fortior esset.

   Inde per Assyriae trahitur commercia ripae ;
hinc fora venalis Galata ductore frequentat
permutatque domos varias ; quis nomina possit   60
tanta sequi ? miles stabuli Ptolemaeus in illis
notior : hic longo lassatus paelicis usu
donat Arinthaeo ; neque enim iam dignus haberi
nec maturus emi. cum fastiditus abiret,
quam gemuit, quanto planxit divortia luctu !   65
" haec erat, heu, Ptolemaee, fides ? hoc profuit aetas
in gremio consumpta tuo lectusque iugalis
et ducti totiens inter praesaepia somni ?
libertas promissa perit ? viduumne relinquis
Eutropium tantasque premunt oblivia noctes,   70
crudelis ? generis pro sors durissima nostri !
femina, cum senuit, retinet conubia partu,

                [1] *codd.* ignem ; *Postgate* imbrem

---

   [1] I take Ptolemy to have been a *stationarius, i.e.* a
servant in a public post-house, but there is possibly some
covert allusion to *stabulum* in the sense of *prostibulum,* a
brothel.

than he becomes a prey to suffering. Up hastens
the Armenian, skilled by operating with unerring
knife to make males womanish and to increase their
loathly value by such loss. He drains the body's
life-giving fluid from its double source and with one
blow deprives his victim of a father's function and
the name of husband. Eutropius lay doubtful of
life, and the severed sinews drew a numbness deep
down into his furthest brain.

Are we to praise the hand that robbed an enemy
of his strength ? Or shall we rather blame the fates ?
It would have been better had he remained a man ;
his very disgrace has proved a blessing to him. Had
he had his full manly vigour he would still have been
a slave.

After this he is dragged from one Assyrian mart
to another ; next in the train of a Galatian slave-
merchant he stands for sale in many a market and
knows many diverse houses. Who could tell the
names of all his buyers ? Among these Ptolemy,
servant of the post-house,[1] was one of the better
known. Then Ptolemy, tired of Eutropius' long
service to his lusts, gives him to Arinthaeus ;—gives,
for he is no longer worth keeping nor old enough
to be bought. How the scorned minion wept at his
departure, with what grief did he lament that
divorce ! "Was this thy fidelity, Ptolemy ? Is
this my reward for a youth lived in thine arms,
for the bed of marriage and those many nights spent
together in the inn ? Must I lose my promised
liberty ? Leav'st thou Eutropius a widow, cruel
wretch, forgetful of such wonderful nights of love ?
How hard is the lot of my kind ! When a woman
grows old her children cement the marriage tie and

uxorisque decus matris reverentia pensat.
nos Lucina fugit, nec pignore nitimur ullo.
cum forma dilapsus amor ; defloruit oris   75
gratia : qua miseri scapulas tutabimur arte ?
qua placeam ratione senex ? "
       Sic fatus acutum
adgreditur lenonis opus, nec segnis ad artem
mens erat officiique capax omnesque pudoris
hauserat insidias.   custodia nulla tuendo   80
fida toro ; nulli poterant excludere vectes :
ille vel aerata Danaën in turre latentem
eliceret.   fletus domini fingebat amantis,
indomitasque mora, pretio lenibat avaras
lascivasque iocis ; non blandior ullus euntis   85
ancillae tetigisse latus leviterque reductis
vestibus occulto crimen mandasse susurro
nec furtis quaesisse locum nec fraude reperta
cautior elusi fremitus vitare mariti.
haud aliter iuvenum flammis Ephyreia Lais   90
e gemino ditata mari ; cum serta refudit
canities, iam turba procax noctisque recedit
ambitus et raro pulsatur ianua tactu,
seque reformidat speculo damnante senectus ;
stat tamen atque alias succingit lena ministras   95
dilectumque diu quamvis longaeva lupanar
circuit et retinent mores, quod perdidit aetas.
144

a mother's dignity compensates for the lost charms of a wife. Me Lucina, goddess of childbirth, will not come near; I have no children on whom to rely. Love perishes with my beauty; the roses of my cheeks are faded. What wits can save my wretched back from blows? How can I, an old man, please?"

So saying he entered upon the skilled profession of a pander. His whole heart was in his work; he knew his business well and was master of every stratagem for the undoing of chastity. No amount of vigilance could protect the marriage-bed from his attack; no bars could shut him out. He would have haled even Danaë from her refuge in the brazen tower. He would represent his patron as dying of love. Was the lady stubborn, he would win her by his patience; was she greedy, by a gift; flighty, he would corrupt her with a jest. None could arrest the attention of a maidservant with so neat a touch as he, none twitch aside a dress so lightly and whisper his shameful message in her ear. Never was any so skilled to choose a scene for the criminal meeting, or so clever at avoiding the wrath of the cuckold husband should the plot be discovered. One thought of Lais of Corinth, to whom the enamoured youth of that city brought wealth from its twin seas, who, when her grey hair could no longer go crowned with roses, when the emulous crowd of her admirers ceased nightly to haunt her doors and but few were left to knock thereat, when before the mirror's verdict age shrank back in horror from itself, yet stood, still faithful to her calling, and as a pander dressed others for the part, haunting still the brothel she had loved so well and so long, and still pandering to the tastes old age forbade her.

Hinc honor Eutropio ; cumque omnibus unica
    virtus
esset in eunuchis thalamos servare pudicos,
solus adulteriis crevit. nec verbera tergo   100
cessavere tamen, quotiens decepta libido
irati caluisset eri, frustraque rogantem
iactantemque suos tot iam per lustra labores
dotalem genero nutritoremque puellae
tradidit. Eous rector consulque futurus   105
pectebat dominae crines et saepe lavanti
nudus in argento lympham gestabat alumnae.
et cum se rapido fessam proiecerat aestu,
patricius roseis pavonum ventilat alis.

Iamque aevo laxata cutis, sulcisque genarum   110
corruerat passa facies rugosior uva :
flava minus presso finduntur vomere rura,
nec vento sic vela tremunt. miserabile turpes
exedere caput tineae ; deserta patebant
intervalla comae : qualis sitientibus arvis   115
arida ieiunae seges interlucet aristae
vel qualis gelidis pluma labente pruinis
arboris inmoritur trunco brumalis hirundo.
scilicet ut trabeis iniuria cresceret olim,
has in fronte notas, hoc dedecus addidit oris   120
luxuriae Fortuna suae : cum pallida nudis
ossibus horrorem dominis praeberet imago
decolor et macies occursu laederet omnes,

Hence sprang Eutropius' fame; for, though a eunuch's one virtue be to guard the chastity of the marriage-chamber, here was one (and one only) who grew great through adulteries. But the lash fell as before on his back whenever his master's criminal passion was through him frustrated. Then it was in vain that he prayed for forgiveness and reminded his lord of all those years of faithful service; he would find himself handed over to a son-in-law as part of the bride's dowry. Thus he would become a lady's-maid, and so the future consul and governor of the East would comb his mistress' locks or stand naked holding a silver vessel of water wherein his charge could wash herself. And when overcome by the heat she threw herself upon her couch, there would stand this patrician fanning her with bright peacock feathers.

And now his skin had grown loose with age; his face, more wrinkled than a raisin, had fallen in by reason of the lines in his cheeks. Less deep the furrows cloven in the cornfield by the plough, the folds wrought in the sails by the wind. Loathsome grubs ate away his head and bare patches appeared amid his hair. It was as though clumps of dry barren corn dotted a sun-parched field, or as if a swallow were dying in winter sitting on a branch, moulting in the frosty weather. Truly, that the outrage to the consul's office might one day be the greater, Fortune added to her gift of wealth this brand upon his brow, this deformity of face. When his pallor and fleshless bones had roused feelings of revulsion in his masters' hearts, and his foul complexion and lean body offended all who came

aut pueris latura metus aut taedia mensis
aut crimen famulis aut procedentibus omen,   125
et nihil exhausto caperent in stipite lucri :
(sternere quippe toros vel caedere ligna culinae
membra negant ; aurum, vestes, arcana tueri
mens infida vetat ; quis enim committere vellet
lenoni thalamum ?): tandem ceu funus acerbum 130
infaustamque suis trusere penatibus umbram.
contemptu iam liber erat : sic pastor obesum
lacte canem ferroque ligat pascitque revinctum,
dum validus servare gregem vigilique rapaces
latratu terrere lupos ; cum tardior idem   135
iam scabie laceras deiecit sordidus aures,
solvit et exuto lucratur vincula collo.

  Est ubi despectus nimius iuvat.   undique pulso
per cunctas licuit fraudes impune vagari
et fatis aperire viam.   pro quisquis Olympi   140
summa tenes, tanto libuit mortalia risu
vertere ?   qui servi non est admissus in usum,
suscipitur regnis, et quem privata ministrum
dedignata domus, moderantem sustinet aula.
ut primum vetulam texere palatia vulpem,   145
quis non ingemuit ? quis non inrepere sacris
obsequiis doluit totiens venale cadaver ?
ipsi quin etiam tali consorte fremebant
regales famuli, quibus est inlustrior ordo
servitii, sociumque diu sprevere superbi.   150

in contact with him, scaring children, disgusting those that sat at meat, disgracing his fellow-slaves, or terrifying as with an evil omen those that met him; when his masters ceased to derive any advantage from that withered trunk (for his wasted limbs refused even to make the beds or cut wood for the kitchen fire, while his faithless nature forbade their entrusting him with the charge of gold or vesture or the secrets of the house—who could bring him to entrust his marriage-chamber to a pander?), then at last they thrust him from their houses like a troublesome corpse or an ill-omened ghost. He was now free—for everyone despised him. So a shepherd chains up a dog and fattens him with milk while yet his strength avails to guard the flock and, ever watchful, to scare away wolves with his barking. But when later this same dog grows old and dirty and droops his mangy ears he looses him, and, taking off his collar, at least saves that.

Universal contempt is sometimes a boon. Driven out by all, he could freely range amid every sort of crime, and open a way for destiny. Oh thou, whosoe'er thou art, that holdest sway in Olympus, was it thy humour to make such mockery of mankind? He who was not suffered to perform the duties of a slave is admitted to the administration of an empire; him whom a private house scorned as a servant, a palace tolerates as its lord. When first the consular residence received this old vixen, who did not lament? Who grieved not to see an oft-sold corpse worm itself into the sacred service of the emperor? Nay, the very palace-servants, holding a prouder rank in slavery, murmured at such a colleague and long haughtily scorned his company.

Cernite, quem Latiis poscant adnectere fastis :
cuius et eunuchos puduit ! sed vilior ante
obscurae latuit pars ignotissima turbae,
donec Abundanti furiis—qui rebus Eois
exitium primumque sibi produxit—ab imis   155
evectus thalamis summos invasit honores.
quam bene dispositum terris, ut dignus iniqui
fructus consilii primis auctoribus instet.
sic multos fluvio vates arente per annos
hospite qui caeso monuit placare Tonantem,   160
inventas primus Busiridis imbuit aras
et cecidit saevi, quod dixerat, hostia sacri.
sic opifex tauri tormentorumque repertor,
qui funesta novo fabricaverat aera dolori,
primus inexpertum Siculo cogente tyranno   165
sensit opus docuitque suum mugire iuvencum.
nullius Eutropius, quam qui se protulit, ante
direptas possedit opes nullumque priorem
perculit exilio solumque hoc rite peregit,
auctorem damnare suum.

                    Postquam obsitus aevo 170
semivir excelsam rerum sublatus in arcem,
quod nec vota pati nec fingere somnia possunt,
vidit sub pedibus leges subiectaque colla
nobilium tantumque sibi permittere fata,
qui nihil optasset plus libertate mereri,   175

---

[1] By birth a Scythian.   Entered the Roman army under
Gratian and reached the position of *magister utriusque
militiae* under Theodosius.   Consul in 393 (Zosim. v. 10. 5)
150

See what manner of man they seek to connect with the annals of Rome : the very eunuchs were ashamed of him. At first of no account, he lay hid, the most unknown unit of an unregarded throng, till thanks to the mad folly of Abundantius [1] (who brought ruin on the empire of the East and, ere that, upon himself) he was advanced from the most menial office to the highest honours. What a happy dispensation of providence it is that in this world the results of ill counsel fall first upon its instigators ! Thus the seer who advised Busiris to placate the Thunderer's wrath, what time Nile's flood had long run dry, with a stranger's blood himself first stained that tyrant's altar with his own and fell a victim of the horrid sacrifice he had advised. Thus he who made the brazen bull and devised that new form of torture, casting the deadly bronze as an instrument of torment, was (at the bidding of the Sicilian tyrant) the first to make trial of the unhanselled image, and to teach his own bull to roar. So with Eutropius : on no man's goods did he sooner seize than on those of him by whom he had been raised to power ; none did he drive sooner into exile and thus, by the condemnation of his patron, was to thank for one righteous action.

When this half-man, worn out with age, had been raised to that pinnacle of glory for which he never would have dared to pray, of which never to dream ; when he had seen law at his feet, the heads of the nobility inclined before him, and fortune heaping such gifts upon one whose only hope and prayer had been to gain his freedom, he straightway forgot

and banished three years later to Pityus, thanks to the machinations of Eutropius.

iamiam dissimulat dominos alteque tumescunt
serviles animi. procerum squalore repletus
carcer et exulibus Meroë campique gemescunt
Aethiopum ; poenis hominum plaga personat ardens ;
Marmaricus claris violatur caedibus Hammon.   180
   Asperius nihil est humili cum surgit in altum :
cuncta ferit dum cuncta timet, desaevit in omnes
ut se posse putent, nec belua taetrior ulla
quam servi rabies in libera terga furentis ;
agnoscit gemitus et poenae parcere nescit,   185
quam subiit, dominique memor, quem verberat, odit.
adde, quod eunuchus nulla pietate movetur
nec generi natisve cavet. clementia cunctis
in similes, animosque ligant consortia damni ;
iste nec eunuchis placidus.
                Sed peius in aurum   190
aestuat ; hoc uno fruitur succisa libido.
quid nervos secuisse iuvat ? vis nulla cruentam
castrat avaritiam. parvis exercita furtis
quae vastare penum neglectaque sueverat arcae
claustra remoliri, nunc uberiore rapina   195
peccat in orbe manus. quidquid se Tigris ab Haemo
dividit, hoc certa proponit merce locandum
institor imperii, caupo famosus honorum.
hic Asiam villa pactus regit ; ille redemit
coniugis ornatu Syriam ; dolet ille paterna   200
Bithynos mutasse domo. subfixa patenti
vestibulo pretiis distinguit regula gentes :

his former masters, and his slave's mind swelled high within him. The prisons were filled with degraded nobles, Meroë and the plains of Ethiopia re-echoed to the weeping of exiles; the desert rang with the punishment of men; the temple of Jupiter Ammon in Africa was stained with gentle blood.

Nothing is so cruel as a man raised from lowly station to prosperity; he strikes everything, for he fears everything; he vents his rage on all, that all may deem he has the power. No beast so fearful as the rage of a slave let loose on free-born backs; their groans are familiar to him, and he cannot be sparing of punishment that he himself has undergone; remembering his own master he hates the man he lashes. Being a eunuch also he is moved by no natural affection and has no care for family or children. All are moved to pity by those whose circumstances are like their own; similitude of ills is a close bond. Yet he is kind not even to eunuchs.

His passion for gold increases—the only passion his mutilated body can indulge. Of what use was emasculation? The knife is powerless against reckless avarice. That hand so well practised in petty thefts, accustomed to rifle a cupboard or remove the bolt from the unwatched coffer, now finds richer spoils and the whole world to rob. All the country between the Tigris and Mount Haemus he exposes for sale at a fixed price, this huckster of empire, this infamous dealer in honours. This man governs Asia for the which his villa has paid. That man buys Syria with his wife's jewels. Another repents of having taken Bithynia in exchange for his paternal mansion. Fixed above the open doors of his hall is a list giving the provinces and their

tot Galatae, tot Pontus eat, tot Lydia nummis ;
si Lyciam tenuisse velis, tot millia ponas,
si Phrygas, adde ; parum ! propriae solacia sorti   205
communes vult esse notas et venditus ipse
vendere cuncta cupit.   certantum saepe duorum
diversum suspendit onus ; cum pondere iudex
vergit, et in geminas nutat provincia lances.
    Non pudet heu, superi, populos venire sub hasta ?
vendentis certe pudeat, quod iure sepultum   211
mancipium tot regna tenet, tot distrahit urbes.
pollentem solio Croesum victoria Cyri
fregit, ut eunucho flueret Pactolus et Hermus ?
Attalus heredem voluit te, Roma, relinqui,   215
restitit Antiochus praescripto margine Tauri,
indomitos curru Servilius egit Isauros
et Pharos Augusto iacuit vel Creta Metello,
ne non Eutropio quaestus numerosior esset ?
in mercem veniunt Cilices, Iudaea, Sophene   220
Romanusque labor Pompeianique triumphi.
    Quo struis hos auri cumulos ? quae pignora tantis
succedent opibus ? nubas ducasve licebit :
numquam mater eris, numquam pater ; hoc tibi
        ferrum,
hoc natura negat. te grandibus India gemmis,   225
te foliis Arabes ditent, te vellere Seres :
nullus inops adeo, nullum sic urget egestas,
ut velit Eutropii fortunam et membra pacisci.
    Iamque oblita sui nec sobria divitiis mens

---

¹ Attalus, King of Pergamum, left his kingdom by will to
Rome, 133 B.C. It became the province of Asia. The terms
mentioned here were imposed on Antiochus, King of Syria,
in 189 B.C. P. Servilius crossed the Taurus and subdued
the Isauri 78 B.C. ; Crete was conquered by Q. Metellus
between 68 and 66 B.C.

prices : so much for Galatia, for Pontus so much,
so much will buy one Lydia. Would you govern
Lycia? Then lay down so many thousands. Phrygia?
A little more. He wishes everything to be marked
with its price to console him for his own fortune and,
himself so often sold, he wants to sell everything.
When two are rivals he suspends in the balance
their opposed payment ; along with the weight
the judge inclines, and a province hangs wavering
in a pair of scales.

Ye gods, are ye not ashamed that whole peoples
are sold beneath the hammer ? At least let it
shame you of the seller, when a slave, a chattel the
law counts dead, possesses so many kingdoms and
retails so many cities. Did Cyrus' victory oust
mighty Croesus from his throne that Pactolus and
Hermus should roll their waves for a eunuch?
Did Attalus make you, Rome, his heir, was Antiochus
confined within the appointed bounds of Taurus,
did Servilius enjoy a triumph over the hitherto
unconquered Isaurians, did Egypt fall before
Augustus, and Crete before Metellus, to ensure
Eutropius a sufficient income ? [1] Cilicia, Judaea,
Sophene, all Rome's labours and Pompey's triumphs,
are there to sell.

Why heap up these riches ? Hast thou children
to succeed to them ? Marry or be married, thou
canst never be a mother or a father : the former
nature hath denied thee, the latter the surgeon's
knife. India may enrich thee with enormous jewels,
Arabia with her spices, China with her silks ; none so
needy, none so poverty-stricken as to wish to have
Eutropius' fortune and therewith Eutropius' body.

And now his mind, forgetful of its true nature and

in miseras leges hominumque negotia ludit.　　230
iudicat eunuchus ; quid iam de consule miror ?
prodigium, quodcumque gerit.　quae pagina lites
sic actas meminit ? quibus umquam saecula terris
eunuchi videre forum ?　sed ne qua vacaret
pars ignominia neu quid restaret inausum,　　235
arma etiam violare parat portentaque monstris
aggerat et secum petulans amentia certat.
erubuit Mavors aversaque risit Enyo
dedecus Eoum, quotiens intenta sagittis
et pharetra fulgens anus exercetur Amazon　　240
arbiter aut quotiens belli pacisque recurrit
adloquiturque Getas.　gaudet cum viderit hostis
et sentit iam deesse viros.　incendia fumant,
muris nulla fides, squalent populatibus agri
et medio spes sola mari.　trans Phasin aguntur　　245
Cappadocum matres, stabulisque abducta paternis
Caucasias captiva bibunt armenta pruinas
et Scythicis mutant Argaei pabula silvis.
extra Cimmerias, Taurorum claustra, paludes
flos Syriae servit.　spoliis nec sufficit atrox　　250
barbarus : in caedem vertunt fastidia praedae.

Ille tamen (quid enim servum mollemque pudebit ?
aut quid in hoc poterit vultu flagrare ruboris ?)
pro victore redit : peditum vexilla sequuntur
et turmae similes eunuchorumque manipli,　　255
Hellespontiacis legio dignissima signis.
obvius ire cliens defensoremque reversum
complecti.　placet ipse sibi laxasque laborat

---

[1] A mountain in Cappadocia.
[2] Claudian is scarcely fair to Eutropius. The reference
here is to the campaign of 398 in which Eutropius succeeded
in driving the Huns back behind the Caucasus.

drunken with riches, makes sport of wretched law
and the affairs of men. A eunuch is judge. Why
now wonder that he is consul? Whatever he does
is a prodigy. Can the annals of the law show cases
so mishandled? What age or what country has
ever witnessed a eunuch's jurisdiction? That
nought might remain undisgraced, nought un-
attempted, he even makes him ready to outrage
arms, heaps portent on portent and wanton folly
seeks to outdo itself. Mars blushed, Bellona scoffed
and turned her from the disgrace of the East whene'er
with arrows strung and flashing quiver the aged
Amazon practises battle or hurries back as arbiter
of peace and war to hold parley with the Getae.
Our enemies rejoiced at the sight and felt that at
last we were lacking in *men*. Towns were set ablaze;
walls offered no security. The countryside was
ravaged and brought to ruin. Mid-ocean alone
gave hope. Women of Cappadocia were driven into
captivity across the river Phasis; stolen from the
stalls of their homesteads, the captive herds drink
the snowy streams of Caucasus, and the flocks
exchange the pastures of Mount Argaeus [1] for the
woods of Scythia. Beyond the Cimmerian marshes,
defence of the Tauric tribes, the youth of Syria are
slaves. Too vast for the fierce barbarians are the
spoils; glutted with booty they turn to slaughter.

Yet Eutropius (can a slave, an effeminate, feel
shame? Could a blush grace such a countenance?),
Eutropius returns in triumph. There follow com-
panies of foot, squadrons like their general, maniples
of eunuchs, an army worthy Priapus' standards.
His creatures meet him and embrace their saviour
on his return.[2] Great is his self-esteem; he struggles

distendisse genas fictumque inflatus anhelat,
pulvere respersus tineas et solibus ora   260
pallidior, verbisque sonat plorabile quiddam
ultra nequitiam fractis et proelia narrat:
perque suam tremula testatur voce sororem,
defecisse vagas ad publica commoda vires;
cedere livori nec sustentare procellas   265
invidiae; mergique fretis spumantibus orat.
exoretque utinam! dum talia fatur ineptas
deterget lacrimas atque inter singula dicta
flebile suspirat: qualis venit arida socrus
longinquam visura nurum; vix lassa resedit   270
et iam vina petit.

          Quid te, turpissime, bellis
inseris aut saevi pertemptas Pallada campi?
tu potes alterius studiis haerere Minervae
et telas, non tela pati, tu stamina nosse,
tu segnes operum sollers urgere puellas   275
et niveam dominae pensis involvere lanam.
vel, si sacra placent, habeas pro Marte Cybeben;
rauca Celaenaeos ad tympana disce furores.
cymbala ferre licet pectusque inlidere pinu
inguinis et reliquum Phrygiis abscidere cultris.   280
arma relinque viris. geminam quid dividis aulam
conarisque pios odiis committere fratres?
te magis, ah demens, veterem si respicis artem,
conciliare decet.

          Gestis pro talibus annum

to swell out his pendulous cheeks and feigns a heavy panting ; his lousy head dust-sprinkled and his face bleached whiter by the sun, he sobs out some pitiful complaint with voice more effeminate than effeminacy's self and tells of battles. In tremulous tones he calls his sister to witness that he has spent his strength for his country's need ; that he yields to envy and cannot stand up against the storms of jealousy and prays to be drowned in the foaming seas. Would God his prayer had been granted ! Thus speaking, he wipes away the silly tears, sighing and sobbing between each word ; like a withered old dame travelled far to visit her son's daughter — scarce seated aweary and already she asks for wine.

Why busy thy foul self with wars ? Why attempt battle on the bloody field ? 'Tis to the arts of that other Minerva thou shouldst apply thyself. The distaff, not the dart should be thine ; thine to spin the thread, and, cunning craftsman that thou art, to urge on the spinning-maids when lazy ; thine to wind the snowy wool for thy mistress' weaving. Or, wouldst thou be a devotee, let Cybele, not Mars, be the object of thy worship. Learn to imitate the madness of the Corybantes to the accompaniment of rolling drums. Thou mayest carry cymbals, pierce thy breast with the sacred pine, and with Phrygian knife destroy what yet is left of thy virility. Leave arms to men. Why seek to divide the two empires and embroil loving brothers in strife ? Madman, remember thy former trade ; 'twere more fitting thou shouldst endeavour to reconcile them.

It is for deeds like this that Eutropius demands

flagitet Eutropius, ne quid non polluat unus,   285
dux acies, iudex praetoria, tempora consul !

   Nil adeo foedum, quod non exacta vetustas
ediderit longique labor commiserit aevi.
Oedipodes matrem, natam duxisse Thyestes
cantatur, peperit fratres Iocasta marito   290
et Pelopea sibi. Thebas ac funera Troiae
tristis Erechthei deplorat scaena theatri.
in volucrem Tereus, Cadmus se vertit in anguem.
Scylla novos mirata canes. hunc arbore figit,
elevat hunc pluma, squamis hunc fabula vestit,   295
hunc solvit fluvio. numquam spado consul in orbe
nec iudex ductorve fuit ! quodcumque virorum
est decus, eunuchi scelus est. exempla creantur
quae socci superent risus luctusque cothurni.

   Quam pulcher conspectus erat, cum tenderet artus
exangues onerante toga cinctuque gravatus   301
indutoque senex obscaenior iret in auro :
humani qualis simulator simius oris,
quem puer adridens pretioso stamine Serum
velavit nudasque nates ac terga reliquit,   305
ludibrium mensis ; erecto pectore dives
ambulat et claro sese deformat amictu.
candida pollutos comitatur curia fasces,
forsitan et dominus. praebet miracula lictor

---

¹ *i.e.* the Emperor.

this year of office, to ensure that by his efforts alone
he leaves nothing not dishonoured, ruining the army
as its general, the courts as their judge, the imperial
fasti as a consul.

No portent so monstrous but time past has given
it birth and the labour of bygone centuries produced
it. Legend tells us that Oedipus married his mother
and Thyestes his daughter ; Jocasta bare brothers
to her husband, Thyestes's daughter gave birth to
her own brother. Athenian tragedy tells the sad
tale of Thebes and the baneful war of Troy. Tereus
was changed into a bird, Cadmus into a snake; Scylla
looked in amaze on the dogs that girt her waist.
Ancient story relates how one was transformed into
a tree and thus attached to earth, how another grew
wings and flew, how a third was clothed with scales
and yet another melted into a river. But no country
has ever had a eunuch for a consul or judge or general.
What in a man is honourable is disgraceful in an emas-
culate. Here is an example to surpass all that is most
laughable in comedy, most lamentable in tragedy.

A pleasant sight in truth to see him strain his
sapless limbs beneath the weight of the toga, borne
down by the wearing of his consular dress ; the
gold of his raiment rendered his decrepitude even
more hideous. 'Twas as though an ape, man's
imitator, had been decked out in sport with precious
silken garments by a boy who had left his back and
quarters uncovered to amuse the guests at supper.
Thus richly dressed he walks upright and seems the
more loathsome by reason of his brilliant trappings.
Dressed in white the senate, perhaps even his
master,[1] accompanies the dishonoured fasces. Be-
hold a portent ! A lictor more noble than the

consule nobilior libertatemque daturus,   310
quam necdum meruit. scandit sublime tribunal
atque inter proprias laudes Aegyptia iactat
somnia prostratosque canit se vate tyrannos.
scilicet in dubio vindex Bellona pependit,
dum spado Tiresias enervatusque Melampus   315
reptat ab extremo referens oracula Nilo.

Obstrepuere avium voces, exhorruit annus
nomen, et insanum gemino proclamat ab ore
eunuchumque vetat fastis accedere Ianus:
sumeret inlicitos etenim si femina fasces,   320
esset turpe minus. Medis levibusque Sabaeis
imperat hic sexus, reginarumque sub armis
barbariae pars magna iacet: gens nulla probatur,
eunuchi quae sceptra ferat. Tritonia, Phoebe,
Terra, Ceres, Cybele, Iuno, Latona coluntur: 325
eunuchi quae templa dei, quas vidimus aras ?
inde sacerdotes ; haec intrat pectora Phoebus ;
inde canunt Delphi ; Troianam sola Minervam
virginitas Vestalis adit flammasque tuetur :
hi nullas meriti vittas semperque profani.   330
nascitur ad fructum mulier prolemque futuram :
hoc genus inventum est ut serviat. Herculis arcu
concidit Hippolyte ; Danai fugere bipennem,
Penthesilea, tuam ; claras Carthaginis arces
creditur et centum portis Babylona superbam   335
femineus struxisse labor. quid nobile gessit

---

¹ In 394 Arcadius had sent Eutropius to the Thebaid
to consult a certain Christian prophet, John, upon the
result of Eugenius' revolt (Sozom. vii. 22. 7, 8).

consul, and a man about to grant to others a liberty
which he has not yet himself won. He mounts the
lofty platform and amid a torrent of self-laudation
boasts of a prophetic dream he had in Egypt[1] and
of the defeat of tyrants which he foretold. No
doubt the goddess of war stayed her avenging hand
and waited till that emasculate Tiresias, that
unmanned Melampus, could crawl back with oracles
culled from farthest Nile.

Loud sang the prophetic birds in warning. The
year shuddered at the thought of bearing Eutropius'
name, and Janus proclaimed the madness of the
choice from his two mouths, forbidding a eunuch
to have access to his annals. Had a woman assumed
the fasces, though this were illegal it were neverthe-
less less disgraceful. Women bear sway among the
Medes and swift Sabaeans; half barbary is governed
by martial queens. We know of no people who
endure a eunuch's rule. Worship is paid to Pallas,
Phoebe, Vesta, Ceres, Cybele, Juno, and Latona;
have we ever seen a temple built or altars raised to
a eunuch god? From among women are priestesses
chosen; Phoebus enters into their hearts; through
their voices the Delphian oracle speaks; none but
the Vestal Virgins approach the shrine of Trojan
Minerva and tend her flame: eunuchs have never
deserved the fillet and are always unholy. A woman
is born that she may bear children and perpetuate
the human race; the tribe of eunuchs was made for
servitude. Hippolyte fell but by the arrow of
Hercules; the Greeks fled before Penthesilea's
axe; Carthage, far-famed citadel, proud Babylon
with her hundred gates, are both said to have been
built by a woman's hand. What noble deed did

eunuchus ? quae bella tulit ? quas condidit urbes ?
illas praeterea rerum natura creavit,
hos fecere manus : seu prima Semiramis astu
Assyriis mentita virum, ne vocis acutae   340
mollities levesve genae se prodere possent,
hos sibi coniunxit similes ; seu Parthica ferro
luxuries vetuit nasci lanuginis umbram
servatoque diu puerili flore coegit
arte retardatam Veneri servire iuventam.   345
    Fama prius falso similis vanoque videri
ficta ioco ; levior volitare per oppida rumor
riderique nefas : veluti nigrantibus alis
audiretur olor, corvo certante ligustris.
atque aliquis gravior morum : " si talibus, inquit, 350
creditur et nimiis turgent mendacia monstris,
iam testudo volat, profert iam cornua vultur ;
prona petunt retro fluvii iuga ; Gadibus ortum
Carmani texere diem ; iam frugibus aptum
aequor et adsuetum silvis delphina videbo ;   355
iam cochleis homines iunctos et quidquid inane
nutrit Iudaicis quae pingitur India velis."
    Subicit et mixtis salibus lascivior alter :
" miraris ? nihil est, quod non in pectore magnum
concipit Eutropius. semper nova, grandia semper
diligit et celeri degustat singula sensu.   361
nil timet a tergo ; vigilantibus undique curis
nocte dieque patet ; lenis facilisque moveri
supplicibus mediaque tamen mollissimus ira
nil negat et sese vel non poscentibus offert ;   365

a eunuch ever do? What wars did such an one fight, what cities did he found? Moreover, nature created the former, the hand of man the latter, whether it was from fear of being betrayed by her shrill woman's voice and her hairless cheeks that clever Semiramis, to disguise her sex from the Assyrians, first surrounded herself with beings like her, or the Parthians employed the knife to stop the growth of the first down of manhood and forced their boys, kept boys by artifice, to serve their lusts by thus lengthening the years of youthful charm.

At first the rumour of Eutropius' consulship seemed false and invented as a jest. A vague story spread from city to city; the crime was laughed at as one would laugh to hear of a swan with black wings or a crow as white as privet. Thus spake one of weighty character: "If such things are believed and swollen lies tell of unheard of monsters, then the tortoise can fly, the vulture grow horns, rivers flow back and mount the hills whence they spring, the sun rise behind Gades and set amid the Carmanians of India; I shall soon see ocean fit nursery for plants and the dolphin a denizen of the woods; beings half-men, half-snails and all the vain imaginings of India depicted on Jewish curtains."

Then another adds, jesting with a more wanton wit: "Dost thou wonder? Nothing great is there that Eutropius does not conceive in his heart. He ever loves novelty, ever size, and is quick to taste everything in turn. He fears no assault from the rear; night and day he is ready with watchful care; soft, easily moved by entreaty, and, even in the midst of his passion, tenderest of men, he never says 'no,' and is ever at the disposal even of

165

quod libet ingenio, subigit traditque fruendum ;
quidquid amas, dabit illa manus ; communiter omni
fungitur officio gaudetque potentia flecti.
hoc quoque conciliis peperit meritoque laborum,
accipit et trabeas argutae praemia dextrae."   370

   Postquam vera fides facinus vulgavit Eoum
gentibus et Romae iam certius impulit aures,
" Eutropiumne etiam nostra dignabimur ira ?
hic quoque Romani meruit pars esse doloris ? "
sic effata rapit caeli per inania cursum   375
diva potens unoque Padum translapsa volatu
castra sui rectoris adit.   tum forte decorus
cum Stilichone gener pacem implorantibus ultro
Germanis responsa dabat, legesque Caucis
arduus et flavis signabat iura Suebis.   380
his tribuit reges, his obside foedera sancit
indicto ; bellorum alios transcribit in usus,
militet ut nostris detonsa Sygambria signis.
laeta subit Romam pietas et gaudia paene
moverunt lacrimas tantoque exultat alumno :   385
sic armenta suo iam defensante iuvenco
celsius adsurgunt erectae cornua matri,
sic iam terribilem stabulis dominumque ferarum
crescere miratur genetrix Massyla leonem.
dimovit nebulam iuvenique adparuit ingens.   390
tum sic orsa loqui :

---

   [1] With a play upon the sexual meaning of the word ;
indeed the whole passage, from l. 358 is a mass of obscene
innuendo.
   [2] *i.e.* the consulship.

those that solicit him not. Whatever the senses desire he cultivates and offers for another's enjoyment. That hand will give whatever thou wouldest have. He performs the functions of all alike ; his dignity loves to unbend. His meetings [1] and his deserving labours have won him this reward,[2] and he receives the consul's robe in recompense for the work of his skilful hand."

When the rumour concerning this disgrace of the eastern empire was known to be true and had impressed belief on Roman ears, Rome's goddess thus spake : " Is Eutropius worthy of mine ire ? Is such an one fit cause for Roman grief ? " So saying the mighty goddess winged her way through the heavens and with one stroke of her pinions passed beyond the Po and approached the camp of her emperor. It happened that even then the august Honorius, assisted by his father-in-law Stilicho, was making answer to the Germans who had come of their own accord to sue for peace. From his lofty throne he was dictating laws to the Cauci and giving a constitution to the flaxen-haired Suebi. Over these he sets a king, with those he signs a treaty now that hostages have been demanded ; others he enters on the list as serviceable allies in war, so that in future the Sygambrians will cut off their flowing locks and serve beneath our banners. Joy and love so fill the goddess' heart that she well nigh weeps, so great is her happy pride in her illustrious foster-child. So when a bullock fights in defence of the herd his mother lifts her own horns more proudly ; so the African lioness gazes with admiration on her cub as he grows to be the terror of the farmsteads and the future king of beasts. Rome lays aside her veil of cloud and towers above the youthful warrior, then thus begins.

"Quantum te principe possim,
non longinqua docent, domito quod Saxone Tethys
mitior aut fracto secura Britannia Picto ;
ante pedes humili Franco tristique Suebo
perfruor et nostrum video, Germanice, Rhenum. 395
sed quid agam ?   discors Oriens felicibus actis
invidet atque alio Phoebi de cardine surgunt
crimina, ne toto conspiret corpore regnum.
Gildonis taceo magna cum laude receptam
perfidiam et fretos Eoo robore Mauros.   400
quae suscepta fames, quantum discriminis urbi,
ni tua vel soceri numquam non provida virtus
australem Arctois pensasset frugibus annum !
invectae Rhodani Tiberina per ostia classes
Cinyphiisque ferax Araris successit aristis.   405
Teutonicus vomer Pyrenaeique iuvenci
sudavere mihi ; segetes mirantur Hiberas
horrea ; nec Libyae senserunt damna rebellis
iam transalpina contenti messe Quirites.
ille quidem solvit meritas (scit Tabraca) poenas, 410
ut pereat quicumque tuis conflixerit armis.

"Ecce repens isdem clades a partibus exit
terrorisque minus, sed plus habitura pudoris
Eutropius consul.   pridem tolerare fatemur
hoc genus, Arsacio postquam se regia fastu   415
sustulit et nostros corrupit Parthia mores.
praefecti sed adhuc gemmis vestique dabantur
custodes sacroque adhibere silentia somno ;

---

¹ She calls him *Germanicus* because of his pacification of
Germany ; see Introduction, p. x.

168

"Examples near at hand testify to the extent of my power now thou art emperor. The Saxon is conquered and the seas safe; the Picts have been defeated and Britain is secure. I love to see at my feet the humbled Franks and broken Suebi, and I behold the Rhine mine own, Germanicus.[1] Yet what am I to do? The discordant East envies our prosperity, and beneath that other sky, lo! wickedness flourishes to prevent our empire's breathing in harmony with one body. I make no mention of Gildo's treason, detected so gloriously in spite of the power of the East on which the rebel Moor relied. For what extremes of famine did we not then look? How dire a danger overhung our city, had not thy valour or the ever-provident diligence of thy father-in-law supplied corn from the north in place of that from the south! Up Tiber's estuary there sailed ships from the Rhine, and the Saône's fertile banks made good the lost harvests of Africa. For me the Germans ploughed and the Spaniards' oxen sweated; my granaries marvel at Iberian corn, nor did my citizens, now satisfied with harvests from beyond the Alps, feel the defection of revolted Africa. Gildo, however, paid the penalty for his treason as Tabraca can witness. So perish all who take up arms against thee!

"Lo! on a sudden from that same clime comes another scourge, less terrible indeed but even more shameful, the consulship of Eutropius. I admit I have long learned to tolerate this unmanned tribe, ever since the court exalted itself with Arsacid pomp and the example of Parthia corrupted our morals. But till now they were but set to guard jewels and raiment, and to secure silence for the imperial slumber. Never beyond the sleeping-

militia eunuchi numquam progressa cubili,
non vita spondente fidem, sed inertia tutum   420
mentis pignus erat. secreta monilia servent,
ornatus curent Tyrios : a fronte recedant
imperii. tenero tractari pectore nescit
publica maiestas. numquam vel in aequore puppim
vidimus eunuchi clavo parere magistri.   425
nos adeo sperni faciles ? orbisque carina
vilior ? auroram sane, quae talia ferre
gaudet, et adsuetas sceptris muliebribus urbes
possideant ; quid belliferam communibus urunt
Italiam maculis nocituraque probra severis   430
ammiscent populis ? peregrina piacula forti
pellantur longe Latio nec transeat Alpes
dedecus ; in solis, quibus extitit, haereat arvis.
scribat Halys, scribat famae contemptor Orontes :
per te perque tuos obtestor Roma triumphos,   435
nesciat hoc Thybris, numquam poscentibus olim
qui dare Dentatis annos Fabiisque solebat.
Martius eunuchi repetet suffragia campus ?
Aemilios inter servatoresque Camillos
Eutropius ? iam Chrysogonis tua, Brute, potestas   440
Narcissisque datur ? natos hoc dedere poenae
profuit et misero civem praeponere patri ?
hoc mihi Ianiculo positis Etruria castris
quaesiit et tantum fluvio Porsenna remotus ?
hoc meruit vel ponte Cocles vel Mucius igne ?   445
visceribus frustra castum Lucretia ferrum

---

[1] Notorious freedmen and tools respectively of Sulla and
the Emperor Claudius.

170

chamber did the eunuch's service pass; not their
lives gave guarantee of loyalty but their dull wits
were a sure pledge. Let them guard hidden store
of pearls and Tyrian-dyed vestments; they must
quit high offices of state. The majesty of Rome
cannot devolve upon an effeminate. Never have
we seen so much as a ship at sea obey the helm
in the hands of a eunuch-captain. Are we then so
despicable? Is the whole world of less account
than a ship? Let eunuchs govern the East by all
means, for the East rejoices in such rulers, let them
lord it over cities accustomed to a woman's sway:
why disfigure warlike Italy with the general brand
and defile her austere peoples with their deadly
profligacy? Drive this foreign pollution from out
the boundaries of manly Latium; suffer not this
thing of shame to cross the Alps; let it remain
fixed in the country of its birth. Let the river
Halys or Orontes, careless of its reputation, add
such a name to its annals: I, Rome, beg thee by
thy life and triumphs, let not Tiber suffer this
disgrace—Tiber whose way was to give the consul-
ship to such men as Dentatus and Fabius though
they asked not for it. Shall the Field of Mars witness
the canvassing of an eunuch? Is Eutropius to stand
with Aemilii and Camilli, saviours of their country?
Is thy office, Brutus, now to be given to a Chryso-
gonus or a Narcissus[1]? Is this the reward for giving
up thy sons to punishment and setting the citizen's
duty before the father's grief? Was it for this that
the Tuscans made their camp on the Janiculum and
Porsenna was but the river's span from our gates?
For this that Horatius kept the bridge and Mucius
braved the flames? Was it all to no purpose that

mersit et attonitum tranavit Cloelia Thybrim ?
Eutropio fasces adservabantur adempti
Tarquiniis ? quemcumque meae vexere curules,
laxato veniat socium aversatus Averno.   450
impensi sacris Decii prorumpite bustis
Torquatique truces animosaque pauperis umbra
Fabricii tuque o, si forte inferna piorum
iugera et Elysias scindis, Serrane, novales.
Poeno Scipiadae, Poeno praeclare Lutati,   455
Sicania Marcelle ferox, gens Claudia surgas[1]
et Curii veteres ; et, qui sub iure negasti
vivere Caesareo, parvo procede sepulcro
Eutropium passure Cato ; remeate tenebris,
agmina Brutorum Corvinorumque catervae.   460
eunuchi vestros habitus, insignia sumunt
ambigui Romana mares ; rapuere tremendas
Hannibali Pyrrhoque togas ; flabella perosi
adspirant trabeis ; iam non umbracula gestant
virginibus, Latias ausi vibrare secures !   465
    " Linquite femineas infelix turba latebras,
alter quos pepulit sexus nec suscipit alter,
execti Veneris stimulos et vulnere casti
(mixta duplex aetas ; inter puerumque senemque
nil medium) : falsi complete sedilia patres ;   470
ite novi proceres infecundoque senatu
Eutropium stipate ducem ; celebrate tribunal
pro thalamis, verso iam discite more curules,
non matrum pilenta sequi.

                    [1] MSS. *have* surgat

chaste Lucretia plunged the dagger into her bosom
and Cloelia swam the astonished Tiber? Were the
fasces reft from Tarquin to be given to Eutropius?
Let Hell ope her jaws and all who have sat in my
curule chair come and turn their backs upon their
colleague. Decii, self-sacrificed for your country's
good, come forth from your graves; and you, fierce
Torquati; and thou, too, great-hearted shade of poor
Fabricius. Serranus, come thou hither, if now thou
ploughest the acres of the holy dead and cleavest
the fallow lands of Elysium. Come Scipios, Lutatius,
famed for your victories over Carthage, Marcellus,
conqueror of Sicily, rise from the dead, thou
Claudian race, you progeny of Curius. Cato, thou
who wouldst not live beneath Caesar's rule, come
thou forth from thy simple tomb and brave the
sight of Eutropius. Immortal bands of Bruti and
Corvini, return to earth. Eunuchs don your robes
of office, sexless beings assume the insignia of Rome.
They have laid hands on the toga that inspired
Hannibal and Pyrrhus with terror. They now despise
the fan and aspire to the consul's cloak. No longer
do they carry the maidenly parasol for they have
dared to wield the axes of Latium.

" Unhappy band, leave your womanly fastnesses,
you whom the male sex has discarded and the female
will not adopt. The knife has cut out the stings of
love and by that wounding you are pure. A mixture
are you of two ages—child and greybeard and nought
between. Take your seats, fathers in name alone.
Come new lords, come sterile senate, throng your
leader Eutropius. Fill the judgement-seat, not the
bedchamber. Change your habits and learn to follow
the consul's chair, not the woman's litter.

                     " Ne prisca revolvam
neu numerem, quantis iniuria mille per annos   475
sit retro ducibus, quanti foedabitur aevi
canities, unam subeant quot saecula culpam :
inter Arinthaei fastos et nomen erile
servus erit dominoque suos aequalis honores
inseret ! heu semper Ptolomaei noxia mundo   480
mancipia ! en alio laedor graviore Pothino
et patior maius Phario scelus. ille cruorem
consulis unius Pellaeis ensibus hausit ;
inquinat hic omnes.
                   " Si nil privata movebunt,
at tu principibus, vestrae tu prospice causae   485
regalesque averte notas. hunc accipit unum
aula magistratum : vobis patribusque recurrit
hic alternus honos. in crimen euntibus annis
parce, quater consul ! contagia fascibus, oro,
defendas ignava tuis neu tradita libris   490
omina vestitusque meos, quibus omne, quod ambit
oceanus, domui, tanta caligine mergi
calcarique sinas. nam quae iam bella geramus
mollibus auspiciis ? quae iam conubia prolem
vel frugem latura seges ? quid fertile terris,   495
quid plenum sterili possit sub consule nasci ?
eunuchi si iura dabunt legesque tenebunt,
ducant pensa viri mutatoque ordine rerum
vivat Amazonio confusa licentia ritu.

---

[1] Arinthaeus had held the high position of *magister
peditum*. He died in 379.

[2] Pothinus, the creature of Ptolemy Dionysius, was
instrumental in killing Pompey in Egypt in 48 B.C.

"I would not cite examples from remote antiquity nor count the countless magistrates of past history whom he thus outrages. But think how the reverence due to all past ages will be impaired, on how many centuries one man's shame will set its mark. Amid the annals that record the name of Arinthaeus,[1] his master, will be found the slave, and he will enter his own honours as equal to those of his owner. The slaves of Egypt's kings have ever been a curse to the world; behold I suffer from a worse than Pothinus and bear a wrong more flagrant than that of which Egypt was once the scene. Pothinus' sword at Alexandria spilled the blood of a single consul;[2] Eutropius brings dishonour on all.

"If the fate of subjects cannot move thee, yet have thou regard for princes, for your common cause, and remove this stain on royalty. The consulship is the sole office the emperor deigns to accept; alternately the honour passes to Court and Senate. Thou who hast thyself been four times consul spare succeeding consuls this infamy. I pray thee, protect the fasces, so often thine, from the pollution of a eunuch's hand; let not the omens handed down in our sacred books, let not those robes of mine wherewith I have subdued everything within Ocean's stream, be plunged in so great darkness and trodden under foot. What kind of wars can we wage now that a eunuch takes the auspices? What marriage, what harvest will be fruitful? What fertility, what abundance is possible beneath a consul stricken with sterility? If eunuchs shall give judgement and determine laws, then let men card wool and live like the Amazons, confusion and licence dispossessing the order of nature.

"Quid trahor ulterius? Stilicho, quid vincere differs,
dum certare pudet? nescis quod turpior hostis   501
laetitia maiore cadit?   piratica Magnum
erigit, inlustrat servilis laurea Crassum.
adnuis.   agnosco fremitum, quo palluit Eurus,
quo Mauri Gildoque ruit.   quid Martia signa   505
sollicitas?   non est iaculis hastisve petendus:
conscia succumbent audito verbere terga,
ut Scytha post multos rediens exercitus annos,
cum sibi servilis pro finibus obvia pubes
iret et arceret dominos tellure reversos,   510
armatam ostensis aciem fudere flagellis:
notus ab inceptis ignobile reppulit horror
vulgus et addictus sub verbere torpuit ensis."

" What need of further words ? Why, Stilicho, dost thou delay to conquer because ashamed to fight ? Knowest thou not that the viler a foe the greater the rejoicing at his overthrow ? His defeat of the pirates extended the fame of great Pompey; his victory in the Servile War gave an added glory to Crassus. Thou acceptest my charge : I recognize the clamour that terrified the East and drove Gildo and his Moors to their destruction. Why sound the trump of war ? No need to attack him with javelin or spear. At the crack of the whip will be bowed the back that has felt its blows. Even so when after many years the Scythian army came back from the wars and was met on the confines of its native land by the usurping crowd of slaves who sought to keep their returning masters from their country ; with displayed whips they routed the armèd ranks ; back from its enterprise the familiar terror drove the servile mob, and at threat of the lash the bondsman's sword grew dull."

IN EUTROPIUM

LIBER SECUNDUS. PRAEFATIO

(XIX.)

Qui modo sublimes rerum flectebat habenas
   patricius, rursum verbera nota timet
et solitos tardae passurus compedis orbes
   in dominos vanas luget abisse minas.
culmine deiectum vitae Fortuna priori   5
   reddidit, insano iam satiata ioco.
scindere nunc alia meditatur ligna securi
   fascibus et tandem vapulat ipse suis.
ille citas consul poenas se consule solvit :
   annus qui trabeas hic dedit exilium.   10
infaustum populis in se quoque vertitur omen ;
   saevit in auctorem prodigiosus honos.
abluto penitus respirant nomine fasti
   maturamque luem sanior aula vomit.
dissimulant socii coniuratique recedunt,   15
   procumbit pariter cum duce tota cohors ;
non acie victi, non seditione coacti ;
   nec pereunt ritu quo periere viri.
concidit exiguae dementia vulnere chartae ;
   confecit saevum littera Martis opus.   20

178

AGAINST EUTROPIUS

BOOK II. PREFACE

(XIX)

The nobly born Eutropius who but lately wielded the reins of supreme power once more fears the familiar blows ; and, soon to feel the wonted shackles about his halting feet, he laments that his threats against his masters have idly vanished. Fortune, having had enough of her mad freak, has thrust him forth from his high office and restored him to his old way of life. He now prepares to hew wood with axe other than the consular and is at last scourged with the rods he once proudly carried. To the punishment set in motion by him when consul he himself as consul succumbed; the year that brought him his robe of office brought him his exile. That omen of evil augury for the people turns against itself, the portent of that consulship brings ruin to the consul. That name erased, our annals breathe once more, and better health is restored to the palace now that it has at last vomited forth its poison. His friends deny him, his accomplices abandon him ; in his fall is involved all the eunuch band, overcome not in battle, subdued not by strife—they may not die a man's death. A mere stroke of the pen has wrought their undoing, a simple letter has fulfilled Mars' savage work.

Mollis feminea detruditur arce tyrannus
  et thalamo pulsus perdidit imperium :
sic iuvenis nutante fide veterique reducta
  paelice defletam linquit amica domum.
canitiem raram largo iam pulvere turpat   25
  et lacrimis rugas implet anile gemens
suppliciterque pias humilis prostratus ad aras
  mitigat iratas voce tremente nurus.
innumeri glomerantur eri sibi quisque petentes
  mancipium solis utile suppliciis.   30
quamvis foedus enim mentemque obscaenior ore,
  ira dabit pretium ; poena meretur emi.

Quas, spado, nunc terras aut quem transibis in axem ?
  cingeris hinc odiis, inde recessit amor.
utraque te gemino sub sidere regia damnat :   35
  Hesperius numquam, iam nec Eous eris.
miror cur, aliis qui pandere fata solebas,
  ad propriam cladem caeca Sibylla taces.
iam tibi nulla videt fallax insomnia Nilus ;
  pervigilant vates iam, miserande, tui.   40
quid soror ? audebit tecum conscendere puppim
  et veniet longum per mare fida comes ?
an fortasse toros eunuchi pauperis odit
  et te nunc inopem dives amare negat ?
eunuchi iugulum primus secuisse fateris ;   45
  sed tamen exemplo non feriere tuo.
vive pudor fatis. en quem tremuere tot urbes,
  en cuius populi sustinuere iugum !

---

¹ Claudian calls Eutropius the Sibyl because both were
" old women." He is referring to Eutropius' consultation
of the Egyptian oracle ; *cf. In Eutrop.* i. 312 and note.

The unsexed tyrant has been routed from out his fastness in the women's quarters and, driven from the bedchamber, has lost his power. Thus sadly, when her lover's fidelity wavers and a former favourite has been recalled, does a mistress leave his house. With handfuls of dust he sprinkles his scanty hairs and floods his wrinkles with senile tears ; as he lies in humble supplication before the altars of the gods his trembling voice seeks to soften the anger of the women. His countless masters gather around, each demanding back his slave, useless except for chastisement. For loathsome though he is and fouler in mind even than in face, yet the very anger they feel against him will make them pay ; he is worth buying simply to punish.

What land or country wilt thou now visit, eunuch ? Here hate surrounds thee, there thy popularity is fled ; both courts have uttered thy condemnation in either half of the world ; never wert thou of the West, now the East repudiates thee too. I marvel that thou, blind Sibyl,[1] who foretold'st the fates of others, art silent about thine own. No longer does fallacious Nile interpret thy dreams ; no longer, poor wretch, do thy prophets see visions. What doth thy sister ? Will she dare to embark with thee and bear thee faithful company over the distant seas ? Mayhap she scorns the couch of an impoverished eunuch, and now that she herself is rich will not love thee who now art poor. Thou dost confess thou wert the first to cut a eunuch's throat, but the example will not secure thine own death. Live on that destiny may blush. Lo ! this is he whom so many cities have held in awe, whose yoke so many peoples have borne. Why lament the loss of that

181

direptas quid plangis opes, quas natus habebit ?
    non aliter poteras principis esse pater.   50
improbe, quid pulsas muliebribus astra querellis,
    quod tibi sub Cypri litore parta quies ?
omnia barbarico per te concussa tumultu.
    crede mihi, terra tutius aequor erit.

Iam non Armenios iaculis terrebis et arcu,   55
    per campos volucrem non agitabis equum ;
dilecto caruit Byzantius ore senatus ;
    curia consiliis aestuat orba tuis :
emeritam suspende togam, suspende pharetram ;
    ad Veneris partes ingeniumque redi.   60
non bene Gradivo lenonia dextera servit.
    suscipiet famulum te Cytherea libens.
insula laeta choris, blandorum mater Amorum :
    nulla pudicitiae cura placere potest.
prospectant Paphiae celsa de rupe puellae   65
    sollicitae, salvam dum ferat unda ratem.
sed vereor, teneant ne te Tritones in alto
    lascivas doctum fallere Nereidas,
aut idem cupiant pelago te mergere venti,
    Gildonis nuper qui tenuere fugam.   70
inclita captivo memoratur Tabraca Mauro,
    naufragio Cyprus sit memoranda tuo.
vecturum moriens frustra delphina vocabis ;
    ad terram solos devehit ille viros.
quisquis adhuc similes eunuchus tendit in actus,   75
    respiciens Cyprum desinat esse ferox.

---

[1] Eutropius had been raised by Arcadius to the highest of
all ranks, that of Patrician. These *patricii* were called the
" fathers " of the Emperor. Hence Eutropius, a patrician,

wealth thy son shall inherit ? In no other way couldst thou have been father to an emperor.[1] Why insatiably weary heaven with a woman's plaints ? A haven of refuge is prepared for thee on the shores of Cyprus. Thou hast plunged the world in war with barbary ; the sea, believe me, is safer than the land.

No longer wilt thou strike terror into the Armenians with javelin and bow, no more scour the plain on thy fleet charger. The senate of Byzantium has been deprived of thy loved voice ; uncertainty holds the august assembly that is now deprived of thy counsels. Hang up thy toga, retired consul ; hang up thy quiver, veteran soldier ; return to Venus' service ; that is thy true calling. The pander's hand knows not to serve Mars featly ; Cytherea will right gladly take back her slave. Dancing fills the island of Cyprus, home of the happy loves ; there purity commands no respect. Paphian maidens gaze forth from the high cliffs, anxious till the wave has brought thy bark safe to land. Yet fear I lest the Tritons detain thee in the deep to teach them how they may seduce the sportive Nereids, or that those same winds which hindered Gildo's flight may seek to drown thee in the sea. Tabraca owes its fame to the overthrow of the Moor ; may Cyprus win prestige from thy shipwreck. In vain will thy last breath be spent in calling on the dolphin to carry thee to shore : his back bears only men.[2] Hereafter should any eunuch attempt to emulate thine actions let him turn his eye towards Cyprus and abate his pride.

left (*i.e.* forfeited) his property on his banishment to Cyprus to his " son " Arcadius.
    [2] A reference to the rescue of Arion by the dolphin.

IN EUTROPIUM

LIBER II.

(XX)

Mygdonii cineres et si quid restat Eoi,
quod pereat, regni : certe non augure falso
prodigii patuere minae, frustraque peracto
vulnere monstriferi praesagia discitis anni.
cautior ante tamen violentum navita Caurum   5
prospicit et tumidae subducit vela procellae.
quid iuvat errorem mersa iam puppe fateri ?
quid lacrimae delicta levant ? stant omina vestri
consulis : inmotis haesere piacula fatis.
tunc decuit sentire nefas, tunc ire recentes   10
detersum maculas. veteri post obruta morbo
corpora Paeonias nequiquam admoveris herbas.
ulcera possessis alte suffusa medullis
non leviore manu, ferro sanantur et igni,
ne noceat frustra mox eruptura cicatrix.   15
ad vivum penetrant flammae, quo funditus umor
defluat et vacuis corrupto sanguine venis

184

AGAINST EUTROPIUS

BOOK II

(XX)

Ashes of Phrygia and you last remnants of the ruined East (if any such remain), the augury was but too true, too clear the threats of heaven: now that the blow has fallen what use to learn the presagings of this year of portents? The sailor is more cautious; he foresees the violence of the North wind and hauls in his canvas before the swelling storm. Of what avail to acknowledge a mistake when his vessel is already sunk? Can tears extenuate a crime? The sinister auspices of your consul live on; the atonement due to unmoved fate remains fixed. Ere the deed was done you should have realized its horror; you should have erased the blot ere it had dried. When the body is overwhelmed by long-standing disease 'tis all in vain that thou makest use of healing medicines. When an ulcer has penetrated to the marrow of the bones the touch of a hand is useless, steel and fire must sane the place that the wound heal not on the surface, like any moment to re-open. The flame must penetrate to the quick to make a way for the foul humours to escape; in order that, once the veins are emptied of corrupted blood, the

185

arescat fons ipse mali ; truncatur et artus,
ut liceat reliquis securum degere membris.
at vos egregie purgatam creditis aulam,   20
Eutropium si Cyprus habet ? vindictaque mundi
semivir exul erit ? qui vos lustrare valebit
oceanus ? tantum facinus quae diluet aetas ?

    Induerat necdum trabeas : mugitus ab axe
redditus inferno, rabies arcana cavernas   25
vibrat et alterno confligunt culmina lapsu.
bacchatus per operta tremor Calchedona movit
pronus et in geminas nutavit Bosphorus urbes.
concurrere freti fauces, radice revulsa
vitant instabilem rursum Symplegada nautae.   30
scilicet haec Stygiae praemittunt signa sorores
et sibi iam tradi populos hoc consule gaudent.
mox oritur diversa lues : hinc Mulciber ignes
sparserat, hinc victa proruperat obice Nereus ;
haec flagrant, haec tecta natant. quam, numina,
      poenam   35
servatis sceleri, cuius tot cladibus omen
constitit ? incumbas utinam, Neptune, tridenti
pollutumque solum toto cum crimine mergas.
unam pro mundo Furiis concedimus urbem.   39

    Utque semel patuit monstris iter, omnia tempus
nacta suum properant : nasci tum decolor imber
infantumque novi vultus et dissona partu
semina, tum lapidum fletus armentaque vulgo
ausa loqui mediisque ferae se credere muris ;
tum vates sine more rapi lymphataque passim   45
186

fountain-head of the evil may be dried up. Nay, even limbs are amputated to assure the healthy life of the rest of the body. Think you the Court fitly cleansed by Eutropius' exile in Cyprus? The world avenged by the banishment of a eunuch? Can any ocean wash away that stain? any age bring forgetfulness of so great a crime?

Ere yet he had donned the consul's robe there came a rumbling from the bowels of the earth; a hidden madness shook the subterranean caverns and buildings crashed one on another. Chalcedon, shaken to the foundations, tottered like a drunken man, and Bosporus, straying from his course, flooded the cities on his either bank. The shores of the strait came together and the sailors once more had to avoid the Clashing Rocks, torn from their foundation and errant. Surely such presages were sent by the sister deities of Styx, rejoicing that under this consul at last all peoples were delivered into their hands. Soon arose divers forms of ruin: here the fire-god spread his flames; there Nereus, god of the sea, brake his bounds. Here men's homes were burned, there flooded. Ye gods, what punishment do ye hold in store for the scoundrel whose rise to power was marked by such portents? O'ercome us, Neptune, with thy trident and overwhelm our defiled soil along with all the guilt. One city we yield to the Furies, a scapegoat for the sins of the world.

Once the way was open for portents, prodigies of every sort hasted to disclose themselves. Rain of blood fell, children of weird form were born and offspring discordant with their breed. Statues wept, not seldom the herds dared to speak, and wild beasts braved an entrance into the city. Then seers raved

pectora terrifici stimulis ignescere Phoebi.
fac nullos cecinisse deos : adeone retusi
quisquam cordis erit, dubitet qui partibus illis
adfore fatalem castrati consulis annum ?
sed quam caecus inest vitiis amor ! omne futurum 50
despicitur suadentque brevem praesentia fructum
et ruit in vetitum damni secura libido,
dum mora supplicii lucro serumque quod instat
creditur.   haud equidem contra tot signa Camillo
detulerim fasces, nedum (pro sexus !) inerti 55
mancipio, cui, cuncta licet responsa iuberent
hortantesque licet sponderent prospera divi,
turpe fuit cessisse viros.

                   Exquirite **retro**
crimina continui lectis annalibus aevi,
prisca recensitis evolvite saecula fastis : 60
quid senis infandi Capreae, quid scaena Neronis
tale ferunt ? spado Romuleo succinctus amictu
sedit in Augustis laribus. vulgata patebat
aula salutantum studiis ; huc plebe senatus
permixta trepidique duces omnisque potestas 65
confluit. advolvi genibus, contingere dextram
ambitus et votum deformibus oscula rugis
figere. praesidium legum genitorque vocatur
principis et famulum dignatur regia patrem.
posteritas, admitte fidem : monumenta petuntur 70
dedecoris multisque gemunt incudibus aera
formatura nefas. haec iudicis, illa togati,

---

[1] Suetonius draws a lurid (and probably exaggerated)
picture of the debaucheries of Tiberius' old age at Capri.
The same author describes the " scaena Neronis." The
curious may find the account in Suet. *Nero*, xxix.

188

strangely and frenzied hearts were everywhere
ablaze, stirred by the fires of the dread god Phoebus.
Yet even had no god warned us, whose mind shall
be so dull as to doubt that the year of an emasculate
consul must be fatal to those lands? Blind folly
ever accompanies crime; of the future no account
is taken; sufficient for the day is its short-lived
pleasure; heedless of loss passion plunges into for-
bidden joys, counting the postponement of punish-
ment a gain and believing distant the retribution
that even now o'erhangs. In face of such portents
I would not have entrusted Camillus' self with the
fasces, let alone a sexless slave (oh! the shame of
it!), to yield it to whom were, for men, a disgrace,
even though every oracle decreed it, and the insis-
tent deities gave pledges of prosperity.

Look back in the annals of crime, read o'er all
past history, unroll the volumes of Rome's story.
What can the Capri of Tiberius' old age, what can
Nero's theatre offer like to this?[1] A eunuch, clad
in the cloak of Romulus, sat within the house of
the emperors; the staled palace lay open to the
eager throng of visitors; hither hasten senators,
mingling with the populace, anxious generals and
magistrates of every degree; all are fain to be the
first to fall at his feet and to touch his hand; the
prayer of all is to set kisses on those hideous wrinkles.
He is called defender of the laws, father of the
emperor, and the court deigns to acknowledge a
slave as its overlord. Ye who come after, acknow-
ledge that it is true! Men must needs erect monu-
ments to celebrate this infamy; on many an anvil
groans the bronze that is to take upon it the form of
this monster. Here gleams his statue as a judge,

haec nitet armati species ; numerosus ubique
fulget eques : praefert eunuchi curia vultus.
ac veluti caveant ne quo consistere virtus   75
possit pura loco, cunctas hoc ore laborant
incestare vias.   maneant inmota precamur
certaque perpetui sint argumenta pudoris.
subter adulantes tituli nimiaeque leguntur
vel maribus laudes : claro quod nobilis ortu   80
(cum vivant domini !), quod maxima proelia solus
impleat (et patitur miles !), quod tertius urbis
conditor (hoc Byzas Constantinusque videbant !).[1]
inter quae tumidus leno producere cenas
in lucem, foetere mero, dispergere plausum   85
empturas in vulgus opes, totosque theatris
indulgere dies, alieni prodigus auri.
at soror et, si quid portentis creditur, uxor
mulcebat matres epulis et more pudicae
coniugis eunuchi celebrabat vota mariti.   90
hanc amat, hanc summa de re vel pace vel armis
consulit, huic curas et clausa palatia mandat
ceu stabulum vacuamque domum. sic magna tueri
regna nihil, patiensque iugi deluditur orbis ?[2]

Mitior alternum Zephyri iam bruma teporem   95
senserat et primi laxabant germina flores,
iamque iter in gremio pacis sollemne parabant
ad muros, Ancyra, tuos, auctore repertum
Eutropio, pelagi ne taedia longa subirent,

---

[1] Mythical founder of Byzantium (=Constantinople):
said to have been contemporaneous with the Argonauts
(Diod. iv. 49. 1).

[2] *i.e.* to prevent his being bored with the view of the
Bosporus.

there as a consul, there as a warrior. On every side
one sees that figure of his mounted on his horse;
before the very doors of the senate-house behold a
eunuch's countenance. As though to rob virtue of
any place where she might sojourn undefiled, men
labour to befoul every street with this vile image.
May they rest for ever undisturbed, indisputable
proofs of our eternal shame; such is my prayer.
Beneath the statues one reads flattering titles and
praises too great even for *men*. Do they tell of
his noble race and lineage while his owners are still
alive? What soldier brooks to read that single-
handed he, Eutropius, won great battles? Are
Byzas[1] and Constantine to be told that he is the
third founder of Rome? Meanwhile the arrogant
pander prolongs his revels till the dawn, stinking
of wine and scattering money amid the crowd to
buy their applause. He spends whole days of
amusement in the theatres, prodigal of another's
money. But his sister and spouse (if such a prodigy
can be conceived) wins the favour of Rome's matrons
by entertainments, and, like a chaste wife, sings the
praises of her eunuch husband. 'Tis her he loves,
her he consults on all matters of importance, be it of
peace or war, to her care he entrusts the keys of the
palace, as one would of a stable or empty house. Is
the guardianship of a mighty empire thus naught? Is
it thus he makes a mockery of a world's obedience?

Winter, passing into spring, had now felt the
returning warmth of Zephyrus' breezes and the
earliest flowers had oped their buds when, in the
lap of peace, they were preparing the annual journey
to thy walls, Ancyra. 'Twas Eutropius' device that
weariness of the sea[2] might not come upon him,

sed vaga lascivis flueret discursibus aestas :   100
unde tamen tanta sublimes mole redibant,
ceu vinctos traherent Medos Indumque bibissent.
ecce autem flavis Gradivus ab usque Gelonis
arva cruentato repetebat Thracia curru :
subsidunt Pangaea rotis altaeque sonoro   105
stridunt axe nives. ut vertice constitit Haemi
femineasque togas pressis conspexit habenis,
subrisit crudele pater cristisque micantem
quassavit galeam ; tunc implacabile numen
Bellonam adloquitur, quae sanguine sordida vestem
Illyricis pingues pectebat stragibus hydros :   111

    " Necdum mollitiae, necdum, germana, mederi
possumus Eoae ? numquam corrupta rigescent
saecula ? Cappadocum tepidis Argaeus acervis
aestuat ; infelix etiamnum pallet Orontes.   115
dum pereunt, meminere mali ; si corda parumper
respirare sinas, nullo tot funera sensu
praetereunt : antiqua levis iactura cruoris !

    " Adspicis obscaenum facinus ? quid crinibus ora
protegis ? en quales sese diffudit in actus   120
parva quies, quantum nocuerunt otia ferri !
qui caruit bellis, eunucho traditur annus.
actum de trabeis esset, si partibus una
mens foret Hesperiis ; rueret derisa vetustas
nullaque calcati starent vestigia iuris,   125
ni memor imperii Stilicho morumque priorum
turpe relegasset defenso Thybride nomen

but a roaming summer might slide away in pleasure journeys. But so magnificent was their return, you would have imagined they brought conquered Persia in their train and had drunk of the waters of Indus. Look you! Mars, returning from the distant lands of the yellow-haired Geloni, was re-seeking the lands of Thrace in his bloody chariot. Pangaeus subsided beneath his wheels, the mountain snows cried out under his sounding axle. Scarce had the father stayed on Haemus' summit and, reining in his coursers, looked upon the toga-clad woman, when he smiled a cruel smile and shook his gleaming crested helm; then he addressed Bellona, implacable goddess, who, her raiment all stained with blood, was combing her snake-hair, fattened on the slaughter of Illyrians.

"Sister, shall we never succeed in curing the East of effeminacy? Will this corrupt age never learn true manliness? Argaeus yet reeks with those heaps of dead Cappadocians not yet cold; Orontes is still pale from misery. But they only remember evil while they suffer it; give them a moment's respite and all their slaughter fades from their minds unfelt; little they reck of bloodshed that is past.

"Seest thou this foul deed? Why veil thy face with thine hair? See what crimes a short spell of peace has wrought! what a curse has the sheathèd sword proved! The year that has known no war has had a eunuch for its consul. The consulship would have been at an end had a like spirit animated Italy; this age-long office had fallen amid mockery and no traces been left of its trampled rights, had not Stilicho, heedful of the empire and of the character and morals of a past age, banished from Tiber's city

intactamque novo servasset crimine **Romam.**
ille dedit portum, quo se pulsata referret
maiestas Latii deformataeque secures ;   130
ille dedit fastos, ad quos Oriente relicto
confugeret sparsum maculis servilibus aevum.

   " Quam similes haec aula viros ! ad moenia visus
dirige : num saltem tacita formidine mussant ?
num damnant animo ? plaudentem cerne senatum 135
et Byzantinos proceres Graiosque Quirites.
o patribus plebes, o digni consule patres !
quid ? quod et armati cessant et nulla virilis
inter tot gladios sexum reminiscitur ira ?
hucine nostrorum cinctus abiere nepotum ?   140
sic Bruti despectus honos ?

                     " Ignosce parenti,
Romule, quod serus temeratis fascibus ultor
advenio : iamiam largis haec gaudia faxo
compensent lacrimis. quid dudum inflare moraris
Tartaream, Bellona, tubam, quid stringere falcem, 145
qua populos a stirpe metis ? molire tumultus,
excute delicias. Thracum Macetumque ruinae
taedet et in gentes iterum saevire sepultas.
damna minus consueta move ; trans aequora saevas
verte faces ; aliis exordia sume rapinis.   150
non tibi Riphaeis hostis quaerendus ab oris,
non per Caucasias accito turbine valles
est opus. Ostrogothis colitur mixtisque Gruthungis
Phryx ager : hos parvae poterunt impellere causae

194

this shameful name and kept Rome unsullied by an
unheard of crime. He has given us a harbour to
which the exiled majesty of Latium and the dis-
graced fasces might retire ; he has given us annals
wherein, abandoning the East, an age polluted with
servile stains might find a refuge.

" How like to its lord the inhabitants of the palace !
Turn your eyes to the city walls. Surely they at
least mutter disapprobation, though fear forbids
them speak out ? Do they not condemn him in
their hearts ? No : list the plaudits of the senate,
of the lords of Byzantium, of the Grecian citizens
of Rome. O people worthy of such a senate, senate
worthy of such a consul ! To think that all these
bear arms and use them not, that manly indignation
reminds not of their sex those many whose thighs
bear a sword ! Has my descendants' robe of office
sunk so low ? Is Brutus' renown thus brought to
scorn ?

" Romulus, forgive thy sire for coming so tardy
an avenger of those outraged fasces. Right soon
will I make them pay for this joy with liberal tears.
Why delayest thou, Bellona, to sound the trumpet of
hell and to arm thyself with the scythe wherewith
thou mowest the people to the ground ? Foment
discord, banish pleasures. I am aweary of the
devastation of Thrace and Macedon, of vengeance
twice wreaked on races already buried. Arouse less
accustomed destruction ; spread fire and sword
beyond the seas, make a beginning of new devasta-
tion. Seek not now thy foe on Riphaeus' heights :
what boots it to rouse the storm of war amid Cau-
casia's ravines ? Ostrogoths and Gruthungi together
inhabit the land of Phrygia ; 'twill need but a touch

in scelus ; ad mores facilis natura reverti.   155
sic eat : in nostro quando iam milite robur
torpuit et molli didicit parere magistro,
vindicet Arctous violatas advena leges ;
barbara Romano succurrant arma pudori."

    Sic fatus clipeo, quantum vix ipse deorum   160
arbiter infesto cum percutit aegida nimbo,
intonuit.   responsat Athos Haemusque remugit ;
ingeminat raucum Rhodope concussa fragorem.
cornua cana gelu mirantibus extulit undis
Hebrus et exanguem glacie timor adligat Histrum. 165
tunc, adamante gravem nodisque rigentibus hastam,
telum ingens nullique deo iaculabile, torsit.
fit late ruptis via nubibus ; illa per auras
tot freta, tot montes uno contenta volatu
transilit et Phrygiae mediis adfigitur arvis.   170
sensit humus ; gemuit Nysaeo palmite felix
Hermus et aurata Pactolus inhorruit urna
totaque summissis fleverunt Dindyma silvis.

    Nec dea praemissae stridorem segnius hastae
consequitur, centumque vias meditata nocendi   175
tandem Tarbigilum (Geticae dux improbus alae [1]
hic erat) adgreditur.   viso tum forte redibat
Eutropio vacuus donis, feritasque dolore
creverat et, teneris etiam quae crimina suadet

      [1] alae *Rubenus ; mss. (followed by Birt) have* aulae

---

    [1] Alluding to the Roman custom of casting a spear as a
sign of the declaration of war ; *cf.* Ovid, *Fasti*, vi. 207—

      Hinc solet hasta manu belli praenuntia mitti
      In regem et gentes cum placet arma capi.

to precipitate them into revolt ; readily does nature
return to her old ways. So be it. Since our soldiers'
valour is numbed and they have learned to obey an
unmanned master, let a stranger from the north
avenge our outraged laws and barbarian arms
bring relief to disgraced Rome."

So spake he and thundered with his shield nigh as
loud as the ruler of the gods when he shakes his
aegis from out the lowering cloud. Athos replies,
Haemus re-echoes ; again and again shaken Rhodope
repeats the hoarse uproar. Hebrus raised from out
the wondering waters his horns hoary with frost,
and bloodless Ister froze in fear. Then the god cast
his javelin,[1] heavy with steel, and stiff with knotted
shaft, a mighty weapon such as none other god
could wield. The clouds part before its onset and
give it free passage ; through the air it speeds o'er
seas and mountains by one mighty cast and comes
to earth amid the plains of Phrygia. The ground
felt the shock ; Hermus blessed with Dionysus' vines
groaned thereat, Pactolus' golden urn shuddered,
all Dindymus bent his forest fleece and wept.

Bellona, too, hastens forth with speed no less than
that of Mars' whistling spear ; a hundred ways of
hurt she pondered and at last approached Tarbigilus,[2]
fierce leader of the Getic squadron. It chanced he
had but late returned with empty hands from a
visit to Eutropius ; disappointment and indignation
aggravated his ferocity, and poverty, that can incite

---

[2] Tarbigilus seems to have belonged to the nation of
the Gruthungi. The exact form of his name is a matter
of uncertainty. The MSS. vary: Zosimus (v. 13. 2) calls him
Τριβίγιλδος. His revolt in Phrygia (cf. ll. 274, etc.) took place
in 399.

ingeniis, Scythicum pectus flammabat egestas.   180
huic sese vultu simulatae coniugis offert
mentitoque ferox incedit barbara gressu,
carbaseos induta sinus : post terga reductas
uberibus propior mordebat fibula vestes,
inque orbem tereti mitra retinente capillum   185
strinxerat et virides flavescere iusserat angues.
advolat ac niveis reducem complectitur ulnis
infunditque animo furiale per oscula virus.
principe quam largo veniat, quas inde reportet
divitias, astu rabiem motura requirit.   190
ille iter ingratum, vanos deflere labores,
quos super eunuchi fastus, quae probra tulisset.
continuo secat ungue genas et tempore pandit
adrepto gemitus :

　　　　　　" I nunc, devotus aratris
scinde solum positoque tuos mucrone sodales   195
ad rastros sudare doce.　bene rura Gruthungus
excolet et certo disponet sidere vites.
felices aliae, quas debellata maritis
oppida, quas magnis quaesitae viribus ornant
exuviae, quibus Argivae pulchraeque ministrant   200
Thessalides, famulas et quae meruere Lacaenas.
me nimium timido, nimium iunxere remisso
fata viro, totum qui degener exuit Histrum,
qui refugit patriae ritus, quem detinet aequi
gloria concessoque cupit vixisse colonus   205
quam dominus rapto.　quid pulchra vocabula pigris

the gentlest heart to crime, inflamed his savage
breast. Taking upon her the similitude of his
wife she comes to meet him ; proudly she steps forth
like the barbarian queen, clothed in linen raiment.
Close to her breast a brooch fastened her dress that
trailed behind her ; she had bound her locks into a
coil that a polished circlet confined, and bidden her
green snakes turn to gold. She hastens to greet
him on his return and throws her snowy arms about
his neck, instilling the poison of the furies into his
soul by her kisses. Guilefully to stir his rage she
asks if the great man has been generous to him ;
if he brings back rich presents. With tears he
recounts his profitless journey, his useless toil, the
pride and insults, moreover, which he had to bear
at the eunuch's hands. At once she seized the
favourable moment, and tearing her cheek with
her nails, discloses her complaints.

" Go then, busy thyself with the plough, cleave the
soil, bid thy followers lay aside their swords and
sweat o'er the harrow. The Gruthungi will make
good farmers and will plant their vines in due
season. Happy those other women whose glory is
seen in the towns their husbands have conquered,
they whose adornment is the spoils so hardly won
from an enemy, whose servants are fair captives
of Argos or Thessaly, and who have won them
slaves from Sparta. Fate has mated me with too
timid, too indolent a husband, a degenerate
who has forgotten the valour of Ister's tribes, who
deserts his country's ways, whom a vain reputation
for justice attracts, while he longs to live as a hus-
bandman by favour rather than as a prince by
plunder. Why give fair names to shameful weak-

praetentas vitiis ?   probitatis inertia nomen,
iustitiae formido subit.   tolerabis iniquam
pauperiem, cum tela geras ? et flebis inultus,
cum pateant tantae nullis custodibus urbes ?   210
    " Quippe metus poenae.   pridem mos ille vigebat,
ut meritos colerent impacatisque rebelles
urgerent odiis ; at nunc, qui foedera rumpit,
ditatur ; qui servat, eget.   vastator Achivae
gentis et Epirum nuper populatus inultam   215
praesidet Illyrico ; iam, quos obsedit, amicos
ingreditur muros illis responsa daturus,
quorum coniugibus potitur natosque peremit.
sic hostes punire solent, haec praemia solvunt
excidiis.   cunctaris adhuc numerumque tuorum   220
respicis exiguamque manum ?   tu rumpe quietem ;
bella dabunt socios.   nec te tam prona monerem,
si contra paterere viros : nunc alter in armis
sexus et eunuchis se defensoribus orbis
credidit ; hos aquilae Romanaque signa sequuntur.
incipe barbaricae tandem te reddere vitae,   226
te quoque iam timeant admirenturque nocentem,
quem sprevere pium.   spoliis praedaque repletus
cum libeat Romanus eris."
                              Sic fata repente
in diram se vertit avem rostroque recurvo   230
turpis et infernis tenebris obscurior alas
auspicium veteri sedit ferale sepulcro.
    Ille, pavor postquam resoluto corde quievit

---

¹ Alaric was made *magister militum* in Illyricum : see
Introduction, p. x.

ness ? Cowardice is called loyalty ; fear, a sense of
justice. Wilt thou submit to humiliating poverty
though thou bearest arms ? Wilt thou weep un-
avenged, though so many cities open to thee their
undefended gates ?

"Dost thou fear the consequences ? Rome's old
way was to reward merit and vent on rebels a hate
that knew no bound. Now he who breaks a treaty
wins riches, while he who observes one lives in want.
The ravager of Achaea and recent devastator of
defenceless Epirus is lord of Illyria[1]; he now enters
as a friend within the walls to which he was laying
siege, and administers justice to those whose wives
he has seduced and whose children he has murdered.
Such is the punishment meted out to an enemy,
such the vengeance exacted for wholesale slaughter
—and dost thou still hesitate ? Hast thou regard
to the small numbers of thy followers ? Nay, have
done with peace : war will give thee allies. Nor
would I urge thee so instantly hadst thou to face
men. It is another sex that is in arms against
thee ; the world has entrusted itself to the pro-
tection of eunuchs ; 'tis such leaders the eagles
and standards of Rome follow. Time it is thou
didst return to a barbarian life ; be thou in thy
turn an object of terror, and let men marvel at
thy crimes who despised thy virtues. Laden with
booty and plunder thou shalt be a Roman when it
pleases thee."

So saying she suddenly changed into an ill-omened
bird, a loathsome sight with its hooked beak and
plumage blacker than Hell's darkness, and perched,
a sinister augury, on an old tomb.

So soon as repose from terror came to his freed

et rigidae sedere comae, non distulit atrox
iussa deae ; sociis, quae viderat, ordine pandit   235
inritatque sequi.   Coniurat barbara pubes
nacta ducem Latiisque palam descivit ab armis.

    Pars Phrygiae, Scythicis quaecumque Trionibus
      alget
proxima, Bithynos, solem quae condit, Ionas,
quae levat, attingit Galatas. utrimque propinqui   240
finibus obliquis Lydi Pisidaeque feroces
continuant australe latus. gens una fuere
tot quondam populi, priscum cognomen et unum
appellata Phryges ; sed (quid non longa valebit
permutare dies ?) dicti post Maeona regem   245
Maeones. Aegaeos insedit Graecia portus ;
Thyni Thraces arant quae nunc Bithynia fertur ;
nuper ab Oceano Gallorum exercitus ingens
illis ante vagus tandem regionibus haesit
gaesaque deposuit, Graio iam mitis amictu,   250
pro Rheno poturus Halyn. dat cuncta vetustas
principium Phrygibus ; nec rex Aegyptius ultra
restitit, humani postquam puer uberis expers
in Phrygiam primum laxavit murmura vocem.

    Hic cecidit Libycis iactata paludibus olim   255
tibia, foedatam cum reddidit umbra Minervam,
hic et Apollinea victus testudine pastor
suspensa memores inlustrat pelle Celaenas.

---

   [1] The reference is to Herodotus ii. 2. Psammetichus,
King of Egypt, wishing to find out which was the most
ancient nation, had two children reared in complete silence.
As the first word they uttered was " Becos," the Phrygian
word for " bread," Phrygia was accorded the honour.
   [2] Minerva is said to have thrown her pipe into the river

heart, and his stiffened hair sank down again, he made all haste to carry out the commands of the goddess. He told his followers all that he had seen and urged them to follow him. Rebellious Barbary had found a champion and openly threw off the Latin yoke.

That part of Phrygia which lies towards the north beneath the cold constellation of the Wain borders on Bithynia; that towards the sunset on Ionia, and that towards the sunrise on Galatia. On two sides runs the transverse boundary of Lydia while the fierce Pisidians hem it in to the south. All these peoples once formed one nation and had one name : they were of old called the Phrygians, but (what changes does time not bring about ?) after the reign of a king Maeon, were known as Maeones. Then the Greeks settled on the shores of the Aegean, and the Thyni from Thrace cultivated the region now called Bithynia. Not long since a vast army of Gauls, nomad hitherto, came at last to rest in the district; these laid by their spears, clothed them in the civilized robe of Greece and drank no longer from Rhine's, but from Halys', waters. All antiquity gives priority to the Phrygian, even Egypt's king had perforce to recognize it when the babe, nourished at no human breast, first opened his lips to lisp the Phrygian tongue.[1]

Here fell the pipe once hurled into the marshes of Libya, what time the stream reflected Minerva's disfigured countenance.[2] Here, too, there perished, conquered by Apollo's lyre, the shepherd Marsyas whose flayed skin brought renown to the city of

when she observed in the reflection the facial contortions apparently necessary to play it ; *cf.* Ovid, *Fasti*, vi. 699.

quattuor hinc magnis procedunt fontibus amnes
auriferi ; nec miror aquas radiare metallo,   260
quae totiens lavere Midan.   diversus ad Austrum
cursus et Arctoum fluviis mare.   Dindyma fundunt
Sangarium, vitrei puro qui gurgite Galli
auctus Amazonii defertur ad ostia Ponti.
Icarium pelagus Mycalaeaque litora iuncti   265
Marsya Maeanderque petunt ; sed Marsya velox,
dum suus est, flexuque carens iam flumine mixtus
mollitur, Maeandre, tuo ; contraria passus,
quam Rhodano stimulatus Arar : quos inter aprica
planities Cererique favet densisque ligatur   270
vitibus et glaucae fructus attollit olivae,
dives equis, felix pecori pretiosaque picto
marmore purpureis, caedit quod Synnada, venis.

   Talem tum Phrygiam Geticis populatibus uri
permisere dei.   securas barbarus urbes   275
inrupit facilesque capi.   spes nulla salutis,
nulla fugae : putribus iam propugnacula saxis
longo corruerant aevo pacisque senecta.

   Interea gelidae secretis rupibus Idae
dum sedet et thiasos spectat de more Cybebe   280
Curetumque alacres ad tympana suscitat enses,
aurea sanctarum decus inmortale comarum
defluxit capiti turris summoque volutus
vertice crinalis violatur pulvere murus.
obstipuere truces omen Corybantes et uno   285
fixa metu tacitas presserunt orgia buxos.
indoluit genetrix, tum sic commota profatur :

Celaenae. Hence flow four broad auriferous rivers. Small wonder that the waters in which King Midas bathed so often glitter with the rare metal. Two flow north, two southwards. Dindymus gives birth to the river Sangarius, which, swollen by the clear stream of the Gallus, hastens on to the Euxine, the sea of the Amazon. The conjoined streams of Marsyas and Meander make for the Icarian main and Mycale's strand. Marsyas flows fast and straight while his course is his own; mingled with thy waters, Meander, he goes slowly—unlike the Saône whose waters are hastened by the Rhone's inflowing. Between these rivers is a sun-kissed plain; kindly is it to the corn, thick-set with vines and displaying the fruit of the grey-green olive; rich, too, in horses, fertile in flocks, and wealthy with the purple-veined marble that Synnada quarries.

Such was Phrygia then when the gods allowed it to be ravaged by Getic brigands. The barbarian burst in upon those cities so peaceful, so easy of capture. There was no hope of safety, no chance of escape. Long and peaceful ages had made the crumbling stones of their battlements to fall.

Meanwhile Cybele was seated amid the hallowed rocks of cold Ida, watching, as is her wont, the dance, and inciting the joyous Curetes to brandish their swords at the sound of the drum, when, lo, the golden-turreted crown, the eternal glory of her blessèd hair, fell from off her head and, rolling from her brow, the castellated diadem is profaned in the dust. The Corybantes stopped in amazement at this omen; general alarm checked their orgies and silenced their pipes. The mother of the gods wept; then spake thus in sorrow.

205

" Hoc mihi iam pridem Lachesis grandaeva canebat
augurium : Phrygiae casus venisse supremos
delapsus testatur apex.   heu sanguine qualis   290
ibit Sangarius quantasque cadavera lenti
Maeandri passura moras!   inmobilis haeret
terminus, haec dudum nato placuere Tonanti.
par et finitimis luctus, frustraque Lyaei
non defensuros implorat Lydia thyrsos.   295
iamque vale Phrygiae tellus perituraque flammis
moenia, conspicuas quae nunc attollitis arces,
mox campi nudumque solum ! dilecta valete
flumina !   non vestris ultra bacchabor in antris
nec iuga sulcabit noster Berecynthia currus."   300
dixit et ad tristes convertit tympana planctus.
labentem patriam sacris ululatibus Attis
personat et torvi lacrimis maduere leones.

   Eutropius, nequeat quamvis metuenda taceri
clades et trepidus vulgaverit omnia rumor,   305
ignorare tamen fingit regnique ruinas
dissimulat : parvam latronum errare catervam,
ad sontes tormenta magis quam tela parari
nec duce frangendas iactat, sed iudice vires :
vasta velut Libyae venantum vocibus ales   310
cum premitur calidas cursu transmittit harenas
inque modum veli sinuatis flamine pennis
pulverulenta volat ; si iam vestigia retro
clara sonent, oblita fugae stat lumine clauso
(ridendum !) revoluta caput creditque latere,   315
quem non ipsa videt.   furtim tamen ardua mittit

"This is the portent that agèd Lachesis foretold long years ago. My fallen crown assures me that Phrygia's final crisis is upon her. Alas for the blood that shall redden Sangarius' waves; for all the corpses that shall retard Meander's slow stream. The hour is fixed irrevocably; such, long since, was my son's, the Thunderer's, will. A like disaster awaits the neighbouring peoples; in vain does Lydia invoke the thyrsus of Bacchus in her defence. Now fare thee well, land of Phrygia, farewell, walls doomed to the flames, walls that now rear aloft proud towers but will soon be levelled with the ground and the bare earth. Farewell, dear rivers: never more shall I hold my inspired revels in your grottoes; no more shall my chariot leave the traces of its wheels on Berecynthus' heights." So spake she, and turned her drums to strains of mourning. Attis filled his devoted country with holy lamentations and Cybele's tawny lions burst into tears.

Eutropius, although this terrible revolt could not be hid and although rumour had spread everywhere the dread news, none the less affects to ignore it and shuts his eyes to the empire's peril. 'Twas some poor troop of wandering brigands; such wretches call for punishment not war; a judge—so he brags —not a general should crush their strength. Even so the great Libyan bird, hard pressed by the cries of its pursuers, runs o'er the burning sands and flies through the dust, curving its wings like sails to catch the breeze; but when it clearly hears the footsteps close behind it, it forgets its flight, standing with closed eyes and hiding its head, believing, poor fool, it cannot be seen by those whom itself cannot see. None the less Eutropius

cum donis promissa novis, si forte rogatus
desinat.   ille semel nota dulcedine praedae
se famulo servire negat, nec grata timentum
munera ; militiam nullam nec prima superbus   320
cingula dignari ; nam quis non consule tali
vilis honos ?
    Postquam precibus mitescere nullis,
non auro cessisse videt creberque recurrit
nuntius incassum nec spes iam foederis extat :
tandem consilium belli confessus agendi   325
ad sua tecta vocat.   iuvenes venere protervi
lascivique senes, quibus est insignis edendi
gloria corruptasque dapes variasse decorum,
qui ventrem invitant pretio traduntque palato
sidereas Iunonis aves et si qua loquendi   330
gnara coloratis viridis defertur ab Indis,
quaesitos trans regna cibos, quorumque profundam
ingluviem non Aegaeus, non alta Propontis,
non freta longinquis Maeotia piscibus explent.
vestis odoratae studium ; laus maxima risum   335
per vanos movisse sales minimeque viriles
munditiae ; compti vultus ; onerique vel ipsa
serica.   si Chunus feriat, si Sarmata portas,
solliciti scaenae ; Romam contemnere sueti
mirarique suas, quas Bosphorus obruat ! aedes ;   340
saltandi dociles aurigarumque periti.
 Pars humili de plebe duces ; pars compede suras

---

[1] Claudian uses the word *cingulum* (=a soldier's belt)
as = military service—a not uncommon late use, *cf.* Serv. *Aen.*
viii. 724 and (frequently) *cingi* =to serve, in the Digests.

[2] *i.e.* the peacock.

sends towering promises with new gifts, if haply
his foe may pause at his entreaty. But the bar-
barian, in whose heart was once waked the old love
of plunder, refuses to submit to a slave; for him
the gifts of fear have no charm; haughtily he
disdains any rank,[1] even the highest, for under
such a consul what honour would not be disgrace?

When Eutropius saw that no prayers could move
him nor any gold win him over; when messenger
after messenger returned, his mission unfulfilled, and
all hopes of an alliance were at an end, he at last
recognized the necessity for war and summoned the
council to his palace. Thither they came—wanton
lads and debauched greybeards whose greatest
glory was gluttony, and whose pride it was to diver-
sify the outraged banquet. Their hunger is only
aroused by costly meats, and they tickle their palates
with foods imported from overseas, the flesh of the
many-eyed fowl of Juno,[2] or of that coloured bird
brought from farthest Ind that knows how to speak.
Not the Aegean, not deep Propontis, not Maeotis'
lake afar can sate their appetites with fish. Per-
fumed garments are their care, their pride to move
foolish laughter with their silly jests. On their
adornment and toilette they bestow a woman's care
and find even the silk they wear too heavy a burden.
Should the Hun, the Sarmatian, strike at the city's
gates yet trouble they for nought but the theatre.
Rome they despise and reserve their admiration
for their own houses—may Bosporus' waters over-
whelm them! Skilful dancers they and clever judges
of charioteers.

Some sprung from the dregs of the people are
generals; some magistrates—though their legs and

cruraque signati nigro liventia ferro
iura regunt, facies quamvis inscripta repugnet
seque suo prodat titulo.   sed prima potestas   345
Eutropium praefert Hosio subnixa secundo.
dulcior hic sane cunctis prudensque movendi
iuris et admoto qui temperet omnia fumo,
fervidus, accensam sed qui bene decoquat iram.
considunt apices gemini dicionis Eoae,   350
hic cocus, hic leno, defossi verbere terga,
servitio, non arte pares, hic saepius emptus,
alter ad Hispanos nutritus verna penates.

  Ergo ubi collecti proceres, qui rebus in artis
consulerent tantisque darent solacia morbis,   355
obliti subito Phrygiae bellisque relictis
ad solitos coepere iocos et iurgia circi
tendere.   nequiquam magna confligitur ira,
quis melius vibrata puer vertigine molli
membra rotet, verrat quis marmora crine supino ?   360
quis magis enodes laterum detorqueat arcus,[1]
quis voci digitos, oculos quis moribus aptet ?
hi tragicos meminere modos ; his fabula Tereus,
his necdum commissa choro cantatur Agave.

  Increpat Eutropius : non haec spectacula tempus
poscere ; nunc alias armorum incumbere curas ;   366
se satis Armenio fessum pro limite cingi

<hr>

    [1] *Birt* artus; *I return to the vulg.* arcus

<hr>

    [1] Hosius, by birth a Spaniard, had been a slave and
a cook—whence these various double meanings. He rose
to be *magister officiorum* at the court of Arcadius (*circa*
396-8).

ankles are still scarred and livid with their wearing
of the fetters of servitude and though their branded
foreheads deny their owners' right to office and
disclose their true title. Among them Eutropius
holds the first place; Hosius, on whom he relies,
comes next. He of a truth is more popular, a
cunning artificer of justice who knows well how to
steam his cases; at times boiling with anger, yet
well able to render down that anger when aroused.[1]
These sit enthroned, joint rulers of the eastern
empire, the one a cook the other a pander. The
backs of both are scarred with the whip, each was
a slave though of a different kind. The one had
been bought and sold a hundred times, the other
brought up a dependant in a Spanish household.

When, therefore, the chief men were gathered
together for consultation in this strait and to
comfort the sickness of the state, forthwith they
forget Phrygia and, setting aside the question of war,
start their accustomed fooling and engage in disputes
about the Circus. With heat as fierce as it is point-
less they wrangle what boy can best whirl quivering
limbs in an easy somersault or sweep the marble
floor with his drooping locks; who can most twist
his flanks into a boneless arch; who can best suit
his gestures to his words and his eyes to his character.
Some recite speeches from tragedy, others chant
the play of Tereus, others again that of Agave,
never before staged.

Eutropius chides them; the present moment,
says he, demands other spectacles than these;
it is war which now should claim all their care.
For his part (for he is an old man and a weary) it is
enough to defend the frontiers of Armenia; single-

211

nec tantis unum subsistere posse periclis ;
ignoscant senio, iuvenes ad proelia mittant :—
qualis pauperibus nutrix invisa puellis   370
adsidet et tela communem quaerere victum
rauca monet ; festis illae lusisse diebus
orant et positis aequaevas visere pensis,
irataeque operi iam lasso pollice fila
turbant et teneros detergent stamine fletus.   375
    Emicat extemplo cunctis trepidantibus audax
crassa mole Leo, quem vix Cyclopia solum
aequatura fames, quem non ieiuna Celaeno
vinceret ; hinc nomen fertur meruisse Leonis.
acer in absentes linguae iactator, abundans   380
corporis exiguusque animi, doctissimus artis
quondam lanificae, moderator pectinis unci.
non alius lanam purgatis sordibus aeque
praebuerit calathis, similis nec pinguia quisquam
vellera per tenues ferri producere rimas.   385
tunc Aiax erat Eutropii lateque fremebat,
non septem vasto quatiens umbone iuvencos,
sed, quam perpetuis dapibus pigroque sedili
inter anus interque colos oneraverat, alvum.
adsurgit tandem vocemque expromit anhelam : 390
    "Quis novus hic torpor, socii ? quonam usque
        sedemus
femineis clausi thalamis patimurque periclum
gliscere desidia ? graviorum turba malorum
texitur, ignavis trahimus dum tempora votis.
me petit hic sudor. numquam mea dextera segnis
ad ferrum. faveat tantum Tritonia coeptis,   396

---

[1] Gainas and Leo were sent by Eutropius to put down
the revolt of Tarbigilus. Gainas, however, never left the
Hellespont and Leo, advancing into Pamphylia, there met,
and was defeated by, Tarbigilus (Zosim. v. 16. 5). We
gather from Claudian that he had once been a weaver.

handed he cannot cope with all these perils. They must pardon his age and send younger men to the war :—it is as though a hated forewoman were sitting among a crowd of poor working-girls and bidding them in her raucous voice ply the loom and gain their livelihood, while they beg to be allowed the enjoyment of a holiday, to lay aside their tasks and visit their friends ; angered at her refusal and wearied of their work they crush the threads in their hands and wipe away their gentle tears with the cloth.

Sudden from out that trembling throng upleaps bold Leo [1] with his vast bulk, he whose single prowess Cyclopean hunger could scarce match, whom starving Celaeno could not outvie. 'Tis to this fact that he is said to have owed his name. Bold (when his foe was absent), brave (as a speaker), great in bulk but small of heart, once a highly skilled spinner of thread and a cunning carder, none other could so well cleanse the dirt from out the fleece and fill the baskets, none other pull the thick wool over the iron teeth of the comb as could he. He was then Eutropius' Ajax and far and near he raged, shaking not a huge shield compact of seven layers of ox-hide, but that belly of his, laden with continuous feastings, as he sat lazily among old dames and distaffs. At length he arose and, panting, said, " What unwonted sluggishness is this, my friends ? How long must we sit closeted in the women's apartments and suffer our perils to increase by reason of our sloth ? Fate weaves for us a network of ill while we waste our time in useless vows. This difficult task demands my action ; never was my hand slow to use iron. Let but Minerva favour

inceptum peragetur opus. iam cuncta furorem
qui gravat, efficiam leviorem pondere lanae
Tarbigilum tumidum, desertoresque Gruthungos
ut miseras populabor oves et pace relata   400
pristina restituam Phrygias ad stamina matres."

His dictis iterum sedit ; fit plausus et ingens
concilii clamor, qualis resonantibus olim
exoritur caveis, quotiens crinitus ephebus
aut rigidam Nioben aut flentem Troada fingit.   405
protinus excitis iter inremeabile signis
adripit infaustoque iubet bubone moveri
agmina Mygdonias mox impletura volucres.

Pulcher et urbanae cupiens exercitus umbrae,
adsiduus ludis, avidus splendere lavacris   410
nec soles imbresve pati, multumque priori
dispar, sub clipeo Thracum qui ferre pruinas,
dum Stilicho regeret, nudoque hiemare sub axe
sueverat et duris haurire bipennibus Hebrum.
cum duce mutatae vires. Byzantia robur   415
fregit luxuries Ancyranique triumphi.
non peditem praecedit eques ; non commoda castris
eligitur regio ; vicibus custodia nullis
advigilat vallo ; non explorantur eundae
vitandaeque viae ; nullo se cornua flectunt   420
ordine : confusi passim per opaca vagantur
lustra, per ignotas angusto tramite valles.

---

¹ *Triumphi* is ironical. Claudian refers to Eutropius'
pleasure journey to Ancyra ; *cf.* l. 98 of this poem.

mine attempts and the work begun will be the work completed. Now will I render proud Tarbigilus, whose madness has caused all this turmoil, of less weight than a ball of wool, the faithless Gruthungi I will drive before me like a flock of wretched sheep; and when I have restored peace I will set the women of Phrygia once more beside their ancient spinning."

So saying he sat down again. Great clamour and applause filled the council-chamber, applause such as rises from the rows of spectators in the theatre when some curled youth impersonates Niobe turned to stone, or Hecuba in tears. Straightway Leo unfolds his banners and starts on the journey whence there is to be no return. To the accompaniment of the screech-owl's ill-omened cry he bids march the host destined so soon to feed the vultures of Mygdonia.

'Tis a well-favoured army, enamoured of the city's shade, ever present at the games, anxious to shine in the baths, not to bear sun-scorch and rain, and oh! how different to that former army who, 'neath the leadership of Stilicho, endured under arms the frosts of Thrace and were wont to winter in the open air and break with their axes the frozen waters of Hebrus for a draught. Changed is the leader and changed their character. Byzantium's luxury and Ancyra's pomp [1] have destroyed their vigour. No longer does the cavalry ride ahead of the foot; suitable ground is not chosen for camps; no constant change of sentries safeguards the ramparts, no scouts are sent forward to discover which roads to take or which to avoid; their evolutions are performed without drill or discipline, in confusion they stray hither and thither amid dark forests, along narrow

215

sic vacui rectoris equi, sic orba magistro
fertur in abruptum casu, non sidere, puppis ;
sic ruit in rupes amisso pisce sodali   425
belua, sulcandas qui praevius edocet undas
inmensumque pecus parvae moderamine caudae
temperat et tanto coniungit foedera monstro ;
illa natat rationis inops et caeca profundi ;
iam brevibus deprensa vadis ignara reverti   430
palpitat et vanos scopulis inlidit hiatus.

    Tarbigilus simulare fugam flatusque Leonis
spe nutrire leves improvisusque repente,
dum gravibus marcent epulis hostique catenas
inter vina crepant, largo sopita Lyaeo   435
castra subit.   pereunt alii, dum membra cubili
tarda levant ; alii leto iunxere soporem ;
ast alios vicina palus sine more ruentes
excipit et cumulis inmanibus aggerat undas.
ipse Leo damma cervoque fugacior ibat   440
sudanti tremebundus equo : qui pondere postquam
decidit, implicitus limo cunctantia pronus
per vada reptabat.   caeno subnixa tenaci
mergitur et pingui suspirat corpore moles
more suis, dapibus quae iam devota futuris   445
turpe gemit, quotiens Hosius mucrone corusco
armatur cingitque sinus secumque volutat,
quas figat verubus partes, quae frusta calenti

---

¹ The *balaena* or whale. According to ancient naturalists
the *balaena* entered into an alliance with the *musculus* or
sea-mouse which, in Pliny's words, "vada praenatans
demonstrat oculorumque vice fungitur" (Pliny, *H.N.* ix.
186).

paths in unexplored valleys. So goes a horse that has lost his rider, thus a ship whose helmsman has been drowned is swept to the abyss, chance guiding her and not the stars. So too the sea monster [1] is dashed to pieces against the rocks when it has lost the comrade fish that swam before it and guided its course through the waves, piloting the great beast with the motion of its tiny tail according to the compact which is between it and its huge companion. Aimlessly the monster swims all unguided through the deep; then, surprised in the shallow water and knowing not how to return to the sea, pants and to no purpose dashes its gaping jaws against the rocks.

Tarbigilus feigns retreat and raises the presumptuous hopes of Leo, then suddenly he bursts all unexpected upon the wine-sodden army, as, overcome by the heavy feast, they brag over their cups of leading the foe in chains. Some are slain as they lift their sluggish limbs from the couch, others know not any break between sleep and death. Others rush pell-mell into a neighbouring swamp and heap the marsh high with their dead bodies. Leo himself, swifter than deer or antelope, fled trembling on his foam-flecked horse, and it falling under his weight Leo sank in the mire and on all fours fought his way through the clinging slime. Held up at first by the thick mud, his fat body gradually settles down panting like a common pig, which, destined to grace the coming feast, squeals when Hosius arms him with flashing knife, and gathers up his garments, pondering the while what portions he will transfix with spits, which pieces of the flesh he will boil and how much sea-urchin

217

mandet aquae quantoque cutem distendat echino.
flagrat opus ; crebro pulsatus perstrepit ictu ;[1]   450
contexit varius penetrans Calchedona nidor.

  Ecce levis frondes a tergo concutit aura :
credit tela Leo ; valuit pro vulnere terror
implevitque vicem iaculi, vitamque nocentem
integer et sola formidine saucius efflat.   455
quis tibi tractandos pro pectine, degener, enses,
quis solio campum praeponere suasit avito ?
quam bene texentum laudabas carmina tutus
et matutinis pellebas frigora mensis !
hic miserande iaces ; hic, dum tua vellera vitas,   460
tandem fila tibi neverunt ultima Parcae.

  Iam vaga pallentem densis terroribus aulam
fama quatit ; stratas acies, deleta canebat
agmina, Maeonios foedari caedibus agros,
Pamphylos Pisidasque rapi. metuendus ab omni 465
Tarbigilus regione tonat ; modo tendere cursum
in Galatas, modo Bithynis incumbere fertur.
sunt qui per Cilicas rupto descendere Tauro,
sunt qui correptis ratibus terraque marique
adventare ferant ; geminantur vera pavoris   470
ingenio : longe spectari puppibus urbes
accensas, lucere fretum ventoque citatas
omnibus in pelago velis haerere favillas.

  Hos inter strepitus funestior advolat alter

---

[1] *I print Birt's text ; but unless* pulsatus *be taken as a substantive (Baehrens' suggestion, cf. P. Lat. Min.* v. *p.* 120 *l.* 169) *it is untranslatable. Emendations proposed are* pulsu Cos . . . icta *Barthius ;* pulsatus aper strepit *Buecheler ;* cultri sus *or* pulpae ius *Birt. The sense demands, however, some such word as* Bosporus *to make a parallelism with* Calchedona. *Possibly the line ended* pulsatur Bosporvs ictu, perstrepit *being a gloss on* pulsatur *and eventually ousting* Bosporus.

stuffing will be needed to fill the empty skin. The work of preparation goes on apace, Bosporus echoes to many a blow and the savoury smell envelops Chalcedon.

Suddenly a gentle breeze stirs the foliage behind Leo's back. He thinks it an arrow, and terror, taking a missile's place, does duty for a wound. Untouched and stricken only by fear he breathes his last. Degenerate Roman, by whose advice didst thou exchange the comb for the sword, thine ancestral calling for the field of battle? How much better to praise in safety the work of the weavers at their looms and keep out the cold by means of morning feasts. Here thou hast suffered a wretched death; here, while thou soughtest to shirk thy spinning, the Fates have at last spun for thee the final thread.

Now spreading rumour shakes the palace, pale with terror upon terror. It told how that the army was destroyed, the troops butchered, the plain of Maeonia red with slaughter, Pamphylia and Pisidia o'errun by the enemy. On all sides rings the dread name of Tarbigilus. He is now said to be bearing down upon Galatia, now to be meditating an attack on Bithynia. Some say he has crossed the Taurus and is descending upon Cilicia, others that he has possessed himself of a fleet and is advancing both by land and sea. Truth is doubled by panic's fancy; they say that from the ships far cities are seen ablaze, that the straits are aglow and that ashes driven by the wind catch in the sails of every ship at sea.

Amid all this confusion comes a yet more terrible

nuntius : armatam rursus Babylona minari   475
rege novo ; resides Parthos ignava perosos
otia Romanae finem iam quaerere paci.
rarus apud Medos regum cruor ; unaque cuncto
poena manet generi : quamvis crudelibus aeque
paretur dominis.   sed quid non audeat annus   480
Eutropii ? socium nobis fidumque Saporem
perculit et Persas in regia vulnera movit
rupturasque fidem, leto pars ne qua vacaret,
Eumenidum taedas trans flumina Tigridis egit.
   Tum vero cecidere animi tantisque procellis   485
deficiunt.   saepti latrantibus undique bellis
infensos tandem superos et consulis omen
agnovere sui, nec iam revocabile damnum
eventu stolido serum didicere magistro.
namque ferunt geminos uno de semine fratres   490
Iapetionidas generis primordia nostri
dissimili finxisse manu : quoscumque Prometheus
excoluit multumque innexuit aethera limo,
hi longe ventura notant dubiisque parati
casibus occurrunt fabro meliore politi.   495
deteriore luto pravus quos edidit auctor,
quem merito Grai perhibent Epimethea vates,
et nihil aetherii sparsit per membra vigoris,
hi pecudum ritu non impendentia vitant
nec res ante vident; accepta clade queruntur   500
et seri transacta gemunt.

---

¹ Varanes IV., who, like his three predecessors, Artaxerxes,
Sapor III., and Varanes III., had observed a truce with Rome,
died in 399 and was succeeded by Isdigerdes. For all
Claudian's real or simulated anxiety this monarch was
as peaceably disposed as the previous ones (see Oros. vii. 34).
Claudian seems to have made an error in calling him Sapor
(l. 481).

rumour—that Babylon is again in arms and, under a
new monarch,[1] threatens our Empire; the Parthians,
long inactive, and now scorning slothful ease, seek
to put an end to the peace imposed by Rome.
Rare among the Medes is the murder of a king, for
punishment falls on the regicide's whole family.
Thus equal obedience is offered to their overlords,
cruel as well as kind. But what would not the year
of Eutropius' consulship dare? 'Tis that has stricken
down our faithful ally Sapor and roused the Per-
sians' swords against their own king; that has cast
the torch of the Furies across the Euphrates, there
to kindle rebellion, that no quarter of the globe
may escape carnage.

Then indeed men's hearts failed them, their cour-
age ebbed away amid all these storms; surrounded
as they were on every side by the din of war, at
last they recognized the wrath of heaven and their
consul's evil omen, learning too late—schooled by
the stubborn issue—their now irrevocable doom.
They say that the twin sons of Iapetus formed our
first parents of the same materials but with unequal
skill. Those whom Prometheus fashioned, and with
whose clay he mingled abundant ether, foresee
the distant future and, thanks to their more careful
making by a better workman, are thus prepared
to meet what fate has in store for them. Those
framed of baser clay by the sorry artificer the Greek
poets so well call Epimetheus, men through whose
limbs no ethereal vigour spreads—these, like sheep,
cannot avoid the dangers that o'erhang them,
nor foresee aught. Not till the blow has fallen do
they protest and weep too late the accomplished
deed.

                       Iam sola renidet
in Stilichone salus, et cuius semper acerbum
ingratumque sibi factorum conscius horror
credidit adventum, quem si procedere tantum
Alpibus audissent, mortem poenasque tremebant,
iam cuncti venisse volunt, scelerumque priorum   506
paenitet ; hoc tantis bellorum sidus in undis
sperant, hoc pariter iusti sontesque precantur :
ceu pueri, quibus alta pater trans aequora merces
devehit, intenti ludo studiisque soluti   510
latius amoto passim custode vagantur ;
si gravis auxilio vacuas invaserit aedes
vicinus laribusque suis proturbet inultos,
tum demum patrem implorant et nomen inani
voce cient frustraque oculos ad litora tendunt.   515

  Omnes supplicio dignos letoque fatentur,
qui se tradiderint famulis Stilichone relicto.
mutati stupuere diu sensuque reducto
paulatim proprii mirantur monstra furoris
avertuntque oculos : proiectis fascibus horret   520
lictor et infames labuntur sponte secures :
quales Aonio Thebas de monte reversae
Maenades infectis Pentheo sanguine thyrsis,
cum patuit venatus atrox matrique rotatum
conspexere caput, gressus caligine figunt   525
et rabiem desisse dolent. quin protinus ipsa
tendit ad Italiam supplex Aurora potentem

AGAINST EUTROPIUS, II

There now shone forth but one hope of salvation
—Stilicho. Him the expectation of whose visits
the consciousness of deeds ill-done had ever rendered
bitter and unpleasant, him whose approach even as
far as the Alps afflicted the Byzantines with fear of
death and punishment, all now wish to come, re-
pentant of their former wrongdoing. To him they
look as to a star amid this universal shipwreck of
war ; to him innocent and guilty alike address their
prayers. So children whose sire carries merchandise
across the sea, wrapt up in their amusements and
heedless of their studies, wander afield more joyfully
now that their guardian is absent, yet, should a
dangerous neighbour invade their defenceless home
and seek to drive them forth unprotected as they
are from their fireside, *then* they beg their father's
help, call upon his name with useless cries and
all to no purpose direct their gaze towards the
shore.

All admit that they deserve punishment and
death for deserting Stilicho and entrusting them-
selves to the governance of slaves. Long they stood
dazed with altered thoughts, and as their senses
slowly return they marvel at the results of their
own madness and turn away their eyes ; flinging
down his rods the lictor shudders, and the dis-
honoured axes fall of their own accord. Even so
the Maenads returning to Thebes from the Aonian
mount, their thyrses dripping with Pentheus' blood,
learning the true character of their dreadful hunting
and seeing the head cast by the mother herself,
hide them in the darkness and lament the end of
their madness. Thereupon suppliant Aurora turned
her flight towards powerful Italy, her hair no

223

non radiis redimita comam, non flammea vultu
nec croceum vestita diem ; stat livida luctu,
qualis erat Phrygio tegeret cum Memnona busto.
quam simul agnovit Stilicho nec causa latebat,　531
restitit ; illa manum victricem amplexa moratur
altaque vix lacrimans inter suspiria fatur :

　" Tantane te nostri ceperunt taedia mundi ?
sic me ludibrium famulis risumque relinquis　535
dux quondam rectorque meus ? solamque tueris
Hesperiam ? domiti nec te post bella tyranni
cernere iam licuit ? sic te victoria nobis
eripuit Gallisque dedit ? Rufinus origo
prima mali : geminas inter discordia partes　540
hoc auctore fuit. sed iam maiora moventi
occurrit iusta rediens exercitus ira,
fortis adhuc ferrique memor. brevis inde reluxit
falsaque libertas ; rursum Stilichonis habenis
sperabam me posse regi. pro caeca futuri　545
gaudia ! fraterno coniungi coeperat orbis
imperio (quis enim tanto terrore recentis
exempli paribus sese committeret ausis ?),
cum subito (monstrosa mihi turpisque relatu
fabula) Rufini castratus prosilit heres,　550
et similes iterum luctus Fortuna reduxit,
ut solum domini sexum mutasse viderer.

　" Hic primum thalami claustris delicta tegebat
clam timideque iubens ; erat invidiosa potestas,
sed tamen eunuchi, necdum sibi publica iura　555

---

¹ *i.e.* that of Rufinus.

longer aureole-crowned and she no more bright of
countenance nor clothed with the saffron of the dawn.
She stands wan with woe, even as when she buried
Memnon in his Phrygian grave. Stilicho recognized
her and stayed, well knowing the reason of her visit.
Long time she clasped his victorious hand and at
length amid tears and sighs addressed him.

"Why art thou so wearied of the world whereon
I shine ? Leavest thou me thus to be the sport and
laughing-stock of slaves and carest only for Italy,
thou that wert once my guide and my leader ?
Since thy victory over the tyrant Eugenius I have
not seen thee. Has victory thus robbed me of
thee and given thee to Gaul ? Rufinus was the
prime cause of the trouble ; 'twas he who wrought
disunion between the two empires. But when he
aimed at more there met him an army returning in
righteous wrath, an army still strong, still mindful
of its former prowess. For a moment I was dazzled
by the mirage of liberty : I hoped that Stilicho
would once more hold the reins of our empire. Alas
for my short-sighted happiness ! The world had
begun to form one single empire under the rule
of the two brothers (for who, with the awful example [1]
so fresh in his mind, would dare embark upon a
like venture ?) when suddenly (it is a monstrous
story which scarce bears the telling) a eunuch came
forward as Rufinus' heir. Thus fortune brought
back my former miseries with this one difference—
that of changing my master's sex.

At first he kept his crimes hidden behind the
doors of his chamber, an unseen and timid ruler ;
power was his that all envied, yet only a eunuch's,
nor dared he yet arrogate to himself the right of

sumere nec totas audebat vertere leges.
at postquam pulsisque bonis et faece retenta
peiores legit socios dignusque satelles
hinc Hosius stetit, inde Leo, fiducia crevit
regnandique palam flagravit aperta libido.   560
patricius, consul maculat quos vendit honores,
plus maculat quos ipse gerit. iam signa tubaeque
mollescunt, ipsos ignavia fluxit in enses.
exultant merito gentes facilisque volenti
praeda sumus. iam Bistoniis Haemoque nivali   565
vastior expulsis Oriens squalescit aratris.
ei mihi, quas urbes et quanto tempore Martis
ignaras uno rapuerunt proelia cursu !
nuper ab extremo veniens equitatus Araxe
terruit Antiochi muros, ipsumque decorae   570
paene caput Syriae flammis hostilibus arsit.
utque gravis spoliis nulloque obstante profunda
laetus caede redit, sequitur mucrone secundo
continuum vulnus ; nec iam mihi Caucasus hostes
nec mittit gelidus Phasis ; nascuntur in ipso   575
bella sinu. legio pridem Romana Gruthungi,
iura quibus victis dedimus, quibus arva domusque
praebuimus, Lydos Asiaeque uberrima vastant
ignibus et si quid tempestas prima reliquit.
nec vi nec numero freti ; sed inertia nutrit   580
proditioque ducum, quorum per crimina miles

governing the state or of trampling on the laws.
But when he had banished the good and, retaining
the dregs of the people, had chosen therefrom
advisers of no worth; when his creature Hosius
stood on his one side and Leo on the other, then
indeed his self-confidence waxed and his lust for
power broke forth into open flame. Patrician and
consul he brought defilement on the honours he
sold; even greater defilement on those he carried
himself. The very standards and trumpets of war
grew feeble; a palsy seized upon our swords.
What wonder the nations rejoiced and we became
the easy prey of any who would subdue us? Gone
are ploughs and ploughmen; the East is more a desert
than Thrace and snowy Haemus. Alas! how many
cities, how long unused to war's alarms, have perished
in a single invasion! Not long since a mounted band
coming from Araxes' farthest banks threatened the
walls of Antioch and all but set fire to the chief city
of the fair province of Syria. Laden with spoil and
rejoicing in the vast carnage it had wrought the band
returned with none to bar its passage; now it
pursues its victorious career inflicting on me wound
upon wound. 'Tis not now Caucasus nor cold Phasis
that send forces against me; wars arise in the very
centre of my empire. Time was when the Gruthungi
formed a Roman legion; conquered we gave them
laws; fields and dwelling-places we apportioned
them. Now they lay waste with fire Lydia and
the richest cities of Asia, ay, and everything that
escaped the earlier storm. 'Tis neither on their
own valour or numbers that they rely; it is our
cowardice urges them on, cowardice and the treason
of generals, through whose guilt our soldiers now

captivis dat terga suis, quos teste subegit
Danuvio partemque timet qui reppulit omnes.

" Aula choris epulisque vacat nec perdita curat,
dum superest aliquid.   ne quid tamen orbe reciso
venditor amittat, provincia quaeque superstes   585
dividitur geminumque duplex passura tribunal
cogitur alterius pretium sarcire peremptae.
sic mihi restituunt populos ; hac arte reperta
rectorum numerum terris pereuntibus augent.   590

" In te iam spes una mihi.   pro fronde Minervae
has tibi protendo lacrimas : succurre ruenti,
eripe me tandem, servilibus eripe regnis.
neve adeo cunctos paucorum crimine damnes
nec nova tot meritis offensa prioribus obstet.   595
iamiam flecte animum.   suprema pericula semper
dant veniam culpae.   quamvis iratus et exul
pro patriae flammis non distulit arma Camillus.
nec te subtrahimus Latio ; defensor utrique
sufficis.   armorum liceat splendore tuorum   600
in commune frui ; clipeus nos protegat idem
unaque pro gemino desudet cardine virtus."

flee before their own captives, whom, as Danube's stream well knows, they once subdued ; and those now fear a handful who once could drive back all.

Meanwhile the palace devotes its attention to dances and feastings, and cares not what be lost so something remain. But lest our salesman lose aught by this dismemberment of the empire he has divided each remaining province into two, and forces the two halves, each under its own governor, to compensate him for the loss of other provinces. 'Tis thus they give me back my lost peoples : by this ingenious device they increase the number of my rulers while the lands they should rule are lost.

In thee is now my only hope; in place of Minerva's supplicating branch I offer thee my tears. Help me in my distress. Save me from this tyranny of a slave master; do not condemn all for the fault of a few, and let not a recent offence cancel former merits. Grant me now my request; extreme danger ever exonerates from blame. Camillus, though justly angered at his banishment, forebore not to succour his country when in flames. I seek not to draw thee away from Italy ; thou art enough defence for both empires. Let both have the benefit of thine illustrious arms ; let the same shield defend us and one hero work the salvation of a twofold world "

FESCENNINA
DE NUPTIIS HONORII AUGUSTI

I. (XI.)

Princeps corusco sidere pulchrior,
Parthis sagittas tendere doctior,
eques Gelonis imperiosior,
quae digna mentis laus erit arduae ?
quae digna formae laus erit igneae ?   5
te Leda mallet quam dare Castorem ;
praefert Achilli te proprio Thetis ;
victum fatetur Delos Apollinem ;
credit minorem Lydia Liberum.
tu cum per altas impiger ilices   10
praedo citatum cornipedem reges
ludentque ventis instabiles comae,
telis iacebunt sponte tuis ferae
gaudensque sacris vulneribus leo
admittet hastam morte superbior.   15
Venus reversum spernit Adonidem,
damnat reductum Cynthia Virbium.
Cum post labores sub platani voles
virentis umbra vel gelido specu
torrentiorem fallere Sirium   20
et membra somno fessa resolveris :
o quantus uret tum Dryadas calor !
quot aestuantes ancipiti gradu
furtiva carpent oscula Naides !

FESCENNINE VERSES IN HONOUR OF THE MARRIAGE OF THE EMPEROR HONORIUS[1]

I (XI)

Prince, fairer than the day-star, who shootest thine arrows with an aim more sure than the Parthian's, rider more daring than the Geloni, what praise shall match thy lofty mind, what praise thy brilliant beauty? Leda would rather have thee her son than Castor; Thetis counts thee dearer than her own Achilles; Delos' isle admits thee Apollo's victor; Lydia puts Bacchus second to thee. When in the heat of the chase thou guidest thy coursing steed amid the towering holm-oaks and thy tossing locks stream out upon the wind, the beasts of their own accord will fall before thine arrows and the lion, right gladly wounded by a prince's sacred hand, will welcome thy spear and be proud so to die. Venus scorns Adonis returned from the dead, Diana disapproves Hippolytus recalled to life.

When after thy toils thou seekest the shade of a green plane-tree or shunnest Sirius' extreme heat in some cool grot and freest thy wearied limbs in sleep, what a passion of love will inflame the Dryads' hearts! how many a Naiad will steal up with trembling foot and snatch an unmarked kiss! Who,

[1] The marriage of Honorius and Maria, daughter of Stilicho, took place at Milan, Feb. 398.

quis vero acerbis horridior Scythis,   25
quis beluarum corde furentior,
qui, cum micantem te prope viderit,
non optet ultro servitium pati,
qui non catenas adripiat libens
colloque poscat vincula libero ?   30
tu si nivalis per iuga Caucasi
saevas petisses pulcher Amazonas,
peltata pugnas desereret cohors
sexu recepto ; patris et inmemor
inter frementes Hippolyte tubas
strictam securim languida poneret   35
et seminudo pectore cingulum
forti negatum solveret Herculi,
bellumque solus conficeret decor.

   Beata, quae te mox faciet virum   40
primisque sese iunget amoribus.

II. (XII.)

Age cuncta nuptiali
    redimita vere tellus
    celebra toros eriles ;
omne nemus cum fluviis,
    omne canat profundum   5
Ligures favete campi,
    Veneti favete montes,
    subitisque se rosetis
    vestiat Alpinus apex
    et rubeant pruinae.   10
Athesis strepat choreis
    calamisque flexuosus
    leve Mincius susurret

though he be more uncivilized than the wild Scythians and more cruel even than the beasts, but will, when he has seen near at hand thy transcendent loveliness, offer thee a ready servitude? Who will not willingly seize the chains of slavery and demand the yoke for a neck as yet free? Hadst thou o'er the heights of snowy Caucasus gone against the cruel Amazons in all thy beauty, that warrior band had fled the fight and called to mind again their proper sex; Hippolyte, amid the trumpets' din, forgetful of her sire, had weakly laid aside her drawn battle-axe, and with half-bared breast loosed the girdle all Hercules' strength availed not to loose. Thy beauty alone would have ended the war.

Blessed is she who will soon call thee husband and unite herself to thee with the bonds of first love.

II (XII)

Come, earth, wreathed about with nuptial spring, do honour to thy master's marriage-feast. Sing, woods and rivers all, sing, deep of ocean. Give your blessing, too, Ligurian plains and yours, Venetian hills. Let Alpine heights on a sudden clothe themselves with rose-bushes and the fields of ice grow red. Let the Adige re-echo the sound of choric lays and meandering Mincius whisper gently through his

et Padus electriferis
   admoduletur alnis;   15
epulisque iam repleto
   resonet Quirite Thybris
   dominique laeta votis
aurea septemgeminas
   Roma coronet arces.   20
procul audiant Hiberi,
   fluit unde semen aulae,
   ubi plena laurearum
imperio feta domus
   vix numerat triumphos.   25
habet hinc patrem maritus,
   habet hinc puella matrem
   geminaque parte ductum
Caesareum flumineo
   stemma recurrit ortu.   30
decorent virecta Baetim,
   Tagus intumescat auro
   generisque procreator
sub vitreis Oceanus
   luxurietur antris.   35
Oriensque regna fratrum
   simul Occidensque plaudat;
   placide iocentur urbes,
quaeque novo quaeque nitent
   deficiente Phoebo.   40
Aquiloniae procellae,
   rabidi tacete Cauri,
   taceat sonorus Auster.
solus ovantem Zephyrus
   perdominetur annum.   45

reeds and Padus make answer with his amber-dripping alders. Let Tiber's banks now ring with the voices of Rome's full-fed citizens and the golden city, rejoicing in her lord's marriage, crown her seven hills with flowers.

Let Spain hear afar, Spain the cradle of the imperial race, where is a house that is mother of emperors, rich in crowns of laurel, whose triumphs can scarce be numbered. Hence came the bridegroom's sire, hence the bride's mother; from either branch flows the blood of the Caesars, like twin streams reunited. Let rich herbage clothe Baetis' banks and Tagus swell his golden flood; may Ocean, ancestor of the imperial race, make merry in his crystal caves. Let East and West, the two brothers' realms, join in their applause, and peace and joy fill the cities illumined by the sun at his rising and at his setting. Be still, ye storms of the north and ye mad blasts of Caurus; sounding Auster, sink to rest. Let Zephyrus have sole rule over this year of triumph.

III. (XIII.)

Solitas galea fulgere comas,
Stilicho, molli necte corona.
cessent litui saevumque procul
Martem felix taeda releget.
tractus ab aula rursus in aulam   5
redeat sanguis.   patris officiis
iunge potenti pignora dextra.
gener Augusti pridem fueras,
nunc rursus eris socer Augusti.
quae iam rabies livoris erit ?   10
vel quis dabitur color invidiae ?
Stilicho socer est, pater est Stilicho.

IV. (XIV.)

Attollens thalamis Idalium iubar
dilectus Veneri nascitur Hesperus.
iam nuptae trepidat sollicitus pudor,
iam produnt lacrimas flammea simplices.
ne cessa, iuvenis, comminus adgredi,   5
impacata licet saeviat unguibus.
non quisquam fruitur veris odoribus
Hyblaeos latebris nec spoliat favos,
si fronti caveat, si timeat rubos ;
armat spina rosas, mella tegunt apes.   10
crescunt difficili gaudia iurgio
accenditque magis, quae refugit, Venus.
quod flenti tuleris, plus sapit osculum.
dices " o ! " quotiens, " hoc mihi dulcius
quam flavos deciens vincere Sarmatas ! "   15

III (XIII)

Twine with a soft garland, Stilicho, the locks whereon a helmet is wont to shine. Let the trumpets of war cease and the propitious torch of marriage banish savage Mars afar. Let regal blood unite once more with regal blood. Perform a father's office and unite these children with thine illustrious hand. Thou didst marry an emperor's daughter, now, in turn, thy daughter shall marry an emperor. What room is here for the madness of jealousy? What excuse for envy? Stilicho is father both of bride and bridegroom.

IV (XIV)

Hesperus, loved of Venus, rises and shines for the marriage with his Idalian [1] rays. Maiden shame now overcomes the anxious bride; her veil now shows traces of innocent tears. Hesitate not to be close in thine attacks, young lover, e'en though she oppose thee savagely with cruel finger-nail. None can enjoy the scents of spring nor steal the honey of Hybla from its fastnesses if he fears that thorns may scratch his face. Thorns arm the rose and bees find a defence for their honey. The refusals of coyness do but increase the joy; the desire for that which flies us is the more inflamed; sweeter is the kiss snatched through tears. How oft wilt thou say: "Better this than ten victories over the yellow-haired Sarmatae"!

[1] Idalian: from Idalium, a mountain in Cyprus, sacred to Venus.

    Adspirate novam pectoribus fidem
mansuramque facem tradite sensibus.
tam iunctis manibus nectite vincula,
quam frondens hedera stringitur aesculus,
quam lento premitur palmite populus,   20
et murmur querula blandius alite
linguis adsiduo reddite mutuis.
et labris animum conciliantibus
alternum rapiat somnus anhelitum.
amplexu caleat purpura regio   25
et vestes Tyrio sanguine fulgidas
alter virgineus nobilitet cruor.
tum victor madido prosilias toro
nocturni referens vulnera proelii.

    Ducant pervigiles carmina tibiae   30
permissisque iocis turba licentior
exultet tetricis libera legibus.
passim cum ducibus ludite milites,
passim cum pueris ludite virgines.
haec vox aetheriis insonet axibus,   35
haec vox per populos, per mare transeat :
" formosus Mariam ducit Honorius."

Breathe a new loyalty into your breasts and let your senses kindle a flame that shall never be extinguished. May your clasped hands form a bond more close than that betwixt ivy and leafy oak tree or poplar and pliant vine. Be the frequent kisses that ye give and receive breathed more softly than those of plaintive doves, and when lips have united soul to soul let sleep still your throbbing breath. Be the purple couch warm with your princely wooing, and a new stain ennoble coverlets ruddy with Tyrian dye. Then leap victorious from the marriage-bed, scarred with the night's encounter.

All night long let the music of the flute resound and the crowd, set free from law's harsh restraints, with larger licence indulge the permitted jest. Soldiers, make merry with your leaders, girls with boys. Be this the cry that re-echoes from pole to pole, among the peoples, over the seas : " Fair Honorius weds with Maria."

EPITHALAMIUM
DE NUPTIIS HONORII AUGUSTI

PRAEFATIO

(IX.)

Surgeret in thalamum ducto cum Pelion arcu
    nec caperet tantos hospita terra deos,
cum socer aequoreus numerosaque turba sororum
    certarent epulis continuare dies
praeberetque Iovi communia pocula Chiron,   5
    molliter obliqua parte refusus equi,
Peneus gelidos mutaret nectare fontes,
    Oetaeis fluerent spumea vina iugis :
Terpsichore facilem lascivo pollice movit
    barbiton et molles duxit in antra choros.   10
carmina nec superis nec displicuere Tonanti,
    cum teneris nossent congrua vota modis.
Centauri Faunique negant.   quae flectere Rhoeton,
    quae rigidum poterant plectra movere Pholum ?

Septima lux aderat caelo totiensque renato   15
    viderat exactos Hesperus igne choros :
tum Phoebus, quo saxa domat, quo pertrahit ornos,
    pectine temptavit nobiliore lyram
venturumque sacris fidibus iam spondet Achillem,
    iam Phrygias caedes, iam Simoënta canit.   20
frondoso strepuit felix Hymenaeus Olympo ;
    reginam resonant Othrys et Ossa Thetim.

EPITHALAMIUM OF HONORIUS AND MARIA

PREFACE

(IX)

When Pelion reared his height to form a bridal chamber with long-drawn arches, and his hospitable land could not contain so many gods ; when Nereus, sire of the bride, and all the throng of her sisters strove to link day to day with feastings ; when Chiron, lying at ease with his horse-flanks curled under him, offered the loving-cup to Jove ; when Peneus turned his cold waters to nectar and frothing wine flowed down from Oeta's summit, Terpsichore struck her ready lyre with festive hand and led the girlish bands into the caves. The gods, the Thunderer himself, disdained not these songs, for they knew that lovers' vows ever harmonized with tender strains. Centaurs and Fauns would have none of it : what lyre could touch Rhoetus or move inhuman Pholus ?

The seventh day had flamed in heaven, seven times had Hesperus relumed his lamp and seen the dances completed ; then Phoebus touched his lyre with that nobler quill, wherewith he leads captive rocks and mountain-ashes, and sang to his sacred strings now the promised birth of Achilles, now the slaughter of the Trojans and the river Simois. The happy marriage-cry re-echoed o'er leafy Olympus, and Othrys and Ossa gave back their mistress Thetis' name.

EPITHALAMIUM

(X.)

Hauserat insolitos promissae virginis ignes
Augustus primoque rudis flagraverat aestu ;
nec novus unde calor nec quid suspiria vellent,
noverat incipiens et adhuc ignarus amandi.
non illi venator equus, non spicula curae,   5
non iaculum torquere libet ; mens omnis aberrat
in vulnus, quod fixit Amor.   quam saepe medullis
erupit gemitus ! quotiens incanduit ore
confessus secreta rubor nomenque beatum
iniussae scripsere manus ! iam munera nuptae   10
praeparat et pulchros Mariae sed luce minores
eligit ornatus, quidquid venerabilis olim
Livia divorumque nurus gessere superbae.
incusat spes aegra moras longique videntur
stare dies segnemque rotam non flectere Phoebe.   15
Scyria sic tenerum virgo flammabat Achillem
fraudis adhuc expers bellatricesque docebat
ducere fila manus et, mox quos horruit Ide,
Thessalicos roseo nectebat pollice crines.
  Haec etiam queritur secum : " quonam usque verendus   20

242

EPITHALAMIUM

(X)

Unfelt before was the fire the Emperor Honorius
had conceived for his promised bride, and he burned,
all unexperienced, with passion's first fever, nor knew
whence came the heat, what meant the sighs—a
tyro and as yet ignorant of love. Hunting, horses,
javelins—for none of these he now cares nor yet to
fling the spear; Love's wound occupies all his
thoughts. How often he groaned from the very
heart; how often a blush, mantling to his cheeks,
betrayed his secret; how often, unbidden of himself,
his hand would write the loved one's name. Already
he prepares gifts for his betrothed and selects to
adorn her (though their beauty is less than hers) the
jewels once worn by noble Livia of old and all the
proud women of the imperial house. The impatient
lover chafes at the delay; the long days seem as
though they stood still and the moon as though
she moved not her slow wheel. Thus Deidamia,
girl of Scyros, e'er yet she sees through his disguise,
inflamed with love the young Achilles, and taught
his warrior hands to draw the slender thread and
passed her rosy fingers through the locks of that Thes-
salian of whom all Ida was soon to stand in awe.

Thus too he communed with himself: " How long

cunctatur mea vota socer ? quid iungere differt,
quam pepigit, castasque preces implere recusat ?
non ego luxuriem regum moremque secutus
quaesivi vultum tabulis [1] ut nuntia formae
lena per innumeros iret pictura penates,   25
nec variis dubium thalamis lecturus [2] amorem
ardua commisi falsae conubia cerae.
non rapio praeceps alienae foedera taedae,
sed quae sponsa mihi pridem patrisque relicta
mandatis uno materni sanguinis ortu   30
communem partitur avum. fastidia supplex
deposui gessique procum ; de limine sacro
oratum misi proceres, qui proxima nobis
iura tenent. fateor, Stilicho, non parva poposci,
sed certe mereor princeps, hoc principe natus   35
qui sibi te generum fraterna prole revinxit,
cui Mariam debes. faenus mihi solve paternum,
redde suos aulae. mater fortasse rogari
mollior. o patrui germen, cui nominis heres
successi, sublime decus torrentis Hiberi,   40
stirpe soror, pietate parens, tibi creditus infans
inque tuo crevi gremio, partuque remoto
tu potius Flaccilla mihi. quid dividis ergo

---

[1] tabulis *vulg.; Birt reads* thalamis *with the better MSS.*
[2] *Birt reads* laturus *with P ; other MSS.* lecturus

---

[1] Serena, daughter of Honorius, the elder, the brother of
Theodosius the Great. Theodosius adopted Serena so that
by adoption Honorius and Serena were brother and sister,

will honoured Stilicho forbear to grant my prayers?
Why postpones he the union of those whose love he
has approved? Why should he refuse to fulfil my
chaste desires? I follow not the example of luxurious
princes in seeking the beauties of a pictured counten-
ance, whereby the pander canvass may pass from
house to house to make known the charms de-
manded; nor yet have I sought to choose the un-
certain object of my love from this house or from
that, and thus entrusted to deceptive wax the difficult
selection of a bride. I sever not in violence the bonds
that unite a wedded woman to her lord; her I seek
who hath long been betrothed to me, who by a
father's orders was left my affianced bride and who
through her mother shares with me a common
grandsire. A suppliant I have laid aside my rank
and acted the suitor. Princes, second only to myself
in rank, have I sent from my imperial palace to
present my petition. 'Tis no small thing I ask,
Stilicho; that I admit; yet surely to me, an emperor,
son of that other emperor who, by giving thee his
brother's adopted daughter to wife, made thee his
son-in-law,—to me thou dost owe Maria. Pay
back to the son the interest due to his sire; restore
to the palace those who are its own. Mayhap
her mother[1] will be less inexorable. Daughter of
mine uncle Honorius, whence I derive my name, chief
glory of the land of swift-flowing Ebro, cousin by
birth, by mother's love a mother, to thy care was
mine infancy entrusted, in thine arms I grew to boy-
hood; save for my birth thou, rather than Flacilla,
art my mother. Why dost thou separate thy two

by birth cousins. Serena was probably born in 376;
Honorius not till Sept. 9, 384.

pignora ?   quid iuveni natam non reddis alumno ?
optatusne dies aderit ?   dabiturne iugalis   45
nox umquam ? "
                    Tali solatur vulnera questu.
risit Amor placidaeque volat trans aequora matri
nuntius et totas iactantior explicat alas.

   Mons latus Ionium Cypri praeruptus obumbrat,
invius humano gressu, Phariumque cubile   50
Proteos et septem despectat cornua Nili.
hunc neque candentes audent vestire pruinae,
hunc venti pulsare timent, hunc laedere nimbi.
luxuriae Venerique vacat.   pars acrior anni
exulat ; aeterni patet indulgentia veris.   55
in campum se fundit apex ; hunc aurea saepes
circuit et fulvo defendit prata metallo.
Mulciber, ut perhibent, his oscula coniugis emit
moenibus et tales uxorius obtulit arces.
intus rura micant, manibus quae subdita nullis   60
perpetuum florent, Zephyro contenta colono,
umbrosumque nemus, quo non admittitur ales,
ni probet ante suos diva sub iudice cantus :
quae placuit, fruitur ramis ; quae victa, recedit.
vivunt in Venerem frondes omnisque vicissim   65
felix arbor amat ; nutant ad mutua palmae
foedera, populeo suspirat populus ictu
et platani platanis alnoque adsibilat alnus.

   Labuntur gemini fontes, hic dulcis, amarus
alter, et infusis corrumpunt mella venenis,   70

children? Why not bestow a daughter born upon an adopted son? Will the longed-for day ever come; the marriage-night ever be sanctioned?"

With such complaint he assuages the wounds of love. Cupid laughed and speeding across the deep bore the news to his gentle mother, proudly spreading his wings to their full extent.

Where Cyprus looks out over the Ionian main a craggy mountain overshadows it; unapproachable by human foot it faces the isle of Pharos, the home of Proteus and the seven mouths of the Nile. The hoar frost dares not clothe its sides, nor the rude winds buffet it nor clouds obscure. It is consecrate to pleasure and to Venus. The year's less clement seasons are strangers to it, whereoever ever brood the blessings of eternal spring. The mountain's height slopes down into a plain; that a golden hedge encircles, guarding its meadows with yellow metal. This demesne, men say, was the price paid by Mulciber for the kisses of his wife, these towers were the gift of a loving husband. Fair is the enclosed country, ever bright with flowers though touched with no labouring hand, for Zephyr is husbandman enough therefor. Into its shady groves no bird may enter save such as has first won the goddess' approval for its song. Those which please her may flit among the branches; they must quit who cannot pass the test. The very leaves live for love and in his season every happy tree experiences love's power: palm bends down to mate with palm, poplar sighs its passion for poplar, plane whispers to plane, alder to alder.

Here spring two fountains, the one of sweet water, the other of bitter, honey is mingled with the first, poison with the second, and in these streams 'tis said

unde Cupidineas armari fama sagittas.
mille pharetrati ludunt in margine fratres,
ore pares, aevo similes, gens mollis Amorum.
hos Nymphae pariunt, illum Venus aurea solum
edidit. ille deos caelumque et sidera cornu   75
temperat et summos dignatur figere reges ;
hi plebem feriunt. nec cetera numina desunt :
hic habitat nullo constricta Licentia nodo
et flecti faciles Irae vinoque madentes
Excubiae Lacrimaeque rudes et gratus amantum 80
Pallor et in primis titubans Audacia furtis
iucundique Metus et non secura Voluptas ;
et lasciva volant levibus Periuria ventis.
quos inter petulans alta cervice Iuventas
excludit Senium luco.   85
                    Procul atria divae
permutant radios silvaque obstante virescunt.
Lemnius haec etiam gemmis extruxit et auro
admiscens artem pretio trabibusque smaragdi
supposuit caesas hyacinthi rupe columnas.
beryllo paries et iaspide lubrica surgunt   90
limina despectusque solo calcatur achates.
in medio glaebis redolentibus area dives
praebet odoratas messes ; hic mitis amomi,
hic casiae matura seges, Panchaeaque turgent
cinnama, nec sicco frondescunt vimina costo   95
tardaque sudanti prorepunt balsama rivo.
  Quo postquam delapsus Amor longasque peregit
penna vias, alacer passuque superbior intrat.
caesariem tunc forte Venus subnixa corusco
fingebat solio. dextra laevaque sorores   100
stabant Idaliae : largos haec nectaris imbres

----

[1] *i.e.* the Graces.

that Cupid dips his arrows. A thousand brother Loves with quivers play all around upon the banks, a tender company like to Cupid himself in face and of equal age. The nymphs are their mothers; Cupid is the only child of golden Venus. He with his bow subdues the stars and the gods and heaven, and disdains not to wound mighty kings; of the others the common people is the prey. Other deities, too, are here: Licence bound by no fetters, easily moved Anger, Wakes dripping with wine, inexperienced Tears, Pallor that lovers ever prize, Boldness trembling at his first thefts, happy Fears, unstable Pleasure, and lovers' Oaths, the sport of every lightest breeze. Amid them all wanton Youth with haughty neck shuts out Age from the grove.

Afar shines and glitters the goddess' many-coloured palace, green gleaming by reason of the encircling grove. Vulcan built this too of precious stones and gold, wedding their costliness to art. Columns cut from rock of hyacinth support emerald beams; the walls are of beryl, the high-builded thresholds of polished jaspar, the floor of agate trodden as dirt beneath the foot. In the midst is a courtyard rich with fragrant turf that yields a harvest of perfume; there grows sweet spikenard and ripe cassia, Panchaean cinnamon-flowers and sprays of oozy balm, while balsam creeps forth slowly in an exuding stream.

Hither Love glided down, winging his way o'er the long journey. Joyfully and with prouder gait than e'er his wont he enters. Venus was seated on her glittering throne, tiring her hair. On her right hand and on her left stood the Idalian sisters.[1] Of these one pours a rich stream of nectar over Venus'

inrigat, haec morsu numerosi dentis eburno
multifidum discrimen arat ; sed tertia retro
dat varios nexus et iusto dividit orbes
ordine, neglectam partem studiosa relinquens :   105
plus error decuit. speculi nec vultus egebat
iudicio ; similis tecto monstratur in omni
et capitur [1] quocumque videt. dum singula cernit,
seque probat, nati venientis conspicit umbram
ambrosioque sinu puerum complexa ferocem   110
" quid tantum gavisus ? " ait ; " quae proelia sudas
improbe ? quis iacuit telis ? iterumne Tonantem
inter Sidonias cogis mugire iuvencas ?
an Titana domas ? an pastoralia Lunam
rursus in antra vocas ? durum magnumque videris
debellasse deum."   116
          Suspensus in oscula matris
ille refert : " Laetare, parens ; inmane tropaeum
rettulimus, nostrum iam sensit Honorius arcum.
scis Mariam patremque ducem, qui cuspide Gallos
Italiamque fovet, nec te praeclara Serenae   120
fama latet. propera ; regalibus adnue votis :
iunge toros."
          Gremio natum Cytherea removit
et crines festina ligat peplumque fluentem
adlevat et blando spirantem numine ceston
cingitur, impulsos pluviis quo mitigat amnes,   125
quo mare, quo ventos irataque fulmina solvit.
ut stetit ad litus, parvos adfatur alumnos :
     " Heus ! quis erit, pueri, vitreas qui lapsus in undas
huc rapidum Tritona vocet, quo vecta per altum

---

[1] *Birt, following the* MSS., rapitur ; capitur *was suggested
by Conington, comparing Virg. Aen.* viii. 311.
250

head, another parts her hair with a fine ivory comb.
A third, standing behind the goddess, braids her
tresses and orders her ringlets in due array, yet
carefully leaving a part untended ; such negligence
becomes her more. Nor did her face lack the mirror's
verdict ; her image is reflected over all the palace
and she is charmed wheresoever she looks. While
she surveys each detail and approves her beauty
she notes the shadow of her son as he approaches
and catches the fierce boy to her fragrant bosom.
" Whence comes thy joy ? " she asks ; " cruel child,
what battles hast thou fought ? What victim has
thine arrow pierced ? Hast thou once more com-
pelled the Thunderer to low among the heifers of
Sidon ? Hast thou overcome Apollo, or again
summoned Diana to a shepherd's cave ? Methinks
thou hast triumphed over some fierce and potent
god."

Hanging upon his mother's kisses he answered :
" Mother, be thou glad ; a great victory is ours.
Now has Honorius felt our arrows. Thou knowest
Maria and her sire, the general whose spear pro-
tects Gaul and Italy ; the fame of noble Serena is
not hidden from thee. Haste thee, assent to their
princely prayers and seal this royal union."

Cytherea freed her from her son's embrace,
hastily bound up her hair, gathered up her flowing
dress and girt herself about with the divine girdle
whose all-compelling charm can stay the rain-swollen
torrent and appease the sea, the winds and angry
thunderbolts. Soon as she stood on the shore she
thus addressed her small foster-children. " Come,
children, which of you will plunge beneath the glassy
wave and summon me hither fleet Triton to bear me

deferar ? haud umquam tanto mihi venerit usu. 130
sacri, quos petimus, thalami. pernicius omnes
quaerite, seu concha Libycum circumsonat aequor,
Aegaeas seu frangit aquas. quicumque repertum
duxerit, aurata donabitur ille pharetra."

Dixerat et sparsa diversi plebe feruntur 135
exploratores. pelagi sub fluctibus ibat
Carpathiis Triton obluctantemque petebat
Cymothoën. timet illa ferum seseque sequenti
subripit et duris elabitur uda lacertis.
" heus," inquit speculatus Amor, " non vestra sub imis
furta tegi potuere vadis. accingere nostram 141
vecturus dominam : pretium non vile laboris
Cymothoën facilem, quae nunc detrectat, habebis.
hac mercede veni."

                Prorupit gurgite torvus
semifer ; undosi verrebant brachia crines ; 145
hispida tendebant bifido vestigia cornu,
qua pistrix commissa viro. ter pectora movit ;
iam quarto Paphias tractu sulcabat harenas.
umbratura deam retro sinuatur in arcum
belua ; tum vivo squalentia murice terga 150
purpureis mollita toris[1] : hoc navigat antro[2]
fulta Venus ; niveae delibant aequora plantae.
prosequitur volucer late comitatus Amorum
tranquillumque choris quatitur mare. serta per
      omnem
Neptuni dispersa domum. Cadmeia ludit 155
Leucothoë, frenatque rosis delphina Palaemon ;
alternas violis Nereus interserit algas ;

---

[1] toris *A, followed by Birt* ; *but* rosis *VP is attractive.*
     [2] antro P^1 ; *vulg.* ostro.

quickly o'er the deep? Never will he have come
to do us better service. Sacred is the marriage
that I seek. Make all speed in your search; may
be the Libyan sea rings to his conch, may be he
cleaves the Aegean main. Whoso shall find and
bring him hither shall have a golden quiver as a
reward."

She spake and, dividing into various bands, the
scouts set out. Triton was swimming beneath the
waves of the Carpathian sea, pursuing reluctant
Cymothoë. She feared her rough lover and eluded
his pursuit, her wet form gliding through the em-
braces of his strong arms. One of the Loves espied
him and cried, " Stay! the deeps cannot hide your
amours. Make ready to carry our mistress; as a
reward for thy services (and 'tis no meagre one) thou
shalt have Cymothoë, a complaisant mistress shall she
be though she flout thee now. Come and win thy
recompense."

The dread monster uprose from the abyss; his
billowing hair swept his shoulders; hoofs of cloven
horn grown round with bristles sprang from where his
fishy tail joined his man's body. He swam three
strokes and at the fourth stranded upon the shore of
Cyprus. To shade the goddess the monster arched
back his tail; then his back, rough with living
purple, was bedded with scarlet coverlets; resting
in such a retreat does Venus voyage, her snowy
feet just dipping in the sea. A great company of
wingèd Loves fly after her, troubling the calm surface
of Ocean. Neptune's palace is all adorned with
flowers. Leucothoë, daughter of Cadmus, sports
on the water, and Palaemon drives his dolphin
with a bridle of roses. Nereus sets violets here

canitiem Glaucus ligat inmortalibus herbis.
nec non et variis vectae Nereides ibant
audito rumore feris (hanc pisce voluto   160
sublevat Oceani monstrum Tartesia tigris ;
hanc timor Aegaei rupturus fronte carinas
trux aries ; haec caeruleae suspensa leaenae
innatat ; haec viridem trahitur complexa iuvencum)
certatimque novis onerant conubia donis.   165
cingula Cymothoë, rarum Galatea monile
et gravibus Psamathe bacis diadema ferebat
intextum, Rubro quas legerat ipsa profundo.
mergit se subito vellitque corallia Doto :
vimen erat dum stagna subit ; processerat undis : 170
gemma fuit.
          Nudae Venerem cinxere catervae
plaudentesque simul tali cum voce sequuntur :
" hos Mariae cultus, haec munera nostra precamur
reginae regina feras. dic talia numquam
promeruisse Thetim nec cum soror Amphitrite 175
nostro nupta Iovi. devotum sentiat aequor,
agnoscat famulum virgo Stilichonia pontum.
victrices nos saepe rates classemque paternam
veximus, attritis cum tenderet ultor Achivis."
   Iam Ligurum terris spumantia pectora Triton 180
adpulerat lassosque fretis extenderat orbes.
continuo sublime volans ad moenia Gallis
condita, lanigeri suis ostentantia pellem,
pervenit. adventu Veneris pulsata recedunt
nubila, clarescunt puris Aquilonibus Alpes. 185

---

[1] *i.e.* Neptune.
[2] Milan ; *cf.* Isid. *Orig.* xv. 1 *vocatum Mediolanum ab eo, quod ibi sus in medio lanea perhibetur inventa*; Sidon. Apol. vii. 17 *et quae lanigero de sue nomen habent.*

and there among the seaweed and Glaucus wreathes his grey hair with deathless flowers. Hearing the tale the Nereids, too, came mounted on various beasts: one (maiden above but fish below) rides the dread sea-tiger of Tartessus; another is carried by that fierce ram, the terror of the Aegean, who shatters ships with his forehead; a third bestrides the neck of a sea-lion; another is borne along by the sea-calf to which she clings. They vie with one another in bringing gifts to the newly-wedded pair. Cymothoë presents a girdle, Galatea a precious necklace, Psamathe a diadem heavily encrusted with pearls gathered by herself from the depths of the Red Sea. Doto suddenly dives to gather coral, a plant so long as it is beneath the water, a jewel once it is brought forth from the waves.

The nude crowd of Nereids throng around Venus, following her and singing praises after this manner: "We beg thee, Venus, our queen, to bear these our gifts, these adornments, to queen Maria. Tell her that never did Thetis receive their like nor even our sister Amphitrite when she espoused our Jupiter.[1] Let the daughter of Stilicho hereby realize the devotion of the sea and know that Ocean is her slave. 'Tis we who bore up her father's fleet, the hope of his victorious land, what time he set out to avenge the ruined Greeks."

And now Triton's foam-flecked breast had touched the Ligurian shore and his wearied coils were extended over the surface of the water. Straightway Venus flew high in the air to the city founded by the Gauls, the city that shows as its device the fleece-covered pelt of a sow.[2] At the coming of the goddess the routed clouds retire; bright shine the Alps be-

laetitiae causas ignorat dicere miles
laetaturque tamen ; Mavortia signa rubescunt
floribus et subitis animantur frondibus hastae.
illa suum dictis adfatur talibus agmen :

" Gradivum, nostri comites, arcete parumper, 190
ut soli vacet aula mihi.   procul igneus horror
thoracum, gladiosque tegat vagina minaces
stent bellatrices aquilae saevique dracones.
fas sit castra meis hodie succumbere signis :
tibia pro lituis et pro clangore tubarum   195
molle lyrae festumque canant.   epulentur ad ipsas
excubias ; mediis spirent crateres in armis.
laxet terribiles maiestas regia fastus
et sociam plebem non indignata potestas
confundat turbae proceres.   solvantur habenis 200
gaudia nec leges pudeat ridere severas.

" Tu festas, Hymenaee, faces, tu, Gratia, flores
elige, tu geminas, Concordia, necte coronas.
vos, pennata cohors, quocumque vocaverit usus,
divisa properate manu, neu marceat ulla   205
segnities : alii funalibus ordine ductis
plurima venturae suspendite lumina nocti ;
hi nostra nitidos postes obducere myrto
contendant ; pars nectareis adspergite tecta
fontibus et flamma lucos adolete Sabaeos ; 210
pars infecta croco velamina lutea Serum
pandite Sidoniasque solo prosternite vestes.
ast alii thalamum docto componite textu ;
stamine gemmato picturatisque columnis

256

neath the clear North wind. The soldier rejoices though he cannot tell why. The standards of war burgeon with red flowers and the spears on a sudden sprout with living leaves. Then Venus thus addresses her attendant throng. " Comrades mine, keep away for a while the god of war that the palace may be mine and mine alone. Banish afar the terror of the flashing breastplate ; let its scabbard sheath the threatening sword. Advance not the standards of war, the eagles and savage dragons. This day the camp shall yield to my standards ; the flute shall sound instead of the bugle, the soft strains of the happy lyre take the place of the trumpets' blare. Let the soldiers feast even when on guard and the beakers foam in the midst of arms. Let regal majesty lay by its awful pride and power, disdaining not to associate with the people, make one the nobles with the crowd. Let joy be unrestrained and sober Law herself be not ashamed to laugh.

" Hymen, choose thou the festal torches, and ye Graces gather flowers for the feast. Thou, Concord, weave two garlands. You, winged band, divide and hasten whithersoever you can be of use : let none be slothful or lazy. You others hang numberless lamps in order from their brackets against the coming of night. Let these haste to entwine the gleaming door-posts with my sacred myrtle. Do you sprinkle the palace with drops of nectar and kindle a whole grove of Sabaean incense. Let others unfold yellow-dyed silks from China and spread tapestries of Sidon on the ground. Do you employ all your arts in decorating the marriage-bed. Woven with jewels and upborne on carved columns be its canopy, such

aedificetur apex, qualem non Lydia dives   215
erexit Pelopi nec quem struxere Lyaeo
Indorum spoliis et opaco palmite Bacchae.
illic exuvias omnes cumulate parentum :
quidquid avus senior Mauro vel Saxone victis,
quidquid ab innumeris socio Stilichone tremendus   220
quaesivit genitor bellis, quodcumque Gelonus
Armeniusve dedit ; quantum crinita sagittis
attulit extremo Meroë circumflua Nilo ;
misit Achaemenio quidquid de Tigride Medus,
cum supplex emeret Romanam Parthia pacem.   225
nobilibus gazis opibusque cubilia surgant
barbaricis ; omnes thalamo conferte triumphos."

    Sic ait et sponsae petit improvisa penates.
illa autem secura tori taedasque parari
nescia divinae fruitur sermone parentis   230
maternosque bibit mores exemplaque discit
prisca pudicitiae Latios nec volvere libros
desinit aut Graios, ipsa genetrice magistra,
Maeonius quaecumque senex aut Thracius Orpheus
aut Mytilenaeo modulatur pectine Sappho   235
(sic Triviam Latona monet ; sic mitis in antro
Mnemosyne docili tradit praecepta Thaliae) :
cum procul augeri nitor et iucundior aër
attonitam lustrare domum fundique comarum
gratus odor.   mox vera fides numenque refulsit. 240
cunctatur stupefacta Venus ; nunc ora puellae,

as rich Lydia ne'er built for Pelops nor yet the
Bacchae for Lyaeus, decked as his was with the
spoils of Ind and the mantling vine. Heap up there
all the gathered wealth of the family, all the spoil
that Honorius the elder, our emperor's grandsire,
won from Moor and Saxon, all that his dread father
with Stilicho at his side gained from numberless
wars, all that the Geloni and Armenians have
contributed or Meroë added—Meroë encircled by
furthermost Nile whose people decorate their hair
with arrows; whatever the Medes sent from the
banks of Persian Tigris when suppliant Parthia
bought peace of Rome. Let the lofty couch be
adorned with the barbaric splendour of kings'
treasuries; be all the wealth of all our triumphs
gathered in that marriage-chamber."

So spake she and all unannounced sought the
bride's home. But Maria, with no thoughts of
wedlock nor knowing that the torches were being
got ready, was listening with rapt attention to the
discourse of her saintly mother, drinking in that
mother's nature and learning to follow the example
of old-world chastity; nor does she cease under
that mother's guidance to unroll the writers of
Rome and Greece, all that old Homer sang, or
Thracian Orpheus, or that Sappho set to music
with Lesbian quill; (even so Latona taught Diana;
so gentle Mnemosyne in her cave gave instruction
to meek Thalia)—when the sky from afar grows more
bright, a sweeter air breathes through the astonished
palace and there is spread the happy fragrance
of scented locks. Soon came the proof; in all
her beauty the goddess bursts upon them. Yet
Venus stands amazed, admiring now the daughter's

nunc flavam niveo miratur vertice matrem.
haec modo crescenti, plenae par altera lunae :
adsurgit ceu forte minor sub matre virenti
laurus et ingentes ramos olimque futuras   245
promittit iam parva comas ; vel flore sub uno
ceu geminae Paestana rosae per iugera regnant :
haec largo matura die saturataque vernis
roribus indulget spatio ; latet altera nodo
nec teneris audet foliis admittere soles.   250

    Adstitit et blande Mariam Cytherea salutat :
" salve sidereae proles augusta Serenae,
magnorum suboles regum parituraque reges.
te propter Paphias sedes Cyprumque reliqui,
te propter libuit tantos explere labores   255
et tantum transnare maris, ne vilior ultra
privatos paterere lares neu tempore longo
dilatos iuvenis nutriret Honorius ignes.
accipe fortunam generis, diadema resume,
quod tribuas natis, et in haec penetralia rursus,   260
unde parens progressa, redi.   fac nulla subesse
vincula cognatae : quamvis aliena fuisses
principibus, regnum poteras hoc ore mereri.
quae propior sceptris facies ? qui dignior aula   264
vultus erit ?   non labra rosae, non colla pruinae,
non crines aequant violae, non lumina flammae.
quam iuncti leviter sese discrimine confert
umbra supercilii !   miscet quam iusta pudorem
temperies nimio nec sanguine candor abundat !

---

¹ The *viola* was probably a pansy or wallflower, Gk
λευκόϊον.

loveliness, now the snowy neck and golden hair
of the mother. The one is like unto the crescent
moon, the other to the full. So grows a young
laurel beneath the shadow of its parent tree and,
small as it now is, gives promise of great branches
and thick foliage to come. Or as 'twere two roses
of Paestum on one stalk; the one day's fulness
has brought to maturity; steeped in the dews of
spring it spreads abroad its petals; the other yet
nestles in its bud nor dares receive the sun's warmth
within its tender heart.

Venus stood and addressed Maria with these gentle
words: "All hail! revered daughter of divine Serena,
scion of great kings and destined to be the mother of
kings. For thy sake have I left my home in Paphos'
isle and Cyprus; for thy sake was I pleased to
face so many labours and cross so many seas lest
thou shouldst continue to live a private life little
befitting thy true worth and lest young Honorius
should still feed in his heart the flame of unrequited
love. Take the rank thy birth demands, resume
the crown to bequeath it to thy children and re-enter
the palace whence thy mother sprang. E'en
though no ties of blood united thee to the royal
house, though thou wert in no way related thereto,
yet would thy beauty render thee worthy of a king-
dom. What face could rather win a sceptre? What
countenance better adorn a palace? Redder than
roses thy lips, whiter than the hoar-frost thy neck,
cowslips[1] are not more yellow than thine hair, fire
not more bright than thine eyes. With how fine
an interspace do the delicate eyebrows meet upon
thy forehead! How just the blend that makes thy
blush, thy fairness not o'ermantled with too much

Aurorae vincis digitos umerosque Dianae ;   270
ipsam iam superas matrem.   si Bacchus amator
dotali potuit caelum signare corona,
cur nullis virgo redimitur pulchrior astris ?
iam tibi molitur stellantia serta Bootes
inque decus Mariae iam sidera parturit aether. 275
i, digno nectenda viro tantique per orbem
consors imperii !   iam te venerabitur Hister ;
nomen adorabunt populi ;   iam Rhenus et Albis
serviet ;   in medios ibis regina Sygambros.
quid numerem gentes Atlanteosque recessus   280
Oceani ?   toto pariter donabere mundo.''
     Dixit et ornatus, dederant quos nuper ovantes
Nereides, collo membrisque micantibus aptat.
ipsa caput distinguit acu, substringit amictus ;
flammea virgineis accommodat ipsa capillis.   285
ante fores iam pompa sonat, pilentaque sacra
praeradiant ductura nurum.   calet obvius ire
iam princeps tardumque cupit discedere solem :
nobilis haud aliter sonipes, quem primus amoris
sollicitavit odor, tumidus quatiensque decoras   290
curvata cervice iubas Pharsalia rura
pervolat et notos hinnitu flagitat amnes
naribus accensis ;   mulcet fecunda magistros
spes gregis et pulchro gaudent armenta marito.
     Candidus interea positis exercitus armis   295
exultat socerum circa ;   nec signifer ullus

---

[1] Venus acts as *pronuba*. The parting of the hair with
the spear was a relic of marriage by capture (*cf.* Catullus
lxi.).

red! Pinker thy fingers than Aurora's, firmer thy shoulders than Diana's; even thy mother dost thou surpass. If Bacchus, Ariadne's lover, could transform his mistress' garland into a constellation how comes it that a more beauteous maid has no crown of stars? Even now Boötes is weaving for thee a starry crown, even now heaven brings new stars to birth to do thee honour. Go, mate with one who is worthy of thee and share with him an empire co-extensive with the world. Ister now shall do thee homage; all nations shall adore thy name. Now Rhine and Elbe shall be thy slaves; thou shalt be queen among the Sygambri. Why should I number the peoples and the Atlantic's distant shores? The whole world alike shall be thy dowry."

She spake and fitted to Maria's neck and shining limbs the rich gear which the happy Nereids had just given her. She parted her hair with the spear's point, girded up her dress, and with her own hands set the veil over the maiden's hair.[1] The procession is halted singing at the door; brightly gleams the holy chariot in which the new bride is to fare. The prince burns to run and meet her and longs for the sun's tardy setting. Even so the noble steed when first the smell that stirs his passions smites upon him proudly shakes his thick, disordered mane and courses over Pharsalia's plains. His nostrils are aflame and with a neighing he greets the streams that saw his birth. His masters smile at the hope of their stud's increase, and the mares take pleasure in their handsome mate.

Meanwhile the army has laid aside its swords: the soldiers are dressed in white and throng around Stilicho, the bride's father. No standard-bearer nor

nec miles pluviae flores dispergere ritu
cessat purpureoque ducem perfundere nimbo.
haec quoque velati lauro myrtoque canebant :

" Dive parens, seu te complectitur axis Olympi,
seu premis Elysias animarum praemia valles,　301
en promissa tibi Stilicho iam vota peregit ;
iam gratae rediere vices ; cunabula pensat ;
acceptum reddit thalamum natoque reponit,
quod dederat genitor. numquam te, sancte, pigebit
iudicii nec te pietas suprema fefellit.　306
dignus cui leges, dignus cui pignora tanti
principis et rerum commendarentur habenae.
dicere possemus, quae proelia gesta sub Haemo
quaeque cruentarint fumantem Strymona pugnae,
quam notus clipeo, quanta vi fulminet hostem,　311
ni prohiberet Hymen. quae tempestiva relatu,
nunc canimus. quis consilio, quis iuris et aequi
nosse modum melior ? quod semper dissilit, in te
convenit, ingenio robur, prudentia forti.　315
fronte quis aequali ? quem sic Romana decerent
culmina ? sufficerent tantis quae pectora curis ?
stes licet in populo, clamet quicumque videbit :
' hic est, hic Stilicho ! ' sic se testatur et offert
celsa potestatis species, non voce feroci,　320
non alto simulata gradu, non improba gestu.
adfectant alii quidquid fingique laborant,
hoc donat natura tibi. pudor emicat una

common soldier fails to scatter flowers like rain
and to drench their leader in a mist of purple blossoms.
Crowned with laurel and myrtle they sing : " Blessed
father, whether the vault of heaven is thy home,
or thou walkest in Elysium, the mansion of the
blest, behold Stilicho hath now fulfilled the promises
he made thee. A happy interchange has now been
made : he compensates thee for his upbringing,
and renders marriage in return for marriage, giving
back to a son what thou, that son's father, gave to
him. Never needst thou repent of thy choice ;
a dying father's love misled thee not. Worthy is he
to be thine heir, worthy to be entrusted with the
child of so powerful a prince and to hold the reins of
government. Now could I tell of the battles fought
beneath the slopes of Mount Haemus, the contests
wherefrom Strymon reeked red with blood ; I could
sing the fame of his arms and how, like a thunder-
bolt, he falls upon his foes, but the marriage-
god says me nay. Our song must be such as now
befits the singing. Who can surpass Stilicho in
counsel ? who in knowledge of law and equity ?
In thee are two opposèd qualities reconciled, wisdom
and strength, prudence and fortitude. Was e'er
so noble a brow ? Whom would Rome's highest
place more befit ? What heart but thine is strong
enough to bear so many troubles ? Shouldst thou
stand amid the crowd whoe'er shall see thee would
exclaim, ' That is Stilicho.' It is thus that the
aspect of supreme majesty brings its own witness—
not with arrogant voice, or pompous walk, or haughty
gesture. The graces which others affect and strive
to seem to possess are thine by nature's gift.
Modesty shines forth together with a noble stern-

formosusque rigor vultusque auctura verendos
canities festina venit. cum sorte remota   325
contingat senio gravitas viresque iuventae,
utraque te cingit propriis insignibus aetas.
ornatur Fortuna viro.   non ulla nocendi
tela nec infecti iugulis civilibus enses.
non odium terrore moves nec frena resolvit   330
gratia ; diligimus pariter pariterque timemus.
ipse metus te noster amat, iustissime legum
arbiter, egregiae pacis fidissime custos,
optime ductorum, fortunatissime patrum.
plus iam, plus domino cuncti debere fatemur,   335
quod gener est, invicte, tuus.   vincire corona ;
insere te nostris contempto iure choreis.
sic puer Eucherius superet virtute parentem ;
aurea sic videat similes Thermantia taedas ;
sic uterus crescat Mariae ; sic natus in ostro   340
parvus Honoriades genibus considat avitis.''

---

¹ Eucherius (born about 388) was the son, and Ther-
mantia the younger daughter, of Stilicho and Serena.
After the death of Maria she became Honorius' second wife.

ness, and white hairs come hastening to increase the reverence of thy face. Though dignity be the crown of age and strength, by a far different lot, of youth, yet either season decks thee with its own peculiar honours. Thou art the ornament of fortune. Never tookst thou up the sword for hurt nor ever didst steep its blade in citizens' blood. No cruelties on thy part aroused men's hatred; favouritism never slacks the reins of justice. We love thee, yet we fear thee. Our very fear testifies to our love, O thou most righteous interpreter of Law, guardian most sure of peace with honour, greatest of our generals, most blessèd among the fathers of our country. We all confess that now we owe our emperor an even firmer allegiance for that thou, hero invincible, art the father of his bride. Crown thy head with a garland, lay aside thy rank for a moment and join our dances. An thou dost this, so may thy son Eucherius[1] surpass the virtues of his sire; so may the fair Thermantia,[1] thy daughter, live to see a marriage such as this; so may Maria's womb grow big and a little Honorius, born in the purple, rest on his grandsire's lap."

PANEGYRICUS
DE TERTIO CONSULATU HONORII AUGUSTI

PRAEFATIO

(VI.)

Parvos non aquilis fas est educere fetus
    ante fidem solis iudiciumque poli.
nam pater, excusso saluit cum tegmine proles
    ovaque maternus rupit hiulca tepor,
protinus implumes convertit ad aethera nidos   5
    et recto flammas imperat ore pati.
consulit ardentes radios et luce magistra
    natorum vires ingeniumque probat.
degenerem refugo torsit qui lumine visum,
    unguibus hunc saevis ira paterna ferit.   10
exploratores oculis qui pertulit ignes
    sustinuitque acie nobiliore diem,
nutritur volucrumque potens et fulminis heres,
    gesturus summo tela trisulca Iovi.
me quoque Pieriis temptatum saepius antris   15
    audet magna suo mittere Roma deo.
iam dominas aures, iam regia tecta meremur
    et chelys Augusto iudice nostra sonat.

PANEGYRIC ON THE THIRD CONSULSHIP OF THE EMPEROR HONORIUS (A.D. 396)

PREFACE

(VI)

Eagles may not rear their young without the sun's permission and the goodwill of heaven. So soon as the chicks have shattered their shells and issued forth, after that the warmth of their mother's body has cracked the opening egg, the father bird makes haste to carry the unfledged nestlings aloft and bids them gaze at the sun's fires with unblinking eye. He takes counsel of those bright beams and under light's schooling makes trial of the strength and temper of his sons. The angry father strikes with pitiless talons the degenerate who turns away his glance, but he whose eye can bear the searching flame, who with bolder sight can outstare the noonday sun, is brought up a king of birds, heir to the thunderbolt, destined to carry Jove's three-forked weapon. So mighty Rome fears not to send me, oft tested e'er now in the Muses' caverns, to face the emperor, her god. Now have I won an emperor's ear, the entrance to an emperor's palace and the emperor himself as judge of my lyre's song.

PANEGYRICUS

(VII.)

Tertia Romulei sumant exordia fasces
terque tuas ducat bellatrix pompa curules ;
festior annus eat cinctusque imitata Gabinos
dives Hydaspeis augescat purpura gemmis ;
succedant armis trabeae, tentoria lictor   5
ambiat et Latiae redeant ad signa secures.
tuque o qui patrium curis aequalibus orbem
Eoo cum fratre regis, procede secundis
alitibus Phoebique novos ordire meatus,
spes votumque poli, quem primo a limine vitae   10
nutrix aula fovet, strictis quem fulgida telis
inter laurigeros aluerunt castra triumphos.
ardua privatos nescit Fortuna penates
et regnum cum luce dedit.   cognata potestas
excepit Tyrio venerabile pignus in ostro   15
lustravitque tuos aquilis victricibus ortus
miles et in mediis cunabula praebuit hastis.
te nascente ferox toto Germania Rheno

---

¹ The *cinctus Gabinus* was one of the insignia of the consul-
ship. It consisted in girding the toga tight round the
body by means of one of its *laciniae* (= loose ends). Servius
(on Virg. *Aen.* vii. 612) has a story that Gabii was invaded
during the performance of a sacrifice and that the parti-
cipants repulsed the enemy in their *cinctus.*

270

PANEGYRIC

(VII)

Let the consular fasces of Romulus open a third year, and for the third time let the warlike procession accompany thy curule litter. More festal in array be the coming year, and let purple, folded in Gabine [1] guise, be proudly enriched with gems of Hydaspes; let the cloak of peace succeed the arms of war; let the lictor guard the consul's tent and the Latin axes return to the standards. [2] And do thou, Honorius, who with thy brother, lord of the East, governest with equal care a world that was once thy sire's, go thy way with favourable omens and order the sun's new course, thyself heaven's hope and desire, palace-nurtured even from life's threshold, to whom the camp, gleaming with drawn swords, gave schooling among the laurels of victory. Thy towering fortune has never known the condition of a private citizen; when thou wast born thou wast born a king. Power which was thine by birth received thee, a precious pledge, amid the purple; soldiers bearing victorious standards inaugurated thy birth and set thy cradle in the midst of arms. When thou wast born fierce Germany trembled along

[2] Claudian suggests the uniting of civil and military power in the hands of Honorius.

intremuit movitque suas formidine silvas
Caucasus et positis numen confessa pharetris   20
ignavas Meroë traxit de crine sagittas.
reptasti per scuta puer, regumque recentes
exuviae tibi ludus erant, primusque solebas
aspera complecti torvum post proelia patrem,
signa triumphato quotiens flexisset ab Histro   25
Arctoa de strage calens, et poscere partem
de spoliis, Scythicos arcus aut rapta Gelonis
cingula vel iaculum Daci vel frena Suebi.
ille coruscanti clipeo te saepe volentem
sustulit adridens et pectore pressit anhelo   30
intrepidum ferri galeae nec triste timentem
fulgur et ad summas tendentem brachia cristas.
tum sic laetus ait : " rex o stellantis Olympi,
talis perdomito redeat mihi filius hoste,
Hyrcanas populatus opes aut caede superbus   35
Assyria, sic ense rubens, sic flamine crebro
turbidus et grato respersus pulvere belli,
armaque gaviso referat captiva parenti."

    Mox ubi firmasti recto vestigia gressu,
non tibi desidias molles nec marcida luxu   40
otia nec somnos genitor permisit inertes,
sed nova per duros instruxit membra labores
et cruda teneras exercuit indole vires :
frigora saeva pati, gravibus non cedere nimbis,
aestivum tolerare iubar, transnare sonoras   45
torrentum furias, ascensu vincere montes,

the Rhine's full course, Caucasus shook his forests in fear, and the people of Meroë, confessing thy divinity, laid aside their quivers and drew the useless arrows from their hair. As a child thou didst crawl among shields, fresh-won spoils of monarchs were thy playthings, and thou wert ever the first to embrace thy stern father on his return from rude battles, when that, reeking with the blood of northern savages, he came home victorious from his conquest over the tribes of the Danube. Then wouldst thou demand thy share of the spoils, a Scythian bow or a belt won from the Geloni, a Dacian spear or Suabian bridle. Often would he smile on thee and uplift thee, eager for the honour, on his shining shield, and clasp thee to his still panting bosom. Thou fearedst not his coat of mail nor the dread gleam of his helmet but stretchedst out thy hands to grasp its lofty plumes. Then in his joy thy father cried: " King of starry Olympus, may this my son return in like manner from the lands of conquered foes, rich with the spoils of Hyrcania or proud with the slaughter of the Assyrians ; his sword thus red with blood, his countenance thus roughened by the constant blasts and stained with the welcome dust of heroic combat, may he bring back to his happy father the arms of his conquered foes."

Soon when thou couldst stand upright and walk with firm step thy sire forbade thee enervating sloth, luxurious ease, time-wasting slumbers. He strengthened thy young limbs with hard toils and rude was the training wherewith he exercised thy tender powers. Thou wert taught to bear winter's cruel cold, to shrink not before storm and tempest, to face the heat of summer, to swim across loud-roaring torrents, to

planitiem cursu, valles et concava saltu,
nec non in clipeo vigiles producere noctes,
in galea potare nives, nunc spicula cornu
tendere, nunc glandes Baleari spargere funda.　50
quoque magis nimium pugnae inflammaret amorem,
facta tui numerabat avi, quem litus adustae
horrescit Libyae ratibusque impervia Thule :
ille leves Mauros nec falso nomine Pictos
edomuit Scottumque vago mucrone secutus　55
fregit Hyperboreas remis audacibus undas
et geminis fulgens utroque sub axe tropacis
Tethyos alternae refluas calcavit harenas.
hos tibi virtutum stimulos, haec semina laudum,
haec exempla dabat.　non ocius hausit Achilles　60
semiferi praecepta senis, seu cuspidis artes
sive lyrae cantus medicas seu disceret herbas.

　Interea turbata fides.　civilia rursus
bella tonant dubiumque quatit discordia mundum.
pro crimen superum, longi pro dedecus aevi :　65
barbarus Hesperias exul possederat urbes
sceptraque deiecto dederat Romana clienti.
iam princeps molitur iter gentesque remotas
colligit Aurorae, tumidus quascumque pererrat　69
Euphrates, quas lustrat Halys, quas ditat Orontes ;
turiferos Arabes saltus, vada Caspia Medi,
Armenii Phasin, Parthi liquere Niphaten.

　Quae tibi tum Martis rabies quantusque sequendi
ardor erat ?　quanto flagrabant pectora voto

---

[1] Pict, to a Roman, means " painted." They were " well-named Picts " because they painted themselves with woad or other stain.

[2] Arbogast is the " barbarian," Eugenius (by trade a rhetorician) the " dependent."　See Introduction, p. ix.

climb mountains, to run o'er the plain, to leap ravines and hollows, to spend sleepless nights of watching under arms, to drink melted snow from thy casque, to shoot the arrow from the bow or hurl the acorn-missiles with a Balearic sling. And the more to inflame thy heart with love of battle he would recount to thee the deeds of thy grandsire, object of dread to Libya's sun-scorched shores and Thule whither no ship can sail. He conquered the fleet Moors and the well-named [1] Picts; his roaming sword pursued the flying Scot; his adventurous oars broke the surface of the northern seas. Crowned with the spoils of triumphs won beneath the northern and the southern sky he trod the wave-swept strand of either Ocean. Thus did he spur thy courage, thus sow the seeds of fame; these were the examples he gave. Not more avidly did Achilles himself drink in the Centaur's precepts when he learnt of him how to wield the spear or play the lyre or discern healing plants.

Meanwhile the world forgot its loyalty: the thunder of civil war sounded afresh and discord shook the tottering earth. O ye guilty gods! O shame everlasting!—a barbarian [2] exile had possessed himself of the cities of Italy and had entrusted the government of Rome to some low-born dependent. But Theodosius was already afoot, rallying to his standard the distant nations of the East, the dwellers on the banks of flooding Euphrates, clear Halys, and rich Orontes. The Arabs left their spicy groves, the Medes the waters of the Caspian Sea, the Armenians the river Phasis, the Parthians the Niphates.

What lust of battle then filled thy heart, what longing to accompany thy father! What would not

275

optatas audire tubas campique cruenta   75
tempestate frui truncisque inmergere plantas ?
ut leo, quem fulvae matris spelunca tegebat
uberibus solitum pasci, cum crescere sensit
ungue pedes et terga iubis et dentibus ora,
iam negat imbelles epulas et rupe relicta   80
Gaetulo comes ire patri stabulisque minari
aestuat et celsi tabo sordere iuvenci.
ille vetat rerumque tibi commendat habenas
et sacro meritos ornat diademate crines.
tantaque se rudibus pietas ostendit in annis,   85
sic aetas animo cessit, quererentur ut omnes
imperium tibi sero datum.
                                        Victoria velox
auspiciis effecta tuis.   Pugnastis uterque :
tu fatis genitorque manu.   te propter et Alpes
invadi faciles cauto nec profuit hosti   90
munitis haesisse locis : spes inrita valli
concidit et scopulis patuerunt claustra revulsis.
te propter gelidis Aquilo de monte procellis
obruit adversas acies revolutaque tela
vertit in auctores et turbine reppulit hastas   95
o nimium dilecte deo, cui fundit ab antris
Aeolus armatas hiemes, cui militat aether
et coniurati veniunt ad classica venti.
Alpinae rubuere nives, et Frigidus amnis

thine eager spirit have given to hear the beloved
clarion's note and to revel in the bloody storm of
battle, trampling upon the slaughtered bodies of thy
foes! Like a young lion in a cave, accustomed to look
for nourishment to the teats of its tawny mother,
who, so soon as he finds talons beginning to grow
from out his paws and a mane sprout from his neck
and teeth arm his jaws, will have none of this in-
glorious food but burns to leave his cavern home and
accompany his Gaetulian sire, to bring death upon
the herds and steep him in the gore of some tall
steer. But Theodosius said thee nay, and put
the reins of government into thy hands, crowning
thy head with the sacred diadem it wore so meetly.
And so did thy virtue show in earliest years, so did
thy soul out-range thy youth that all complained
that to thee empire was granted late.

Swiftly beneath thy auspices was victory achieved.
Both fought for us—thou with thy happy influence,
thy father with his strong right arm. Thanks to thee
the Alps lay open to our armies, nor did it avail
the careful foe to cling to fortified posts. Their
ramparts, and the trust they put therein, fell; the
rocks were torn away and their hiding-places exposed.
Thanks to thine influence the wind of the frozen North
overwhelmed the enemy's line with his mountain
storms, hurled back their weapons upon the throwers
and with the violence of his tempest drove back their
spears. Verily God is with thee, when at thy behest
Aeolus frees the armèd tempests from his cave, when
the very elements fight for thee and the allied winds
come at the call of thy trumpets. The Alpine snows
grew red with slaughter, the cold Frigidus, its waters
turned to blood, ran hot and steaming, and would

mutatis fumavit aquis turbaque cadentum   100
staret, ni rapidus iuvisset flumina sanguis.
    At ferus inventor scelerum traiecerat altum
non uno mucrone latus, duplexque tepebat
ensis, et ultrices in se converterat iras
tandem iusta manus. iam libertate reducta,   105
quamvis emeritum peteret natura reverti
numen et auratas astrorum panderet arces
nutaretque oneris venturi conscius Atlas,
distulit Augustus cupido se credere caelo,
dum tibi pacatum praesenti traderet orbem.   110
nec mora : Bistoniis alacer consurgis ab oris,
inter barbaricas ausus transire cohortes
impavido vultu ; linquis Rhodopeia saxa
Orpheis animata modis ; iuga deseris Oetes
Herculeo damnata rogo ; post Pelion intras   115
Nereis inlustre toris ; te pulcher Enipeus
celsaque Dodone stupuit rursusque locutae
in te Chaoniae moverunt carmina quercus.
Illyrici legitur plaga litoris ; arva teruntur
Dalmatiae ; Phrygii numerantur stagna Timavi. 120
gaudent Italiae sublimibus oppida muris
adventu sacrata tuo, summissus adorat
Eridanus blandosque iubet mitescere fluctus
et Phaëthonteas solitae deflere ruinas
roscida frondosae revocant electra sorores.   125
    Quanti tum iuvenes, quantae sprevere pudorem
spectandi studio matres, puerisque severi

---

¹ This is obscure. Zosimus (iv. 58. 6) and Socrates (v. 25)
merely mention suicide, but from Claudian's account it looks
as though, like Nero, Arbogast's courage had failed him and
an attendant had had to help him to his death.
    ² The Fons Timavi (near Aquileia and the river Frigidus)
is called Trojan from the story of the colonization of Venetia
by the Trojan Antenor (Livy i. 1. 3).

have been choked with the heaps of corpses had not their own fast-flowing gore helped on its course.

Meanwhile Arbogast, the cause of this wicked war, had pierced his side deep not with a single blade: two swords [1] reeked with his blood, and his own hand, learning justice at last, had turned its savage fury against himself. Thus was liberty restored; but though Nature demanded the return to heaven of divine Theodosius whose work was now accomplished, though the sky threw open the golden palaces of its starry vault and Atlas staggered knowing the burden he was to bear, yet did the emperor forbear to entrust him to expectant Olympus until he could in thy presence hand over to thee a world at peace. Straightway didst thou, Honorius, leave the coasts of Thrace, and, braving the dangers of the journey, pass without a tremor through the hordes of barbarians. Thou leavest the rocks of Rhodope to which Orpheus' lyre gave life; thou quittest the heights of Oeta, scene of Hercules' ill-omened funeral pyre; next thou climbest Pelion, famed for the marriage of Peleus and Thetis. Fair Enipeus and lofty Dodona look upon thee in amaze, and the oaks of Chaonia, finding tongues once more, utter oracles in thine honour. Thou skirtest the extreme coasts of Illyria and, passing over Dalmatia's fields, dost cross in turn the nine sources of Trojan Timavus.[2] The high-walled cities of Italy rejoice in the blessings of thy presence. Eridanus bows his head and worships, bidding his waves flow gently to the sea; and Phaëthon's leafy sisters, that ever weep their brother's death, check the flow of their dewy amber.

How many youths, how many matrons set modesty aside in eagerness to behold thee! Austere grey-

certavere senes, cum tu genitoris amico
exceptus gremio mediam veherere per urbem
velaretque pios communis laurea currus !　　130
quis non Luciferum roseo cum Sole videri
credidit aut iunctum Bromio radiare Tonantem ?
floret cristatis exercitus undique turmis,
quisque sua te voce canens.　praestringit aena
lux oculos, nudique seges Mavortia ferri　　135
ingeminat splendore diem.　pars nobilis arcu,
pars longe iaculis, pars comminus horrida contis ;
hi volucres tollunt aquilas, hi picta draconum
colla levant, multusque tumet per nubila serpens
iratus stimulante Noto vivitque receptis　　140
flatibus et vario mentitur sibila tractu.

　Ut ventum ad sedes, cunctos discedere tectis
dux iubet et generum compellat talibus ultro :
" bellipotens Stilicho, cuius mihi robur in armis,
pace probata fides : quid enim per proelia gessi　145
te sine ? quem merui te non sudante triumphum ?
Odrysium pariter Getico foedavimus Hebrum
sanguine, Sarmaticas pariter prostravimus alas
Riphaeaque simul fessos porreximus artus
in glacie stantemque rota sulcavimus Histrum :　150
ergo age, me quoniam caelestis regia poscit,
tu curis succede meis, tu pignora solus
nostra fove : geminos dextra tu protege fratres.
280

beards struggle with boys for places whence to see
thee in the tender embraces of thy sire, borne
through the midst of Rome on a triumphal chariot
decked but with the shade of a simple laurel branch.
Who did not then think that he beheld the morning-
star together with the rosy sun, or the Thunderer
shine in concert with Bacchus? On every side
stretches the host of plumed warriors, each hymning
thy praises in his own tongue; the brightness of
bronze dazzles the eye and the martial glint of a
forest of unsheathed swords redoubles the light
of day. Some are decked with bows, others bristle
with far-flung javelins or pikes for fighting at close
quarters. These raise standards adorned with
flying eagles, or with embroidered dragons or
writhing serpents, that in their thousands seem to be
roused to angry life by the breath of the wind which,
as it blows them this way and that, causes them
to rustle with a sound like the hiss of a living snake.

When they reached the palace the emperor bade
all depart and thus unbidden addressed his son-in-
law: "Victorious Stilicho, of whose courage in
war, of whose loyalty in peace I have made proof
— what warlike feat have I performed without
thine aid? What triumph have I won that thou
helpedst me not in the winning? Together we
caused Thracian Hebrus to run red with Getic blood,
together overthrew the squadrons of the Sarmatae,
together rested our weary limbs on the snows of
Mount Riphaeus and scarred the frozen Danube
with our chariot's wheel—come, therefore, since
heaven's halls claim me, do thou take up my
task; be thou sole guardian of my children, let
thy hand protect my two sons. I adjure thee by

281

per consanguineos thalamos noctemque beatam,
per taedas, quas ipsa tuo regina levavit   155
coniugio sociaque nurum produxit ab aula,
indue mente patrem, crescentes dilige fetus
ut ducis, ut soceri.   Iamiam securus ad astra
te custode ferar ; rupta si mole Typhoeus
prosiliat, vinclis Tityos si membra resolvat,   160
si furor Enceladi proiecta mugiat Aetna,
opposito Stilichone cadent."
                              Nec plura locutus,
sicut erat, liquido signavit tramite nubes
ingrediturque globum Lunae limenque relinquit
Arcados et Veneris clementes advolat auras.   165
hinc Phoebi permensus iter flammamque nocentem
Gradivi placidumque Iovem ; stetit arce suprema,
algenti qua zona riget Saturnia tractu.
machina laxatur caeli rutilaeque patescunt
sponte fores.   Arctoa parat convexa Bootes,   170
australes reserat portas succinctus Orion
invitantque novum sidus, pendentque vicissim
quas partes velit ipse sequi, quibus esse sodalis
dignetur stellis aut qua regione morari.
o decus aetherium, terrarum gloria quondam,   175
te tuus Oceanus natali gurgite lassum
excipit et notis Hispania proluit undis.
fortunate parens, primos cum detegis ortus,
adspicis Arcadium ; cum te proclivior urges,
occiduum visus remoratur Honorius ignem ;   180
et quocumque vagos flectas sub cardine cursus,

that marriage that makes thee kin with me, by the
night that saw its consummation, by the torch
which at thy wedding-feast the queen carried in
her own hand when she led thy bride-elect from out
the imperial palace, take on thee a father's spirit,
guard the years of their childhood. Was not their sire
thy master and thy wife's father? Now, now I shall
mount untroubled to the stars for thou wilt watch over
them. Even should Typhoeus rend away the rocks
and leap forth, should Tityus free his captive limbs,
should Enceladus, hurling Etna from him, roar in
rage—each and all will fall before Stilicho's attack."

He spake no more but still in human form clove
a furrow of light through the clouds; he passes
to Luna's globe, leaves Mercury's threshold and
hastens to the gentle airs of Venus. Hence he tra-
verses Phoebus' path, Mars' baleful fires and Jupiter's
quiet quarters, and stands upon the very crown of
the sky, cold Saturn's frozen zone. Heaven's fabric
opens, unbidden the shining doors swing back.
Boötes prepares a place in the vault of the northern
sky, sword-girt Orion unbars the portals of the south;
they offer welcome to the new star, uncertain
each in turn to what region he will betake himself,
what constellation he will grace with his presence,
or in what quarter he will elect to shine alone.
O glory of heaven as once thou wert of earth, the
ocean that laves the shores of the land of thy birth
receives thee wearied with thy nightly course, Spain
bathes thee in thy natal waves. Happy father, when
first thou risest above the horizon thou lookest upon
Arcadius, when thou dippest to thy setting the sight
of Honorius delays thy westering fires. Through
whichever hemisphere thou takest thy wandering

natorum per regna venis, qui mente serena
maturoque regunt iunctas moderamine gentes,
saecula qui rursus formant meliore metallo.
luget Avarities Stygiis innexa catenis   185
cumque suo demens expellitur Ambitus auro.
non dominantur opes nec corrumpentia sensus
dona valent : emitur sola virtute potestas.

    Unanimi fratres, quorum mare terraque fatis
debetur, quodcumque manus evasit avitas,   190
quod superest patri : vobis iam Mulciber arma
praeparat et Sicula Cyclops incude laborat,
Brontes innumeris exasperat aegida signis,
altum fulminea crispare in casside conum
festinat Steropes, nectit thoraca Pyragmon   195
ignifluisque gemit Lipare fumosa cavernis.
vobis Ionia virides Neptunus in alga
nutrit equos, qui summa freti per caerula possint
ferre viam segetemque levi percurrere motu,
nesciat ut spumas nec proterat ungula culmos.   200
iam video Babylona rapi Parthumque coactum
non ficta trepidare fuga, iam Bactra teneri
legibus et famulis Gangen pallescere ripis
gemmatosque humilem dispergere Persida cultus.
ite per extremum Tanaim pigrosque Triones,   205
ite per ardentem Libyam, superate vapores
solis et arcanos Nili deprendite fontes,
Herculeum finem, Bacchi transcurrite metas :
vestri iuris erit, quidquid complectitur axis.
vobis Rubra dabunt pretiosas aequora conchas,   210
Indus ebur, ramos Panchaia, vellera Seres.

journey, thou passest over the domains of sons who with tranquil mind and ripe control rule over allied peoples, who once again fashion the ages from a nobler ore. Avarice is left to weep in Stygian chains, mad Ambition and his gold banished afar. Wealth does not hold sway ; sense-corrupting gifts are of no avail ; virtue alone can purchase power.

Brothers twain, with the heart of one, brothers to whose rule fate has entrusted sea and land, if there is aught that has escaped your grandsire's conquering hand, aught your father has left unsubdued, even now Vulcan prepares the arms for their subjection and Cyclops labours on the Sicilian anvil. Brontes carves countless figures on the shield, Steropes hastes to bend the lofty peak of the flashing helmet, Pyragmon knits the coat of mail, smoky Lipare roars throughout its fire-belching caves. 'Tis for you that Neptune pastures in the sea-weed meadows of the Ionian main green sea-horses who can fly o'er the surface of the blue waters with so light a step that their hoofs are unflecked with foam, and course o'er fields of corn so delicately that the ears do not bend beneath their weight. E'en now I see the sack of Babylon and the Parthian driven to flight that is not feigned, Bactria subjected to the Law, the fearful pallor of the Ganges' servile banks, the humbled Persian throwing off his gem-encrusted robes. Mount to Tanais' source, explore the frozen North, traverse sun-scorched Libya, o'ercome the fires of Titan and surprise Nile's hidden spring ; pass the Pillars of Hercules, the bourne, too, whence Bacchus returned ; whatever heaven enfolds shall own your dominion. To you the Red Sea shall give precious shells, India her ivory, Panchaia perfumes, and China silk.

285

PANEGYRICUS
DE QUARTO CONSULATU HONORII AUGUSTI

(VIII.)

Auspiciis iterum sese regalibus annus
induit et nota fruitur iactantior aula,
limina nec passi circum privata morari
exultant reduces Augusto consule fasces.
cernis ut armorum proceres legumque potentes   5
patricios sumant¹ habitus? et more Gabino
discolor incedit legio positisque parumper
bellorum signis sequitur vexilla Quirini.
lictori cedunt aquilae ridetque togatus
miles et in mediis effulget curia castris.   10
ipsa Palatino circumvallata senatu
iam trabeam Bellona gerit parmamque removit
et galeam sacras umeris vectura curules.
nec te laurigeras pudeat, Gradive, secures
pacata gestare manu Latiaque micantem   15
loricam mutare toga, dum ferreus haeret
currus et Eridani ludunt per prata iugales.
   Haud indigna coli nec nuper cognita Marti
Ulpia progenies et quae diademata mundo
sparsit Hibera domus. nec tantam vilior unda   20

---

¹ sumant *B; Birt reads* sumunt, *following the other* MSS.

---

¹ As marking a festival; see note on vii. 3.

286

PANEGYRIC ON THE FOURTH CONSULSHIP OF THE EMPEROR HONORIUS (A.D. 398)

(VIII)

Once more the year opens under royal auspices and enjoys in fuller pride its famous prince; not brooking to linger around private thresholds the returning fasces rejoice in Caesar's consulship Seest thou how the armed chiefs and mighty judges don the raiment of senators? and the soldiers step forth in garb of peaceful hue worn Gabine [1] wise, and laying aside for a season the standards of war follow the banner of Quirinus. The eagles give way to the lictors, the smiling soldier wears the toga of peace and the senate-house casts its brilliance in the midst of the camp. Bellona herself, surrounded by a noble band of senators, puts on the consul's gown and lays by her shield and helmet in order to harness the sacred curule chair to her shoulders. Think it no shame, Gradivus, to bear the laurel-crowned axes in a hand of peace and to exchange thy shining breastplate for the Latin toga while thine iron chariot remains unused and thy steeds disport them in the pastures of Eridanus.

Not unworthy of reverence nor but newly acquainted with war is the family of Trajan and that Spanish house which has showered diadems upon the world. No common stream was held worthy

promeruit gentis seriem : cunabula fovit
Oceanus ; terrae dominos pelagique futuros
inmenso decuit rerum de principe nasci.
hinc processit avus, cui post Arctoa frementi
classica Massylas adnexuit Africa laurus,   25
ille, Caledoniis posuit qui castra pruinis,
qui medios Libyae sub casside pertulit aestus,
terribilis Mauro debellatorque Britanni
litoris ac pariter Boreae vastator et Austri.
quid rigor aeternus, caeli quid frigora prosunt   30
ignotumque fretum ?   maduerunt Saxone fuso
Orcades ; incaluit Pictorum sanguine Thyle ;
Scottorum cumulos flevit glacialis Hiverne.
quid calor obsistit forti ?   per vasta cucurrit
Aethiopum cinxitque novis Atlanta maniplis,   35
virgineum Tritona bibit sparsosque venenis
Gorgoneos vidit thalamos et vile virentes
Hesperidum risit, quos ditat fabula, ramos.
arx incensa Iubae, rabies Maurusia ferro
cessit et antiqui penetralia diruta Bocchi.   40

  Sed laudes genitor longe transgressus avitas
subdidit Oceanum sceptris et margine caeli
clausit opes, quantum distant a Tigride Gades,
inter se Tanais quantum Nilusque relinquunt :
haec tamen innumeris per se quaesita tropaeis,   45

---

[1] Claudian is thinking of such passages in Homer as *e.g.*
Il. xiv. 245-246 :

$$\rho\acute{\epsilon}\epsilon\theta\rho\alpha$$
Ὠκεανοῦ, ὅς περ γένεσις πάντεσσι τέτυκται,

or perhaps Vergil's *Oceanumque patrem rerum* (Virg. *Georg.*
iv. 382).
288

to water the homeland of so illustrious a race;
Ocean laved their cradle, for it befitted the future
lords of earth and sea to have their origin in the
great father [1] of all things.   Hence came Theodosius,
grandfather of Honorius, for whom, exultant after
his northern victories, Africa twined fresh laurels
won from the Massylae.   'Twas he who pitched his
camp amid the snows of Caledonia,[2] who never
doffed his helmet for all the heat of a Libyan summer,
who struck terror into the Moors, brought into
subjection the coasts of Britain and with equal
success laid waste the north and the south.   What
avail against him the eternal snows, the frozen air,
the uncharted sea?   The Orcades ran red with
Saxon slaughter; Thule was warm with the blood
of Picts; ice-bound Hibernia wept for the heaps
of slain Scots.   Could heat stay the advance of a
courageous general?   No; he overran the deserts
of Ethiopia, invested Atlas with troops strange to
him, drank of lake Triton where was born the virgin
goddess Minerva, beheld the Gorgon's empoisoned
lair, and laughed to see the common verdure of
those gardens of the Hesperides which story had
clothed with gold. Juba's fortress was burned
down, the frenzied valour of the Moor yielded to
the sword and the palace of ancient Bocchus was
razed to the ground.

But thy father's fame far surpassed that of thy
grandsire: he subdued Ocean to his governance
and set the sky for border to his kingdom, ruling
from Gades to the Tigris, and all that lies 'twixt
Tanais and Nile; yet all these lands won by count-
less triumphs of his own, he gained them not by gift

[2] *Cf.* note on xv. 216.

non generis dono, non ambitione potitus.
digna legi virtus. ultro se purpura supplex
obtulit et solus meruit regnare rogatus.
nam cum barbaries penitus commota gementem
inrueret Rhodopen et mixto turbine gentes   50
iam deserta suas in nos transfunderet Arctos,
Danuvii totae vomerent cum proelia ripae,
cum Geticis ingens premeretur Mysia plaustris
flavaque Bistonios operirent agmina campos,
omnibus adflictis et vel labentibus ictu   55
vel prope casuris : unus tot funera contra
restitit extinxitque faces agrisque colonos
reddidit et leti rapuit de faucibus urbes.
nulla relicta foret Romani nominis umbra,
ni pater ille tuus iamiam ruitura subisset   60
pondera turbatamque ratem certaque levasset
naufragium commune manu : velut ordine rupto
cum procul insanae traherent Phaëthonta quadrigae
saeviretque dies terramque et stagna propinqui
haurirent radii, solito cum murmure torvis   65
sol occurrit equis ; qui postquam rursus eriles
agnovere sonos, rediit meliore magistro
machina concentusque poli, currusque recepit
imperium flammaeque modum.
                              Sic traditus ille
servatusque Oriens. at non pars altera rerum   70
tradita : bis possessa manu, bis parta periclis.
per varium gemini scelus erupere tyranni
tractibus occiduis : hunc saeva Britannia fudit ;

of birth or from lust of power. It was his own
merit secured his election. Unsought the purple
begged his acceptance of itself; he alone when asked
to rule was worthy to do so. For when unrest at
home drove barbarian hordes over unhappy Rhodope
and the now deserted north had poured its tribes
in wild confusion across our borders, when all the
banks of Danube poured forth battles and broad
Mysia rang beneath the chariots of the Getae, when
flaxen-haired hordes covered the plains of Thrace and
amid this universal ruin all was either prostrate or
tottering to its fall, one man alone withstood the tide
of disaster, quenched the flames, restored to the
husbandmen their fields and snatched the cities
from the very jaws of destruction. No shadow of
Rome's name had survived had not thy sire borne
up the tottering mass, succoured the storm-tossed
bark and with sure hand averted universal ship-
wreck. As when the maddened coursers broke from
their path and carried Phaëthon far astray, when
day's heat grew fierce and the sun's rays, brought
near to earth, dried up both land and sea, Phoebus
checked his fierce horses with his wonted voice;
for they knew once more their master's tones, and
with a happier guide heaven's harmonious order was
restored; for now the chariot again accepted govern-
ment and its fires control.

Thus was the East entrusted to him and thus was
its salvation assured; but the other half of the
world was not so entrusted: twice was the West
gained by valour, twice won by dangers. In those
lands of the sunset by manifold crime there arose
to power tyrants twain: wild Britain produced
one (Maximus), the other (Eugenius) was chosen

hunc sibi Germanus famulum delegerat exul :
ausus uterque nefas, domini respersus uterque   75
ınsontis iugulo.   novitas audere priori
suadebat cautumque dabant exempla sequentem.
hic nova moliri praeceps, hic quaerere tuta
providus ; hic fusis, collectis viribus ille ;
hic vagus excurrens, hic intra claustra reductus.   80
dissimiles, sed morte pares.   evadere neutri
dedecus aut mixtis licuit procumbere telis.
amissa specie, raptis insignibus ambo
in vultus rediere suos manibusque revinctis
oblati gladiis summittunt colla paratis   85
et vitam veniamque rogant.   pro damna pudoris !
qui modo tam densas nutu movere cohortes,
in quos iam dubius sese libraverat orbis,
non hostes victore cadunt, sed iudice sontes ;
damnat voce reos, petiit quos Marte tyrannos.   90
amborum periere duces : hic sponte carina
decidit in fluctus, illum suus abstulit ensis ;
hunc Alpes, hunc pontus habet.   solacia caesis
fratribus haec ultor tribuit : necis auctor uterque
labitur ; Augustas par victima mitigat umbras.   95
has dedit inferias tumulis, iuvenumque duorum
purpureos merito placavit sanguine manes.
    Illi iustitiam confirmavere triumphi,

---

[1] Maximus was responsible for the murder of the Emperor Gratian, Eugenius for that of Valentinian II. See Introduction, p. viii.

as a tool by a Frankish outlaw (Arbogast). Both
dared monstrous guilt; both stained their hands with
an innocent emperor's[1] blood. Sudden elevation
inspired Maximus with audacity, his failure taught
his successor caution. Maximus was quick to arm
rebellion, Eugenius careful to attempt only what
was safe. The one o'erran the country, spreading
his forces in all directions, the other kept his troops
together and himself secure behind a rampart.
Different were they, but in their deaths alike. To
neither was it granted to escape an ignominious end
and to fall in the thick of the fight. Gone was their
glory, their weapons were reft from them and they
reduced to their former state; their arms were
bound behind their backs and they stretched forth
their necks to the sword's imminent stroke, begging
for pardon and for life. What a fall did pride there
suffer! They who but lately had moved such
countless cohorts with but a nod, into whose palm
a wavering world had hung ready to drop, fall
not as warriors at a victor's hand but as malefactors
before a judge; he sentences with his voice as
criminals those whom he assailed in war as tyrants.
With both perished their lieutenants: Andragathius
hurled himself from his ship into the waves, Arbo-
gast took his life with his own sword; the Alps
mark the tomb of the one, the sea of the other.
This solace at least the avenger afforded to those mur-
dered brothers that both the authors of their deaths
themselves were slain; two victims went to appease
those royal ghosts. Such was Theodosius' oblation
at their tomb and with the blood of the guilty he
appeased the shades of the two young emperors.

Those triumphs stablished Justice on her throne

praesentes docuere deos. hinc saecula discant
indomitum nihil esse pio tutumve nocenti :　　100
nuntius ipse sui longas incognitus egit
praevento rumore vias, inopinus utrumque
perculit et clausos montes, ut plana, reliquit.
extruite inmanes scopulos, attollite turres,
cingite vos fluviis, vastas opponite silvas,　　105
Garganum Alpinis Appenninumque nivalem
permixtis sociate iugis et rupibus Haemum
addite Caucasiis, involvite Pelion Ossae :
non dabitis murum sceleri. qui vindicet, ibit :
omnia subsident meliori pervia causae.　　110

Nec tamen oblitus civem cedentibus atrox
partibus infremuit ; non insultare iacenti
malebat : mitis precibus, pietatis abundans,
poenae parcus erat ; paci non intulit iram ;
post acies odiis idem qui terminus armis.　　115
profuit hoc vincente capi, multosque subactos
prospera[1] laturae commendavere catenae.
magnarum largitor opum, largitor honorum
pronus et in melius gaudens convertere fata.
hinc amor, hinc validum devoto milite robur.　　120
hinc natis mansura fides.

　　　　　　　　　　Hoc nobilis ortu
nasceris aequaeva cum maiestate creatus
nullaque privatae passus contagia sortis.
omnibus acceptis ultro te regia solum
protulit et patrio felix adolescis in ostro,　　125

---

[1] *Birt, with the* MSS., aspera; *I return to the* prospera
of the edit. princeps.

---

[1] *i.e.* by winning first the pity and then the favour of
Theodosius.
[2] "Only," because Arcadius was born *before* Theodosius
became emperor.

and taught that heaven gives help. From them
let the ages learn that righteousness need fear no
foe and guilt expect no safety. Himself his own
messenger, outstripping the rumour of his approach,
Theodosius traversed those long journeys undetected
by his enemies. Suddenly he fell on both, passing
over entrenched mountains as if they were a plain.
Build up monstrous rocks, raise towers, surround
yourselves with rivers, set limitless forests to protect
you, put Garganus and the snowy Apennines upon
the summits of the Alps that all form one vast moun-
tain barrier, plant Haemus on the crags of Caucasus,
roll Pelion on Ossa, yet will ye not gain security
for guilt. The avenger will come ; for the better
cause all things shall sink to make a path.

Yet never did Theodosius forget that he and
the vanquished were fellow-citizens, nor was his
anger implacable against those who yielded. Not
his the choice to exult over the fallen. His ears
were open to prayers, his clemency unbounded, his
vengeance restrained. His anger did not survive
the war to darken the days of peace ; the day that
set an end to the combat set an end to his wrath.
Capture by such a victor was a gain ; and many a
conquered foe did their chains commend to future
fortune.[1] As liberal of money as of honours he
was ever bent to redress the injuries of fate.
Hence the love, the fortitude, the devotion of his
troops ; hence their abiding loyalty to his sons.

Child of so noble a sire, thy kingly state was
coëval with thy birth nor ever knewest thou the
soilure of a private lot. To thee all things came
unsought ; thee only [2] did a palace rear ; thy happy
growth was in ancestral purple, and thy limbs, never

membraque vestitu numquam violata profano
in sacros cecidere sinus.   Hispania patrem
auriferis eduxit aquis, te gaudet alumno
Bosphorus.   Hesperio de limine surgit origo,
sed nutrix Aurora tibi ; pro pignore tanto   130
certatur, geminus civem te vindicat axis.
Herculis et Bromii sustentat gloria Thebas,
haesit Apollineo Delos Latonia partu
Cretaque se iactat tenero reptata Tonanti ;
sed melior Delo, Dictaeis clarior oris   135
quae dedit hoc numen regio ; non litora nostro
sufficerent angusta deo.   nec inhospita Cynthi
saxa tuos artus duro laesere cubili :
adclinis genetrix auro, circumflua gemmis
in Tyrios enixa toros ; ululata verendis   140
aula puerperiis.   quae tunc documenta futuri ?
quae voces avium ?   quanti per inane volatus ?
qui vatum discursus erat ?   tibi corniger Hammon
et dudum taciti rupere silentia Delphi,
te Persae cecinere magi, te sensit Etruscus   145
augur et inspectis Babylonius horruit astris,
Chaldaei stupuere senes Cumanaque rursus
intonuit rupes, rabidae delubra Sibyllae.
nec te progenitum Cybeleius aere sonoro
lustravit Corybas : exercitus undique fulgens   150
adstitit ; ambitur signis augustior infans,
sentit adorantes galeas, redditque ferocem
vagitum lituus.

> Vitam tibi contulit idem

outraged by garb profane, were laid upon a hallowed lap. Spain with its rivers of gold gave birth to thy sire ; Bosporus boasts thee among its children. The West is the cradle of thy race but the East was thine own nurse ; rivals are they for so dear a pledge, either hemisphere claims thee as its citizen. The fame of Hercules and Bacchus has immortalized Thebes ; when Latona gave birth to Apollo in Delos that island stayed its errant course ; it is Crete's boast that over its fields the infant Thunderer crawled. But the land that brought divine Honorius to birth is a greater than Delos, a more famous than Crete. Such narrow shores would not suffice our god. Nor did the bleak rocks of Cynthus hurt thy body with their rough bed ; on couch of gold, clothed in jewelled raiment, thy mother gave birth to thee amid Tyrian purples ; a palace rang with joy at that royal deliverance. What presages were there not then of future prosperity ? what songs of birds, what flights of good omen in the heavens ? What was the hurrying to and fro of seers ? Hornèd Ammon and Delphi so long dumb at length broke their silence; Persian magi prophesied thy triumphs; Tuscan augurs felt thine influence ; seers of Babylon beheld the stars and trembled ; amazement seized the Chaldaean priests ; the rock of Cumae, shrine of raging Sibyl, thundered once again. Cybele's corybants surrounded not thy cradle with the clatter of their brazen shields; a shining host stood by thee on every side. Standards of war hedged in the royal babe who marked the bowed helmets of the worshipping soldiery while the trumpet's blare answered his warlike cries.

The day that gave thee birth gave thee a kingdom ;

imperiumque dies ; inter cunabula consul
proveheris, signas posito modo nomine fastos   155
donaturque tibi, qui te produxerat, annus.
ipsa Quirinali parvum te cinxit amictu
mater et ad primas docuit reptare curules.
uberibus sanctis inmortalique dearum
crescis adoratus gremio : tibi saepe Diana   160
Maenalios arcus venatricesque pharetras
suspendit, puerile decus ; tu saepe Minervae
lusisti clipeo fulvamque impune pererrans
aegida tractasti blandos interritus angues ;
saepe tuas etiam iam tum gaudente marito   165
velavit regina comas festinaque voti
praesumptum diadema dedit, tum lenibus ulnis
sustulit et magno porrexit ad oscula patri.
nec dilatus honos : mutatur principe Caesar ;
protinus aequaris fratri.   170
                           Non certius umquam
hortati superi, nullis praesentior aether
adfuit ominibus.   tenebris involverat atra
lumen hiems densosque Notus collegerat imbres.
sed mox, cum solita miles te voce levasset,
nubila dissolvit Phoebus pariterque dabantur   175
sceptra tibi mundoque dies : caligine liber
Bosphorus adversam patitur Calchedona cerni.
nec tantum vicina nitent, sed tota repulsis
nubibus exuitur Thrace, Pangaea renident
insuetosque palus radios Maeotia vibrat.   180

---

[1] Honorius, who was born Sept. 9, 384, was made consul
for 386.

[2] Arcadius was made Augustus Jan. 16 (? 19), 383 :
Honorius not till Nov. 20, 393.   Both succeeded to the throne
Jan. 17, 395.

in thy cradle thou wast raised to the consulship.[1] With the name so recently bestowed upon thee thou dowerest the fasti and the year wherein thou wert born is consecrated to thee. Thy mother herself wrapped thy small form in the consular robe and directed thy first steps to the curule chair. Nourished at a goddess' breasts, honoured with the embraces of immortal arms thou grewest to maturity. Oft to grace thy boyish form Diana hung upon thy shoulders her Maenalian bow and huntress' quiver; oft thou didst sport with Minerva's shield and, crawling unharmed over her glittering aegis, didst caress its friendly serpents with fearless hand. Often even in those early days thy mother beneath thy sire's happy gaze crowned thy tender locks and, anticipating the answer to her prayers, gave thee the diadem that was to be thine hereafter; then raising thee in her gentle arms she held thee up to receive thy mighty father's kiss. Nor was that honour long in coming; thou, then Caesar, didst become emperor and wert straightway made equal with thy brother.[2]

Never was the encouragement of the gods more sure, never did heaven attend with more favouring omens. Black tempest had shrouded the light in darkness and the south wind gathered thick rain-clouds, when of a sudden, so soon as the soldiers had borne thee aloft with customary shout, Phoebus scattered the clouds and at the same moment was given to thee the sceptre, to the world light. Bosporus, freed from clouds, permits a sight of Chalcedon on the farther shore; nor is it only the vicinity of Byzantium that is bathed in brightness; the clouds are driven back and all Thrace is cleared; Pangaeus shows afar and lake Maeotis makes quiver the rays he

nec Boreas nimbos aut sol ardentior egit :
imperii lux illa fuit ; praesagus obibat
cuncta nitor risitque tuo natura sereno.
visa etiam medio populis mirantibus audax
stella die, dubitanda nihil nec crine retuso   185
languida, sed quantus numeratur nocte Bootes,
emicuitque plagis alieni temporis hospes
ignis et agnosci potuit, cum luna lateret :
sive parens Augusta fuit, seu forte reluxit
divi sidus avi, seu te properantibus astris   190
cernere sol patiens caelum commune remisit.
adparet quid signa ferant.   ventura potestas
claruit Ascanio, subita cum luce comarum
innocuus flagraret apex Phrygioque volutus
vertice fatalis redimiret tempora candor.   195
at tua caelestes inlustrant omina flammae.
talis ab Idaeis primaevus Iuppiter antris
possessi stetit arce poli famulosque recepit
natura tradente deos ; lanugine nondum
vernabant vultus nec adhuc per colla fluebant   200
moturae convexa comae ; tum scindere nubes
discebat fulmenque rudi torquere lacerto.

   Laetior augurio genitor natisque superbus
iam paribus duplici fultus consorte redibat
splendebatque pio complexus pignora curru.   205
haud aliter summo gemini cum patre Lacones,
progenies Ledaea, sedent : in utroque relucet
frater, utroque soror ; simili chlamys effluit auro ;

---

¹ Virgil mentions the portent (*Aen.* ii. 682).

rarely sees. 'Tis not Boreas nor yet Phoebus' warmer breath that has put the mists to flight. That light was an emperor's star. A prophetic radiance was over all things, and with thy brightness Nature laughed. Even at midday did a wondering people gaze upon a bold star ('twas clear to behold)—no dulled nor stunted beams but bright as Boötes' nightly lamp. At a strange hour its brilliance lit up the sky and its fires could be clearly seen though the moon lay hid. May be it was the Queen mother's star or the return of thy grandsire's now become a god, or may be the generous sun agreed to share the heavens with all the stars that hasted to behold thee. The meaning of those signs is now unmistakable. Clear was the prophecy of Ascanius' coming power when an aureole crowned his locks, yet harmed them not, and when the fires of fate encircled his head and played about his temples.[1] Thy future the very fires of heaven foretell. So the young Jove, issuing from the caves of Ida, stood upon the summit of the conquered sky and received the homage of the gods whom Nature handed to his charge. The bloom of youth had not yet clothed his cheeks nor flowed there o'er his neck the curls whose stirrings were to shake the world. He was yet learning how to cleave the clouds and hurl the thunderbolt with unpractised hand.

Gladdened by that augury and proud of his now equal sons the sire returned, upstayed on the two princes and lovingly embracing his children in glittering car. Even so the Spartan twins, the sons of Leda, sit with highest Jove; in each his brother is mirrored, in each their sister; round each alike flows a golden dress, and star-crowned are the

stellati pariter crines. iuvat ipse Tonantem
error et ambiguae placet ignorantia matri ;   210
Eurotas proprios discernere nescit alumnos.
    Ut domus excepit reduces, ibi talia tecum
pro rerum stabili fertur dicione locutus :
    " Si tibi Parthorum solium Fortuna dedisset,
care puer, terrisque procul venerandus Eois   215
barbarus Arsacio consurgeret ore tiaras :
sufficeret sublime genus luxuque fluentem
deside nobilitas posset te sola tueri.
altera Romanae longe rectoribus aulae
condicio. virtute decet, non sanguine niti.   220
maior et utilior fato coniuncta potenti,
vile latens virtus. quid enim ? submersa tenebris
proderit obscuro veluti sine remige puppis
vel lyra quae reticet vel qui non tenditur arcus.
    " Hanc tamen haud quisquam, qui non agnoverit
        ante   225
semet et incertos animi placaverit aestus,
inveniet ; longis illuc ambagibus itur.
disce orbi, quod quisque sibi. cum conderet artus
nostros, aetheriis miscens terrena, Prometheus,
sinceram patri mentem furatus Olympo   230
continuit claustris indignantemque revinxit
et, cum non aliter possent mortalia fingi,
adiunxit geminas. illae cum corpore lapsae
intereunt, haec sola manet bustoque superstes
evolat. hanc alta capitis fundavit in arce   235
mandatricem operum prospecturamque labori ;

---

[1] Claudian here follows the Platonic psychology which
divides the soul into τὸ ἐπιθυμητικόν, τὸ θυμοειδές, the two
(" geminas ") baser elements, and τὸ λογιστικόν (the " haec "
of l. 234).

locks of both. The Thunderer rejoices in his very uncertainty, and to their hesitating mother her ignorance brings delight; Eurotas cannot make distinction between his own nurslings.

When all had returned to the palace, Theodosius, anxious for the world's just governance, is said to have addressed thee in these terms:

"Had fortune, my dear son, given thee the throne of Parthia, hadst thou been a descendant of the Arsacid house and did the tiara, adored by Eastern lands afar, tower upon thy forehead, thy long lineage would be enough, and thy birth alone would protect thee, though wantoning in idle luxury. Very different is the state of Rome's emperor. 'Tis merit, not blood, must be his support. Virtue hidden hath no value, united with power 'tis both more effective and more useful. Nay, o'erwhelmed in darkness it will no more advantage its obscure possessor than a vessel with no oars, a silent lyre, an unstrung bow.

"Yet virtue none shall find that has not first learned to know himself and stilled the uncertain waves of passion within him. Long and winding is the path that leads thereto. What each man learns in his own interests learn thou in the interests of the world. When Prometheus mixed earthly and heavenly elements and so formed human kind, he stole man's spirit pure from his own heavenly home, held it imprisoned and bound despite its outcries, and since humanity could be formed in no other way he added two more souls.[1] These fail and perish with the body; the first alone remains, survives the pyre and flies away. This soul he stationed in the lofty fastness of the brain to control and oversee the work and labours of the body. The other

illas inferius collo praeceptaque summae
passuras dominae digna statione locavit.
quippe opifex veritus confundere sacra profanis
distribuit partes animae sedesque removit.   240
iram sanguinei regio sub pectore cordis
protegit imbutam flammis avidamque nocendi
praecipitemque sui.   rabie succensa tumescit,
contrahitur tepefacta metu.   cumque omnia secum
duceret et requiem membris vesana negaret,   245
invenit pulmonis opem madidumque furenti
praebuit, ut tumidae ruerent in mollia fibrae.
at sibi cuncta petens, nil conlatura cupido
in iecur et tractus imos compulsa recessit,
quae, velut inmanis reserat dum belua rictus,   250
expleri pascique nequit : nunc verbere curas
torquet avaritiae, stimulis nunc flagrat amorum,
nunc gaudet, nunc maesta dolet satiataque rursus
exoritur caesaque redit pollentius hydra.

  " Hos igitur potuit si quis sedare tumultus,   255
inconcussa dabit purae sacraria menti.
tu licet extremos late dominere per Indos,
te Medus, te mollis Arabs, te Seres adorent :
si metuis, si prava cupis, si duceris ira,
servitii patiere iugum ; tolerabis iniquas   260
interius leges.   tunc omnia iure tenebis,
cum poteris rex esse tui.   proclivior usus
in peiora datur suadetque licentia luxum
inlecebrisque effrena favet.   tum vivere caste
304

two he set below the neck in a place befitting their
functions, where it is their part to obey the com-
mands of the directing soul. Doubtless our creator,
fearing to mix the heavenly with the mortal, placed
the different souls in different parts and kept their
dwelling-places distinct. Near to the heart whence
springs our blood there is within the breast a place
where fiery anger lurks, eager to hurt and uncon-
trolled. This cavity swells when heated by rage
and contracts when cooled by fear. Then, since
anger swept everything away with it and in its fury
gave the limbs no rest, Prometheus invented the
lungs to aid the body and applied their humidity
to the raging of anger to soothe our wrath-swollen
flesh. Lust, that asks for everything and gives
nought, was driven down into the liver and of neces-
sity occupied the lowest room. Like a beast, open-
ing its capacious jaws, lust can never be full fed nor
satisfied ; it is a prey now to the cruel lash of sleep-
less avarice, now to the fiery goads of love ; is
swayed now by joy, now by misery, and is no sooner
fed than fain to be fed again, returning with more
insistence than the oft-beheaded hydra.

" Can any assuage this tumult he will assure an
inviolable sanctuary for a spotless soul. Thou
mayest hold sway o'er farthest India, be obeyed by
Mede, unwarlike Arab or Chinese, yet, if thou
fearest, hast evil desires, art swayed by anger,
thou wilt bear the yoke of slavery ; within thyself
thou wilt be a slave to tyrannical rule. When thou
canst be king over thyself then shalt thou hold
rightful rule over the world. The easier way often
trod leads to worse ; liberty begets licence and,
when uncontrolled, leads to vice. Then is a chaste

asperius, cum prompta Venus ; tum durius irae   265
consulitur, cum poena patet. sed comprime motus
nec tibi quid liceat, sed quid fecisse decebit
occurrat, mentemque domet respectus honesti.

  " Hoc te praeterea crebro sermone monebo,
ut te totius medio telluris in ore   270
vivere cognoscas, cunctis tua gentibus esse
facta palam nec posse dari regalibus usquam
secretum vitiis ; nam lux altissima fati
occultum nihil esse sinit, latebrasque per omnes
intrat et abstrusos explorat fama recessus.   275

  " Sis pius in primis ; nam cum vincamur in omni
munere, sola deos aequat clementia nobis.
neu dubie suspectus agas neu falsus amicis
rumorumve avidus : qui talia curat, inanes
horrebit strepitus nulla non anxius hora.   280
non sic excubiae, non circumstantia pila
quam tutatur amor. non extorquebis amari ;
hoc alterna fides, hoc simplex gratia donat.
nonne vides, operum quod se pulcherrimus ipse
mundus amore liget, nec vi conexa per aevum   285
conspirent elementa sibi ? quod limite Phoebus
contentus medio, contentus litore pontus
et, qui perpetuo terras ambitque vehitque,
nec premat incumbens oneri nec cesserit aër ?
qui terret, plus ipse timet ; sors ista tyrannis   290
convenit ; invideant claris fortesque trucident,

life harder when love is at call; then is it a sterner task to govern anger when vengeance is to hand. Yet master thine emotions and ponder not what thou mightest do but what thou oughtest to do, and let regard for duty control thy mind.

" Of this too I cannot warn thee too often : remember that thou livest in the sight of the whole world, to all peoples are thy deeds known; the vices of monarchs cannot anywhere remain hid. The splendour of their lofty station allows nought to be concealed; fame penetrates every hiding-place and discovers the inmost secrets of the heart.

" Above all fail not in loving-kindness; for though we be surpassed in every virtue yet mercy alone makes us equal with the gods. Let thine actions be open and give no grounds for suspicion, be loyal to thy friends nor lend an ear to rumours. He who attends to such will quake at every idle whisper and know no moment's peace. Neither watch nor guard nor yet a hedge of spears can secure thee safety; only thy people's love can do that. Love thou canst not extort; it is the gift of mutual faith and honest goodwill. Seest thou not how the fair frame of the very universe binds itself together by love, and how the elements, not united by violence, are for ever at harmony among themselves ? Dost thou not mark how that Phoebus is content not to outstep the limits of his path, nor the sea those of his kingdom, and how the air, which in its eternal embrace encircles and upholds the world, presses not upon us with too heavy a weight nor yet yields to the burden which itself sustains ? Whoso causes terror is himself more fearful; such doom befits tyrants. Let them be jealous of another's fame, murder the

muniti gladiis vivant saeptique venenis,
ancipites habeant arces trepidique minentur :
tu civem patremque geras, tu consule cunctis,
non tibi, nec tua te moveant, sed publica vota.   295

   " In commune iubes si quid censesque tenendum,
primus iussa subi : tunc observantior aequi
fit populus nec ferre negat, cum viderit ipsum
auctorem parere sibi.   componitur orbis
regis ad exemplum, nec sic inflectere sensus   300
humanos edicta valent quam vita regentis :
mobile mutatur semper cum principe vulgus.

   " His tamen effectis neu fastidire minores
neu pete praescriptos homini transcendere fines.
inquinat egregios adiuncta superbia mores.   305
non tibi tradidimus dociles servire Sabaeos,
Armeniae dominum non te praefecimus orae,
nec damus Assyriam, tenuit quam femina, gentem.
Romani, qui cuncta diu rexere, regendi,
qui nec Tarquinii fastus nec iura tulere   310
Caesaris.   annales veterum delicta loquuntur :
haerebunt maculae   quis non per saecula damnat
Caesareae portenta domus ?   quem dira Neronis
funera, quem rupes Caprearum taetra latebit
incesto possessa seni ?   victura feretur   315
gloria Traiani, non tam quod Tigride victo
nostra triumphati fuerint provincia Parthi,
alta quod invectus fractis Capitolia Dacis,

---

[1] *i.e.* Tiberius.

brave, live hedged about with swords and fenced with poisons, dwelling in a citadel that is ever exposed to danger, and threaten to conceal their fears. Do thou, my son, be at once a citizen and a father, consider not thyself but all men, nor let thine own desires stir thee but thy people's.

" If thou make any law or establish any custom for the general good, be the first to submit thyself thereto ; then does a people show more regard for justice nor refuse submission when it has seen their author obedient to his own laws. The world shapes 'tself after its ruler's pattern, nor can edicts sway men's minds so much as their monarch's life ; the unstable crowd ever changes along with the prince.

" Nor is this all : show no scorn of thine inferiors nor seek to overstep the limits established for mankind. Pride joined thereto defaces the fairest character. They are not submissive Sabaeans whom I have handed over to thy rule, nor have I made thee lord of Armenia ; I give thee not Assyria, accustomed to a woman's rule. Thou must govern Romans who have long governed the world, Romans who brooked not Tarquin's pride nor Caesar's tyranny. History still tells of our ancestors' ill deeds ; the stain will never be wiped away. So long as the world lasts the monstrous excesses of the Julian house will stand condemned. Will any not have heard of Nero's murders or how Capri's foul cliffs were owned by an agèd lecher [1] ? The fame of Trajan will never die, not so much because, thanks to his victories on the Tigris, conquered Parthia became a Roman province, not because he brake the might of Dacia and led their chiefs in triumph up the slope of the Capitol, but because

quam patriae quod mitis erat.   ne desine tales,
nate, sequi.

        " Si bella canant, prius agmina duris
exerce studiis et saevo praestrue Marti.   321
non brumae requies, non hibernacula segnes
enervent torpore manus.   ponenda salubri
castra loco ;   praebenda vigil custodia vallo.
disce, ubi denseri cuneos, ubi cornua tendi   325
aequius aut iterum flecti ; quae montibus aptae,
quae campis acies, quae fraudi commoda vallis,
quae via difficilis.   fidit si moenibus hostis,
tum tibi murali libretur machina pulsu ;
saxa rota ;   praeceps aries protectaque portas   330
testudo feriat ;   ruat emersura iuventus
effossi per operta soli.   si longa moretur
obsidio, tum vota cave secura remittas
inclusumve putes ; multis damnosa fuere
gaudia ; dispersi pereunt somnove soluti ;   335
saepius incautae nocuit victoria turbae.
neu tibi regificis tentoria larga redundent
deliciis, neve imbelles ad signa ministros
luxuries armata trahat.   neu flantibus Austris
neu pluviis cedas, neu defensura calorem   340
aurea summoveant rapidos umbracula soles.
inventis utere cibis.   solabere partes
aequali sudore tuas : si collis iniquus,

---

¹ A well-known Roman method of attack by which the
troops advanced to the point of attack in close formation,
each man holding his shield above his head.   The protection
thus afforded to the assaulting band was likened to the
shell of the tortoise (*testudo*).

he was kindly to his country. Fail not to make such as he thine example, my son.

" Should war threaten, see first that thy soldiers are exercised in the practices of war and prepare them for the rigours of service. The ease of winter months spent in winter quarters must not weaken nor unnerve their hands. Establish thy camps in healthy places and see that watchful sentries guard the ramparts. Learn how to know when to mass your troops and when it is better to extend them or face them round ; study the formations suitable for mountain warfare and those for fighting on the plain. Learn to recognize what valleys may conceal an ambush and what routes will prove difficult. If thine enemy trusts in his walls to defend him then let thy catapults hurl stones at his battlements ; fling rocks thereat and let the swinging ram and shield-protected testudo[1] shake his gates. Your troops should undermine the walls and issuing from this tunnel should rush into the town. Should a long siege delay thee, then take care thou unbend not thy purpose in security or count thine enemy thy prisoner. Many ere this have found premature triumph their undoing, scattered or asleep they have been cut to pieces ; indeed victory itself has not seldom been the ruin of careless troops. Not for thee let spacious tents o'erflow with princely delights nor luxury don arms and drag to the standards her unwarlike train. Though the storm winds blow and the rain descends yield not to them and use not cloth of gold to guard thee from the sun's fierce rays. Eat such food as thou canst find. It will be a solace to thy soldiers that thy toil is as heavy as theirs ; be the first to mount the arduous hill and, should

primus ini ; silvam si caedere provocat usus,
sumpta ne pudeat quercum stravisse bipenni.   345
calcatur si pigra palus, tuus ante profundum
pertemptet sonipes. fluvios tu protere cursu
haerentes glacie, liquidos tu scinde natatu.
nunc eques in medias equitum te consere turmas ;
nunc pedes adsistas pediti. tum promptius ibunt
te socio, tum conspicuus gratusque geretur   351
sub te teste labor."

               Dicturum plura parentem
voce subis : " equidem, faveant modo numina coeptis,
haec effecta dabo, nec me fratrique tibique
dissimilem populi commissaque regna videbunt.   355
sed cur non potius, verbis quae disseris, usu
experior ? gelidas certe nunc tendis in Alpes.
duc tecum comitem ; figant sine nostra tyrannum
spicula ; pallescat nostro sine barbarus arcu.
Italiamne feram furiis praedonis acerbi   360
subiectam ? patiar Romam servire clienti ?
usque adeone puer ? nec me polluta potestas
nec pia cognati tanget vindicta cruoris ?
per strages equitare libet. da protinus arma.
cur annos obicis ? pugnae cur arguor impar ?
aequalis mihi Pyrrhus erat, cum Pergama solus   365
verteret et patri non degeneraret Achilli.
denique si princeps castris haerere nequibo,
vel miles veniam."

              Delibat dulcia nati
oscula miratusque refert : " laudanda petisti ;   370
sed festinus amor. veniet robustior aetas ;
ne propera. necdum decimas emensus aristas
adgrederis metuenda viris : vestigia magnae

necessity demand the felling of a forest, be not ashamed to grasp the axe and hew down the oak. If a stagnant marsh must be crossed let thy horse be the first to test the depth of it. Boldly tread the frozen river ; swim the flood. Mounted thyself, ride amid thy squadrons of horse or again stand foot to foot with the infantry. They will advance the bolder for thy presence, and with thee to witness glorious and glad shall be the fulfilment of their task."

More would he have spoken but Honorius broke in and said : " All this will I do, so God favour my attempts. The peoples and kingdoms committed to my care shall find me not unworthy of thee nor of my brother. But why should I not experience in action what thou has taught in words ? Thou goest to the wintry Alps : take me with thee. Let mine arrows pierce the tyrant's body, and the barbarians pale at my bow. Shall I allow Italy to become the prey of a ruthless bandit ? Rome to serve one who is himself but a servant ? Am I still such a child that neither power profaned nor just revenge for an uncle's blood shall move me ? Fain would I ride through blood. Quick, give me arms. Why castest thou my youth in my teeth ? Why thinkest me unequal to the combat ? I am as old as was Pyrrhus when alone he o'erthrew Troy and proved himself no degenerate from his father Achilles. If I may not remain in thy camp as a prince I will come even as a soldier."

Theodosius kissed his son's sweet lips and answered him wondering : " Nought have I but praise for thy petition, but this love of glory has bloomed too early. Thy strength will increase with years ; till then be patient. Though thou hast not yet completed ten summers thou wouldst hansel dangers that a man

indolis agnosco. fertur Pellaeus, Eoum
qui domuit Porum, cum prospera saepe Philippi 375
audiret, laetos inter flevisse sodales
nil sibi vincendum patris virtute relinqui.
hos video motus. fas sit promittere patri :
tantus eris. nostro nec debes regna favori,
quae tibi iam natura dedit. sic mollibus olim 380
stridula ducturum pratis examina regem
nascentem venerantur apes et publica mellis
iura petunt traduntque favos ; sic pascua parvus
vindicat et necdum firmatis cornibus audax
iam regit armentum vitulus. sed proelia differ 385
in iuvenem patiensque meum cum fratre tuere
me bellante locum. vos impacatus Araxes,
vos celer Euphrates timeat, sit Nilus ubique
vester et emisso quidquid sol imbuit ortu.
si pateant Alpes, habeat si causa secundos 390
iustior eventus, aderis partesque receptas
suscipies, animosa tuas ut Gallia leges
audiat et nostros aequus modereris Hiberos.
tunc ego securus fati laetusque laborum
discedam, vobis utrumque regentibus axem 395
    " Interea Musis animus, dum mollior, instet
et quae mox imitere legat ; nec desinat umquam
tecum Graia loqui, tecum Romana vetustas.
antiquos evolve duces, adsuesce futurae

---

¹ As is well known, the ancients mistook the sex of the
queen bee.

might fear: I mark the tokens of a noble nature.
It is said that Alexander, conqueror of eastern
Porus, wept at the constant news of Philip's fortune,
telling his companions who rejoiced thereat that his
sire's valour left him nought to conquer. In thee
I see like spirit. May a father be allowed this
prophecy—"thou shalt be as great"! It is not to
my goodwill thou owest the kingdom, for nature
has already made it thine. So even from his birth
bees reverence the king[1] who is to lead their
buzzing swarms through the soft meadows, ask his
public laws for the gathering of the honey and
entrust to him their combs. So the spirited young
bull-calf claims sovereignty over the grazing-grounds
and, though as yet his horns are not grown strong,
lords it over the herd. Nay: postpone thy cam-
paigns till thou art a man and while I do battle
patiently help thy brother to fulfil my office. Be
you two the terror of untamed Araxes and of swift
Euphrates; may Nile throughout all his length
belong to you and all the lands upon which the
morning sun lets fall his beam. Should I force a
passage over the Alps, should success crown the
juster cause, thou shalt come and govern the re-
covered provinces, whereby fierce Gaul shall obey
thy laws and my native Spain be guided by thy
just rule. Then, careless of doom and rejoicing in
my labours, I shall quit this mortal life, while you,
my sons, rule either hemisphere.

"Meanwhile cultivate the Muses whilst thou art
yet young; read of deeds thou soon mayest rival;
never may Greece's story, never may Rome's, cease
to speak with thee. Study the lives of the heroes
of old to accustom thee for wars that are to be.

militiae, Latium retro te confer in aevum.   400
libértas quaesita placet ? mirabere Brutum.
perfidiam damnas ? Metti satiabere poenis.
triste rigor nimius ? Torquati despice mores.
mors impensa bonum ? Decios venerare ruentes.
vel solus quid fortis agat, te ponte soluto   405
oppositus Cocles, Muci te flamma docebit ;
quid mora perfringat, Fabius ; quid rebus in artis
dux gerat, ostendet Gallorum strage Camillus.
discitur hinc nullos meritis obsistere casus :
prorogat aeternam feritas tibi Punica famam,   410
Regule ; successus superant adversa Catonis.
discitur hinc quantum paupertas sobria possit :
pauper erat Curius, reges cum vinceret armis,
pauper Fabricius, Pyrrhi cum sperneret aurum ;
sordida dictator flexit Serranus aratra :   415
lustratae lictore casae fascesque salignis
postibus adfixi ; collectae consule messes
et sulcata diu trabeato rura colono."

  Haec genitor praecepta dabat : velut ille carinae
longaevus rector, variis quem saepe procellis   420
exploravit hiems, ponto iam fessus et annis
aequoreas alni nato commendat habenas
et casus artesque docet : quo dextra regatur
sidere ; quo fluctus possit moderamine falli ;
quae nota nimborum ; quae fraus infida sereni ;   425

---

[1] The story of the punishment of Mettius Fufetius, the
Alban dictator, by the Roman king Tullus Hostilius for his
treachery in the war against Fidenae is told by Livy (i. 28. 10)
and referred to by Claudian (xv. 254). For Mucius (Scaevola)
holding his arm in the flame to show Lars Porsenna how
little he, a Roman, minded bodily pain see Livy ii. 12.

Go back to the Latin age. Admirest thou a fight for liberty? Thou wilt admire Brutus. Does treachery rouse thine indignation? The punishment of Mettius[1] will fill thee with satisfaction. Dost thou hate undue severity? Abominate Torquatus' savagery. Is it a virtue to die for one's country? Honour the self-devotion of the Decii. Horatius Cocles, facing the foe on the broken bridge, Mucius holding his arm in the flames,[2] these shall show thee what, single-handed, brave men can do. Fabius will show thee what overthrow delay can cause; Camillus and his slaughter of the Gauls what in face of odds a leader can effect. From history thou mayest learn that no ill fortune can master worth; Punic savagery extends thy fame, Regulus, to eternity; the failure of Cato outdoes success. From history thou mayest learn the power of frugal poverty; Curius was a poor man when he conquered kings in battle; Fabricius was poor when he spurned the gold of Pyrrhus; Serranus, for all he was dictator, drove the muddy plough. In those days the lictors kept watch at a cottage door, the fasces were hung upon a gateway of wood; consuls helped to gather in the harvest, and for long years the fields were ploughed by husbandmen who wore the consular robe."

Such were the precepts of the sire. Even so an aged helmsman oft proved by winter's various storms, aweary now of the sea and his weight of years, commends to his son the rudder of his bark, tells him of dangers and devices—by what art the helmsman's hand is guided; what steerage may elude the wave; what is a sign of storms; what the treachery of a cloudless sky, the promise of the

quid sol occiduus prodat; quo saucia vento
decolor iratos attollat Cynthia vultus.
adspice nunc, quacumque micas, seu circulus Austri,
magne parens, gelidi seu te meruere Triones,
adspice : completur votum.   iam natus adaequat   430
te meritis et, quod magis est optabile, vincit
subnixus Stilichone tuo, quem fratribus ipse
discedens clipeum defensoremque dedisti.
pro nobis nihil ille pati nullumque recusat
discrimen temptare sui, non dura viarum,   435
non incerta maris, Libyae squalentis harenas
audebit superare pedes madidaque cadente
Pleiade Gaetulas intrabit navita Syrtes.

   Hunc tamen in primis populos lenire feroces
et Rhenum pacare iubes.   volat ille citatis   440
vectus equis nullaque latus stipante caterva,
aspera nubiferas qua Raetia porrigit Alpes,
pergit et hostiles (tanta est fiducia) ripas
incomitatus adit.   totum properare per amnem
attonitos reges humili cervice videres.   445
ante ducem nostrum flavam sparsere Sygambri
caesariem pavidoque orantes murmure Franci
procubuere solo : iuratur Honorius absens
imploratque tuum supplex Alamannia nomen.
Bastarnae venere truces, venit accola silvae   450
Bructerus Hercyniae latisque paludibus exit
Cimber et ingentes Albim liquere Cherusci.

setting sun; what storm-wind frets the Moon so that discoloured she uplifts an angry face. Behold now, great father, in whatsoever part of heaven thou shinest, be it the southern arch or the cold constellation of the Plough that has won the honour of thy presence; see, thy prayer has been answered; thy son now equals thee in merit, nay, a consummation still more to be desired, he surpasseth thee, thanks to the support of thy dear Stilicho whom thou thyself at thy death didst leave to guard and defend the brothers twain. For us there is nought that Stilicho is not ready to suffer, no danger to himself he is not willing to face, neither hardships of the land nor hazards of the sea. His courage will carry him on foot across the deserts of Libya, at the setting of the rainy Pleiads his ship will penetrate the Gaetulian Syrtes.

To him, however, thy first command is to calm fierce nations and bring peace to the Rhine. On wind-swift steed, no escort clinging to his side, he crosses the cloud-capped summits of the Raetian Alps, and, so great is his trust in himself, approaches the river unattended. Then mightest thou have seen from source to mouth come hastening up Rhine's princes, bending their heads in fearful submission. Before our general the Sygambri abased their flaxen locks and the Franks cast themselves upon the ground and sued with trembling voice for pardon. Germany swears allegiance to the absent Honorius and addresses her suppliant prayers to him. Fierce Bastarnae were there and the Bructeri who dwell in the Hercynian forest. The Cimbrians left their broad marsh-lands, the tall Cherusci came from the river Elbe. Stilicho listens

accipit ille preces varias tardeque rogatus
adnuit et magno pacem pro munere donat.
nobilitant veteres Germanica foedera Drusos,   455
Marte sed ancipiti, sed multis cladibus empta—
quis victum meminit sola formidine Rhenum?
quod longis alii bellis potuere mereri,
hoc tibi dat Stilichonis iter.

                           Post otia Galli
limitis hortaris Graias fulcire ruinas.   460
Ionium tegitur velis ventique laborant
tot curvare sinus servaturasque Corinthum
prosequitur facili Neptunus gurgite classes,
et puer, Isthmiaci iam pridem litoris exul,
secura repetit portus cum matre Palaemon.   465
plaustra cruore natant: metitur pellita iuventus:
pars morbo, pars ense perit.   non lustra Lycaei,
non Erymantheae iam copia sufficit umbrae
innumeris exusta rogis, nudataque ferro
sic flagrasse suas laetantur Maenala silvas.   470
excutiat cineres Ephyre, Spartanus et Arcas
tutior exanguis pedibus proculcet acervos
fessaque pensatis respiret Graecia poenis!
gens, qua non Scythicos diffusior ulla Triones
incoluit, cui parvus Athos angustaque Thrace,   475
cum transiret, erat, per te viresque tuorum
fracta ducum lugetque sibi iam rara superstes,
et, quorum turbae spatium vix praebuit orbis,
uno colle latent.   sitiens inclusaque vallo

---

¹ =Corinth.

to their various prayers, gives tardy assent to their
entreaties and of his great bounty bestows upon
them peace. A covenant with Germany gave glory
to the Drusi of old, but purchased by what uncer-
tain warfare, by how many disasters! Who can
recall the Rhine conquered by terror alone? That
which others were enabled to win by long wars—
this, Honorius, Stilicho's mere march gives thee.

Thou biddest Stilicho after restoring peace in
Gaul save Greece from ruin. Vessels cover the
Ionian sea; scarce can the wind fill out so many
sails. Neptune with favouring currents attends the
fleet that is to save Corinth, and young Palaemon,
so long an exile from the shores of his isthmus,
returns in safety with his mother to the harbour.
The blood of barbarians washes their wagons; the
ranks of skin-clad warriors are mowed down, some by
disease, some by the sword. The glades of Lycaeus,
the dark and boundless forests of Erymanthus, are
not enough to furnish such countless funeral pyres;
Maenalus rejoices that the axe has stripped her of her
woods to provide fuel for such a holocaust. Let
Ephyre [1] rise from her ashes while Spartan and Arca-
dian, now safe, tread under foot the heaps of slain;
let Greece's sufferings be made good and her weary
land be allowed to breathe once more. That nation,
wider spread than any that dwells in northern
Scythia, that found Athos too small and Thrace too
narrow when it crossed them, that nation, I say,
was conquered by thee and thy captains, and now,
in the persons of the few that survive, laments its
own overthrow. One hill now shelters a people whose
hordes scarce the whole world could once contain.
Athirst and hemmed within their rampart they

ereptas quaesivit aquas, quas hostibus ante   480
contiguas alio Stilicho deflexerat actu
mirantemque novas ignota per avia valles
iusserat averso fluvium migrare meatu.

Obvia quid mirum vinci, cum barbarus ultro
iam cupiat servire tibi ? tua Sarmata discors   485
sacramenta petit ; proiecta pelle Gelonus
militat ; in Latios ritus transistis Alani.
ut fortes in Marte viros animisque paratos,
sic iustos in pace legis longumque tueris
electos crebris nec succedentibus urges.   490
iudicibus notis regimur, fruimurque quietis
militiaeque bonis, ceu bellatore Quirino,
ceu placido moderante Numa. non inminet ensis,
nullae nobilium caedes ; non crimina vulgo
texuntur ; patria maestus non truditur exul ;   495
impia continui cessant augmenta tributi ;
non infelices tabulae ; non hasta refixas
vendit opes ; avida sector non voce citatur,
nec tua privatis crescunt aeraria damnis.
munificus largi, sed non et prodigus, auri.   500
perdurat non empta fides nec pectora merces
adligat ; ipsa suo pro pignore castra laborant ;
te miles nutritor amat.

                              Quae denique Romae

---

[1] *i.e.* lists of the proscribed and of their properties put up
for sale.

sought in vain for the stolen waters, that, once within our foemen's reach, Stilicho had turned aside in another course, and commanded the stream, that marvelled at its strange channel amid unknown ways, to shift its altered track.

What wonder that the nations barring thy path should fall before thee, since the barbarian of his own choice now seeks to serve thee ? The Sarmatae, ever a prey to internal strife, beg to swear allegiance to thee ; the Geloni cast off their cloaks of hide and fight for thee ; you, O Alans, have adopted the customs of Latium. As thou choosest for war men that are brave and eager for the fray, so thou choosest for the offices of peace men that are just, and once chosen keepest them long in their charge, not ousting them by ever new successors. We know the magistrates who govern us, and we enjoy the blessings of peace while we reap the advantages of war, as though we lived at one and the same time in the reign of warlike Romulus and peace-loving Numa. A sword is no longer hung over our heads ; there are no massacres of the great ; gone is the mob of false accusers ; no melancholy exiles are driven from their fatherland. Unholy increase of perpetual taxes is at an end ; there are no accursed lists,[1] no auctions of plundered wealth ; the voice of greed summons not the salesman, nor is thy treasury increased by private losses. Thou art liberal with thy money, yet not wasteful of it. The loyalty of thy soldiers is a lasting loyalty, for it is not bought, nor is it gifts that win their love ; the army is anxious for the success of its own child and loves thee who wast its nursling.

And how deep is thy devotion to Rome herself !

cura tibi ! quam fixa manet reverentia patrum !
firmatur senium iuris priscamque resumunt   505
caniticm leges emendanturque vetustae
acceduntque novae.   talem sensere Solonem
res Pandioniae ; sic armipotens Lacedaemon
despexit muros rigido munita Lycurgo.
quae sub te vel causa brevis vel iudicis error   510
neglegitur ? dubiis quis litibus addere finem
iustior et mersum latebris educere verum ?
quae pietas quantusque rigor tranquillaque magni
vis animi nulloque levis terrore moveri
nec nova mirari facilis ! quam docta facultas   515
ingenii linguaeque modus ! responsa verentur
legati, gravibusque latet sub moribus aetas.

   Quantus in ore pater radiat ! quam torva voluptas
frontis et augusti maiestas grata pudoris !
iam patrias imples galeas ; iam cornus avita   520
temptatur vibranda tibi ; promittitur ingens
dextra rudimentis Romanaque vota moratur.
quis decor, incedis quotiens clipeatus et auro
squameus et rutilus cristis et casside maior !
sic, cum Threïcia primum sudaret in hasta,   525
flumina laverunt puerum Rhodopeia Martem.
quae vires iaculis vel, cum Gortynia tendis
spicula, quam felix arcus certique petitor
vulneris et iussum mentiri nescius ictum !
scis, quo more Cydon, qua dirigat arte sagittas   530

---

[1] *i.e.* Athens.

How fixed abides thy reverence for the Senate!
Old customs are preserved, law has recovered its
ancient sanctity in the amendment of former statutes
and by the addition of new ones. Such an one as
thee Pandion's city [1] found in Solon; even so did
warrior Lacedaemon disdain walls, for unyielding
Lycurgus gave it defence. What case so petty,
what judicial error so slight that it escapes thy
notice? Who with truer justice put an end to
dishonest suits and brought forth lurking truth
from her hiding-place? What mercy, yet what
firmness; thine is the quiet strength of a great soul,
too firm to be stirred by fear, too stable to be swayed
by the attraction of novelty. How stored with
learning thy ready wit, how controlled thy speech;
ambassadors are awe-stricken at thine answers, and
thy grave manners make them forget thy years.

How thy father's nobility shines in thy face!
How awful is thy winning brow, how charming
the majesty of a blushing emperor! Boy though
thou art, thou canst wear thy sire's helmet and
brandish thy grandsire's spear. These exercises
of thy youth foreshadow vast strength in man-
hood and convince Rome that the ruler of her
prayers is come. How fair art thou in shield and
golden armour girt, with waving plumes and taller
by the altitude of a helmet! So looked the youthful
Mars when after the toil and sweat of his first battle
he bathed him in Thracian Rhodope's mountain
stream. With what vigour thou hurlest the javelin,
and, when thou stretchest the Cretan bow, what
success attends thy shaft! Sure is the wound it
seeks; it knows not how to fail the appointed
stroke. Thou knowest in what fashion the Cretan,

Armenius, refugo quae sit fiducia Partho :
sic Amphioniae pulcher sudore palaestrae
Alcides pharetras Dircaeaque tela solebat
praetemptare feris olim domitura Gigantes
et pacem latura polo, semperque cruentus   535
ibat et Alcmenae praedam referebat ovanti ;
caeruleus tali prostratus Apolline Python
implicuit fractis moritura volumina silvis.

   Cum vectaris equo simulacraque Martia ludis,
quis mollis sinuare fugas, quis tendere contum   540
acrior aut subitos melior flexisse recursus ?
non te Massagetae, non gens exercita campo
Thessala, non ipsi poterunt aequare bimembres ;
vix comites alae, vix te suspensa sequuntur
agmina ferventesque tument post terga dracones.   545
utque tuis primum sonipes calcaribus arsit,
ignescunt patulae nares, non sentit harenas
ungula discussaeque iubae sparguntur in armos ;
turbantur phalerae, spumosis morsibus aurum
fumat, anhelantes exundant sanguine gemmae.   550
ipse labor pulvisque decet confusaque motu
caesaries ; vestis radiato murice solem
combibit, ingesto crispatur purpura vento.
si dominus legeretur equis, tua posceret ultro
verbera Nereidum stabulis nutritus Arion   555
serviretque tuis contempto Castore frenis

with what skill the Armenian, directs his arrows ; in what the retreating Parthian puts his trust. Thus was Alcides, graced with the sweat of the wrestling-ground at Thebes, wont to try his bow and Boeotian arrows on the beasts of the forest ere he turned them against the Giants and so secured peace for heaven. Stains of blood were ever upon him and proud was his mother Alcmena of the spoils he brought back home. Such was Apollo when he slew the livid serpent that enfolded and brake down forests in his dying coils.

When mounted on thy horse thou playest the mimicry of war, who is quicker smoothly to wheel in flight, who to hurl the spear, or more skilled to sweep round in swift return ? There the Massagetae are not thy peers nor the tribes of Thessaly, well versed though they be in riding, no, nor the very Centaurs themselves. Scarce can the squadrons and flying bands that accompany thee keep pace, while the wind behind thee bellies the fierce dragons on the flags. So soon as the touch of thy spur has fired thy steed, flames start from his swelling nostrils ; his hoof scarce touches the ground and his mane is outspread over his shoulders. His harness rattles and the golden bit grows warm in his foam-flecked mouth. The jewels that stud his quivering bridle are red with blood. The signs of toil, the dust stains, the disorder of thy hair all do but increase thy beauty. Thy brilliant scarlet cloak drinks in the sunlight as the wind blows its gay surface into folds. Could horses choose their riders then surely would Arion, full fed in the stables of the Nereids, have prayed for the very whip of such a master, Cyllarus would have had none of Castor, but would have looked

Cyllarus et flavum Xanthus sprevisset Achillem.
ipse tibi famulas praeberet Pegasus alas
portaretque libens melioraque pondera passus
Bellerophonteas indignaretur habenas.   560
quin etiam velox Aurorae nuntius Aethon,
qui fugat hinnitu stellas roseoque domatur
Lucifero, quotiens equitem te cernit ab astris,
invidet inque tuis mavult spumare lupatis.

   Nunc quoque quos habitus, quantae miracula
     pompae   565
vidimus, Ausonio cum iam succinctus amictu
per Ligurum populos solito conspectior ires
atque inter niveas alte veherere cohortes,
obnixisque simul pubes electa lacertis
sidereum gestaret onus. sic numina Memphis   570
in vulgus proferre solet ; penetralibus exit
effigies, brevis illa quidem : sed plurimus infra
liniger imposito suspirat vecte sacerdos
testatus sudore deum ; Nilotica sistris
ripa sonat Phariosque modos Aegyptia ducit   575
tibia ; summissis admugit cornibus Apis.
omnis nobilitas, omnis tua sacra frequentat
Thybridis et Latii suboles ; convenit in unum
quidquid in orbe fuit procerum, quibus auctor honoris
vel tu vel genitor. numeroso consule consul   580
cingeris et socios gaudes admittere patres.
inlustri te prole Tagus, te Gallia doctis
civibus et toto stipavit Roma senatu.
portatur iuvenum cervicibus aurea sedes
ornatuque novo gravior deus. asperat Indus   585
velamenta lapis pretiosaque fila smaragdis

to thy reins for guidance and Xanthus have scorned to bear golden-haired Achilles. Pegasus himself had lent thee his subject wings and been glad to carry thee and, now that a mightier rider bestrode him, had turned in proud disdain from Bellerophon's bridle. Nay, Aethon, swift messenger of dawn, who routs the stars with his neigh and is driven by rosy Lucifer, seeing thee from heaven as thou ridest by, is filled with envy and would choose rather to hold thy bit in his foaming mouth.

What raiment, too, have we not seen, what miracles of splendour, when, girt with the robe of Italy, thou didst go, still more glorious than thou art wont, through the peoples of Liguria, borne aloft amid thy troops clad in triumphal white and carried upon the shoulders of chosen warriors who so proudly upheld their godlike burden! 'Tis thus that Egypt brings forth her gods to the public gaze. The image issues from its shrine; small it is, indeed, yet many a linen-clad priest pants beneath the pole, and by his sweat testifies that he bears a god; Nile's banks resound to the holy rattles, and Egypt's pipe drones its native measure; Apis abases his horns and lows in reply. All the nobles, all whom Tiber and Latium rear, throng thy festival; gathered in one are all the great ones of the earth that owe their rank either to thee or to thy sire. Many a consular surrounds thee, the consul whose good pleasure it is to associate the senate in thy triumph. The nobles of Spain, the wise men of Gaul, and the senators of Rome all throng round thee. On young men's necks is borne thy golden throne, and new adorning adds weight to deity. Jewels of India stud thy vestment, rows of green emeralds enrich

ducta virent ; amethystus inest et fulgor Hiberus
temperat arcanis hyacinthi caerula flammis.
nec rudis in tali suffecit gratia textu ;
auget acus meritum picturatumque metallis   590
vivit opus : multa remorantur iaspide cultus [1]
et variis spirat Nereia baca figuris.
quae tantum potuit digitis mollire rigorem
ambitiosa colus ? vel cuius pectinis arte
traxerunt solidae gemmarum stamina telae ?   595
invia quis calidi scrutatus stagna profundi
Tethyos invasit gremium ? quis divitis algae
germina flagrantes inter quaesivit harenas ?
quis iunxit lapides ostro ? quis miscuit ignes
Sidonii Rubrique maris ? tribuere colorem   600
Phoenices, Seres subtegmina, pondus Hydaspes.
hoc si Maeonias cinctu graderere per urbes,
in te pampineos transferret Lydia thyrsos,
in te Nysa choros ; dubitassent orgia Bacchi,
cui furerent ; irent blandae sub vincula tigres.   605
talis Erythraeis intextus nebrida gemmis
Liber agit currus et Caspia flectit eburnis
colla iugis : Satyri circum crinemque solutae
Maenades adstringunt hederis victricibus Indos ;
ebrius hostili velatur palmite Ganges.   610

   Auspice mox laetum sonuit clamore tribunal
te fastos ineunte quater. sollemnia ludit
omina libertas ; deductum Vindice morem
lex celebrat, famulusque iugo laxatus erili

      [1] *Birt* vultus ; *cod. Ambrosianus* cultus

  [1] Vindex (or Vindicius) was the name of the slave who
was granted his liberty by Brutus for giving information of
the royalist plot in which Brutus' own sons were implicated.
For the story (probably an aetiological myth to explain
vindicta, another word for *festuca*) see Livy ii. 5.

the seams; there gleams the amethyst and the glint of Spanish gold makes the dark-blue sapphire show duller with its hidden fires. Nor in the weaving of such a robe was unadorned beauty enough; the work of the needle increases its value, thread of gold and silver glows therefrom; many an agate adorns the embroidered robes, and pearls of Ocean breathe in varied pattern. What bold hand, what distaff had skill enough to make thus supple elements so hard? What loom so cunning as to weave jewels into close-textured cloth? Who, searching out the uncharted pools of hot Eastern seas, despoiled the bosom of Tethys? Who dared seek o'er burning sands rich growth of coral? Who could broider precious stones on scarlet and so mingle the shining glories of the Red Sea and of Phoenicia's waters? Tyre lent her dyes, China her silks, Hydaspes his jewels. Shouldst thou traverse Maeonian cities in such a garb, to thee would Lydia hand over her vine-wreathed thyrsus, to thee Nysa her dances; the revels of Bacchus would have doubted whence came their madness; tigers would pass fawning beneath thy yoke. Even such, his fawn-skin enwoven with orient gems, doth the Wine-god drive his car, guiding the necks of Hyrcanian tigers with ivory yoke; around him satyrs and wild-haired Maenads fetter Indians with triumphant ivy, while drunken Ganges twines his hair with the vine tendril.

Already shouts of joy and of good omen resound about the consul's throne to welcome this thy fourth opening of Rome's year. Liberty enacts her wonted ceremonies; Law observes the custom dating back to Vindex [1] whereby a slave freed from his master's service is introduced into thy presence and thence

ducitur et grato remeat securior ictu.   615
tristis condicio pulsata fronte recedit ;
in civem rubuere genae, tergoque removit
verbera permissi felix iniuria voti.

Prospera Romuleis sperantur tempora rebus
in nomen ventura tuum.   praemissa futuris   620
dant exempla fidem : quotiens te cursibus aevi
praefecit, totiens accessit laurea patri.
ausi Danuvium quondam transnare Gruthungi
in lintres fregere nemus ; ter mille ruebant
per fluvium plenae cuneis inmanibus alni.   625
dux Odothaeus erat.   tantae conamina classis
incipiens aetas et primus contudit annus :
summersae sedere rates ; fluitantia numquam
largius Arctoos pavere cadavera pisces ;
corporibus premitur Peuce ; per quinque recurrens
ostia barbaricos vix egerit unda cruores,   631
confessusque parens Odothaei regis opima
rettulit exuviasque tibi.   civile secundis
conficis auspiciis bellum.   tibi debeat orbis
fata Gruthungorum debellatumque tyrannum :   635
Hister sanguineos egit te consule fluctus ;
Alpinos genitor rupit te consule montes.

Sed patriis olim fueras successibus auctor,
nunc eris ipse tuis.   semper venere triumphi
cum trabeis sequiturque tuos victoria fasces.   640

---

[1] A reference to the Roman method of manumitting a
slave *alapa et festuca,* *i.e.* by giving him a slight blow
(*alapa*) with a rod (*festuca*).   See Gaius on *vindicatio* (iv. 16)
and on the whole question R. G. Nisbet in *Journal of Roman
Studies,* viii. Pt. 1.
[2] The campaign of Theodosius against Odothaeus, King
of the Gruthungi (Zosimus iv. 35 calls him 'Οδόθεος) is thus

dismissed—a freeman thanks to that envied stroke.[1]
A blow upon the brow and his base condition is
gone ; reddened cheeks have made him a citizen,
and with the granting of his prayer a happy insult
has given his back freedom from the lash.

Prosperity awaits our empire ; thy name is earnest
for the fulfilment of our hopes. The past guarantees
the future ; each time that thy sire made thee chief
magistrate of the year the laurels of victory crowned
his arms. Once the Gruthungi, hewing down a
forest to make them boats, dared to pass beyond
the Danube. Three thousand vessels, each crowded
with a barbarous crew, made a dash across the river.
Odothaeus was their leader. Thy youth, nay, the
first year of thy life, crushed the attempt of that
formidable fleet. Its boats filled and sank ; never
did the fish of that northern river feed more lavishly
on the bodies of men. The island of Peuce was
heaped high with corpses. Scarce even through
five mouths could the river rid itself of barbarian
blood, and thy sire, owning thine influence, gave
thanks to thee for the spoils won in person from
King Odothaeus. Consul a second time thou didst
end civil war by thine auspices. Let the world
thank thee for the overthrow of the Gruthungi and
the defeat of their king ; thou wast consul when the
Danube ran red with their blood, thou wast consul,
too, when thy sire crossed the Alps to victory.[2]

But thou, once author of thy father's successes,
shalt now be author of thine own. Triumph has ever
attended thy consulship and victory thy fasces.

dated as 386, the year of Honorius' first consulship (see
note on viii. 153). Honorius' second consulship (394) saw
the defeat of Eugenius.

sis, precor, adsiduus consul Mariique relinquas
et senis Augusti numerum.   quae gaudia mundo,
per tua lanugo cum serpere coeperit ora,
cum tibi protulerit festas nox pronuba taedas !
quae tali devota toro, quae murice fulgens   645
ibit in amplexus tanti regina mariti ?
quaenam tot divis veniet nurus, omnibus arvis
et toto donanda mari ?   quantusque feretur
idem per Zephyri metas Hymenaeus et Euri !
o mihi si liceat thalamis intendere carmen   650
conubiale tuis, si te iam dicere patrem !
tempus erit, cum tu trans Rheni cornua victor,
Arcadius captae spoliis Babylonis onustus
communem maiore toga signabitis annum ;
crinitusque tuo sudabit fasce Suebus,   655
ultima fraternas horrebunt Bactra secures.

---

[1] Marius was consul seven, Augustus thirteen, times.

Heaven grant thou mayest be our perpetual consul and outnumber Marius [1] and old Augustus. Happy universe that shall see the first down creep over thy cheeks, and the wedding-night that shall lead forth for thee the festal torches. Who shall be consecrated to such a couch; who, glorious in purple, shall pass, a queen, to the embraces of such a husband? What bride shall come to be the daughter of so many gods, dowered with every land and the whole sea? How gloriously shall the nuptial song be borne at once to farthest East and West! O may it be mine to sing thy marriage-hymn, mine presently to hail thee father! The time will come when, thou victorious beyond the mouths of the Rhine, and thy brother Arcadius laden with the spoil of captured Babylon, ye shall endow the year with yet more glorious majesty; when the long-haired Suebian shall bear the arms of Rome and the distant Bactrian tremble beneath the rule of thyself and thy brother.

PANEGYRICUS
DICTUS MANLIO THEODORO CONSULI

PRAEFATIO

(XVI.)

Audebisne, precor, tantae subiecta catervae,
    inter tot proceres, nostra Thalia, loqui ?
nec te fama vetat, vero quam celsius auctam
    vel servasse labor vel minuisse pudor ?
an tibi continuis crevit fiducia castris   5
    totaque iam vatis pectora miles habet ?
culmina Romani maiestatemque senatus
    et, quibus exultat Gallia, cerne viros.
omnibus audimur terris mundique per aures
    ibimus.   ah nimius consulis urget amor !   10
Iuppiter, ut perhibent, spatium cum discere vellet
    naturae regni nescius ipse sui,
armigeros utrimque duos aequalibus alis
    misit ab Eois Occiduisque plagis.
Parnasus geminos fertur iunxisse volatus ;   15
    contulit alternas Pythius axis aves.
Princeps non aquilis terras cognoscere curat ;
    certius in vobis aestimat imperium.
hoc ego concilio collectum metior orbem ;
    hoc video coetu quidquid ubique micat.   20

---

[1] See Introduction, p. xv. Judging from this poem
Manlius started by being an *advocatus* in the praetorian
prefect's court, was then *praeses* of some district in Africa,
then governor (*consularis*) of Macedonia, next recalled to
Rome as Gratian's *magister epistularum*, then *comes*

PANEGYRIC ON THE CONSULSHIP OF
FL. MANLIUS THEODORUS [1] (A.D. 399)

PREFACE

(XVI)

Wilt dare to sing, my Muse, when so great, so
august an assembly shall be thy critic ? Does not
thine own renown forbid thee ? 'Tis greater now than
thou deservest; how hard then to enhance, how
disgraceful to diminish it ! Or has thine assurance
grown through ever dwelling in the camp, and does
the soldier now wholly possess the poet's breast ?
Behold the flower of the Roman senate, the majesty,
the pride, the heroes of Gaul. The whole earth
is my audience, my song shall sound in the ears
of all the world. Alack ! Love for our consul
constrains too strongly. Jove, 'tis said, when he
would fain learn its extent (for he knew not the
bounds of his own empire) sent forth two eagles
of equal flight from the East and from the West.
On Parnassus, as they tell, their twin flights met ;
the Delphic heaven brought together the one bird
and the other. Our Emperor needs no eagles to
teach him the magnitude of his domains ; yourselves
are preceptors more convincing. 'Tis this assembly
that gives to me the measure of the universe ; here
I see gathered all the brilliance of the world.

sacrarum largitionum (=ecclesiastical treasurer) and after
that praetorian prefect of Gaul (ll. 50-53).

PANEGYRICUS

(XVII.)

Ipsa quidem Virtus pretium sibi, solaque late
Fortunae secura nitet nec fascibus ullis
erigitur plausuve petit clarescere vulgi.
nil opis externae cupiens, nil indiga laudis,
divitiis animosa suis inmotaque cunctis
casibus ex alta mortalia despicit arce.
attamen invitam blande vestigat et ultro
ambit honor : docuit totiens a rure profectus
lictor et in mediis consul quaesitus aratris.
te quoque naturae sacris mundique vacantem,   10
emeritum pridem desudatisque remotum
iudiciis eadem rursum complexa potestas
evehit et reducem notis imponit habenis.
accedunt trabeae : nil iam, Theodore, relictum,
quo virtus animo crescat vel splendor honori.[1]   1
culmen utrumque tenes : talem te protinus anni
formavere rudes, et dignum vita curuli
traxit iter primaeque senes cessere iuventae.
iam tum canities animi, iam dulce loquendi

            [1] honori *conject. Birt* ; honore *codd.*

PANEGYRIC

(XVII)

Virtue is its own reward; alone with its far-flung splendour it mocks at Fortune; no honours raise it higher nor does it seek glory from the mob's applause. External wealth cannot arouse its desires, it asks no praise but makes its boast of self-contained riches, and unmoved by all chances it looks down upon the world from a lofty citadel. Yet in its own despite importunate honours pursue it, and offer themselves unsought; that the lictor coming from the farm hath ofttimes proved and a consul sought for even at the plough. Thou, too, who wert at leisure to study the mysteries of nature and the heavens, thou who hadst served thy time and retired from the law courts where thou hadst toiled so long, art once more enfolded by a like dignity, which, raising thee aloft, sets in thy returning hands the familiar rein. The consulship now is thine, Theodorus, nor is there now aught left to add to thy virtues or to the glory of thy name. Thou art now at the summit of both; from thine earliest years thy character was thus formed, the whole course of thy life was worthy of the curule chair; thy earliest youth outrivalled age. Even then thy mind was hoar, thy pleasant talk weighty, thy

pondus et attonitas sermo qui duceret aures.   20
mox undare foro victrix opulentia linguae
tutarique reos.   ipsa haec amplissima sedes
orantem stupuit, bis laudatura regentem.
hinc te pars Libyae moderantem iura probavit,
quae nunc tota probat ; longi sed pignus amoris   25
exiguae peperere morae populumque clientem
publica mansuris testantur vocibus aera.
inde tibi Macetum tellus et credita Pellae
moenia, quae famulus quondam ditavit Hydaspes ;
tantaque commissae revocasti gaudia genti   30
mitibus arbitriis, quantum bellante Philippo
floruit aut nigri cecidit cum regia Pori.

Sed non ulterius te praebuit urbibus aula :
maluit esse suum ; terris edicta daturus,
supplicibus responsa venis.   oracula regis   35
eloquio crevere tuo, nec dignius umquam
maiestas meminit sese Romana locutam.
hinc sacrae mandantur opes orbisque tributa
possessi, quidquid fluviis evolvitur auri,
quidquid luce procul venas rimata sequaces   40
abdita pallentis fodit sollertia Bessi.

Ac velut expertus [1] lentandis navita tonsis
praeficitur lateri custos ; hinc ardua prorae
temperat et fluctus tempestatesque futuras
edocet ; adsiduo cum Dorida vicerit usu,   45
iam clavum totamque subit torquere carinam :

[1] expertus *Barthius ; Birt keeps MSS.* exertus.

340

converse the admiration and delight of all that heard it. The wealth of thy triumphant eloquence soon overflowed the forum and brought safety to the accused. Yea, this most august assembly was astonied at thy pleading, as it was twice to applaud thy governance. Next, a part of Libya approved the administration which it now in its entirety enjoys; but thy brief stay won for thee a pledge of perpetual love, and public statues bear witness with enduring eloquence that thou wert a nation's guardian. Macedonia was next committed to thy care and the walls of Pella, enriched once by conquered Hydaspes. The mildness of thy rule brought to the country entrusted to thee such joy as it once knew under warlike Philip or when the empire of Indian Porus fell to Alexander's arms.

But Rome could not spare thy services longer to the provinces; she chose rather to have thee for her own; thou comest to give edicts to the world, to make reply to suppliants. A monarch's utterance has won dignity from thine eloquence, never can the majesty of Rome recall when she spoke more worthily. After this the offerings and wealth of the world, the tribute of the empire, is entrusted to thy care; the gold washed down by the rivers and that dug out of deep Thracian mines by the skill of pale-faced Bessi who track the hidden seams —all is thine.

As a sailor skilled in wielding the oar is at first set in charge of but a side of the vessel, then, when he can manage the lofty prow and is able, thanks to his long experience of the sea, to know beforehand what storms and tempests the vessel is like to encounter, he has charge of the helm and is entrusted with the

sic cum clara diu mentis documenta dedisses,
non te parte sui, sed in omni corpore sumpsit
imperium cunctaque dedit tellure regendos
rectores.   Hispana tibi Germanaque Tethys   50
paruit et nostro diducta Britannia mundo,
diversoque tuas coluerunt gurgite voces
lentus Arar Rhodanusque ferox et dives Hiberus.
o quotiens doluit Rhenus, qua barbarus ibat,
quod te non geminis frueretur iudice ripis !   55
unius fit cura viri, quodcumque rubescit
occasu, quodcumque dies devexior ambit.

    Tam celer adsiduos explevit cursus honores ;
una potestatum spatiis interfuit aetas
totque gradus fati iuvenilibus intulit annis.   60

    Postquam parta quies et summum nacta cacumen
iam secura petit privatum gloria portum,
ingenii redeunt fructus aliique labores,
et vitae pars nulla perit : quodcumque recedit
litibus, incumbit studiis, animusque vicissim   65
aut curam imponit populis aut otia Musis.
omnia Cecropiae relegis secreta senectae
discutiens, quid quisque novum mandaverit aevo
quantaque diversae producant agmina sectae.

    Namque aliis princeps rerum disponitur aër ;   70
hic confidit aquis ; hic procreat omnia flammis.

---

¹ Claudian refers to the early Ionian philosophers.
Anaximenes believed that air was the first principle of all
things, Thales said water, Heraclitus fire. l. 72 refers to
Empedocles who postulated the four elements and two
principles, love and hate, which respectively made and
unmade the universe out of the elements. The "*hic*" of
l. 75 may be Democritus or it may refer to the Sceptic,
Pyrrho. The "*hic*" of l. 76 is Anaxagoras, the friend of
Pericles. "*Ille*" (79) may be taken to refer to Leucippus,
the first of the atomic philosophers ; he postulated infinite

direction of the entire ship; so when thou hadst
long given illustrious proofs of thy character, the
empire of Rome summoned thee to govern not a
part but the whole of itself, and set thee as ruler over
all the rulers of the world. The seas of Spain, the
German ocean obeyed thee and Britain, so far
removed from our continent. Rivers of all lands
observed thy statutes, slow-flowing Saône, swift
Rhone, and Ebro rich in gold. How often did the
Rhine, in those districts where the barbarians dwell,
lament that the blessings of thy rule extended
not to both banks ! All the lands the setting sun
bathes in its rays, all that its last brilliance illumines
are entrusted to the charge of one man.

So swiftly did thy career fill office after office;
a single period of life was enough for the round of
dignities and gave to thy youthful years every step
on fortune's ladder.

When repose was earned and now, after reaching
the highest place, glory, laying care aside, seeks
refuge in a private life, genius again wins reward
from other tasks. No part of life is lost : all that is
withdrawn from the law courts is devoted to the
study, and thy mind in turn either bestows its efforts
on the State or its leisure on the Muses. Once
more thou readest the secrets of ancient Athens,
examining the discoveries with which each sage
has enriched posterity and noting what hosts of
disciples the varying schools produce.

For some hold that air [1] is the first beginning of
all things, others that water is, others again derive
the sum of things from fire. Another, destined to

space. " *Hi* " (82) = Democritus, Epicurus, and other
atomists. " *Alii* " (83) are the Platonists.

alter in Aetnaeas casurus sponte favillas
dispergit revocatque deum rursusque receptis
nectit amicitiis quidquid discordia solvit.
corporis hic damnat sensus verumque videri   75
pernegat. hic semper lapsurae pondera terrae
conatur rapido caeli fulcire rotatu
accenditque diem praerupti turbine saxi.
ille ferox unoque tegi non passus Olympo
inmensum per inane volat finemque perosus   80
parturit innumeros angusto pectore mundos.
hi vaga collidunt caecis primordia plagis.
numina constituunt alii casusque relegant.

   Graiorum obscuras Romanis floribus artes
inradias, vicibus gratis formare loquentes   85
suetus et alterno verum contexere nodo.
quidquid Socratico manavit ab ordine, quidquid
docta Cleantheae sonuerunt atria turbae,
inventum quodcumque tuo, Chrysippe, recessu,
quidquid Democritus risit dixitque tacendo   90
Pythagoras, uno se pectore cuncta vetustas
condidit et maior collectis viribus exit.
ornantur veteres et nobiliore magistro
in Latium spretis Academia migrat Athenis,
ut tandem propius discat, quo fine beatum   95
dirigitur, quae norma boni, qui limes honesti ;
quaenam membra sui virtus divisa domandis
obiectet vitiis ; quae pars iniusta recidat,
quae vincat ratione metus, quae frenet amores ;
aut quotiens elementa doces semperque fluentis 100

---

[1] Claudian's way of saying that Manlius translates Greek
philosophy into clear and elegant Latin, throwing his
translation into the form of a dialogue.

fall self-immolated into Etna's fiery crater, reduces God to principles of dispersion and re-collection and binds again in resumed friendship all that discord separates. This philosopher allows no authority to the senses and denies that the truth can be perceived. Another seeks to explain the suspension of the world in space by the rapid revolution of the sky (whence else the world would fall) and kindles day's fires by the whirl of a rushing rock. That fearless spirit, not content with the covering of but one sky, flies through the limitless void and, scorning a limit, conceives in one small brain a thousand worlds. Others make wandering atoms clash with blind blows, while others again set up deities and banish chance.

Thou dost adorn the obscure learning of Greece with Roman flowers,[1] skilled to shape speech in happy interchange and weave truth's garland with alternate knots. All the lore of Socrates' school, the learning that echoed in Cleanthes' lecture-room, the thoughts of the stoic Chrysippus in his retreat, all the laughter of Democritus, all that Pythagoras spoke by silence—all the wisdom of the ancients is stored in that one brain whence it issues forth the stronger for its concentration. The ancients gain fresh lustre and, scorning Athens, the Academy migrates to Latium under a nobler master, the more exactly at last to learn by what end happiness guides its path, what is the rule of the good, the goal of the right ; what division of virtue should be set to combat and overthrow each separate vice, and what part of virtue it is that curbs injustice, that causes reason to triumph over fear, that holds lust in check. How often hast thou taught us the nature

materiae causas : quae vis animaverit astra
impuleritque choros ; quo vivat machina motu ;
sidera cur septem retro nitantur in ortus
obluctata polo ; variisne meatibus idem
arbiter an geminae convertant aethera mentes ;
sitne color proprius rerum, lucisne repulsu   106
eludant aciem ; tumidos quae luna recursus
nutriat Oceani ; quo fracta tonitrua vento,
quis trahat imbriferas nubes, quo saxa creentur
grandinis ; unde rigor nivibus ; quae flamma per
    auras   110
excutiat rutilos tractus aut fulmina velox
torqueat aut tristem figat crinita cometem.

    Iam tibi compositam fundaverat ancora puppim,
telluris iam certus eras ; fecunda placebant
otia ; nascentes ibant in saecula libri :   115
cum subito liquida cessantem vidit ab aethra
Iustitia et tanto viduatas iudice leges.
continuo frontem limbo velata pudicam
deserit Autumni portas, qua vergit in Austrum
Signifer et noctis reparant dispendia Chelae.   120
pax avibus, quacumque volat, rabiemque frementes
deposuere ferae ; laetatur terra reverso
numine, quod prisci post tempora perdidit auri.
illa per occultum Ligurum se moenibus infert
et castos levibus plantis ingressa penates   125
invenit aetherios signantem pulvere cursus,
quos pia sollicito deprendit pollice Memphis :
346

of the elements and the causes of matter's cease-
less change; what influence has given life to the
stars, moving them in their courses; what quickens
with movement the universal frame. Thou tellest
why the seven planets strive backward towards the
East, doing battle with the firmament; whether
there is one lawgiver to different movements or
two minds govern heaven's revolution; whether
colour is a property of matter or whether objects
deceive our sight and owe their colours to reflected
light; how the moon causes the ebb and flow of the
tide; which wind brings about the thunder's crash,
which collects the rain clouds and by which the hail-
stones are formed; what causes the coldness of snow
and what is that flame that ploughs its shining furrow
through the sky, hurls the swift thunderbolt, or sets
in heaven's dome the tail of the baleful comet.

Already had the anchor stayed thy restful bark,
already thou wert minded to go ashore; fruitful
leisure charmed and books were being born for im-
mortality, when, of a sudden, Justice looked down
from the shining heaven and saw thee at thine ease,
saw Law, too, deprived of her great interpreter. She
stayed not but, wreathing her chaste forehead with a
band, left the gates of Autumn where the Standard-
bearer dips towards the south and the Scorpion makes
good the losses of the night. Where'er she flies a
peace fell upon the birds, and howling beasts laid
aside their rage. Earth rejoices in the return of a
deity lost to her since the waning of the age of gold.
Secretly Justice enters the walls of Milan, Liguria's
city, and penetrating with light step the holy palace
finds Theodorus marking in the sand those heavenly
movements which reverent Memphis discovered by

347

quae moveant momenta polum, quam certus in astris
error, quis tenebras solis causisque meantem
defectum indicat numerus, quae linea Phoeben   130
damnet et excluso pallentem fratre relinquat.
ut procul adspexit fulgentia Virginis ora
cognovitque deam, vultus veneratus amicos
occurrit scriptaeque notas confundit harenae.

    Tum sic diva prior : " Manli, sincera bonorum   135
congeries, in quo veteris vestigia recti
et ductos video mores meliore metallo :
iam satis indultum studiis, Musaeque tot annos
eripuere mihi.   pridem te iura reposcunt :
adgredere et nostro rursum te redde labori   140
nec tibi sufficiat transmissae gloria vitae.
humanum curare genus quis terminus umquam
praescripsit ?   nullas recipit prudentia metas.
adde quod haec multis potuit contingere sedes,
sed meriti tantum redeunt actusque priores   145
commendat repetitus honos, virtusque reducit
quos fortuna legit.[1]   melius magnoque petendum
credis in abstrusa rerum ratione morari ?
scilicet illa tui patriam praecepta Platonis
erexere magis, quam qui responsa secutus   150
obruit Eoas classes urbemque carinis
vexit et arsuras Medo subduxit Athenas ?
Spartanis potuit robur praestare Lycurgus
matribus et sexum leges vicere severae

    [1] *Birt* regit *with the* MSS. (*he suggests* nequit); *Heinsius* legit

    [1] Virgo (=Astraea) was a recognized synonym for the goddess Justice ; see Virg. *Ec.* iv. 6.
    [2] *i.e.* Themistocles.

anxious reckoning. He sought the forces that move
the heavens, the fixed (though errant) path of the
planets, the calculation which predicts the over-
shadowing of the sun and its surely-fixed eclipse,
and the line that sentences the moon to be left in
darkness by shutting out her brother. Soon as
from afar he beheld the shining face of the Maiden[1]
and recognized the goddess, reverencing that dear
countenance, he hurries to meet her, effacing from
the sand the diagrams he had drawn.

The goddess was the first to speak. " Manlius,
in whom are gathered all the virtues unalloyed, in
whom I see traces of ancient justice and manners
moulded of a purer metal, thou hast devoted time
enough now to study ; all these years have the
Muses reft from me my pupil. Long has Law de-
manded thy return to her allegiance. Come, devote
thyself once more to my service, and be not content
with the glory of thy past. To the service of man-
kind what boundary ever set the limits ? Wisdom
accepts no ends for herself. Then, too, to many
has this office fallen, as well it might, but only
the worthy return thereto ; reappointment to office
is the best commendation of office well held, and
virtue brings back him whom chance elects. Deemst
thou it a better and a worthier aim to spend thy
days in exploring Nature's secret laws ? Dost thou
think it was thy Plato's precepts raised his country
to glory rather than he [2] who, in obedience to the
oracle, sank the Persian fleet, put his city on ship-
board and saved from the Medes Athens destined
for the flames ? Lycurgus could dower the mothers
of Sparta with a man's courage and by his austere
laws correct the weakness of their sex ; by for-

civibus et vetitis ignavo credere muro 155
tutius obiecit nudam Lacedaemona bellis :
at non Pythagorae monitus annique silentes
famosum Oebalii luxum pressere Tarenti.

" Quis vero insignem tanto sub principe curam
respuat ?   aut quando meritis maiora patebunt 160
praemia ?   quis demens adeo qui iungere sensus
cum Stilichone neget ?   similem quae protulit aetas
consilio vel Marte virum ?   nunc Brutus amaret
vivere sub regno, tali succumberet aulae
Fabricius, cuperent ipsi servire Catones. 165
nonne vides, ut nostra soror Clementia tristes
obtundat gladios fratresque amplexa serenos
adsurgat Pietas, fractis ut lugeat armis
Perfidia et laceris morientes crinibus hydri
lambant invalido Furiarum vincla veneno ? 170
exultat cum Pace Fides.   iam sidera cunctae
liquimus et placidas inter discurrimus urbes.
nobiscum, Theodore, redi."

                      Subit ille loquentem
talibus : " agrestem dudum me, diva, reverti
cogis et infectum longi rubigine ruris 175
ad tua signa vocas.   nam quae mihi cura tot annis
altera quam duras sulcis mollire novales,
nosse soli vires, nemori quae commoda rupes,
quis felix oleae tractus, quae glaeba faveret
frugibus et quales tegeret vindemia colles ? 180
terribiles rursum lituos veteranus adibo
et desueta vetus temptabo caerula vector ?

350

bidding his fellow-citizens to put a coward's trust in walls, he set Lacedemon to face wars more securely in her nakedness; but all the teaching of Pythagoras and his years of silence never crushed the infamous licentiousness of Sparta's colony Tarentum.

"Besides, beneath such an emperor, who could refuse office? Was ever merit more richly rewarded? Who is so insensate as not to wish to meet Stilicho in council? Has ever any age produced his equal in prudence or in bravery? Now would Brutus love to live under a king; to such a court Fabricius would yield, the Catos themselves long to give service. Seest thou not how my sister Mercy blunts the cruel sword of war; how Piety rises to embrace the two noble brothers; how Treason laments her broken weapons and the snakes, writhing in death upon the Furies' wounded heads, lick their chains with enfeebled venom? Peace and loyalty are triumphant. All the host of heaven leaves the stars and wanders from peaceful city to peaceful city. Return thou with us, Theodorus."

Then Theodorus made answer: "From my long accustomed fields, goddess, thou urgest me to return, summoning to thy standard one grown rusty in the distant countryside. What else has been my care all these years but to break up the stubborn fallow-land into furrows, to know the nature of the soil, the rocky land suitable to the growth of trees, the country where the olive will flourish, the fields that will yield rich harvests of grain or the hills which my vineyards may clothe? I have served my time; am I to hearken once more to the dreadful trumpet? Is the old helmsman again to brave the seas whose lore he has forgotten?

351

collectamque diu et certis utcumque locatam
sedibus in dubium patiar deponere famam ?
nec me, quid valeat natura fortior usus,   185
praeterit aut quantum neglectae defluat arti.
desidis aurigae non audit verbera currus,
nec manus agnoscit quem non exercuit arcum.
esse sed iniustum fateor quodcumque negatur
iustitiae.   tu prima hominem silvestribus antris 190
elicis et foedo deterges saecula victu.
te propter colimus leges animosque ferarum
exuimus.   nitidis quisquis te sensibus hausit,
inruet intrepidus flammis, hiberna secabit
aequora, confertos hostes superabit inermis.   195
ille vel Aethiopum pluviis solabitur aestus ;
illum trans Scythiam vernus comitabitur aër."

   Sic fatus tradente dea suscepit habenas
quattuor ingenti iuris temone refusas.
prima Padum Thybrimque ligat crebrisque micantem
urbibus Italiam ; Numidas [1] Poenosque secunda 201
temperat ; Illyrico se tertia porrigit orbi ;
ultima Sardiniam, Cyrnum trifidamque retentat
Sicaniam et quidquid Tyrrhena tunditur unda
vel gemit Ionia.   nec te tot lumina rerum   205
aut tantum turbavit onus ; sed ut altus Olympi
vertex, qui spatio ventos hiemesque relinquit,
perpetuum nulla temeratus nube serenum
celsior exurgit pluviis auditque ruentes

---

[1] Numidas *Heinsius ;* Birt †Lydos

My fame has long been gathered in and where it is 'tis in safe custody; am I to suffer its being put to the hazard? Full well do I realize that habit is a stronger force than nature, nor am I ignorant of the rapidity with which we forget an art that we have ceased to exercise. The whip of an unpractised charioteer is powerless to urge on his horses; the hand that is unaccustomed thereto cannot bend the bow. And yet it were unjust, I admit, to refuse aught to Justice. Thou first didst draw man from his woodland cave and free the human race from its foul manner of life. Thanks to thee we practise law and have put off the temper of wild beasts. Whosoever has drunk of thee with pure heart will rush fearless through flames, will sail the wintry seas, and overcome unarmed the densest company of foemen. Justice is to the just as rain to temper even the heat of Ethiopia, a breath of spring to journey with him across the deserts of Scythia."

So spake he and took from the goddess' hand the four reins that lay stretched along the huge pole of Justice's car. The first harnesses the rivers Po and Tiber and Italy with all her glittering towns; the second guides Numidia and Carthage; the third runs out across the land of Illyria; the last holds Sardinia, Corsica, three-cornered Sicily and the coasts beaten by the Tyrrhenian wave or that echo to the Ionian. The splendour and magnitude of the undertaking troubled thee not one whit; but as the lofty summit of Olympus, far removed from the winds and tempests of the lower air, its eternal bright serene untroubled by any cloud, is lifted above the rain storms and hears the hurricane rushing

sub pedibus nimbos et rauca tonitrua calcat: 210
sic patiens animus per tanta negotia liber
emergit similisque sui, iustique tenorem
flectere non odium cogit, non gratia suadet.
nam spretas quis opes intactaque pectora lucro
commemoret? fuerint aliis haec forte decora: 215
nulla potest laus esse tibi, quae crimina purget.
servat inoffensam divina modestia vocem:
temperiem servant oculi; nec lumina fervor
asperat aut rabidas suffundit sanguine venas,
nullaque mutati tempestas proditur oris. 220
quin etiam sontes expulsa corrigis ira
et placidus delicta domas; nec dentibus umquam
instrepis horrendum, fremitu nec verbera poscis.

   Qui fruitur poena, ferus est, legumque videtur
vindictam praestare sibi; cum viscera felle 225
canduerint, ardet stimulis ferturque nocendi
prodigus, ignarus causae: dis proximus ille,
quem ratio, non ira movet, qui facta rependens
consilio punire potest. mucrone cruento
se iactent alii, studeant feritate timeri 230
addictoque hominum cumulent aeraria censu.
lene fluit Nilus, sed cunctis amnibus extat
utilior nullo confessus murmure vires;
acrior ac rapidus tacitas praetermeat ingens
Danuvius ripas; eadem clementia sani 235
gurgitis inmensum deducit in ostia Gangen.
torrentes inmane fremant lassisque minentur

beneath its feet while it treads upon the thunder's roar; so thy patient mind, unfettered by cares so manifold, rises high above them; thou art ever the same, no hatred can compel thee, no affection induce thee, to swerve from the path of justice. For why should any speak of riches scorned and a heart unallured by gain? These might perhaps be virtues in others: absence of vice is no praise to bestow on thee. The calm of a god banishes anger from thy voice; the spirit of moderation shines from thine eyes; passion never inflames that glance or fills with blood the angry veins; never is a tempest heralded on thy changed countenance. Nay, thou punishest the very criminals without show of anger and checkest their evil-doing with unruffled calm. Never dost thou gnash with thy teeth upon them nor shout orders for them to be chastised.

He is a savage who delights in punishment and seems to make the vengeance of the laws his own; when his heart is inflamed with the poison of wrath he is goaded by fury and rushes on knowing nothing of the cause and eager only to do hurt. But he whom reason, not anger, animates is a peer of the gods, he who, weighing the guilt, can with deliberation balance the punishment. Let others boast them of their bloody swords and wish to be feared for their ferocity, while they fill their treasuries with the goods of the condemned. Gently flows the Nile, yet is it more beneficent than all rivers for all that no sound reveals its power. More swiftly the broad Danube glides between its quiet banks. Huge Ganges flows down to its mouths with gently moving current. Let torrents roar horribly, threaten weary

pontibus et volvant spumoso vertice silvas :
pax maiora decet ; peragit tranquilla potestas,
quod violenta nequit, mandataque fortius urget 240
imperiosa quies.

     Idem praedurus iniquas
accepisse preces, rursus, quae digna petitu,
largior et facilis ; nec quae comitatur honores,
ausa tuam leviter temptare superbia mentem.
frons privata manet nec se meruisse fatetur,   245
quae crevisse putat ; rigidi sed plena pudoris
elucet gravitas fastu iucunda remoto.
quae non seditio, quae non insania vulgi
te viso lenita cadat ? quae dissona ritu
barbaries, medii quam non reverentia frangat ? 250
vel quis non sitiens sermonis mella politi
deserat Orpheos blanda testudine cantus ?
qualem te legimus teneri primordia mundi
scribentem aut partes animae, per singula talem
cernimus et similes agnoscit pagina mores.   255

 Nec dilata tuis Augusto iudice merces
officiis, illumque habitum, quo iungitur aulae
curia, qui socio proceres cum principe nectit,
quem quater ipse gerit, perfecto detulit anno
deposuitque suas te succedente curules.   260
crescant virtutes fecundaque floreat aetas.
ingeniis patuit campus certusque merenti
stat favor : ornatur propriis industria donis.
surgite sopitae, quas obruit ambitus, artes.
nil licet invidiae, Stilicho dum prospicit orbi 265

---

[1] *i.e.* Manlius modestly regards his honours as a natural growth, not as the reward of merit.

bridges, and sweep down forests in their foaming whirl ; 'tis repose befits the greater ; quiet authority accomplishes what violence cannot, and that mandate compels more which comes from a commanding calm.

" Thou art as deaf to the prayers of injustice as thou art generous and attentive where the demand is just. Pride, that ever accompanies office, has not so much as dared to touch thy mind. Thy look is a private citizen's nor allows that it has deserved what it thinks to have but grown [1] ; but full of stately modesty shines forth a gravity that charms because pride is banished. What sedition, what madness of the crowd could see thee and not sink down appeased ? What country so barbarous, so foreign in its customs, as not to bow in reverence before thy mediation ? Who that desires the honied charm of polished eloquence would not desert the lyre-accompanied song of tuneful Orpheus ? In every activity we see thee as we see thee in thy books, describing the creation of the newly-fashioned earth or the parts of the soul ; we recognize thy character in thy pages.

The Emperor has not been slow in rewarding thy merit. The robe that links Senate-house and palace, that unites nobles with their prince—the robe that he himself has four times worn, he hath at the year's end handed on to thee, and left his own curule chair that thou mightest follow him. Grow, ye virtues ; be this an age of prosperity ! The path of glory lies open to the wise ; merit is sure of its reward ; industry dowered with the gifts it deserves. Arts, rise from the slumber into which depraved ambition had forced you ! Envy cannot hold up her head while Stilicho and his godlike

sidereusque gener.   non hic violata curulis,
turpia non Latios incestant nomina fastos ;
fortibus haec concessa viris solisque gerenda
patribus et Romae numquam latura pudorem.

   Nuntia votorum celeri iam Fama volatu   270
moverat Aonios audito consule lucos.
concinuit felix Helicon fluxitque Aganippe
largior et docti riserunt floribus amnes.
Uranie redimita comas, qua saepe magistra
Manlius igniferos radio descripserat axes,   275
sic alias hortata deas : " patimurne, sorores,
optato procul esse die nec limina nostri
consulis et semper dilectas visimus aedes ?
notior est Helicone[1] domus.   gestare curules
et fasces subiisse libet.   miracula plebi   280
colligite et claris nomen celebrate theatris.

   " Tu Iovis aequorei summersam fluctibus aulam
oratum volucres, Erato, iam perge quadrigas,
a quibus haud umquam palmam rapturus Arion.
inlustret circum sonipes, quicumque superbo   285
perstrepit hinnitu Baetin, qui splendida potat
stagna Tagi madidoque iubas adspergitur auro.

   " Calliope, liquidas Alciden posce palaestras :
cuncta Palaemoniis manus explorata coronis
adsit et Eleo pubes laudata Tonanti.   290

   " Tu iuga Taygeti frondosaque Maenala, Clio,
i Triviae supplex ; non aspernata rogantem
amphitheatrali faveat Latonia pompae.

---

[1] *codd. have* Stilichone ; *Birt obelizes the line ; it is only found in* V ; Helicone *Gevartius.*

---

[1] Claudian is thinking of Eutropius, Manlius' eastern colleague.

son-in-law direct the state. Here is no pollution of the consul's office, no shameful names disgrace the Latin fasti; here the consulship is an honour reserved for the brave, given only to senators, never a source of scandal to Rome's city.[1]

Now had Fame, announcing our good fortune, winged her way to Aonia whose groves she stirred with the tidings of the new consul. Helicon raised a hymn of praise, Aganippe flowed with waters more abundant, the streams of song laughed with flowers. Then Urania, her hair wreath-crowned, Urania whose hand had oft directed Manlius' compass in marking out the starry spheres, thus addressed the other Muses: "Sisters, can we bear to be absent this longed-for day? Shall we not visit our consul's door and the house we have always loved? Better known to us is it than Helicon; gladly we draw the curule chair and bear the fasces. Bring marvels for the people's delight and make known his name in the famed theatres.

" Do thou, Erato, go visit the palace of Neptune beneath the sea and beg for four swift coursers such that even Arion could not snatch the prize from them. Let the Circus be graced by every steed to whose proud neighing Baetis re-echoes, who drinks of Tagus' shining pools and sprinkles his mane with its liquid gold.

" Calliope, ask thou of Alcides the oil of the wrestling-ground. Let all the company proved in the games at Elis follow thee and the athletes who have won fame with Olympian Jove.

" Fly, Clio, to Taygetus' heights and leafy Maenalus and beg Diana not to spurn thy petition but help the amphitheatre's pomp. Let the goddess herself

audaces legat ipsa viros, qui colla ferarum
arte ligent certoque premant venabula nisu.   295
ipsa truces fetus captivaque ducat ab antris
prodigia et caedis sitientem differat arcum.
conveniant ursi, magna quos mole ruentes
torva Lycaoniis Helice miretur ab astris,
perfossique rudant populo pallente leones,   300
quales Mygdonio curru frenare Cybebe
optet et Herculei mallent fregisse lacerti.
obvia fulminei properent ad vulnera pardi
semine permixto geniti, cum forte leaenae
nobiliorem uterum viridis corrupit adulter ;   305
hi maculis patres referunt et robore matres.
quidquid monstriferis nutrit Gaetulia campis,
Alpina quidquid tegitur nive, Gallica siquid
silva tenet, iaceat ; largo ditescat harena
sanguine ; consumant totos spectacula montes.   310
   " Nec molles egeant nostra dulcedine ludi :
qui laetis risum salibus movisse facetus,
qui nutu manibusque loquax, cui tibia flatu,
cui plectro pulsanda chelys, qui pulpita socco
personat aut alte graditur maiore cothurno,   315
et qui magna levi detrudens murmura tactu
innumeras voces segetis moderatus aenae
intonet erranti digito penitusque trabali
vecte laborantes in carmina concitet undas,
vel qui more avium sese iaculentur in auras   320

---

¹ Helice=the Great Bear ; so does the phrase " Lycaon's
stars," for Lycaon was the father of Callisto who was trans-
formed by the jealous Juno into a bear and as such trans-
lated by Jupiter to the sky.   Claudian means that he wants
the Great Bear to observe this assemblage of earthly bears.
   ² The *hydraulus* or water organ was known in Cicero's day
(*Tusc.* iii. 18. 43).   It is illustrated by a piece of sculpture in the
Museum at Arles (see Grove, *Dict. of Music*, under " Organ ").

choose out brave hunters cunningly to lasso the necks
of wild animals and to drive home the hunting-
spear with unfailing stroke. With her own hand let
her lead forth from their caverns fierce beasts and
captive monsters, laying aside her bloodthirsty bow.
Let bears be gathered together, whereat, as they
charge with mighty bulk, Helice may gaze in wonder
from Lycaon's stars.[1] Let smitten lions roar till the
people turn pale, lions such as Cybele would be
fain to harness to her Mygdonian chariot or
Hercules strangle in his mighty arms. May leopards,
lightning-swift, hasten to meet the spear's wound,
beasts that are born of an adulterous union what
time the spotted sire did violence to the nobler lion's
mate : of such beasts their markings recall the sire,
their courage the dam. Whatsoever is nourished
by the fields of Gaetulia rich in monsters, whatsoever
lurks beneath Alpine snows or in Gallic woods, let
it fall before the spear. Let large streams of
blood enrich the arena and the spectacle leave
whole mountains desolate.

" Nor let gentler games lack the delights we bring :
let the clown be there to move the people's laughter
with his happy wit, the mime whose language is
in his nod and in the movements of his hands, the
musician whose breath rouses the flute and whose
finger stirs the lyre, the slippered comedian to whose
voice the theatre re-echoes, the tragedian towering
on his loftier buskin ; him too whose light touch can
elicit loud music from those pipes of bronze that
sound a thousand diverse notes beneath his wander-
ing fingers and who by means of a lever stirs to song
the labouring water.[2] Let us see acrobats who hurl
themselves through the air like birds and build

corporaque aedificent celeri crescentia nexu,
quorum compositam puer amentatus in arcem
emicet et vinctu plantae vel cruribus haerens
pendula librato figat vestigia saltu.
mobile ponderibus descendat pegma reductis   325
inque chori speciem spargentes ardua flammas
scaena rotet varios et fingat Mulciber orbis
per tabulas impune vagus pictaeque citato
ludant igne trabes et non permissa morari
fida per innocuas errent incendia turres.   330
lascivi subito confligant aequore lembi
stagnaque remigibus spument inmissa canoris.
   " Consul per populos idemque gravissimus auctor
eloquii, duplici vita subnixus in aevum
procedat pariter libris fastisque legendus.   335
accipiat patris exemplum tribuatque nepoti
filius et coeptis ne desit fascibus heres.
decurrat trabeata domus tradatque secures
mutua posteritas servatoque ordine fati
Manlia continuo numeretur consule proles."   340

---

[1] We do not hear of Claudian's hopes coming true. This
son was, however, proconsul of Africa (Augustine, *Contra
Crescon.* iii. 62).

pyramids that grow with swift entwining of their bodies, to the summit of which pyramid rushes a boy fastened by a thong, a boy who, attached there by the foot or leg, executes a step-dance suspended in the air. Let the counterweights be removed and the mobile crane descend, lowering on to the lofty stage men who, wheeling chorus-wise, scatter flames; let Vulcan forge balls of fire to roll innocuously across the boards, let the flames appear to play about the sham beams of the scenery and a tame conflagration, never allowed to rest, wander among the untouched towers. Let ships meet in mimic warfare on an improvised ocean and the flooded waters be lashed to foam by singing oarsmen.

" As consul at once and stateliest master, upborne by a twofold fame, let Manlius go forth among the peoples, read in his own books and in our calendars. May the sire's example be followed by the son [1] and handed on to a grandson, nor these first fasces ever lack succession. May his race pass on purple-clad, may the generations, each to each, hand on the axes, and obedient to the ordinance of fate, Manlius after Manlius add one more consul to the tale."

DE CONSULATU STILICHONIS

LIBER I.

(XXI.)

Continuant superi pleno Romana favore
gaudia successusque novis successibus augent :
conubii necdum festivos regia cantus
sopierat, cecinit fuso Gildone triumphos,
et calidis thalami successit laurea sertis,   5
sumeret ut pariter princeps nomenque mariti
victorisque decus ; Libyae post proelia crimen
concidit Eoum, rursusque Oriente subacto
consule defensae surgunt Stilichone secures.
ordine vota meant.   equidem si carmen in unum 10
tantarum sperem cumulos advolvere rerum,
promptius imponam glaciali Pelion Ossae.
si partem tacuisse velim, quodcumque relinquam
maius erit. veteres actus primamque iuventam
prosequar ? ad sese mentem praesentia ducunt. 15
narrem iustitiam ? resplendet gloria Martis.
armati referam vires ? plus egit inermis.
quod floret Latium, Latio quod reddita servit
Africa, vicinum quod nescit Hiberia Maurum,

364

ON STILICHO'S CONSULSHIP (A.D. 400)

BOOK I

(XXI)

Ceaseless are the blessings the gods shower with
full bounty upon Rome, crowning success with new
successes. Scarce had the happy songs of marriage
ceased to echo in the palace when the defeat of
Gildo brought material for a hymn of triumph.
Hard upon the garlands of passionate love followed
the crown of laurel, so that the emperor won alike
the name of husband and the fame of conqueror.
After the war in Africa eastern sedition waned ;
the Orient once more was laid low and, guarded
by the consul Stilicho, the axes rose in triumph.
In due order are vows fulfilled. Should I hope to
roll into one poem all my lofty themes, more easily
should I pile Pelion on frozen Ossa. Were I silent
anent a part, what I leave unsung will prove the
greater. Am I to recall his deeds of old and earliest
manhood ? His present deeds lure away my mind.
Am I to tell of his justice ? His military glory
outshines it. Shall I mention his prowess in war ?
He has done more in peace. Shall I relate how
Latium flourishes, how Africa has returned to her
allegiance and service, how Spain knows no more

tuta quod imbellem miratur Gallia Rhenum,   20
aut gelidam Thracen decertatosque labores
Hebro teste canam ?   magnum mihi panditur aequor,
ipsaque Pierios lassant proclivia currus
laudibus innumeris.

                Etenim mortalibus ex quo
tellus coepta coli, numquam sincera bonorum   25
sors ulli concessa viro.   quem vultus honestat,
dedecorant mores ;   animus quem pulchrior ornat,
corpus destituit.   bellis insignior ille,
sed pacem foedat vitiis.   hic publica felix,
sed privata minus.   partitum ; singula quemque   30
nobilitant : hunc forma decens, hunc robur in armis,
hunc rigor, hunc pietas, illum sollertia iuris,
hunc suboles castique tori.   sparguntur in omnes,
in te mixta fluunt ; et quae divisa beatos
efficiunt, collecta tenes.   35

              Ne facta revolvam
militiamque patris, cuius producere famam,
si nihil egisset clarum nec fida Valenti
dextera duxisset rutilantes crinibus alas,
sufficeret natus Stilicho : mens ardua semper
a puero, tenerisque etiam fulgebat in annis   40
fortunae maioris honos.   erectus et acer
nil breve moliri, nullis haerere potentum
liminibus fatisque loqui iam digna futuris.
iam tum conspicuus, iam tum venerabilis ibas
spondebatque ducem celsi nitor igneus oris   45

---

¹ We know really nothing of Stilicho's parentage save
that the family was a Vandal one : *Vandalorum genere
editus*, Oros. vii. 38.

the Moor as her neighbour, how Gaul has now
nought to fear from a disarmed Germany? Or
shall I sing of wintry Thrace and those fierce
struggles whereof Hebrus was witness? Limitless
is the expanse that opens before me and even
on the slopes of Helicon this weight of praise
retards my muse's chariot.

For truly since man inhabited this globe never
has one mortal been granted all earth's blessings
without alloy. This man's face is fair but his char-
acter is evil; another has a beauteous soul but an
ugly body. One is renowned in war but makes
peace hideous with his vices. This man is happy in
his public but unhappy in his private life. Each
takes a part; each owes his fame to some one gift,
to bodily beauty, to martial prowess, to strength,
to uprightness of life, to knowledge of law, to
his offspring and a virtuous wife. To all men else
blessings come scattered, to thee they flow com-
mingled, and gifts that separately make happy are
all together thine.

I will not unfold the tale of thy sire's [1] warlike
deeds. Had he done nothing of note, had he in
loyalty to Valens never led to battle those yellow-
haired companies, yet to be the father of Stilicho
would have spread abroad his fame. Ever from thy
cradle did thy soul aspire, and in the tender years
of childhood shone forth the signs of loftier estate.
Lofty in spirit and eager, nothing paltry didst thou
essay; never didst thou haunt any rich man's
doorstep; thy speech was such as to befit thy future
dignities. A mark wert thou even then for all
eyes, even then an object of reverence; the fiery
brightness of thy noble countenance, the very mould

367

membrorumque modus, qualem nec carmina fingunt
semideis.   quacumque alte gradereris in urbe,
cedentes spatiis adsurgentesque videbas
quamvis miles adhuc.   taciti suffragia vulgi
iam tibi detulerant, quidquid mox debuit aula.   50

   Vix primaevus eras, pacis cum mitteris auctor
Assyriae ; tanta foedus cum gente ferire
commissum iuveni.   Tigrim transgressus et altum
Euphraten Babylona petis.   stupuere severi
Parthorum proceres, et plebs pharetrata videndi   55
flagravit studio, defixaeque hospite pulchro
Persides arcanum suspiravere calorem.
turis odoratae cumulis et messe Sabaea
pacem conciliant arae ; penetralibus ignem
sacratum rapuere adytis rituque iuvencos   60
Chaldaeo stravere magi.   rex ipse micantem
inclinat dextra pateram secretaque Beli
et vaga testatur volventem sidera Mithram.
si quando sociis tecum venatibus ibant,
quis Stilichone prior ferro penetrare leones   65
comminus aut longe virgatas figere tigres ?
flectenti faciles cessit tibi Medus habenas ;
torquebas refugum Parthis mirantibus arcum.

   Nubilis interea maturae virginis aetas
urgebat patrias suspenso principe curas,   70
quem simul imperioque ducem nataeque maritum
prospiceret ; dubius toto quaerebat ab axe
dignum coniugio generum thalamisque Serenae.

---

¹ By Assyria Claudian means Persia. He refers to the
dispatch of Stilicho in 387 as ambassador to the court of
Sapor III. (383–388) to arrange about the partition of
Armenia.

of thy limbs, greater even than poets feign of demi-gods, marked thee out for a leader of men. Whithersoever thy proud form went in the city thou didst see men rise and give place to thee; yet thou wast then but a soldier. The silent suffrage of the people had already offered thee all the honours the court was soon to owe.

Scarce hadst thou reached man's estate when thou wast sent to negotiate peace with Assyria[1]; to make a treaty with so great a people was the charge entrusted to thy youth. Crossing the Tigris and the deep Euphrates thou cam'st to Babylon. The grave lords of Parthia looked at thee in amaze and the quiver-bearing mob burned with desire to behold, while the daughters of Persia gazing on their beauteous guest sighed out their hidden love. The peace is sworn at altars sweet with the fragrance of incense and the harvests of Saba. Fire is brought forth from the innermost sanctuary and the Magi sacrifice heifers according to the Chaldean ritual. The king himself dips the jewelled bowl of sacrifice and swears by the mysteries of Bel and by Mithras who guides the errant stars of heaven. Whenever they made thee sharer of their hunting, whose sword struck down the lion in close combat before that of Stilicho, whose arrow pierced the striped tiger afar before thine? When thou didst guide the easy rein the Mede gave way to thee, and the Parthian marvelled at the bow thou didst discharge in flight.

Meanwhile a maiden of years full ripe for marriage troubled a father's heart, and the emperor doubted whom to select as her husband and as future ruler of the world; right anxiously did he search east and west for a son-in-law worthy of being wedded

369

iudicium virtutis erat ; per castra, per urbes,
per populos animi cunctantis libra cucurrit.   75
tu legeris tantosque viros, quos obtulit orbis,
intra consilium vincis sensumque legentis,
et gener Augustis olim socer ipse futurus
accedis.   radiis auri Tyriaque superbit
maiestate torus ; comitata parentibus exit   80
purpureis virgo.   stabat pater inde tropaeis
inclitus ; inde pium matris regina gerebat
obsequium gravibus subnectens flammea gemmis.
tunc et Solis equos, tunc exultasse choreis
astra ferunt mellisque lacus et flumina lactis   85
erupisse solo, cum floribus aequora vernis
Bosphorus indueret roseisque evincta coronis
certantes Asiae taedas Europa levaret.

 Felix arbitrii princeps, qui congrua mundo
iudicat et primus censet, quod cernimus omnes.   90
talem quippe virum natis adiunxit et aulae,
cui neque luxuries bello nec blanda periclis
otia nec lucis fructus pretiosior umquam
laude fuit.   quis enim Visos in plaustra feroces
reppulit aut saeva Promoti caede tumentes   95
Bastarnas una potuit delere ruina ?
Pallantis iugulum Turno moriente piavit
Aeneas, tractusque rotis ultricibus Hector
irato vindicta fuit vel quaestus Achilli.
tu neque vesano raptas venalia curru   100
funera nec vanam corpus meditaris in unum
saevitiam ; turmas equitum peditumque catervas

---

¹ Promotus, who had rescued Theodosius from an ambush
in his war against the Visigoths in 390, lost his life in the
same war the year after.   Stilicho succeeded to his command.

to Serena. Merit alone had to decide ; through
camps, through cities, through nations roamed his
poised and hesitating thoughts. But thou wast
chosen, thus in the opinion and judgement of him
who selected thee surpassing all the candidates of the
whole world and becoming a son-in-law in the
imperial family where thou wast shortly to become
a father-in-law. The marriage - bed was ablaze
with flashing gold and regal purple. The maiden
steps forth accompanied by her parents clad in
scarlet. On one side stood her sire, famed for his
triumphs, on the other was the queen, fulfilling a
mother's loving office and ordering the bridal veil
beneath a weight of jewels. Then, so men say, the
horses of the sun and the stars of heaven danced
for joy, pools of honey and rivers of milk welled
forth from the earth. Bosporus decked his banks
with vernal flowers, and Europe, entwined with rosy
garlands, uplifted the torches in rivalry with Asia.

Happy our emperor in his choice ; he judges
and the world agrees ; he is the first to value what
we all see. Ay, for he has allied to his children
and to his palace one who never preferred ease to
war nor the pleasures of peace to danger, nor yet
his life to his honour. Who but he could have
driven back the savage Visigoths to their wagons or
overwhelmed in one huge slaughter the Bastarnae
puffed up with the slaying of Promotus[1]? Aeneas
avenged the slaughter of Pallas with the death of
Turnus, Hector, dragged behind the chariot-wheels,
was to wrathful Achilles either revenge or gain ;
thou dost not carry off in mad chariot dead bodies
for ransom nor plot idle savagery against a single
corpse ; thou slayest at thy friend's tomb whole

hostilesque globos tumulo prosternis amici ;
inferiis gens tota datur.   nec Mulciber auctor
mendacis clipei fabricataque vatibus arma   105
conatus iuvere tuos : tot barbara solus
milia iam pridem miseram vastantia Thracen
finibus exiguae vallis conclusa tenebas.
nec te terrisonus stridor venientis Alani
nec vaga Chunorum feritas, non falce Gelonus,   110
non arcu pepulere Getae, non Sarmata conto.
extinctique forent penitus, ni more maligno
falleret Augustas occultus proditor aures
obstrueretque moras strictumque reconderet ensem,
solveret obsessos, praeberet foedera captis.   115
    Adsiduus castris aderat, rarissimus urbi,
si quando trepida princeps pietate vocaret ;
vixque salutatis Laribus, vix coniuge visa,
deterso necdum repetebat sanguine campum.
nec stetit Eucherii dum carperet oscula saltem   120
per galeam.   patris stimulos ignisque mariti
vicit cura ducis.   quotiens sub pellibus egit
Edonas hiemes et tardi flabra Bootae
sub divo Riphaea tulit !   cumque igne propinquo
frigora vix ferrent alii, tunc iste rigentem   125
Danuvium calcabat eques nivibusque profundum
scandebat cristatus Athon lateque corusco
curvatas glacie silvas umbone ruebat.
nunc prope Cimmerii tendebat litora Ponti,

squadrons of horse, companies of foot, and hordes of enemies. To his ghost a whole nation is offered up. Neither Vulcan's fabulous shield nor such armour as that of which poets sing the forging assisted thine efforts. Single-handed thou didst succeed in penning within the narrow confines of a single valley the vast army of barbarians that were long since ravaging the land of Thrace. For thee the fearful shriek of the onrushing Alan had no terrors nor the fierceness of the nomad Hun nor the scimitar of the Geloni, nor the Getae's bow or Sarmatian's club. These nations would have been destroyed root and branch had not a traitor by a perfidious trick abused the emperor's ear and caused him to withhold his hand; hence the sheathing of the sword, the raising of the siege, and the granting of a treaty to the prisoners.

He was always with the army, seldom in Rome, and then only when the young emperor's anxious love summoned him thither. Scarce had he greeted the gods of his home, scarce seen his wife when, still stained with the blood of his enemies, he hastened back to the battle. He did not stay to catch at least a kiss from Eucherius through his vizor; the anxieties of a general o'ercame a father's yearning and a husband's love. How often has he bivouacked through the Thracian winter and endured beneath the open sky the blasts that slow Boötes sends from mount Riphaeus. When others, huddled over the fire, could scarce brook the cold, he would ride his horse across the frozen Danube and climb Athos deep in snow, his helmet on his head, thrusting aside the frozen branches of the ice-laden trees with his far gleaming targe. Now he pitched his tent by the shores of Cimmerian Pontus, now

nunc dabat hibernum Rhodope nimbosa cubile.   130
vos Haemi gelidae valles, quas saepe cruentis
stragibus aequavit Stilicho, vos Thracia testor
flumina, quae largo mutastis sanguine fluctus ;
dicite, Bisaltae vel qui Pangaea iuvencis
scinditis, offenso quantae sub vomere putres   135
dissiliant glaebis galeae vel qualia rastris
ossa peremptorum resonent inmania regum.

   Singula complecti cuperem ; sed densior instat
gestorum series laudumque sequentibus undis
obruimur.   genitor caesi post bella tyranni   140
iam tibi commissis conscenderat aethera terris.
ancipites rerum ruituro culmine lapsus
aequali cervice subis : sic Hercule quondam
sustentante polum melius librata pependit
machina nec dubiis titubavit Signifer astris   145
perpetuaque senex subductus mole parumper
obstupuit proprii spectator ponderis Atlas.

   Nulli barbariae motus ; nil turbida rupto
ordine temptavit novitas, tantoque remoto
principe mutatas orbis non sensit habenas.   150
nil inter geminas acies, ceu libera frenis,
ausa manus.   certe nec tantis dissona linguis
turba nec armorum cultu diversior umquam
confluxit populus : totam pater undique secum
moverat Auroram ; mixtis hic Colchus Hiberis,   155
hic mitra velatus Arabs, hic crine decorus
Armenius ; hic picta Saces fucataque Medus,

---

[1] *i.e.* Eugenius.
[2] *i.e.* of East and West.

misty Rhodope afforded him a winter's bed. I call
you to witness, cold valleys of Haemus, that Stilicho
has often filled with bloody slaughter; and you,
rivers of Thrace, your waters turned to blood;
say, ye Bisaltae, or you whose oxen plough Pangaeus'
slopes, how many a rotting helm has not your
share shattered neath the soil, how oft have not
your mattocks rung against the giant bones of
slaughtered kings.

Fain would I embrace each separate one; but
thine exploits press on in too close array, and I am
overwhelmed by the pursuing flood of glorious
deeds. When Theodosius had warred against, and
slain, the tyrant [1] he ascended into heaven, leaving
the governance of the world to thee. With a
strength equal to his thou dost bear up the tottering
structure of the empire that threatens each moment
to collapse. Thus, when once Hercules upheld the
world, the universal frame hung more surely poised,
the Standard-bearer did not reel with tottering
stars, and old Atlas, relieved for a moment of the
eternal load, was confounded as he gazed upon his
own burden.

Barbary was quiet, no revolution troubled the
empire's peace and though so great a prince was dead
the world knew not that the reins had passed into
another's hands. No company in the two armies [2]
dared aught as though set loose from control. Yet
surely never had such diversities of language and
arms met together to form one united people.
Theodosius had unified the whole East beneath his
rule. Here were mingled Colchian and Iberian,
mitred Arab, beautifully coifed Armenian; here the
Sacian had pitched his painted tent, the Mede his

hic gemmata niger tentoria fixerat Indus ;
hic Rhodani procera cohors, hic miles alumnus
Oceani.   ductor Stilicho tot gentibus unus,   160
quot vel progrediens vel conspicit occiduus sol.
in quo tam vario vocum generumque tumultu
tanta quies iurisque metus servator honesti
te moderante fuit, nullis ut vinea furtis
vel seges erepta fraudaret messe colonum,   165
ut nihil aut saevum rabies aut turpe libido
suaderet, placidi servirent legibus enses.
scilicet in vulgus manant exempla regentum,
utque ducum lituos, sic mores castra sequuntur.

Denique felices aquilas quocumque moveres,   170
arebant tantis epoti milibus amnes.
Illyricum peteres : campi montesque latebant.
vexillum navale dares : sub puppibus ibat
Ionium.   nullas[1] succincta Ceraunia nimbis
nec iuga Leucatae feriens spumantia fluctu   175
deterrebat hiems.   tu si glaciale iuberes
vestigare fretum, securo milite ducti
stagna reluctantes quaterent Saturnia remi ;
si deserta Noti, fontem si quaerere Nili,
Aethiopum medios penetrassent vela vapores.   180

Te memor Eurotas, te rustica Musa Lycaei,
te pastorali modulantur Maenala cantu
Partheniumque nemus, quod te pugnante resurgens
aegra caput mediis erexit Graecia flammis.
plurima Parrhasius tunc inter corpora Ladon   185

---

[1] *AΠ* nullum; *other* MSS. nullis, *which Birt prints. But*
deterrebat *needs an object (as A and Π indicate). Possibly,
then,* nullas

376

stained tent, the dusky Indian his embroidered tent :
here were the tall company of warriors from the
Rhone and the warlike children of Ocean. Stilicho
and Stilicho alone commanded all the nations looked
on by the rising and the setting sun. Amid this com-
pany so diverse in blood and speech such peace
reigned beneath thy rule, so did fear of justice secure
right, that not a single vineyard was robbed, nor did
a single field cheat the husbandman of its plundered
crop ; rage incited to no violence, passion to no
deeds of shame ; the peaceful sword was obedient
to law. Of a truth their leaders' pattern passes to
the crowd, and the soldier follows not only the
standards but also the example of his general.

Whithersoever thou didst lead thy victorious eagles
there rivers grew dry, drunk up by so many thousands
of men. Didst thou march towards Illyria, plain and
mountain were hidden ; didst thou give the signal
to thy fleet, the Ionian main was lost beneath thy
ships. Cloud-girt Ceraunia, the storms that dash
the waves in foam on Leucas' promontory—these
could not affright any. Shouldst thou bid them
explore some frozen sea, thy untroubled soldiers
would shatter the congealed waters with counter-
vailing oar ; had they to seek the deserts of
the south, to search out the sources of the Nile,
their sails would penetrate into Ethiopia's midmost
heat.

Thee mindful Eurotas, thee Lycaeus' rustic muse,
thee Maenalus celebrates in pastoral song, and there-
with the woods of Parthenius, where, thanks to thy
victorious arms, weary Greece has raised once more
her head from amid the flames. Then did Ladon, river
of Arcadia, stay his course amid the countless bodies,

haesit et Alpheus Geticis angustus acervis
tardior ad Siculos etiamnunc pergit amores.

Miramur rapidis hostem succumbere bellis,
cum solo terrore ruant ? non classica Francis
intulimus : iacuere tamen. non Marte Suebos   190
contudimus, quis iura damus. quis credere possit ?
ante tubam nobis audax Germania servit.
cedant, Druse, tui, cedant, Traiane, labores :
vestra manus dubio quidquid discrimine gessit,
transcurrens egit Stilicho totidemque diebus   195
edomuit Rhenum, quot vos potuistis in annis ;
quem ferro, adloquiis ; quem vos cum milite, solus.
impiger a primo descendens fluminis ortu
ad bifidos tractus et iuncta paludibus ora
fulmineum perstrinxit iter ; ducis impetus undas   200
vincebat celeres, et pax a fonte profecta
cum Rheni crescebat aquis. ingentia quondam
nomina, crinigero flaventes vertice reges,
qui nec principibus donis precibusque vocati
paruerant, iussi properant segnique verentur   205
offendisse mora ; transvecti lintribus amnem
occursant ubicumque velit. nec fama fefellit
iustitiae : videre pium, videre fidelem.
quem veniens timuit, rediens Germanus amavit.
illi terribiles, quibus otia vendere semper   210
mos erat et foeda requiem mercede pacisci,
natis obsidibus pacem tam supplice vultu

---

¹ *i.e.* Arethusa.

and Alphaeus, choked with heaps of slaughtered
Getae, won his way more slowly to his Sicilian love.[1]

Do we wonder that the foe so swiftly yields in
battle when they fall before the sole terror of his
name? We did not declare war on the Franks;
yet they were overthrown. We did not crush in
battle the Suebi on whom we now impose our laws.
Who could believe it? Fierce Germany was our
slave or ever the trumpets rang out. Where are
now thy wars, Drusus, or thine, Trajan? All that
your hands wrought after doubtful conflict that
Stilicho did as he passed along, and o'ercame the
Rhine in as many days as you could do in years;
you conquered with the sword, he with a word; you
with an army, he single-handed. Descending from
the river's source to where it splits in twain and to
the marshes that connect its mouths he flashed his
lightning way. The speed of the general outstripped
the river's swift course, and Peace, starting with him
from Rhine's source, grew as grew Rhine's waters.
Chieftains whose names were once so well known,
flaxen-haired warrior-kings whom neither gifts nor
prayers could win over to obedience to Rome's
emperors, hasten at his command and fear to offend
by dull delay. Crossing the river in boats they
meet him wheresoever he will. The fame of his
justice did not play them false: they found him
merciful, they found him trustworthy. Him whom
at his coming the German feared, at his departure
he loved. Those dread tribes whose wont it was
ever to set their price on peace and let us purchase
repose by shameful tribute, offered their children
as hostages and begged for peace with such sup-
pliant looks that one would have thought them

captivoque rogant, quam si post terga revincti
Tarpeias pressis subeant cervicibus arces.
omne, quod Oceanum fontesque interiacet Histri, 215
unius incursu tremuit ; sine caede subactus
servitio Boreas exarmatique Triones.

    Tempore tam parvo tot proelia sanguine nullo
perficis et luna nuper nascente profectus
ante redis, quam tota fuit, Rhenumque minacem 220
cornibus infractis adeo mitescere cogis,
ut Salius iam rura colat flexosque Sygambrus
in falcem curvet gladios, geminasque viator
cum videat ripas, quae sit Romana, requirat ;
ut iam trans fluvium non indignante Chauco 225
pascat Belga pecus, mediumque ingressa per Albim
Gallica Francorum montes armenta pererrent ;
ut procul Hercyniae per vasta silentia silvae
venari tuto liceat, lucosque vetusta
religione truces et robur numinis instar 230
barbarici nostrae feriant impune bipennes.

    Ultro quin etiam devota mente tuentur
victorique favent.   quotiens sociare catervas
oravit iungique tuis Alamannia signis !
nec doluit contempta tamen, spretoque recessit 235
auxilio laudata fides.   provincia missos
expellet citius fasces quam Francia reges,
quos dederis.   acie nec iam pulsare rebelles,
sed vinclis punire licet ; sub iudice nostro
regia Romanus disquirit crimina carcer : 240

captives, their hands bound behind their backs, and they mounting the Tarpeian rock with the chains of slavery upon their necks. All those lands that lie between Ocean and the Danube trembled at the approach of one man. Boreas was brought into servitude without a blow; the Great Bear was disarmed.

In so short a time didst thou win so many battles without loss of blood, and, setting out with the moon yet new, thou didst return or ever it was full; so didst thou compel the threatening Rhine to learn gentleness with shattered horns, that the Salian now tills his fields, the Sygambrian beats his straight sword into a curved sickle, and the traveller, as he looks at the two banks, asks over which Rome rules. The Belgian, too, pastures his flock across the river and the Chauci heed it not; Gallic herds cross the middle Elbe and wander over the hills of the Franks. Safe it is to hunt amid the vast silence of the distant Hercynian forest, and in the woods that old-established superstition has rendered awful our axes fell the trees the barbarian once worshipped and nought is said.

Nay more, devoted to their conqueror this people offers its arms in his defence. How oft has Germany begged to add her troops to thine and to join her forces with those of Rome! Nor yet was she angered when her offer was rejected, for though her aid was refused her loyalty came off with praise. Provence will sooner drive out the governor thou sendest than will the land of the Franks expel the ruler thou hast given them. Not to rout rebels in the field but to punish them with chains is now the law; under our judge a Roman prison holds inquest

Marcomeres Sunnoque docet; quorum alter Etruscum
pertulit exilium; cum se promitteret alter
exulis ultorem, iacuit mucrone suorum:
res avidi concire novas odioque furentes
pacis et ingenio scelerumque cupidine fratres.   245
    Post domitas Arctos alio prorupit ab axe
tempestas et, ne qua tuis intacta tropaeis
pars foret, Australis sonuit tuba.   moverat omnes
Maurorum Gildo populos, quibus inminet Atlas
et quos interior nimio plaga sole relegat: 250
quos vagus umectat Cinyps et proximus hortis
Hesperidum Triton et Gir notissimus amnis
Aethiopum, simili mentitus gurgite Nilum;
venerat et parvis redimitus Nuba sagittis
et velox Garamas, nec quamvis tristibus Hammon 255
responsis alacrem potuit Nasamona morari.
stipantur Numidae campi, stant pulvere Syrtes
Gaetulae, Poenus iaculis obtexitur aër.
hi virga moderantur equos; his fulva leones
velamenta dabant ignotarumque ferarum   260
exuviae, vastis Meroë quas nutrit harenis;
serpentum patulos gestant pro casside rictus;
pendent vipereae squamosa pelle pharetrae.
non sic intremuit Simois, cum montibus Idae
nigra coloratus produceret agmina Memnon,   265
non Ganges, cum tela procul vibrantibus Indis
inmanis medium vectaret belua Porum.

---

¹ Marcomeres and Sunno, brother chiefs of the Ripuarian
Franks, had (? in connexion with Maximus' revolt) invaded
Roman territory near Cologne in 388 and been defeated by
Arbogast.   Stilicho's successful campaign against them, of
which we read here, is to be dated 395 (? March).

on the crimes of kings. Marcomeres and Sunno [1] give proof : the one underwent exile in Etruria, the other, proclaiming himself the exile's avenger, fell beneath the swords of his own soldiers. Both were eager to arouse rebellion, both hated peace—true brothers in character and in a common love of crime.

After the conquest of the north arose a fresh storm in another quarter. The trumpets of war rang out in the south that there might be no part of the world untouched by thy victories. Gildo stirred up all the Moorish tribes living beneath mount Atlas and those whom the excessive heat of the sun cuts off from us in the interior of Africa, those too whom Cinyps' wandering stream waters, and Triton, neighbour of the garden of the Hesperides ; those who dwell beside the waters of Gir, most famous of the rivers of Ethiopia, that overflows his banks as it had been another Nile. There came at his summons the Nubian with his head-dress of short arrows, the fleet Garamantian, the Nasamonian whose impetuous ardour not even the sinister predictions of Ammon could restrain. The plain of Numidia was overrun, their dust covered the Gaetulian Syrtes ; the sky of Carthage was darkened with their arrows. Some, mounted, guide their horses with sticks, others are clad in tawny lion-skins and pelts of the nameless animals that range the vast deserts of Meroë. Severed heads of serpents with gaping jaws serve them for helmets, the bright scaly skin of the viper fashions their quivers. Simois trembled not so violently when swart Memnon led his dusky troops o'er Ida's summit. Not so fearful was Ganges when Porus approached, mounted on his towering elephant and surrounded with his far-shooting Indian soldiery.

Porus Alexandro, Memnon prostratus Achilli,
Gildo nempe tibi.

Nec solum fervidus Austrum,
sed partes etiam Mavors agitabat Eoas.   270
quamvis obstreperet pietas, his ille regendae
transtulerat nomen Libyae scelerique profano
fallax legitimam regni praetenderat umbram.
surgebat geminum varia formidine bellum,
hoc armis, hoc triste dolis.   hoc Africa saevis   275
cinxerat auxiliis, hoc coniuratus alebat
insidiis Oriens.   illinc edicta meabant
corruptura duces ; hinc frugibus atra negatis
urgebat trepidamque fames obsederat urbem.
exitiale palam Libycum ; civile pudoris   280
obtentu tacitum.

Tales utrimque procellae
cum fremerent lacerumque alternis ictibus anceps
imperium pulsaret hiems, nil fessa remisit
officii virtus contraque minantia fata
pervigil eventusque sibi latura secundos   285
maior in adversis micuit : velut arbiter alni,
nubilus Aegaeo quam turbine vexat Orion,
exiguo clavi flexu declinat aquarum
verbera, nunc recta, nunc obliquante carina
callidus, et pelagi caelique obnititur irae.   290
   Quid primum, Stilicho, mirer? quod cautus ad omnes
restiteris fraudes, ut te nec noxia furto
littera nec pretio manus inflammata lateret ?
quod nihil in tanto circum terrore locutus
indignum Latio ?   responsa quod ardua semper 295
Eois dederis, quae mox effecta probasti—

---

[1] Africa belonged to the West. Gildo, in the words of
Zosimus (v. 11. 2), ἀφίστησι τὴν χώραν τῆς Ὀνωρίου βασιλείας
καὶ τῇ Ἀρκαδίου προστίθησιν.

Yet Porus was defeated by Alexander, Memnon by Achilles, and Gildo by thee.

It was not, however, only the South that fierce Mars aroused but also the East. Though loyalty cried out against it Gildo had transferred the nominal rule of Libya to the Eastern empire, cloaking his base treason under the name of legitimate government.[1] Thus with diverse terror a twofold war arose ; here were arms, there were wiles. Africa supported the one with her savage tribes, the other the conspiring East nurtured with treachery. From Byzantium came edicts to subvert the loyalty of governors ; from Africa that refused her crops black famine pressed and had beleaguered trembling Rome. Libya openly meditated our destruction ; over the civic strife shame had laid her veil of silence.

Though such storms raged on either hand, though the twofold tempest buffeted the torn empire on this side and on that, no whit did our consul's courage yield to weariness, but ever watchful against threatening doom and soon to win prosperous issue, shone greater amid dangers : as the ship's pilot, tossed in mid Aegean by the storms of rainy Orion, eludes the waves' buffeting by the least turn of the tiller, skilfully guiding his vessel now on straight, now on slanting course, and struggles successfully against the conjoint fury of sea and sky.

At what, Stilicho, shall I first marvel ? At the providence that resisted all intrigues, whereby no treacherous missive, no bribe-fraught hand escaped thy notice ? Or because that amid the general terror thou spakest no word unworthy of Latium ? Or because thou didst ever give haughty answer to the East and later made that answer

securus, quamvis et opes et rura tenerent
insignesque domos? levis haec iactura; nec
    umquam
publica privatae cesserunt commoda causae.
dividis ingentes curas teque omnibus unum   300
obicis, inveniens animo quae mente gerenda,
efficiens patranda manu, dictare paratus
quae scriptis peragenda forent. quae brachia centum,
quis Briareus aliis numero crescente lacertis
tot simul obiectis posset confligere rebus :   305
evitare dolos ; veteres firmare cohortes,
explorare novas ; duplices disponere classes,
quae fruges aut bella ferant ; aulaeque tumultum
et Romae lenire famem ? quot nube soporis
inmunes oculi per tot discurrere partes,   310
tot loca sufficerent et tam longinqua tueri ?
Argum fama canit centeno lumine cinctum
corporis excubiis unam servasse iuvencam !
  Unde tot adlatae segetes ? quae silva carinas
texuit ? unde rudis tanto tirone iuventus   315
emicuit senioque iterum vernante resumpsit
Gallia bis fractas Alpino vulnere vires ?
non ego dilectu, Tyrii sed vomere Cadmi
tam subitas acies concepto dente draconis
exiluisse reor : Dircaeis qualis in arvis   320
messis cum proprio mox bellatura colono
cognatos strinxit gladios, cum semine iacto
terrigenae galea matrem nascente ferirent

---

[1] In the wars against, respectively, Eugenius and the
Goths.

good ? They held thy goods, thy lands, thy houses, yet wast thou unmoved. This thou didst account a trifling loss nor ever preferred private to public interest. Thy mighty task thou dost parcel out, yet dost thou face it all alone, debating the problems that must needs be thought out, acting where deeds are called for, ever ready to dictate where aught is to be accomplished by writing. What hundred-handed monster, what Briareus, whose arms ever grew more numerous as they were lopped off, could cope with all these things at once ? To avoid the snares of treachery, to strengthen existing regiments and enroll new ones, to equip two fleets, one of corn-ships, one of men-of-war, to quell the tumult of the court and alleviate the hunger of the Roman populace—what eyes, never visited by the veil of sleep, have had the strength to turn their gaze in so many directions and over so many lands or to pierce so far ? Fame tells how Argus girt with a hundred eyes could guard but one heifer with his body's watch.

Whence comes this mass of corn ? What forest fashioned all those vessels ? Whence has sprung this untutored army with all its young recruits ? Whence has Gaul, its age once more at the spring, won back the strength that Alpine blows twice shattered [1] ? Methinks 'tis no levy but the plough-share of the Phoenician Cadmus that has raised up thus suddenly a host sprung from the sowing of the dragon's teeth ; 'tis like the crop that in the fields of Thebes drew the sword of kin in threatened battle with its own sower when, the seed once sown, the earth-born giants clave the earth, their mother's womb, with their springing helms and a harvest of

armifer et viridi floreret milite sulcus.
hoc quoque non parva fas est cum laude relinqui, 325
quod non ante fretis exercitus adstitit ultor,
ordine quam prisco censeret bella senatus.
neglectum Stilicho per tot iam saecula morem
rettulit, ut ducibus mandarent proelia patres
decretoque togae felix legionibus iret   330
tessera.   Romuleas leges rediisse fatemur,
cum procerum iussis famulantia cernimus arma.

   Tyrrhenum poteras cunctis transmittere signis
et ratibus Syrtes, Libyam complere maniplis ;
consilio stetit ira minor, ne territus ille   335
te duce suspecto Martis graviore paratu
aut in harenosos aestus zonamque rubentem
tenderet aut solis fugiens transiret in ortus
missurusve sibi certae solacia mortis
oppida dirueret flammis.   res mira relatu :   340
ne timeare times et, quem vindicta manebat,
desperare vetas.   quantum fiducia nobis
profuit !   hostilis salvae Carthaginis arces ;
inlaesis Tyrii gaudent cultoribus agri,
quos potuit vastare fuga.   spe captus inani   345
nec se subripuit poenae nostrisque pepercit :
demens, qui numero tantum, non robore mensus
Romanos rapidis ibat ceu protinus omnes
calcaturus equis et, quod iactare solebat,
solibus effetos mersurus pulvere Gallos.   350

young soldiery burgeoned along the armèd furrows. This too must not be passed over without full meed of praise, that the avenging expedition did not embark until the senate had, in accordance with antique usage, declared war. Stilicho re-established this custom, neglected for so many ages, that the Fathers should give generals charge to fight, and by decree of the toga-clad Senate the battle-token pass auspiciously among the legions. We acknowledge that the laws of Romulus have now returned when we see arms obedient to our ministers.

Thou couldst have filled the Tyrrhene sea with all thy standards, the Syrtes with thy fleet and Libya with thy battalions, but wrath was stayed o'ercome by prudent fear lest Gildo, terrified at the thought that thou wast in arms against him and suspecting that thy forces were of overwhelming strength, might retire into the hot desert and the torrid zone, or travel east in flight or, to console him for the certainty of death, might destroy his cities with fire. Marvellous it is to tell: thou wast fearful of being feared and forbade him to despair whom thy vengeance awaited. How greatly was his confidence our gain! Safe are the towers of hostile Carthage, and the Phoenician fields rejoice in their unharmed husbandmen, fields he might have laid waste in his flight. Deluded by a vain hope he spared what was ours without escaping chastisement for himself. Madman, to measure Rome by the numbers instead of the valour of her soldiers! He advanced as though he would ride them all down by means of his fleet cavalry and, as he often boasted, would overwhelm in the dust the Gauls enervated by the sun's heat. But he soon learned that neither wounds

sed didicit non Aethiopum geminata venenis
vulnera, non fusum crebris hastilibus imbrem,
non equitum nimbos Latiis obsistere pilis.
sternitur ignavus Nasamon, nec spicula supplex
iam torquet Garamas ; repetunt deserta fugaces 355
Autololes ; pavidus proiecit missile Mazax.
cornipedem Maurus nequiquam hortatur anhelum ;
praedonem lembo profugum ventisque repulsum
suscepit merito fatalis Tabraca portu
expertum quod nulla tuis elementa paterent   360
hostibus, et laetae passurum iurgia plebis
fracturumque reos humili sub iudice vultus.
    Nil tribuat Fortuna sibi. sit prospera semper
illa quidem ; sed non uni certamina pugnae
credidimus totis nec constitit alea castris   365
nutatura semel ; si quid licuisset iniquis
casibus, instabant aliae post terga biremes ;
venturus dux maior erat.
                              Victoria nulla
clarior aut hominum votis optatior umquam
contigit. an quisquam Tigranen armaque Ponti 370
vel Pyrrhum Antiochique fugam vel vincla Iugurthae
conferat aut Persen debellatumque Philippum ?
hi propagandi ruerant pro limite regni ;
hic stabat Romana salus. ibi tempora tuto
traxerunt dilata moras ; hic vincere tarde   375
vinci paene fuit. discrimine Roma supremo
inter supplicium populi deforme pependit ;
et tantum Libyam fructu maiore recepit
quam peperit, quantum graviorem amissa dolorem
quam necdum quaesita movent. quis Punica gesta,
390

made more deadly by the poisoned arrow of Ethiopia nor thick hail of javelins nor clouds of horsemen can withstand Latin spears. The cowardly Nasamonian troops are scattered, the Garamantian hurls not his spears but begs for mercy, the swift-footed Autololes fly to the desert, the terror-stricken Mazacian flings away his arms, in vain the Moor urges on his flagging steed. The brigand flees in a small boat and driven back by the winds met with his just fate in the harbour of Tabraca, discovering that no element offered refuge, Stilicho, to thine enemies. There he was destined to undergo the insults of the overjoyed populace and to bow his guilty head before a lowly judgement-seat.

Let not Fortune claim aught for herself. Let her be ever favourable ; but we trusted not the issue to a single fight, nor was the hazard set with all our force to be lost at a single throw. Had hard chance at all prevailed, a second fleet pressed on behind, a greater leader was yet to come.

Never was a more famous victory nor one that was the object of more heart-felt prayers. Will anyone compare with this the defeat of Tigranes, of the king of Pontus, the flight of Pyrrhus or Antiochus, the capture of Jugurtha, the overthrow of Perses or Philip ? Their fall meant but the enlargement of the empire's bounds ; on Gildo's depended the very existence of Rome. In those cases delay entailed no ill ; in this a late-won victory was all but a defeat. On this supreme issue, while leanness racked her people, hung the fate of Rome ; and to win back Libya was a greater gain than its first conquest, even as to lose a possession stirs a heavier pain than never to have had it. Who would

quis vos, Scipiadae, quis te iam, Regule, nosset, 380
quis lentum caneret Fabium, si iure perempto
insultaret atrox famula Carthagine Maurus ?
haec omnes veterum revocavit adorea lauros ;
restituit Stilicho cunctos tibi, Roma, triumphos. 385

now be telling of the Punic wars, of you, ye Scipios, or of thee, Regulus ; who would sing of cautious Fabius, if, destroying right, the fierce Moor were trampling on an enslaved Carthage ? This victory, Rome, has revived the laurels of thy heroes of old ; Stilicho has restored to thee all thy triumphs.

(35)

Printed in Great Britain by R. & R. CLARK, LIMITED, *Edinburgh*

THE LOEB CLASSICAL LIBRARY

VOLUMES ALREADY PUBLISHED

LATIN AUTHORS

AMMIANUS MARCELLINUS. J. C. Rolfe. 3 Vols.

APULEIUS : THE GOLDEN ASS (METAMORPHOSES). W. Adlington (1566). Revised by S. Gaselee.

ST. AUGUSTINE : CITY OF GOD. 7 Vols. Vol. I. G. E. McCracken. Vol. II. W. M. Green. Vol. III. D. Wiesen. Vol. IV. P. Levine. Vol. V. E. M. Sanford and W. M. Green. Vol. VI. W. C. Greene. Vol. VII. W. M. Green.

ST. AUGUSTINE, CONFESSIONS OF. W. Watts (1631). 2 Vols.

ST. AUGUSTINE : SELECT LETTERS. J. H. Baxter.

AUSONIUS. H. G. Evelyn White. 2 Vols.

BEDE. J. E. King. 2 Vols.

BOETHIUS : TRACTS AND DE CONSOLATIONE PHILOSOPHIAE. Rev. H. F. Stewart and E. K. Rand. Revised by S. J. Tester.

CAESAR : ALEXANDRIAN, AFRICAN AND SPANISH WARS. A. G. Way.

CAESAR : CIVIL WARS. A. G. Peskett.

CAESAR : GALLIC WAR. H. J. Edwards.

CATO AND VARRO : DE RE RUSTICA. H. B. Ash and W. D. Hooper.

CATULLUS. F. W. Cornish ; TIBULLUS. J. B. Postgate ; and PERVIGILIUM VENERIS. J. W. Mackail.

CELSUS : DE MEDICINA. W. G. Spencer. 3 Vols.

CICERO : BRUTUS AND ORATOR. G. L. Hendrickson and H. M. Hubbell.

CICERO : DE FINIBUS. H. Rackham.

CICERO : DE INVENTIONE, etc. H. M. Hubbell.

CICERO : DE NATURA DEORUM AND ACADEMICA. H. Rackham.

CICERO : DE OFFICIIS. Walter Miller.

CICERO : DE ORATORE, etc. 2 Vols. Vol. I : DE ORATORE, Books I and II. E. W. Sutton and H. Rackham. Vol. II : DE ORATORE, Book III ; DE FATO ; PARADOXA STOICORUM ; DE PARTITIONE ORATORIA. H. Rackham.

CICERO : DE REPUBLICA, DE LEGIBUS. Clinton W. Keyes.

1

THE LOEB CLASSICAL LIBRARY

Ovid : The Art of Love and other Poems. J. H. Mozley.

Ovid : Fasti. Sir James G. Frazer.

Ovid : Heroides and Amores. Grant Showerman.

Ovid : Metamorphoses. F. J. Miller. 2 Vols.

Ovid : Tristia and Ex Ponto. A. L. Wheeler.

Petronius. M. Heseltine ; Seneca : Apocolocyntosis. W. H. D. Rouse.

Phaedrus and Babrius (Greek). B. E. Perry.

Plautus. Paul Nixon. 5 Vols.

Pliny : Letters, Panegyricus. B. Radice. 2 Vols.

Pliny : Natural History. 10 Vols. Vols. I-V. H. Rackham. Vols. VI-VIII. W. H. S. Jones. Vol. IX. H. Rackham. Vol. X. D. E. Eichholz.

Propertius. H. E. Butler.

Prudentius. H. J. Thomson. 2 Vols.

Quintilian. H. E. Butler. 4 Vols.

Remains of Old Latin. E. H. Warmington. 4 Vols. Vol. I (Ennius and Caecilius). Vol. II (Livius, Naevius, Pacuvius, Accius). Vol. III (Lucilius, Laws of the XII Tables). Vol. IV (Archaic Inscriptions).

Sallust. J. C. Rolfe.

Scriptores Historiae Augustae. D. Magie. 3 Vols.

Seneca : Apocolocyntosis. *Cf.* Petronius.

Seneca : Epistulae Morales. R. M. Gummere. 3 Vols.

Seneca : Moral Essays. J. W. Basore. 3 Vols.

Seneca : Naturales Quaestiones. T. H. Corcoran. 2 Vols.

Seneca : Tragedies. F. J. Miller. 2 Vols.

Seneca the Elder : Controversiae Suasoriae. M. Winterbottom. 2 Vols.

Sidonius : Poems and Letters. W. B. Anderson. 2 Vols.

Silius Italicus. J. D. Duff. 2 Vols.

Statius. J. H. Mozley. 2 Vols.

Suetonius. J. C. Rolfe. 2 Vols.

Tacitus : Agricola and Germania. M. Hutton ; Dialogus. Sir Wm. Peterson. Revised by R. M. Ogilvie, E. H. Warmington, M. Winterbottom.

Tacitus : Histories and Annals. C. H. Moore and J. Jackson. 4 Vols.

Terence. John Sargeaunt. 2 Vols.

Tertullian : Apologia and De Spectaculis. T. R. Glover ; Minucius Felix. G. H. Rendall.

Valerius Flaccus. J. H. Mozley.

Varro : De Lingua Latina. R. G. Kent. 2 Vols.

Velleius Paterculus and Res Gestae Divi Augusti. F. W. Shipley.

3

THE LOEB CLASSICAL LIBRARY

VIRGIL. H. R. Fairclough. 2 Vols.
VITRUVIUS: DE ARCHITECTURA. F. Granger. 2 Vols.

GREEK AUTHORS

ACHILLES TATIUS. S. Gaselee.
AELIAN: ON THE NATURE OF ANIMALS. A. F. Scholfield.
  3 Vols.
AENEAS TACTICUS, ASCLEPIODOTUS AND ONASANDER. The
  Illinois Greek Club
AESCHINES. C. D. Adams.
AESCHYLUS. H. Weir Smyth. 2 Vols.
ALICIPHRON, AELIAN AND PHILOSTRATUS: LETTERS. A. R.
  Benner and F. H. Fobes.
APOLLODORUS. Sir James G. Frazer. 2 Vols.
APOLLONIUS RHODIUS. R. C. Seaton.
THE APOSTOLIC FATHERS. Kirsopp Lake. 2 Vols.
APPIAN'S ROMAN HISTORY. Horace White. 4 Vols.
ARATUS. Cf. CALLIMACHUS: HYMNS AND EPIGRAMS.
ARISTIDES. C. A. Behr. 4 Vols. Vol. I.
ARISTOPHANES. Benjamin Bickley Rogers. 3 Vols. Verse
  trans.
ARISTOTLE: ART OF RHETORIC. J. H. Freese.
ARISTOTLE: ATHENIAN CONSTITUTION, EUDEMIAN ETHICS,
  VIRTUES AND VICES. H. Rackham.
ARISTOTLE: THE CATEGORIES. ON INTERPRETATION. H. P.
  Cooke; PRIOR ANALYTICS. H. Tredennick.
ARISTOTLE: GENERATION OF ANIMALS. A. L. Peck.
ARISTOTLE: HISTORIA ANIMALIUM. A. L. Peck. 3 Vols.
  Vols. I and II.
ARISTOTLE: METAPHYSICS. H. Tredennick. 2 Vols.
ARISTOTLE: METEOROLOGICA. H. D. P. Lee.
ARISTOTLE: MINOR WORKS. W. S. Hett. "On Colours,"
  "On Things Heard," "Physiognomics," "On Plants,"
  "On Marvellous Things Heard," "Mechanical Prob-
  lems," "On Invisible Lines," "Situations and Names of
  Winds," "On Melissus, Xenophanes, and Gorgias."
ARISTOTLE: NICOMACHEAN ETHICS. H. Rackham.
ARISTOTLE: OECONOMICA AND MAGNA MORALIA. G. C.
  Armstrong. (With METAPHYSICS, Vol. II.)
ARISTOTLE: ON THE HEAVENS. W. K. C. Guthrie.
ARISTOTLE: ON THE SOUL, PARVA NATURALIA, ON BREATH.
  W. S. Hett.

4

THE LOEB CLASSICAL LIBRARY

ARISTOTLE: PARTS OF ANIMALS. A. L. Peck; MOVEMENT
AND PROGRESSION OF ANIMALS. E. S. Forster.
ARISTOTLE: PHYSICS. Rev. P. Wicksteed and F. M. Corn-
ford. 2 Vols.
ARISTOTLE: POETICS; LONGINUS ON THE SUBLIME. W. Ham-
ilton Fyfe; DEMETRIUS ON STYLE. W. Rhys Roberts.
ARISTOTLE: POLITICS. H. Rackham.
ARISTOTLE: POSTERIOR ANALYTICS. H. Tredennick; TOPICS.
E. S. Forster.
ARISTOTLE: PROBLEMS. W. S. Hett. 2 Vols.
ARISTOTLE: RHETORICA AD ALEXANDRUM. H. Rackham.
(With PROBLEMS, Vol. II.)
ARISTOTLE: SOPHISTICAL REFUTATIONS. COMING-TO-BE AND
PASSING-AWAY. E. S. Forster; ON THE COSMOS. D. J.
Furley.
ARRIAN: HISTORY OF ALEXANDER AND INDICA. 2 Vols.
Vol. I. P. Brunt. Vol. II. Rev. E. Iliffe Robson.
ATHENAEUS: DEIPNOSOPHISTAE. C. B. Gulick. 7 Vols.
BABRIUS AND PHAEDRUS (Latin). B. E. Perry.
ST. BASIL: LETTERS. R. J. Deferrari. 4 Vols.
CALLIMACHUS: FRAGMENTS. C. A. Trypanis; MUSAEUS:
HERO AND LEANDER. T. Gelzer and C. Whitman.
CALLIMACHUS: HYMNS AND EPIGRAMS, AND LYCOPHRON.
A. W. Mair; ARATUS. G. R. Mair.
CLEMENT OF ALEXANDRIA. Rev. G. W. Butterworth.
COLLUTHUS. Cf. OPPIAN.
DAPHNIS AND CHLOE. Cf. LONGUS.
DEMOSTHENES I: OLYNTHIACS, PHILIPPICS AND MINOR
ORATIONS: I-XVII AND XX. J. H. Vince.
DEMOSTHENES II: DE CORONA AND DE FALSA LEGATIONE.
C. A. Vince and J. H. Vince.
DEMOSTHENES III: MEIDIAS, ANDROTION, ARISTOCRATES,
TIMOCRATES, ARISTOGEITON. J. H. Vince.
DEMOSTHENES IV-VI: PRIVATE ORATIONS AND IN NEAERAM.
A. T. Murray.
DEMOSTHENES VII: FUNERAL SPEECH, EROTIC ESSAY, EX-
ORDIA AND LETTERS. N. W. and N. J. DeWitt.
DIO CASSIUS: ROMAN HISTORY. E. Cary. 9 Vols.
DIO CHRYSOSTOM. 5 Vols. Vols. I and II. J. W. Cohoon.
Vol. III. J. W. Cohoon and H. Lamar Crosby. Vols. IV
and V. H. Lamar Crosby.
DIODORUS SICULUS. 12 Vols. Vols. I-VI. C. H. Oldfather.
Vol. VII. C. L. Sherman. Vol. VIII. C. B. Welles. Vols.
IX and X. Russel M. Geer. Vols. XI and XII. F. R.
Walton. General Index. Russel M. Geer.

5

Diogenes Laertius. R. D. Hicks. 2 Vols. New Introduction by H. S. Long.

Dionysius of Halicarnassus: Critical Essays. S. Usher. 2 Vols.

Dionysius of Halicarnassus: Roman Antiquities. Spelman's translation revised by E. Cary. 7 Vols.

Epictetus. W. A. Oldfather. 2 Vols.

Euripides. A. S. Way. 4 Vols. Verse trans.

Eusebius: Ecclesiastical History. Kirsopp Lake and J. E. L. Oulton. 2 Vols.

Galen: On the Natural Faculties. A. J. Brock.

The Greek Anthology. W. R. Paton. 5 Vols.

The Greek Bucolic Poets (Theocritus, Bion, Moschus). J. M. Edmonds.

Greek Elegy and Iambus with the Anacreontea. J. M. Edmonds. 2 Vols.

Greek Mathematical Works. Ivor Thomas. 2 Vols.

Herodes. Cf. Theophrastus: Characters.

Herodian. C. R. Whittaker. 2 Vols.

Herodotus. A. D. Godley. 4 Vols.

Hesiod and the Homeric Hymns. H. G. Evelyn White.

Hippocrates and the Fragments of Heracleitus. W. H. S. Jones and E. T. Withington. 4 Vols.

Homer: Iliad. A. T. Murray. 2 Vols.

Homer: Odyssey. A. T. Murray. 2 Vols.

Isaeus. E. S. Forster.

Isocrates. George Norlin and LaRue Van Hook. 3 Vols.

[St. John Damascene]: Barlaam and Ioasaph. Rev. G. R. Woodward, Harold Mattingly and D. M. Lang.

Josephus. 9 Vols. Vols. I-IV. H. St. J. Thackeray. Vol. V. H. St. J. Thackeray and Ralph Marcus. Vols. VI and VII. Ralph Marcus. Vol. VIII. Ralph Marcus and Allen Wikgren. Vol. IX. L. H. Feldman.

Julian. Wilmer Cave Wright. 3 Vols.

Libanius: Selected Works. A. F. Norman. 3 Vols. Vols. I and II.

Longus: Daphnis and Chloe. Thornley's translation revised by J. M. Edmonds; and Parthenius. S. Gaselee.

Lucian. 8 Vols. Vols. I-IV. A. M. Harmon. Vol. VI. K. Kilburn. Vols. VII and VIII. M. D. Macleod.

Lycophron. Cf. Callimachus: Hymns and Epigrams.

Lyra Graeca. J. M. Edmonds. 3 Vols.

Lysias. W. R. M. Lamb.

Manetho. W. G. Waddell; Ptolemy: Tetrabiblos. F. E. Robbins.

THE LOEB CLASSICAL LIBRARY

MARCUS AURELIUS. C. R. Haines.

MENANDER. F. G. Allinson.

MINOR ATTIC ORATORS. 2 Vols. K. J. Maidment and J. O. Burtt.

MUSAEUS: HERO AND LEANDER. *Cf.* CALLIMACHUS: FRAGMENTS.

NONNOS: DIONYSIACA. W. H. D. Rouse. 3 Vols.

OPPIAN, COLLUTHUS, TRYPHIODORUS. A. W. Mair.

PAPYRI. NON-LITERARY SELECTIONS. A. S. Hunt and C. C. Edgar. 2 Vols. LITERARY SELECTIONS (Poetry). D. L. Page.

PARTHENIUS. *Cf.* LONGUS.

PAUSANIAS: DESCRIPTION OF GREECE. W. H. S. Jones. 4 Vols. and Companion Vol. arranged by R. E. Wycherley.

PHILO. 10 Vols. Vols. I-V. F. H. Colson and Rev. G. H. Whitaker. Vols. VI-X. F. H. Colson. General Index. Rev. J. W. Earp.
Two Supplementary Vols. Translation only from an Armenian Text. Ralph Marcus.

PHILOSTRATUS: THE LIFE OF APOLLONIUS OF TYANA. F. C. Conybeare. 2 Vols.

PHILOSTRATUS: IMAGINES; CALLISTRATUS: DESCRIPTIONS. A. Fairbanks.

PHILOSTRATUS AND EUNAPIUS: LIVES OF THE SOPHISTS. Wilmer Cave Wright.

PINDAR. Sir J. E. Sandys.

PLATO: CHARMIDES, ALCIBIADES, HIPPARCHUS, THE LOVERS, THEAGES, MINOS AND EPINOMIS. W. R. M. Lamb.

PLATO: CRATYLUS, PARMENIDES, GREATER HIPPIAS, LESSER HIPPIAS. H. N. Fowler.

PLATO: EUTHYPHRO, APOLOGY, CRITO, PHAEDO, PHAEDRUS. H. N. Fowler.

PLATO: LACHES, PROTAGORAS, MENO, EUTHYDEMUS. W. R. M. Lamb.

PLATO: LAWS. Rev. R. G. Bury. 2 Vols.

PLATO: LYSIS, SYMPOSIUM, GORGIAS. W. R. M. Lamb.

PLATO: REPUBLIC. Paul Shorey. 2 Vols.

PLATO: STATESMAN, PHILEBUS. H. N. Fowler; ION. W. R. M. Lamb.

PLATO: THEAETETUS AND SOPHIST. H. N. Fowler.

PLATO: TIMAEUS, CRITIAS, CLITOPHO, MENEXENUS, EPISTULAE. Rev. R. G. Bury.

PLOTINUS. A. H. Armstrong. 6 Vols. Vols. I-III.

PLUTARCH: MORALIA. 17 Vols. Vols. I-V. F. C. Babbitt. Vol. VI. W. C. Helmbold. Vol. VII. P. H. De Lacy and

CAMBRIDGE, MASS.   LONDON
HARVARD UNIV. PRESS   WILLIAM HEINEMANN LTD

8

DUE DATE

Printed
in USA